Talking it Through
Responses to Sorcery and Witchcraft Beliefs
and Practices in Melanesia

Talking it Through

Responses to Sorcery and Witchcraft Beliefs and Practices in Melanesia

Edited by Miranda Forsyth and Richard Eves

PRESS

Published by ANU Press
The Australian National University
Canberra ACT 0200, Australia
Email: anupress@anu.edu.au
This title is also available online at http://press.anu.edu.au

National Library of Australia Cataloguing-in-Publication entry

Title: Talking it through : responses to sorcery and witchcraft beliefs and practices in Melanesia / Miranda Forsyth, Richard Eves (editors).

ISBN: 9781925021561 (paperback) 9781925021578 (ebook)

Subjects: Witchcraft--Melanesia.
Witchcraft--Papua New Guinea.
Melanesia--Social life and customs.
Papua New Guinea--Social life and customs.
Melanesia--Religion.
Papua New Guinea--Religion.

Other Creators/Contributors:
Forsyth, Miranda, editor.
Eves, Richard, editor.

Dewey Number: 133.43

All rights reserved. No part of this publication may be reproduced, stored in a retrieval system or transmitted in any form or by any means, electronic, mechanical, photocopying or otherwise, without the prior permission of the publisher.

Cover design and layout by ANU Press

Cover photo: Woman who had been accused of sorcery and tortured returning for the first time to her village following reconciliation. Photo courtesy of Father Philip Gibbs.

This edition © 2015 ANU Press

Contents

Foreword: Sorcery- and Witchcraft-Related Killings in
Papua New Guinea. vii
Gairo Onagi

The Problems and Victims of Sorcery and Witchcraft Practices
and Beliefs in Melanesia: An Introduction 1
Miranda Forsyth and Richard Eves

Part 1: Social, Economic and Cultural Dimensions to the Belief in Witchcraft and Sorcery

1. The Spread of Sorcery Killing and its Social Implications. 23
   Jack Urame

2. Sorcery, Christianity and the Decline of Medical Services 37
   John Cox and Georgina Phillips

3. Witchcraft, Sorcery, Violence: Matrilineal and Decolonial
   Reflections. 55
   Salmah Eva-Lina Lawrence

4. Sorcery and Witchcraft as a Negative Force on Economic and
   Social Development in Solomon Islands 75
   Lawrence Foana'ota

5. Huli Customary Beliefs and Tribal Laws about Witches
   and Witch Spirits. 85
   John Himugu

6. Talking *Sanguma*: The Social Process of Discernment of Evil
   in Two Sepik Societies 111
   Patrick F. Gesch

7. The *Haus Man* Cleansing at Nahu Rawa 131
   Patrick F. Gesch and Jonathan Julius

8. 'The Land Will Eat You': Land and Sorcery in North Efate,
   Vanuatu. 137
   Siobhan McDonnell

9. Sorcery, Poison and Politics: Strategies of Self-Positioning in
   South Malekula, Vanuatu 161
   Laurent Dousset

Part 2: Legal Dimensions to the Belief in Witchcraft and Sorcery

10. The Courts, the Churches, the Witches and their Killers . . . 183
    Christine Stewart

11. The Western Legal Response to Sorcery in Colonial
    Papua New Guinea 197
    Mel Keenan

12. A Pluralist Response to the Regulation of Sorcery and
    Witchcraft in Melanesia 213
    Miranda Forsyth

13. Sorcery- and Witchcraft-Related Killings in Papua New Guinea:
    The Criminal Justice System Response 241
    Ravunamu Auka, Barbara Gore and Pealiwan Rebecca Koralyo

14. Sorcery Violence in Bougainville Through the Lens of Human
    Rights Law: A Critical View 255
    Mark Evenhuis

15. The Belief in Sorcery in Solomon Islands. 281
    Philip Kanairara and Derek Futaiasi

Part 3: Positive Directions in Overcoming Violence

16. *Kumo Koimbo*: Accounts and Responses to Witchcraft in
    Gor, Simbu Province 299
    Clara Bal

17. Practical Church Interventions on Sorcery and Witchcraft
    Violence in the Papua New Guinea Highlands 309
    Fr Philip Gibbs

Author Biographies 329

Foreword: Sorcery- and Witchcraft-Related Killings in Papua New Guinea

Gairo Onagi

Papua New Guinea (PNG) is no exception when it comes to the practices of witchcraft and sorcery. Different names are used to describe these practices. Some call them *sanguma*; others call them *puri puri* and *malira*. Whatever the names used for these practices that are dubbed as evil and antisocial, such behaviour exists in many countries throughout the world and is particularly associated with social stress and dislocation. I believe that this volume forms part of a constructive dialogue to develop practical and workable solutions to the negative societal issues posed by the problems of sorcery- and witchcraft-related social ills and, in particular, the horrendous killings that are so frequently experienced now in PNG.

Our women, when accused of sorcery, are blamed and branded as witches with horrific and traumatic consequences. The PNG and global media have taken a big interest in this matter and we are widely known for these brutal murders of innocent people, especially women. When people die, especially men, people start asking, 'Who is behind this?'. In PNG, we view sorcery or witchcraft as causes for sickness or death before medical reasons are considered. This is a commonly held belief across PNG, even among educated PNG citizens. Thus, the belief in sorcery and witchcraft is embedded in the fabric of PNG society.

Respect for the rule of law and the rights of others are pillars of modern democracy, and we would like to think that PNG falls in this category. But this is not the case. We hear stories of witchcraft used in the general elections. We hear stories of sorcery used in sporting competitions to win games. We hear stories about witchcraft used in negotiations and job interviews.

One rural person, when asked about sorcery said:

> Why take my *puri puri* away. I use my *puri puri* to catch fish to feed my family. Why take my *puri puri* away from me? I use it for planting to get good harvest. Why take it away from me when I use it for health … I make people well. Why take it away when I use it for love? Why outlaw it? Go get the murders [and] killers [and] put them behind bars, not me.

> Those who harm people are the ones the law should deal with. My good *puri puri* is my sacred knowledge. My ancestors passed it to me. It is my heritage. Don't outlaw my sacred knowledge.

Different perceptions are held as to the nature of sorcery and witchcraft. This perception begs an important question: how widespread will be the laws that will be created to help a stable and harmonious society without sorcery? Enacting laws and penalties against certain behaviour is easy to do. But executing these laws relating to sorcery and witchcraft is another matter. Village courts were set up for the purpose of dealing with village issues and one of them is sorcery. Evidence has shown that we have not been successful. Moreover, our parliament passed a law on capital punishment to deter sorcerers from killing. The courts have not sentenced a single person to death yet. And so, we the citizens carry out the punishment ourselves. The state is not helping at all and must do more to protect innocent lives.

People, including perpetrators, are 'taking the law into their own hands'. They become the judge and jury, simultaneously carry out acts of justice, sentencing and punishing outside the courts. In doing so, they create more injustices to the society because innocent lives are affected. Moreover, the most affected are women who are being brutally murdered outside the state laws. The gendered nature of sorcery and witchcraft assumes that females are the best hosts for such practices. The female anatomy is depicted as the pathway for possible transformation and existence of these practices. There is little evidence to back this but traditional beliefs have strong indications and so women face gross physical abuses, injuries and death.

We all know the phrase 'innocent until proven guilty'. If we go by that then we have a challenge. Sorcery and witchcraft are spiritual matters. In many cases, the eyes will not see nor the ears hear. How will the evidence be collected to charge and subsequently sentence an alleged practitioner? This is a big challenge. In many cases alleged practitioners have been innocent yet they are jailed or inhumanely treated. Kepari Leniata's brutal murder is an example of high suspicion and speculation, yet she was publicly humiliated, doused in petrol and torched! In many instances, the accusers are not dealt with. So I am posing this question: where is the law to protect the citizens? The killings are continuing!

Will the state laws relating to sorcery and witchcraft protect its citizens? The laws, in my mind, do not govern the rural people. Traditional norms and practices in tribal societies still rule over our rural people. Sorcery and witchcraft are deeply embedded in the lives of our people. More than 129 years of Christianity has not eradicated this so-called evil. We ask ourselves 'WHY?'. It could be the methods used that must be reviewed.

Churches in PNG must work collaboratively and address the issue through collective approaches with other stakeholders. This is a spiritual matter and must be addressed through spiritual approaches, with the backing of the law. Human bodies can be possessed by such evil spirits. I have witnessed reformation of sorcery/witchcraft practitioners through spiritual means. I have heard stories of two schools that were rid of sorcery and witchcraft effects. Churches also operate in locations that see little of government representatives and are well placed to understand the local situations, and can utilise local knowledge to provide pathways to educate people on impacts of sorcery and witchcraft. Further, I strongly call for the government and relevant stakeholders to work closely with churches.

Many innocent lives have fallen victim to sorcery- and witchcraft-related killings. The brutal case of the burning of Kepari Leniata in Mount Hagen in 2013 sparked domestic and global outrage. This challenges the establishment and application of PNG laws to punish offenders. It also challenges the context whether people in our rural societies fully understand, can adhere to, and comply with the laws respectfully.

Belief systems cannot be simply erased from people's minds. In modern times the nature of sorcery and witchcraft is associated with money. Practitioners ply their wares for money. They are likened to 'hired killers'. With a certain fee, they can fulfil the sponsor's request. Thus, sorcery and witchcraft practitioners are now assuming respectable positions as power wielders and brokers. Reports and evidence indicate sorcery and witchcraft as growing industries in certain areas of PNG.

Sorcery-related violence will continue unless we educate our people on the negative impacts of sorcery and witchcraft beliefs. Heinous murders of innocent lives on suspicions of sorcery or witchcraft will continue to rise. So what are the best holistic approaches that we can use to arrest this issue? One way is to focus on local conditions by using anthropological and sociological pathways to understand people's beliefs and practices. Another approach that I have strong conviction in is through churches' input. Revisiting established laws that govern offences and penalties relating to the practices are vital. International conventions on human rights abuses in all forms have taken a strong foothold in our country's adoption, practice and application of the relevant laws.

The way forward for us is to develop national plans and policies to address sorcery and witchcraft, delivered through different mechanisms and approaches.

Acknowledgements

The editors would like to acknowledge the efforts of all those who contributed to, and participated in, the two conferences that this book is based upon. Particular thanks are due to Ume Wainetti, who initiated the Goroka conference and who was a key driver in it, Donald Gumbis and his colleagues at the University of Goroka, who did such an amazing coordinating job in Goroka, and other members of the coordinating committee including Josephine Advent, Isi Oru, Jack Urame, Winifred Oraka, Roselyne Kenneth, Susan Ferguson, Rudolph Lies, Father Philip Gibbs and Nicole Haley. We also acknowledge the support of the Department of Foreign Affairs and Trade and The Australian National University's Research School of Asia and the Pacific. Finally we would like to thank all the contributing authors and also Tracy Harwood for her outstanding copyediting work.

The Problems and Victims of Sorcery and Witchcraft Practices and Beliefs in Melanesia: An Introduction

Miranda Forsyth and Richard Eves

The belief that illness, death and misfortune of all sorts is frequently caused by the deliberate interventions of individuals with special powers or magical knowledge is pervasive throughout Melanesia. As a result, sorcery and witchcraft beliefs and practices exert a powerful influence on many aspects of day-to-day life, as well as being significant vectors for community tensions, conflict and violence. Moreover, rather than disappearing under the influence of Christianity and modern life, sorcery and witchcraft practices and beliefs are proving extremely resilient, with many claiming that they are increasing and spreading. In recent years, most of the attention given to the problems arising from sorcery and witchcraft beliefs and practices has been on the attacks and killings of accused sorcerers and witches. Three widely publicised events in 2013 and 2014 brought these forcibly into public focus. In Mount Hagen in 2013 a woman was tortured and then burnt alive in front of hundreds of onlookers, including members of her community and police officers. Later that year, a female teacher in Bougainville was publicly tortured and beheaded. Then, in November 2014, two men in Vanuatu were publicly hanged in a community hall following accusations that they had been practising witchcraft. However, sorcery and witchcraft beliefs and practices also give rise to a range of social problems that are not as visible, including the retarding of economic development, poor public health, undermining of social cohesion, incentivising crime and creating insecurity.

Today, as in the past, many communities, individuals, church organisations and policymakers in Melanesia are trying very hard to grapple with these negative societal impacts of belief in sorcery and witchcraft. Partly as a result of the three incidents detailed above, the 'problem' of sorcery and witchcraft is increasingly a focus of international attention, such as through special rapporteur reports and the work of international non-government organisations (NGOs) (e.g. Heyns 2014; Manjoo 2013). The chapters in this book document and discuss the ways in which different actors are addressing and exploring the different facets of the problems associated with these beliefs in Melanesia. As such, this book's emphasis is on trying to understand what is happening, and also on the types of interventions that are being trialled and their successes and failures.

At the outset it is important to observe that understandings about what the actual problems are differ widely depending upon the world view of the person concerned. For the overwhelming majority of the population across Melanesia, the problem of sorcery and witchcraft is the harm that sorcerers and witches do to their communities, killing and harming innocent people, undermining local businesses and national development projects, and leading to fear and insecurity. From this perspective, victims of sorcery are those people who are believed to have been killed or otherwise negatively affected by the actions of a witch or a sorcerer. In contrast, most international NGOs and human rights bodies consider the problem to be the violence that sometimes emanates from sorcery or witchcraft accusations, and characterise victims as those who are accused of *being* witches or sorcerers and consequently attacked or expelled from their community.

This radical difference that world view makes has resulted in much confusion, misunderstanding and lack of traction in the well-meaning efforts of different groups to address the 'problem'. It has also meant that meaningful dialogue between those with different world views has been limited. Partly in response to this, this book seeks to engage with, and interconnect, a variety of viewpoints on both what the problems of sorcery and witchcraft practices and beliefs entail, and who the victims are and how they are suffering. The authors in this book are Melanesians and non-Melanesians, academics from a variety of disciplines including anthropology and law, policymakers, lawyers and members of church organisations. Taken together, their insights demonstrate the multifaceted nature of the issues arising from sorcery and witchcraft practices and beliefs, and lead to the conclusion that any redress must be alive to the interwoven elements involved. Similarly, the chapters in this book highlight the futility in distinguishing between 'traditional' and 'modern' causes or expressions of sorcery, suggesting that such dualistic ways of thinking are unhelpful to the analysis (see also Herriman 2014).

It is also critical to acknowledge that sorcery and witchcraft beliefs and practices do not always lead to harm, and, from a local perspective, these powers often have a range of associated positives such as healing, gardening and weather magic. By and large, however, this book is not about these positive elements, except in a tangential way that respects their existence and continued beneficial importance. The focus of this book is rather on the problems associated with these beliefs and practices, problems that are the focus of struggle and concern for communities around Melanesia. It aims to contextualise these problems in ways that avoid simplistic solutions and provoke deeper investigation into creative and realistic paths forward.

This volume originates from two multidisciplinary conferences in 2013, one in Australia and one in Papua New Guinea (PNG), focusing on the negative social consequences of belief in sorcery and witchcraft in Melanesia.¹ Both involved academics, policymakers, human rights activists, church organisations, NGOs, international organisations and aid donors. Participants and speakers came from PNG, Vanuatu, Solomon Islands, Australia, New Zealand, Europe and North America.² This volume brings together a selection of papers from both conferences, and although the majority concern PNG, two chapters deal with Solomon Islands and two with Vanuatu. While there are a number of similarities in the experiences of these three countries, and indeed within them, there are also crucial differences, especially in regard to the extent of violence associated with the beliefs.

This collection forms part of an extensive body of literature about sorcery and witchcraft in Melanesia (e.g. Fortune 1963; Knauft 1985; Lindenbaum 1979; Patterson 1974–75; Stephen 1987; Zelenietz and Lindenbaum 1981; Zocca 2009) and around the globe in general (e.g. Ellen and Watson 1993; Kapferer 1997; Siegel 2006; Whitehead and Wright 2004), a full overview of which is beyond the scope of this introduction. Historically, the topic has been dominated by anthropological writings in the form of classic ethnographies that have largely sought to describe in detail such beliefs to illustrate their inherent logic, often in comparison to science. The classic here is Evans-Pritchard's (1937) *Witchcraft, oracles and magic among the Azande*. Contemporary anthropologists have turned to consider sorcery and witchcraft beliefs as indigenous critiques or commentaries on modernity, capitalism and unequal development (e.g. Ashforth 2005; Comaroff and Comaroff 1993; Geschiere 1997; Moore and Sanders 2001; Niehaus et al. 2001; Smith 2008). More recently this topic has been addressed by academics from a range of disciplines, such as lawyers concerned with the possibilities and limitations of legislative change (e.g. Forsyth 2006), academics concerned with the relevance of human rights for addressing attacks on those accused of sorcery and witchcraft, public health academics (e.g. Baskind and Birbeck 2005) and development academics concerned about ways in which these beliefs undermine development (e.g. Ashforth 2005; Brain 1982; Fisiy and Geschiere 2001; Golooba-Mutebi 2005; Kohnert 1996; Leistner 2014; Petrus 2012; Smith 2005). There is also an increasing amount of grey literature being produced in this area, including by church organisations, NGOs, international NGOs, United Nations agencies and others.³ The increasingly wide range of commentators interested in this topic is reflected in the varied backgrounds of the authors in this volume.

---

1 Sorcery and Witchcraft-Related Killings in Melanesia: Culture, Law and Human Rights Perspectives Conference, The Australian National University, Canberra, 5–7 June 2013; and Sorcery and Witchcraft Accusations: Developing a National Response to Overcome the Violence Conference, Goroka, PNG, December 2013.
2 For further details of the conferences, see Forsyth (2013a, 2013b, 2013c).
3 See, for example, the 'resources' page on the Witchcraft and Human Rights Information Network website, www.whrin.org; Amnesty International (2011); HSIMR (2004); and Oxfam International (2010).

The book is structured into three parts. The chapters in Part 1 discuss the social, economic and cultural dimensions to the belief in witchcraft and sorcery. Part 2 contains a number of chapters that deal with the legal dimensions to the belief in witchcraft and sorcery. Finally, the chapters in Part 3 explore some positive ways forward in overcoming one of the most problematic aspects of sorcery and witchcraft beliefs and practices today, namely sorcery accusation-related violence.

Terminology and cosmological perspective

As mentioned above, terminology in this area is problematic and frequently misleading, as both the problems of sorcery and witchcraft and the victims of those problems depend upon the world view of the person concerned. This book aims to be neutral in relation to the question of whether sorcery and witchcraft 'really' occur, and as such refers to sorcery and witchcraft beliefs and practices. A number of authors also refer to sorcery and witchcraft accusation-related violence to clearly distinguish that group of victims from those considered to have been harmed by sorcery and witchcraft itself.

Definitional clarity is also needed in respect of terms such as sorcery, witchcraft and magic. It is clear that there is much confusion around the use of these terms, that they are often used interchangeably, and that none of them adequately describe the particular nature of the phenomenon as it is experienced around the region. These terms can also be viewed as dangerously neo-colonial, and reference European traditions that are highly inappropriate in the Melanesian context. Following the work of Evans-Pritchard (1937) among the Azande in Africa, anthropologists around the world have tended to distinguish between sorcery and witchcraft on the basis that witches are seemingly possessed of an innate and unconscious propensity to harm others, whereas sorcery involves the conscious and deliberate manipulation of objects and/or spells to achieve a desired outcome (Eves 2013). However, as always in Melanesia, distinctions and categorisations of any sort are often confounded by the multiple variations that are present in almost everything, sorcery and witchcraft practices and beliefs included. The diverse nature of what is understood by sorcery or witchcraft in the region is reflected in the range of vernacular terms used to describe it: *puri puri, mura mura, dikana, vada, mea mea,* or *sanguma* in PNG; *vele* and *arua* in Solomon Islands; and *nakaemas, posen* and black magic in Vanuatu. As a general rule, the authors in this volume use the terminology that best suits their particular context.

Part 1: Social, economic and cultural dimensions to the belief in witchcraft and sorcery

The first part of this volume contains chapters that analyse the social, economic and cultural context of witchcraft and sorcery practices and beliefs, written by Melanesian and non-Melanesian anthropologists and policymakers. These authors demonstrate that such beliefs and practices give rise to, and are associated with, a wide range of negative social problems, from poor economic development, public health and social cohesion, to crime and insecurity. Belief in sorcery discourages entrepreneurism because jealousy derived from economic inequality is a key source of sorcery and witchcraft accusations. Crime and insecurity arise because people react to deaths, sickness and misfortune by seeking to punish, expel, cure or get revenge on those identified as being the sorcerer or witch responsible. While sorcery and witchcraft accusations often occur within communities or even families, in some areas they are also implicated in intercommunity warfare. As well as physical attacks and murders of those accused, such accusations can also lead to civil unrest, property destruction, and the fostering of a pervasive culture of insecurity for relatives of the accused.

Here we identify a number of common themes in the chapters in this part, and also incorporate a number of relevant observations made during the two conferences by presenters whose papers are not included in this volume.

The modern nature of witchcraft- and sorcery-related beliefs and practices (and some of their potential causes)

It is clear from many of the chapters that the actions following witchcraft and sorcery accusations, and indeed the underlying expressions of beliefs today, vary markedly from precolonial times. The very public nature of many witchcraft-related attacks today, and the associated prolonged sexualised torture of the victim that has been witnessed recently in PNG, are said to differ from traditional practices, when victims were dispatched secretly, often by kin. Attention is also drawn to the fact that witchcraft- and sorcery-related beliefs are being transported around PNG, and Melanesia in general, to places where they never previously existed. One participant in the Canberra conference commented that people are reacting to new social ideas in terms of old belief systems, and so for example are talking about witches using helicopters and mobile phones. Other speakers observed that in the past people referred to stones being used to 'poison' people, but now it is chemicals that are said to be used. Sorcery practices are also being commodified and increasingly able to be 'bought' at local markets as new modes of accessing power, meaning that a far greater range of people have access to them than previously. The variety of forms of sorcery and witchcraft seem to be increasing, rather than dying out.

Many of these changes are discussed in Chapter 1 by Jack Urame, Director of the Melanesian Institute. His chapter, which is based on several years of research into the issue, details the extent of the violence associated with sorcery accusations, the various ways in which the rate and pattern of sorcery-accusation violence has grown and changed, and also the different types of violence associated with it. He identifies a number of contributing factors to sorcery-related violence, including lack of development, collapse of traditional systems, economic imbalance, lifestyle diseases, generational conflict, and lack of information or misguided information from medical workers.

Chapter 2, by John Cox and Georgina Phillips, also provides an important insight into a significant contributor to the prevalence of the sorcery and witchcraft complex in PNG today, namely the failing health system. They explore these issues through a focus on emergency departments in hospitals and explore the ways in which notionally biomedical spaces can be places where meanings of illness and death are contested. They call for reinvestment in medical services and training as a strategy for combating sorcery-related violence.

Perpetrators of violence against accused witches and sorcerers

Some authors argue that it is 'useless', disenfranchised young men who are carrying out the physical attacks on alleged witches and sorcerers, although the accusations may have been first made by women or older men (Urame, Chapter 1, this volume). Young men are associated with drugs, alcohol, small arms and frustration, and are positioned as unable to find a meaningful role for themselves in their communities. Conversely, they see themselves as local heroes in the role of protecting their communities. These authors therefore suggest that strategies targeted towards working with such men, and confronting the troubled forms of postcolonial masculinity, are necessary in dealing with sorcery and witchcraft practices today. However, others complicate this picture, presenting research that suggests there is far more community support for the violence than these descriptions depict, and that violence is often carried out with widespread public approbation (Eves and Kelly-Hanku 2014). This is certainly an area that requires more research.

The gendered nature of sorcery and witchcraft

The gendered nature of sorcery and witchcraft is a subject on which many different viewpoints are expressed. Although there has been a tendency for the problem of sorcery and witchcraft to be described in international discourse as a problem experienced by women, in fact those accused of perpetrating acts of sorcery and witchcraft, and the victims of sorcery- and witchcraft-related attacks, are both men and women (e.g. Jorgensen 2014). One speaker at the Canberra conference commented that a common theme in the victims of these attacks was that they are either 'strangers on the inside' such as women who have married-in, or else 'insiders who have become strangers', such as community members who predominantly live away from their communities in urban settings, returning home sporadically. However, certain geographical areas tend to target one gender or the other, depending upon local cultural understandings and beliefs about sorcery and witchcraft. For example, a speaker at the Goroka conference was adamant that in Mekeo, PNG, no woman is associated with sorcery practices, and this is the realm of men who use the powers to attack neighbouring tribes or defend their communities from such attacks. Overall, however, women appear to be greater targets of witchcraft accusations than men, particularly in PNG (Amnesty International 2009; Eves and Kelly-Hanku 2014). In addition, where women are the victims of sorcery accusation-related violence, they are often more vulnerable and at risk than men, due to unequal power relations, lack of support structures, and lack of access to land or income.

Social changes and breakdown of traditional authorities

Classical analyses of sorcery and witchcraft have correlated the increase of such beliefs, in particular places at particular times, with periods of illness, misfortune and uncertainty. They explain witchcraft and sorcery in terms of anxieties born of radical social change, suggesting that accusations arise when communities experience dramatic upheavals and conflicts precipitated by epidemics, labour migration, incorporation into the cash economy and political insecurity (Behringer 2004; Comaroff and Comaroff 1993; Eves 2000; Zocca 2009). These observations appear to hold true for Melanesia today, where the beliefs are associated with unexplained deaths and sickness, social stress and change, poverty, uneven development, issues of jealousy, and the problem of drugs and alcohol. New forms of wealth, and trends towards individualism and materialism, are leading to economic disparities and provoking jealousy and envy, which also feeds witchcraft- and sorcery-related suspicions and accusations. This is associated with the growth of settlements, people living in larger communities, and with people traditionally considered as 'outsiders' moving into communities. It is also clear that service delivery failure, particularly in health services, education and transport infrastructure, are major contributors to the premature deaths that are fuelling accusations of sorcery and witchcraft, particularly in PNG. Finally, intergenerational tensions were also highlighted as a significant contributing factor to sorcery-accusation violence. Paul Barker, the head of PNG's Institute of National Affairs and MC at the Goroka conference, observed that when young men carry out this violence, 'They're also demonstrating their power versus that of the traditional leadership, including the more modern leadership, the local village court magistrates and other leaders' (ABC News 2014).

Many speakers referred to the disintegration of traditional authority structures, in particular control over young men by community leaders, as being a particular problem. Even if there is a desire to stop sorcery and witchcraft accusations getting out of control, there is limited power to do so at a local level, meaning that there is a frequent theme of requiring more state engagement in managing the issues. Jack Urame (Chapter 1) observes, 'Unlike in traditional societies, today traditional leaders are often reluctant to intervene when sorcery accusations occur because they are afraid of being physically attacked or blamed for being sorcerers themselves'. Again, this is less marked in Vanuatu where the customary governance structures are relatively stronger.

The role of churches

There are differing views about whether churches contribute to sorcery accusation-related violence or whether they help to overcome it. Many speakers at both conferences stressed that Pentecostal churches with their emphasis on Satan and their campaigns of 'spiritual warfare' and need for exorcisms were fomenting beliefs in witchcraft and sorcery. Some observed that there is a need to control the proliferation of such churches. However, positive examples were also given of strategies developed and adopted by the more established churches to control sorcery and witchcraft accusations. Philip Gibbs (Chapter 17) describes the Catholic Church's 'five-point strategy' that has had a restraining effect on sorcery-related violence. There was considerable discussion during the conferences of the sometimes contradictory roles played by the Melanesian Brotherhood in Vanuatu and Solomon Islands in relation to these issues.

The role of the media

Questions were asked during the two conferences about the role of the media in engendering 'copycat' sorcery- and witchcraft-related violence in PNG. Responses to these concerns stressed that news about sorcery- and witchcraft-related attacks were being transmitted through informal networks (particularly mobile phones) as much as, or more than, through formal media;

that the more informed the debate can be the better; that the power of the media can be harnessed in positive ways such as through the enormously successful *Haus Krai* movement in 2013 and the 'Remembering Kepari Leniata Campaign' on Facebook;[4] and that standing by and watching the most vulnerable members of communities be attacked and victimised is not a palatable alternative. The comment was also made that a major problem is that the message of impunity in relation to these attacks as a result of police unwillingness or incapacity to act has already gotten out loud and clear.

Sorcery and violence

Many speakers at the two conferences drew attention to the different forms of sorcery-related violence. The attacks on the two women accused of witchcraft in PNG mentioned above were shown to be just one particular manifestation of violence, although media exposure on this suggests to outsiders that it is the only type. For example, sorcery was also demonstrated to be a trigger for intercommunity tribal warfare in the highlands, and also to have been causative in disputes between different clans in Bougainville. Some speakers also discussed the fact that most accusations of sorcery and witchcraft do not end up in violence, particularly in Vanuatu and Solomon Islands, and this is also a point compellingly articulated by Salmah Eva-Lina Lawrence (Chapter 3).

In this volume, the relationship between sorcery and tribal warfare is demonstrated through a case study by Father Patrick Gesch and Jonathan Julius (Chapter 7), which seeks to investigate what lay behind the killings of seven men and a three-year-old boy in Madang Province in April 2014. This chapter describes a cycle of violence that was contributed to by the gradual withdrawal of all government services from the communities involved, ongoing disputes over land, and cult-like practices associated with the *haus man* group.

Overall, many speakers at both conferences considered sorcery-accusation violence to be part of a wider problem of the pervasiveness of violence throughout PNG society, including domestic violence and sexual violence, that urgently needs to be addressed. To this end, a decision was made in the planning stages for the Goroka conference to focus on breaking the link between sorcery accusations and violence. This was a pragmatic decision that recognised that violence is the most problematic aspect of the beliefs in PNG today. It was also intended to allow some conceptual separation between the beliefs themselves and the violent responses to accusations of sorcery or witchcraft, although there is considerable debate about the extent to which this separation can in fact be made.

---

4   www.facebook.com/NationalHausKrai; www.facebook.com/TheLeniataLegacy.

Finally, it should be noted that the problem of violence arising from sorcery and witchcraft accusations in Melanesia today is by no means unique.[5] Rather, it is part of a growing global phenomenon, with new pockets of what has been termed an 'epidemic' appearing in many diaspora communities worldwide, and developing in new and troubling directions in many parts of Africa and Latin America.[6]

Differences in sorcery- and witchcraft-related beliefs across Melanesia

The chapters in this part of the book highlight the diversity of witchcraft- and sorcery-related beliefs across Melanesia. It is clear that understanding the particular cultural context involved is fundamental to an understanding of the problems associated with the beliefs, as is argued by John Himugu (Chapter 5). He describes in some detail the beliefs of the Huli people in PNG and the way in which they have developed their own mechanisms to deal with the social issues they generate. As a result of this diversity, there are limits to the extent to which valid generalisations can be made in the context of sorcery- and witchcraft-related beliefs and practices. Further, accusations and counter-accusations are often embedded in particular local political landscapes, a point convincingly made by Siobhan McDonnell (Chapter 8) on the linkages between tensions over land and sorcery accusations in Vanuatu. She shows how land is a major source of social tension in rural areas in Vanuatu, and argues that solutions to *nakaemas* must recognise the social circumstances and relations that surround sorcery and that this must be built into any regulatory model.

For the East Sepik, Father Patrick Gesch (Chapter 6) reports that the institutions of sorcery and witchcraft have their supporters in the leaders of the communities. They are social forms of review of what is happening or what harm evildoers are bringing to the village, and as such these institutions serve particular roles in the community that must be understood within their particular context.

Multifaced nature of sorcery

At the Canberra conference, it was noted by Professor Margaret Jolly that divine power has many faces in Melanesia, and commonly those who are thought to have the power to harm also have the power to heal. Although the focus of this volume, and the two conferences, is and was on the negative social effects of sorcery and witchcraft beliefs, participants also stressed positive aspects

---

5   It is also a problem for Indonesia; see Herriman (2007).
6   For Africa, see Ashforth (2002, 2005); Comaroff and Comaroff (1993); Geschiere (1997); Moore and Sanders (2001); Niehaus et al. (2001); and Smith (2008). For Latin America, see Whitehead and Wright (2004).

of the beliefs, such as gardening and healing magic, and the need for these to be taken into account in policy responses. In Chapter 3, Salmah Eva-Lina Lawrence describes how sorcery and witchcraft empowers and contributes to the status of Milne Bay women. She characterises witchcraft into three types — harming, protecting and healing — and notes the importance of these bodies of knowledge as key community resources, for example, by giving women control over their own fertility. Some speakers suggested that the polarising of sorcery into good and evil is a product of Christianisation with its emphasis on evil and Satan, and that previously spirits were neither good nor bad, just powerful.

In Chapter 9, Laurent Dousset reminds us that in many respects the narrative of sorcery is a means by which communities deal with social change. He argues that sorcery is 'a place where belonging and being are reconfigured and therefore where notions of the "person", the "group", "ethnicity" or "power" are redefined and adapted to changing historical and material conditions'. Comparing his analysis of Malekula in Vanuatu with the accounts reported by Maurice Bloch for Madagascar, he suggests that sorcery incorporates both a generalised sociocognitive and a localised historical component. Through the former, sorcery constitutes the process in which 'boundaries' between humanity and animality, or between 'self' or similarity and 'other' or difference, are challenged. The localised historical component, on the other hand, reflects the particular material and immaterial conditions that trigger this process of boundary reconfiguration with as a possible corollary important changes in the local sociocultural and political order.

Sorcery as impeding economic development/jealousy

A number of speakers linked fear of sorcery with jealousy and envy, leading to an unwillingness of some in the region to work towards advancing their own living standards. Setting up businesses and becoming successful (especially if wealth is shown outwardly, such as in building new houses) is widely seen as being risky and as inviting a premature death through a sorcery attack. These fears are to an extent supported by the sudden deaths of apparently successful (and hence often overweight, stressed, physically inactive and so forth) middle-aged men and women due to heart attacks and other non-communicable diseases such as hypertension and diabetes. It was generally agreed that these concerns have to date been largely invisible in development discourse. Lawrence Foana'ota (Chapter 4) sets out in some detail how the belief in sorcery and witchcraft in Solomon Islands has pervasive negative effects on social and economic development, and is often blamed for the failure of development projects. This in turn is problematic, as it deflects attention from alternative explanations of such failures, such as corruption.

Part 2: Legal dimensions to the belief in witchcraft and sorcery

The belief in sorcery and witchcraft also raises a host of complicated legal issues that are explored through six chapters in Part 2 of the book, focusing firstly on PNG and then Solomon Islands. Christine Stewart (Chapter 10) and Mel Keenan (Chapter 11) contextualise the legal treatment of sorcery and witchcraft in a historical setting, providing the background to the enactment of the PNG *Sorcery Act 1971* and its colonial antecedents. Miranda Forsyth (Chapter 12) then updates these discussions in the light of recent developments in the region, including the repeal of the *Sorcery Act 1971* in 2013. She sets out a number of overarching questions central to any criminal justice response, including whether sorcery or witchcraft should be a crime in the criminal justice legislation, whether beliefs in sorcery and witchcraft should be available as a criminal defence or be able to be taken into account in mitigation of sentence, and whether the state should provide forums (such as courts or mediation centres) for dealing with allegations of witchcraft and sorcery, and if so where and how.

The chapter by Ravunamu Auka, Barbara Gore and Rebecca Koralyo (Chapter 13), all legal officers in the PNG Office of the Public Prosecutor, sheds a number of insights into the operational difficulties of prosecuting sorcery- and witchcraft-related cases in the state criminal justice system. They demonstrate the extremely limited way in which the state criminal justice system has been able to operationalise the *Sorcery Act 1971*, and also to deal with the perpetrators of sorcery accusation-related violence. Their statistical analysis was supported by Monica Paulus and Mary Kini of the Highlands Human Rights Defenders Network, who presented at both conferences. They stated that in the 36 cases of sorcery accusation-related violence they have been involved with, only one had led to a successful prosecution and that was because the victim in question had money to pursue the issue. This chapter is also an important reflection of the limitations of a regulatory approach that focuses solely on a legislative response, demonstrating the critical need for engagement of the whole of the criminal justice system, particularly the police. Auka and colleagues argue that '[i]n PNG the police are inadequately paid and infrastructure relating to their work needs either maintenance or restructure. With a police force in this situation, PNG cannot possibly contain sorcery-related violence, because the violence is usually a group attack and everyone in the community usually takes part. Police are often outnumbered and outgunned.'

Their chapter also demonstrates the influence of social attitudes on the operation of the criminal justice system. For instance, their statistics show that only 25 per cent of the cases that have ended up in the state courts have involved a female victim of sorcery-accusation violence, despite evidence from elsewhere that women are far more likely than men to be victims. They surmise that this 'could possibly mean that the death of a woman may be less significant or may go unnoticed in the community or may not be seen to warrant an action taken against the offenders'. These statistics were supported by a presentation at the Goroka conference from the village courts secretariat, whose statistics showed that a significant majority of cases coming before the village courts involved male complainants and also male defendants.[7] Clearly, addressing this issue requires challenging fundamental stereotypes about the respective worth of women and men, and also issues of real and perceived barriers to women's access to the state justice system.

The campaign against sorcery accusation-related violence is being increasingly articulated within the discourse of human rights, both at international levels and also at very local levels, such as with the Highlands Human Rights Defenders Network. Mark Evenhuis (Chapter 14) interrogates the promise and limitations of relying upon the language of human rights to know about and respond to these issues, focusing particularly on Bougainville. He argues that human rights law inevitably conceptualises sorcery-related violence as a traditional practice productive of societal disorder, which demands state-led interventions involving law and cultural transformation. He suggests a more productive approach would take into account the broader political and socio-economic contexts in which accusations of sorcery arise. He shows how the violence that is the subject of critique by the developed world through the language of human rights is, ironically, actually in large part a result of the economic pressures on Bougainville caused by its economic exploitation by those developed countries. Salmah Eva-Lina Lawrence (Chapter 3) also notes that in discourse and praxis there is an absence of 'acknowledge[ment] [of] the negative effects of Eurocentric modernity and its contemporary guise of development, and consideration of its impact upon civil unrest and criminal activity, and indeed upon gender violence'.

Since 2013 the law reform commissions in Vanuatu, PNG and Solomon Islands have started to review their laws against sorcery and witchcraft in attempts to better deal with the legal issues involved. The final chapter in this part, by Philip Kanairara and Derek Futaiasi of the Solomon Islands Law Reform Commission, gives an insight into the preliminary findings of the commission on the issue and outlines possible future directions. These are seen to involve enrolling local courts, chiefs or community leaders and the churches. The authors recommend that if this is to happen, the state must provide training in areas of natural justice, human rights principles and other basic legal principles for those who

---

7   Presentation by Miriam Dondo, Village Courts and Land Mediation Secretariat, Goroka conference, 2013.

will be involved in dealing with issues arising from the belief in sorcery. This will empower them to conduct and discharge fair hearings and settlements for parties who seek remedies from them.

Part 3: Positive directions in overcoming violence

The final section of the book is concerned with identifying positive directions in managing sorcery-related social problems in non-violent ways. In fact, this was a central concern of the Canberra conference, and as organisers we were disappointed by the limited number of abstracts we received that provided good examples of such actions. This disappointment was subsequently partially alleviated by some inspiring presentations given formally and informally at both conferences, albeit without academic papers, by individuals and organisations involved in managing disputes at the grassroots level in PNG. These presenters included Monica Paulus and Lily Be'soer for the Highlands Human Rights Defenders Network, Mary Kini for KUP Women for Peace, Josephine Siviri's work in Bougainville, Bishop Bal's work in Simbu Province, and Dr Jan Jaworski of Kundiawa Hospital. All demonstrated the enormous power of individuals to overcome violence and to offer real comfort and support to a wide range of victims. For example, at the Goroka conference Dr Jaworski described an occasion when he gave the relatives of a person with important political connections a thorough biomedical explanation of his death. They asked him to address 100 distraught relatives and he did so. After he had finished, someone stood up and said to him 'thank you doctor, we will not search for *sanguma*'. Dr Jaworski observed that such an explanation can bring relief and also allows people to stop searching for the person responsible.

The potential of communities to overcome sorcery accusation-related violence is also powerfully demonstrated by Clara Bal (Chapter 16), who describes the way in which the Gor community in Simbu Province has written new laws for itself and created a local police force to assist in enforcing these laws, drawing upon a group of young men who may otherwise be tempted to turn to victimising 'sorcerers' in a quest for community recognition. At the Goroka conference there were also a number of examples of positive initiatives that could be extended to deal with sorcery and witchcraft practices and beliefs. For example, the male champions program involves men acting as agents of change by seeking to change problematic perceptions about women in their daily interactions with other men within their own communities.

The final chapter by Philip Gibbs, as mentioned above, sets out a five-point plan developed by the Catholic Church to deal with the problems of sorcery and witchcraft practices and beliefs. Father Gibbs identifies the crucial role that individual leadership can have, especially when combined with pastoral support from a local priest and biomedical explanations of death and sickness from health professionals. The chapter also powerfully reflects upon what can be done in restoring community relationships that have been horribly fractured by sorcery accusations and violence.

A common thread running through all these interventions is the need for communities to engage in internal discussions about the problems of sorcery and witchcraft practices and beliefs as they see them, in order to identify ways forward that fit within their own sets of priorities and world views. Advice, assistance and gentle guidance from trusted outsiders can be catalytic in such discussions, and different communities and individuals have and will continue to derive strength and support from a variety of sources, such as Christian faith and human rights discourses. Continuing examples of these and similar positive community actions are documented on a new website, Stop Sorcery Violence Papua New Guinea.[8] However, it is also clear that solutions coming from outside that are imposed upon communities in paternalistic or doctrinal fashion are unlikely to achieve any traction.

In conclusion, it is perhaps helpful to sketch out the series of events that have occurred in PNG following the initial conference on the topic in Canberra in 2013. As already noted, this led first to a follow-up conference at Goroka, which in turn led to the development by the participants of an outcome statement that sketched in general terms a way forward. The participants were of the view that any solution to the problems raised by sorcery and witchcraft has to be holistic, multipronged and pay close attention to local conditions. Dealing comprehensively with the issues relating to sorcery and witchcraft beliefs was felt to require working across multiple government departments, in particular health, education and justice, in addition to working with a range of non-state institutions and organisations. Legislative responses, although important, are not sufficient in and of themselves to stem sorcery- and witchcraft-related violence. Similarly, a regular law-and-order approach (for example, recruiting more police and increasing penalties) is not likely to be effective unless coupled with other interventions.

This outcome statement was further refined through a workshop on 12–13 June 2014 in Port Moresby, in which 80 or so participants from a range of government departments and civil society, church and academic organisations drafted a national action plan to overcome sorcery- and witchcraft-related violence. The plan involves a number of government ministries and their departments, including the Department of Health, the Department of Education, the Royal

---

8   www.stopsorceryviolence.org.

Papua New Guinea Constabulary, the Department for Community Development and Religion, and the Department of Justice and Attorney General. It also includes a range of NGOs, such as Oxfam, the Highlands Human Rights Defenders, the Family and Sexual Violence Action Committee's networks, church organisation networks, and international development partners, such as the Australian Government Department of Foreign Affairs and Trade, and the United Nations. It has five core areas: legal and protection, health, advocacy and communication, care and counselling, and research. Each area contains a few key recommendations and sets out concrete activities to be taken in both the short- and medium-term to implement the recommendations (Forsyth 2014). It will take some time to see the extent to which the government and other stakeholders commit to, and then implement, the action plan. However, the commitment to date to developing a comprehensive approach is highly encouraging, and we hope that this volume will provide a firm foundation on which such new initiatives can be based.

References

ABC News 2014. Local 'Power Plays' Behind Rise in Sorcery-Related Violence in PNG, Says Institute of National Affairs. ABC News online 2 August. www.abc.net.au/news/2014-08-01/png-sorcery-violence-on-the-rise/5642190, viewed 5/8/2014.

Amnesty International 2009. Women Killed for Witchcraft in PNG. 29 January. www.amnesty.org.au/svaw/comments/20139/, viewed 17/2/2015.

Amnesty International 2011. *Papua New Guinea Violence against Women, Sorcery-Related Killings and Forced Evictions*. Amnesty International Submission to the UN Universal Periodic Review, May 2011. www.amnesty.org/en/library/asset/ASA34/005/2010/en/8fac8481-2baf-46df-afaf-0b13d1ce33f2/asa340052010en.html, viewed 17/2/2015.

Ashforth, A. 2002. An Epidemic of Witchcraft? The Implications of AIDS for the Post-Apartheid State. *African Studies* 61(1):121–43. users.polisci.wisc.edu/schatzberg/ps657/Ashforth2002.pdf, viewed 17/2/2015.

Ashforth, A. 2005. *Witchcraft, Violence, and Democracy in South Africa*. Chicago: University of Chicago Press.

Baskind, R. and G.L. Birbeck 2005. Epilepsy-Associated Stigma in Sub-Saharan Africa: The Social Landscape of a Disease. *Epilepsy & Behavior* 7:68–73.

Behringer, W. 2004. *Witches and Witch-Hunts: A Global History*. Cambridge: Polity Press.

Brain, J.L. 1982. Witchcraft and Development. *African Affairs* 81:83–111.

Comaroff, J. and J. Comaroff (eds) 1993. *Modernity and Its Malcontents: Ritual Power in Postcolonial Africa*. Chicago: University of Chicago Press.

Ellen, R. and C.W. Watson (eds) 1993. *Understanding Witchcraft and Sorcery in Southeast Asia*. Honolulu: University of Hawai'i Press.

Evans-Pritchard, E.E. 1937. *Witchcraft, Oracles and Magic among the Azande*. The Clarendon Press.

Eves, R. 2000. Sorcery's the Curse: Modernity, Envy and the Flow of Sociality in a Melanesian Society. *The Journal of the Royal Anthropological Institute* 6(3):453–68.

Eves, R. 2013. Sorcery and Witchcraft in Papua New Guinea: Problems in Definition. *SSGM In Brief* 2013/12. Canberra: State, Society and Governance in Melanesia Program, The Australian National University.

Eves, R. and A. Kelly-Hanku 2014. Witch-Hunts in Papua New Guinea's Eastern Highlands Province: A Fieldwork Report. *SSGM In Brief* 2014/4. Canberra: State, Society and Governance in Melanesia Program, The Australian National University.

Fisiy, C.F. and P. Geschiere 2001. Witchcraft, Development and Paranoia in Cameroon: Interactions between Popular, Academic and State Discourse. In H.L. Moore and T. Sanders (eds), *Magical Interpretations, Material Realities: Modernity, Witchcraft and the Occult in Postcolonial Africa*. London: Routledge, 226–46.

Forsyth, M. 2006. Sorcery and the Criminal Law in Vanuatu. *Lawasia Journal* 1:1–27.

Forsyth, M. 2013a. Witchcraft and Sorcery-Related Killings in Melanesia: The Legal Issues. *SSGM In Brief* 2013/1. Canberra: State, Society and Governance in Melanesia Program, The Australian National University.

Forsyth, M. 2013b. Summary of Main Themes Emerging from the Conference on Sorcery & Witchcraft-Related Killings in Melanesia, 5–7 June 2013, ANU, Canberra. Outrigger: Blog of the Pacific Institute. pacificinstitute.anu.edu.au/outrigger/2013/06/18/summary-sorcery-witchcraft-related-killings-in-melanesia-5-7-june-2013/, viewed 5/8/2014.

Forsyth, M. 2013c. Witchcraft and Sorcery Related Killings in Melanesia: Culture, Law and Human Rights Perspectives. *NZ Human Rights Working Paper* 20. www.humanrights.auckland.ac.nz/webdav/site/humanrights/shared/Research/HRWorkingpaper20-Forsyth.pdf, viewed 5/8/2014.

Forsyth, M. 2014. New Draft National Action Plan to Address Sorcery Accusation-Related Violence in Papua New Guinea. *SSGM In Brief* 2014/18. Canberra: State, Society and Governance in Melanesia Program, The Australian National University.

Fortune, R.F. 1963. *Sorcerers of Dobu: The Social Anthropology of the Dobu Islanders of the Western Pacific*. New York: E.P. Dutton.

Geschiere, P. 1997. *The Modernity of Witchcraft: Politics and the Occult in Postcolonial Africa*. Charlottesville: University of Virginia Press.

Golooba-Mutebi, F. 2005. Witchcraft, Social Cohesion and Participation in a South African Village. *Development and Change* 36(5):937–58.

Herriman, N. 2007. 'Sorcerer' Killings in Banyuwangi: A Re-Examination of State Responsibility for Violence. *Asian Studies Review* 31(1):61–78.

Herriman, N. 2014. The Morbid Nexus: Reciprocity and Sorcery in Rural East Java. *TAJA: The Australian Journal of Anthropology* (early view 24/11/2014).

Heyns, C. 2014. Preliminary Observations on the Official Visit to Papua New Guinea by Mr Christof Heyns, United Nations Special Rapporteur on Extrajudicial, Summary or Arbitrary Executions, 3–14 March 2014. Press statement, Office of the High Commissioner for Human Rights. www.ohchr.org/EN/NewsEvents/Pages/DisplayNews.aspx?NewsID=14373&LangID=E, viewed 5/8/2014.

HSIMR (Health Services and Institute of Medical Research) 2004. Final Report into the Study of *Sanguma* in the Eastern Highlands and Simbu Provinces. HSIMR.

Jorgensen, D. 2014. Preying on Those Close to Home: Witchcraft Violence in a Papua New Guinea Village. *TAJA: The Australian Journal of Anthropology* 25:267–86.

Kapferer, B. 1997. *The Feast of the Sorcerer: Practices of Consciousness and Power*. Chicago: University of Chicago Press.

Knauft, B.M. 1985. *Good Company and Violence: Sorcery and Social Action in a Lowland New Guinea Society*. Berkeley: University of California Press.

Kohnert, D. 1996. Magic and Witchcraft: Implications for Democratization and Poverty-Alleviating Aid in Africa. *World Development* 24(8):1347–355.

Leistner, E. 2014. Witchcraft and African Development. *African Security Review* 23(1):53–77.

Lindenbaum, S. 1979. *Kuru Sorcery: Disease and Danger in the New Guinea Highlands*. California: Mayfield Publishing Company.

Manjoo, R. 2013. Report of the Special Rapporteur on Violence against Women, its Causes and Consequences. 13/3/2013, A/HRC/23/49/Add.2.

Moore, H.L. and T. Sanders (eds) 2001. *Magical Interpretations, Material Realities: Modernity, Witchcraft and the Occult in Postcolonial Africa*. London: Routledge.

Niehaus, I. with E. Mohlala and K. Shokane 2001. *Witchcraft, Power and Politics: Exploring the Occult in the South African Lowveld*. London: Pluto Press.

Oxfam International Papua New Guinea 2010. *Sorcery Beliefs and Practices in Gumine: A Source of Conflict and Insecurity*. Oxfam International. <archive.org/details/SorceryReportFINAL>, viewed 5/8/2014.

Patterson, M. 1974–75. Sorcery and Witchcraft in Melanesia. *Oceania* 45(2&3):132–60, 212–34.

Petrus, T. 2012. Influence, Insecurities and Evil: The Political and Economic Context of Witchcraft-Related Crime in the Eastern Cape, South Africa. *International Journal of Sociology and Anthropology* 4(6):179–89.

Siegel, J. 2006. *Naming the Witch*. Stanford: Stanford University Press.

Smith, J.H. 2005. Buying a Better Witch Doctor: Witch-Finding, Neoliberalism, and the Development Imagination in the Taita Hills, Kenya. *American Ethnologist* 32(1):141–58.

Smith, J.H. 2008. *Bewitching Development: Witchcraft and the Reinvention of Development in Neoliberal Kenya*. Chicago: University of Chicago Press.

Stephen, M. (ed.) 1987. *Sorcerer and Witch in Melanesia*. Carlton: Melbourne University Press.

Whitehead, N.L. and R. Wright (eds) 2004. *In Darkness and Secrecy: The Anthropology of Assault Sorcery and Witchcraft in Amazonia*. Durham: Duke University Press.

Zelenietz, M. and S. Lindenbaum (eds) 1981. *Sorcery and Social Change in Melanesia. Social Analysis* No. 8 (Special Issue). Adelaide: Association for Social Anthropology in Oceania.

Zocca, F. (ed.) 2009. *Sanguma* in Paradise: Sorcery, Witchcraft and Christianity in Papua New Guinea. *Point* No. 33. Goroka: Melanesian Institute.

Part 1: Social, Economic and Cultural Dimensions to the Belief in Witchcraft and Sorcery

1. The Spread of Sorcery Killing and its Social Implications

Jack Urame

Introduction

In changing times when sickness and death can be scientifically explained, people continue to use sorcery and witchcraft beliefs to provide explanations and express their frustrations, confusion and stress when bad events happen. As a result, sorcery-related violence remains a huge social phenomenon in Papua New Guinea (PNG). Many families have suffered social stress from sorcery and witchcraft accusations, the marginalised have been displaced, the weak have been expelled from their communities and the defenceless have been killed in horrific circumstances.

Due to the diversity of sorcery and witchcraft beliefs and practices in PNG, sorcery-related killing is common in some societies but not in others. Media reports and stories are insufficient to generalise the phenomenon of sorcery killing or witch-hunts across PNG. In some societies people use direct physical force to kill, while in others people use counter-sorcery as a means of revenge without direct physical violence. Using physical violence in the pretext of sorcery is common in the highlands of PNG, in some parts of the Sepik, Madang, Bougainville and a few other places in PNG.

In this chapter, I will discuss two practical aspects of sorcery and witchcraft violence: accusations on the pretext of sorcery and witchcraft beliefs and the spread of sorcery killing or witch-hunts. I use the phrase 'sorcery-related killing' to refer to murder in the pretext of sorcery beliefs. Sorcery-related violence results from the belief that bad events are caused by evil people. I attempt to answer why sorcery accusations have increased in recent times and why the culture of killing has spread to new locations where it was uncommon or unknown in the past. To avoid terminology and conceptual inconsistency I use sorcery as an inclusive term for witchcraft. However, in some parts of PNG the term witchcraft or its pidgin equivalent *sanguma* is common.

Reported cases of sorcery-related killings

Some few years back I conducted research on media reports of sorcery-related violence. My aim was to find out the extent sorcery cases were reported in the media, whether sorcery issues gained sufficient publicity and how the community, the police and the courts responded to sorcery cases. I searched in three PNG newspapers: the daily *National* and *Post-Courier* and the weekly *Wantok* papers. I did an electronic search through the papers, which were scanned and electronically stored in a database at the Melanesian Institute. I began this task in 2007 and selected newspaper reports from 2000 to 2006. Within that seven-year period I identified 75 cases with 147 victims reported in the newspapers (Zocca and Urame 2008). These figures were not convincing to claim that there was an average of 10.7 cases of sorcery accusations per year or a monthly average of 0.9 cases of sorcery involving torture and murder. However, those figures are likely to under-represent the real numbers because sorcery-related violence was not always reported to appropriate authorities or to the media. The number of victims I identified in the media search was much lower than what was revealed in research conducted by the Melanesian Institute around the same period. For instance, Kundiawa Hospital in Simbu Province registered many sorcery victims who sought medical treatment but many of those cases were not reported in the media (Zocca 2009).

Comparing sorcery cases involving violence during that period, the Highlands Region was leading followed by Momase Region, Southern Region and New Guinea Islands Region. At present the sequence from highest to lowest cases of sorcery involving violence in the four regions still stands in this order. Since 2007, the number of cases involving torture and murder around the country has not been consistently followed up, therefore the actual figure is unknown. Without actual data it is difficult to establish the average number of killings annually in the country. However, from research conducted by the Melanesian Institute as well as cases reported in the media, sorcery killings have increased in recent times (Zocca 2009; Zocca and Urame 2008).

There are several factors why many sorcery-related cases have not been exposed in the media or in public. These are described below.

Protection of the community

Often sorcery-related killings are concealed within the clan or tribal communities. From the community's perspective, killing a suspected sorcerer is an act of defence for the good of the community. The young people in the communities who usually take the lead in accusations and killings are supported by the members of the community because the accusers are considered as defenders and protectors of the community. The negative response of the members of the community is influenced by this general perception; therefore sometimes they do not support the police or cooperate in police investigations on sorcery killing. Often members of the community are reluctant to report because of the belief that sorcerers are a threat to the well-being of the community and therefore must be removed.

Fear of consequences

Many cases have never been reported to appropriate authorities because people are afraid of risking their own lives. Those who attempt to report or defend the accused are often themselves in danger of being accused for supporting sorcerers or in danger of being labelled as sorcerers. Due to threats and intimidation, relatives and family members are afraid of losing their own lives if they report or retaliate. Fear of possible negative consequences continues to suppress people, hence sorcery-related violence often remains unreported.

Lack of police presence

Police response has been very limited. Not all sorcery-related violence has been attended to and followed up by police. There are several reasons why police response has been minimal. Some of these are unavailability of vehicles, no fuel, lack of manpower and police expectations for complainants to pay money or buy diesel before cases are attended to. These are expressions of police reluctance or ignorance to reduce sorcery-related violence. When this happens people simply give up, seek other alternatives or resort to further violence.

Geographic limitations

Many villages are situated in remote places and the nearest government stations from which to seek help are located kilometres away from the villages. Due to geographic hardship and absence of government stations, many cases of sorcery-related violence are not made known to the public or attended to by state authorities. Sometimes cases are not attended to because the roads have deteriorated or bridges collapsed, preventing access to the area so sorcery cases remain isolated from the police or other state authorities.

The culture of silence

The factors listed above contribute to the culture of silence. In places where sorcery-related violence occurs, people remain silent and accept sorcery killing as a way of life because the belief in sorcery is deeply embedded in Melanesian spirituality.

Violence was a way of life in traditional societies and continues to be so across societies in Melanesia today, because people are reluctant or do not easily accept alternative world views. When sorcery talk begins, young people in the community often claim authority over others and exercise control over the situation. They intimidate members of the community who may feel threatened and powerless and do not speak up or speak against the young people. So the culture of silence on one hand promotes sorcery violence, and on the other hand prevents cases of sorcery-related violence from being reported to state authorities.

New trends of sorcery killing

In Melanesian societies where social relationships and kinship ties are central to life in rural communities, sorcery violence often breaks families and clan communities apart.

There are several reasons why family members suffer sorcery accusations. First, it is believed that the blood of the relatives is 'hot', so sorcery power is inwardly projected, therefore sorcery issues begin within the family. Second, the power of sorcery is effective within the family line so when someone dies, an immediate family member is most likely to be accused. Third, sorcery power is believed to be passed from one person to another through the social network of family and lineage. Fourth, when family members react against the accusation or when they do not support the community, they are blamed for protecting or supporting the sorcerer. Fifth, the accusers feel much safer blaming people within the family than outside the family due to fear of retaliation from accusations directed at people from another line or clan.

However, despite the general perception of the connection between sorcery and family violence, in the past accusations were targeted at individuals and rarely on families. Today, accusations involving families and groups are increasing. For instance, from the 75 cases of sorcery accusation I identified in the media reports, half of them involved families or groups of people who are socially related. Here are some examples: in one case, three families were tortured and their houses burnt down completely; in another case, a family was held at gunpoint, slowly tortured for hours and eventually murdered; in a different case a husband was chased out of the community while his wife was chopped to death and their children were left in complete desolation; in a further case, a baby was split in half when the mother who was carrying the baby tried to avoid a bush knife that was swung at her. The list of such violent attacks on families is not exhaustive and new incidents are added every year.

The traditional patterns of sorcery accusation have also changed. Various techniques of accusation were used by perpetrators, ranging from verbal abuse to physical assault and murder in various forms. Particularly in the highlands where sorcery-related killing is common, some of the punishment methods now applied to suspected sorcerers are new compared to methods used in traditional societies. For instance, suspected sorcerers are tied with cords, publicly interrogated and disgraced, thrown alive into rivers, tied and thrown alive over cliffs, locked indoors and burnt alive, buried in pit toilets, suffocated, hung on trees, slowly tortured for hours or days, burnt with flammable liquids, axed to death, chopped with bush knives, shot with guns, tied up and burnt with hot iron, stripped naked and tortured in public, or tied with rope and dragged behind moving vehicles. These are some methods used recently to eliminate suspected sorcerers from communities.

Sorcery-related violence using modern technologies like guns, vehicles, iron, axes, bush knives or chemicals on families indicates the collapse of social order in communities and the lack of social control in the midst of social crisis. The victims are those perceived to be on the periphery of society and the marginalised whose social status is considered insignificant by the community. Victims of sorcery violence are often old people and women who are not able to defend themselves. Due to their weak social status in the community, they become vulnerable to sorcery-related violence when social crises like sickness and death strike the community.

Factors of increase in sorcery killing

In traditional societies, sorcery-related killing was not common in all parts of PNG. In places where sorcery belief was strong, traditional social structures provided control mechanisms through which issues were addressed, and therefore sorcery-related killing was minimal. In chieftain societies there was hierarchal order, which kept the behaviour of young people in control. The chiefs often relied on the sorcerer for his advantage and for the good of the community. Therefore in times of social crisis sorcerers were not penalised or removed from the community by young people. In traditional big-man societies, particularly in the highlands, young people respected the authority of traditional leaders. In Simbu Province, for example, sorcery issues were publicly discussed in the presence of the members of the community and not among a few in private to execute murder. Previously, in times of social disorder, young people, whose social status was less significant in the community, were afraid to act violently against suspected sorcerers without the approval of the traditional leaders.

However, today there is a changing trend where sorcery-related violence is often initiated and executed by young people in isolation and the community becomes aware only during or after the accusation or removal of the sorcerers. Unlike in traditional societies, today traditional leaders are often reluctant to intervene when sorcery accusations occur because they are afraid of being physically attacked or blamed for being sorcerers themselves. Compared to tribal warfare, which often caused extreme social stress and communal disorder, sorcery-related violence in the past was less destructive because of social controls within clans. In some societies, suspected sorcerers were publicly disgraced, but they were rarely burnt, hanged or killed as happens today in some PNG societies.

Today sorcery-related violence, in particular witch-hunts, are spreading from one place to another. In societies where sorcery killing seldom happened, it occurs quite frequently today, and in places where it was never experienced before, it is beginning to happen. These new trends of sorcery violence bring new challenges and therefore it is important to understand the underlying factors of the increase and spread of sorcery killing. Some of the contributing factors are discussed below.

Lack of development

Lack of development causes social stress among people and contributes to the increase in sorcery-related violence. New development alters people's perception of life while rapid changes create confusion, disorientation and social tension. While lack of development is evident in many places, people's expectations for a better life are high. However, when expectations are not met, people resort to sorcery as a means of seeking answers or as a shortcut to meet their expectations. Lack of economic development in rural areas, failure in business, failure in school examinations, failure to find employment and so on are also attributed to sorcery. As a result of development failures, innocent people are blamed and accused on the pretext of sorcery.

Collapse of traditional systems

In today's changing PNG, our Melanesian social structures and systems, which hold societies together, are becoming weak or gradually collapsing. Village elders and traditional leaders are no longer being respected by young people who seek identity and recognition in society. Social cohesion within families and clan communities declines as sorcery-related violence causes social fragmentation. Traditional values of communal life and social systems are increasingly being challenged as the trend towards materialism and individualism increases. This results in the culture of greed and corruption, and the social and economic life of sharing, caring and helping is gradually losing its value. The collapse of traditional social systems promotes the culture of sorcery accusations.

Economic imbalance

Economic disparity also contributes to the increase in sorcery violence. The rising cost of living in the country creates inequality between those who have and those who do not, and the gap between them widens. This often leads to jealousy within communities between the economically advantaged and disadvantaged groups. As a result, when sorcery issues arise, people take advantage of the situation to release their frustration. The discontent of economic imbalances in society is often expressed through the existing belief in sorcery.

Lifestyle diseases

The increase in lifestyle diseases in PNG today also contributes to sorcery accusations. The availability of imported food like lamb flaps, alcohol and fast food, which contain too much sugar and fat, affects the health of many people and causes new sicknesses, which were unknown in traditional societies. Many people also lack knowledge about health, hygiene and healthy lifestyles. As a result, when people die of lifestyle diseases, innocent people are blamed. People die young due to risky behaviour and unhealthy lifestyles, yet relatives often attribute the deaths to sorcery.

Generational conflict

The breakdown in social order and generational conflict between the old and young also leads to the increase in sorcery accusations. Today a new social group is emerging in the communities. They are known as 'drug bodies', made up of young people who have no perspective in life and who have no hope for the future. They become a threat to communities because of their association with drugs and violence. In times of social crisis such as sickness and death, sorcery discussions are often led by drugtakers and accusations are made by these young people.

Lack of information or misguided information from medical workers

Sometimes there is insufficient or irrelevant information from hospitals. In my research with the Melanesian Institute on sorcery, I found that families of patients were not properly informed when the patient could not recover. When medical help was exhausted and the patient was at the point of death, medical workers say it is '*sik bilong ples*' therefore '*go long ples na stretim tok*', which implies that the sickness is caused by someone at home, so go home and seek answers there. Nonsense talk like this confirms the belief that sicknesses are caused by evil people and therefore sorcerers must be blamed. When patients die at the hospital, doctors provide medical reports but, despite this, people continue to accuse innocent people of sorcery and witchcraft (see also Cox and Phillips, Chapter 2, this volume).

Lack of positive knowledge

People are so deeply rooted in their belief systems that they are not able to accept alternative world views. People with positions of authority and responsibilities, such as medical workers, police, church pastors and educated elites, continue to believe in the power of sorcery and witchcraft. They sometimes become a party to sorcery violence through direct involvement in it, or through their influence on others. This implies that in PNG the level of education, social standing, profession and leadership of many people do not play a significant role in influencing people's belief systems. Thus lack of positive knowledge can lead to the increase in sorcery violence.

Spread of sorcery killing

In the past, witch-hunts were practised only in some societies. While witch-hunts were uncommon in traditional Enga society and in parts of Western Highlands, Eastern Highlands, Southern Highlands and Hela provinces, they were common in Simbu and other parts of Eastern Highlands, Western Highlands and Jiwaka provinces. However, in recent times, sorcery killing has spread to societies where the practice was unknown or infrequent in the past. Today there are reported cases of people being accused or murdered for sorcery in almost all the highlands provinces.

When the Melanesian Institute conducted research on sorcery in PNG, I did over 50 interviews between 2006 and 2008 in various locations (Urame 2009). After the publication of that research I continued to do random interviews with various people from different provinces to understand the spread of sorcery killing. I interviewed people from different places in Morobe, Madang, Eastern Highlands, Simbu, Jiwaka, Western Highlands and Enga provinces. They were a mixture of ordinary people, educated elites, village leaders, students, church workers, academics and missionaries. In the interviews I asked, 'Is witch-hunt common in your area and if so was it also practised in the past or is it a new culture in your area? If it is a new culture how did it spread into your area?' Except in Simbu, respondents from other provinces gave similar responses. They claimed that witch-hunts are a new social phenomenon and they are not sure how it was brought into their area. In an interview in 2007 with a church pastor from Enga, I found that sorcery accusations were uncommon although the belief in harmful spirits was already present in traditional Enga spirituality. The common threat to human life in Enga was tribal enemies and not sorcery. However, in an interview in 2014 with another pastor from Enga, I found that the culture of sorcery accusations is now beginning to penetrate the province. It has spread from Western Highlands to Wapenamanda in Enga Province. Cases of sorcery fear and accusations were already reported in Porgera and Wapenamanda. Therefore, it is very likely that in a few years the culture of witch-killing will grip Enga society as in other highlands societies.

Several factors have contributed to the spread of witch-hunts in recent times. These are described below.

Geographic mobility

Geographic mobility has increased and people continue to move between villages and towns. When people migrate they go with their beliefs and in times of sickness, death or other misfortune they use their beliefs to resolve crises. Today witch-hunts are no longer isolated in villages or remote parts of the country, but have spread to towns and urban settlements.

Intermarriage

In traditional societies, marriage was limited to neighbouring clans or tribes and rarely extended beyond those limits. The pattern of marriage is changing today. People are exposed to new cultures through intermarriage. They come into contact with people whose belief systems are different from their own. As a result, traditional beliefs such as sorcery and its related violence spread from one cultural group to another through marriage connections and social networks.

Media

Media publicity of sorcery killing also contributes to the spread of sorcery violence. When what happens in one part of the country is published in the media, it spreads to the other parts of the country. While the media serves its purpose of publicity, people digest the information and reinterpret it in the context of their own belief systems. The information either informs or reinforces the existing beliefs. Therefore media publicity of sorcery cases has in a way unintentionally fuelled the spread of the belief and the violence associated with it.

Importation of culture

People have selective memories and tend to remember events or stories that confirm their beliefs. Hence sorcery accusations confirm and reinforce their beliefs. People hear or learn about sorcery violence from other places and they try it out in their own cultures. The common belief in bad spirits and evil powers provides the basis through which sorcery accusation has spread from one society to another.

Conclusion

Sorcery accusations are used as a means of revenge, resolving conflict and settling hostilities, and as a means to redress social and economic imbalances in society. The perpetrators of sorcery violence are not strangers, but people who are biologically or socially related to the accused. For example, in a personal interview with a highly educated man, he told me of his approval for the death of his biological mother in 2010 in Simbu. He ordered the young men in his village to murder her because he believed that she planned to bewitch him. In another personal interview in 2011 with a man in Simbu, he said he mobilised with his clansman and murdered his own niece because they suspected her of causing the death of a cousin brother. There are examples of many similar cases.

If sorcery killing is permitted to happen between people who are socially connected, there must be another underlying value that lies deep within society other than the value of the social bond. In the centre of society lies man's religious beliefs — be it sorcery or Christianity or something else. The value of religious belief outweighs the value of social bond. In several interviews, this idea was explicitly expressed. One said, 'if we don't remove the sorcerers we will all die and our clan will be empty'. Another said, 'if the government imposes the death penalty on the young men in the communities for witch-hunts our defence will be removed and the sorcerers will be happy and wipe us all out'. If this is indicative of a mindset dilemma influenced by their Melanesian world view, it is not sufficient to address sorcery-related violence on the surface, but necessary to go a step further to understand the Melanesian belief systems. Therefore the most crucial attempt would be to work towards changing the mindset of the people, so that through the process of change sorcery belief and its consequential violence may one day be eliminated.

References

Bartle, N. 2005. Death, Witchcraft and the Spirit World in the Highlands of Papua New Guinea. *Point* No. 29. Goroka: Melanesian Institute.

Bogner, P. 1988. *Sangguma – Schwarze Magie der Papua: Bericht aus einer anderen Wirklichkiet*. München, Germany: Wilhelm Goldmann Verlag.

Bowden, R. 1987. Sorcery, Illness and Social Control in Kwoma Society. In M. Stephen (ed.) *Sorcerer and Witch in Melanesia*. Carlton: Melbourne University Press, 183–207.

Brown, P. 1997. Kumo Witchcraft at Mintima, Chimbu Province. *Oceania* XLVIII(1):26–29.

Fortune, R.F. 1963. *Sorcery of Dobu: The Social Anthropology of the Dobu Islanders of the Western Pacific*. New York: E.P. Dutton.

Gesch, P. 1979. Magic as a Process of Social Discernment. In N.C. Habel (ed.) *Powers, Plumes and Piglets: Phenomena of Melanesian Religion*. Australian Association for the Study of Religions, 137–48.

Gibbs, P. 2010. Witch Killing and Engendered Violence in Simbu. *Catalyst* 40(1):24–64.

Hughes, J.R. 1985. Chimbu Worlds: Experiences of Continuity and Change by a Papua New Guinea Highland People. PhD thesis, La Trobe University, Melbourne.

Kelly, R. 1976. Witchcraft and Sexual Relations. In P. Brown and G. Buchbinder (ed.) *Man and Woman in the New Guinea Highlands*. Washington DC: American Anthropological Association, 36–53.

Kelly, R.C. 1993. *Constructing Inequality: The Fabrication of a Hierarchy of Virtue among the Etoro*. Ann Arbor: University of Michigan Press.

Kuehling, S. 2005. *Dobu: Ethics of Exchange on a Massim Island, Papua New Guinea*. Honolulu: University of Hawai'i Press.

Leonard, B.G. 1973. Sorcery and Witchcraft. In I. Hogbin (ed.) *Anthropology in Papua New Guinea*. Carlton: Melbourne University Press, 182–86.

Lindenbaum, S. 1978. Sorcery and Danger. *Oceania* XLVI(1):68–75.

Lindenbaum, S. 1979. *Kuru Sorcery: Disease and Danger in the New Guinea Highlands*. California: Mayfield Publishing Company.

Longgar, W. 2009. Sorcery and Christianity in the Gazelle Peninsula. In F. Zocca (ed.) *Sanguma* in Paradise: Sorcery, Witchcraft and Christianity in Papua New Guinea. *Point* No. 33. Goroka: Melanesian Institute, 305–59.

MacDonald, M. 1981. Sorcery and Society. *Catalyst* 11(3):168–79.

MacDonald, M.N. 1990. *Mararoko: A Study in Melanesian Religion*. New York: Peter Lang.

Malinowski, B. 1985. *Crime and Custom in Savage Society*. Totowa, NJ: Rowman & Allanheld.

Sillitoe, P. 1987. Sorcery Divination among the Wola. In M. Stephen (ed.) *Sorcerer and Witch in Melanesia*. Carlton: Melbourne University Press, 121–46.

Steadman, L. 1978. Sorcery and Danger. *Oceania* XLVI(1):114–21.

Stephen, M. 1979. Sorcery, Magic and the Mekeo World View. In N.C. Habel (ed.) *Powers, Plumes and Piglets: Phenomena of Melanesian Religion*. Australian Association for the Study of Religions, 149–60.

Stephen, M. 1987. Constructing Images of Power. In M. Stephen (ed.) *Sorcerer and Witch in Melanesia*. Carlton: Melbourne University Press, 249–99.

Strathern, M. 1972. *Women In Between: Female Roles in a Male World: Mount Hagen, New Guinea*. London: Seminar Press.

Strathern, M. 1988. *The Gender of the Gift*. Berkeley: University of California Press.

Trompf, G.W. 1991. *Melanesian Religions*. Cambridge: Cambridge University Press.

Trompf, G.W. 1994. *Payback: The Logic of Retribution in Melanesian Religions*. Cambridge: Cambridge University Press.

Urame, J. 2008. A Review on Some Researches Done on the Belief and Practices of Sorcery and Witchcraft in the Simbu Province. *Catalyst* 38(2):181–201.

Urame, J. 2009. Sorcery Beliefs, Practices and Mission among the Kote of Finschaffen, Morobe Province. In F. Zocca (ed.) *Sanguma* in Paradise: Sorcery, Witchcraft and Christianity in Papua New Guinea. *Point* No. 33. Goroka: Melanesian Institute, 96–166.

Zocca, F. (ed.) 2009. *Sanguma* in Paradise: Sorcery, Witchcraft and Christianity in Papua New Guinea. *Point* No. 33. Goroka: Melanesian Institute.

Zocca, F. 2010. Gender and Accusation of Malevolent Sorcery and Witchcraft in Papua New Guinea. *Catalyst* 40(2):192–206.

Zocca, F. and J. Urame 2008. Sorcery, Witchcraft and Christianity in Melanesia. *Melanesian Mission Studies* No. 5. Goroka: Melanesian Institute.

2. Sorcery, Christianity and the Decline of Medical Services

John Cox and Georgina Phillips

Introduction

In Papua New Guinea (PNG), witchcraft and sorcery accusations appear to be proliferating and, in many cases, leading to horrific violence, torture and murder of those thought to be sorcerers (Chandler 2013). Our contribution to the debates about sorcery-related violence is to see it as the result of poverty and failing services. Following the medical anthropologist and infectious diseases physician Paul Farmer, we reject interpretations of sorcery accusations and violence as grounded in the ancient traditional culture of Melanesia.[1] Instead, we see the resurgence of sorcery as an effect of poverty and social inequality, particularly the neglect of medical services and training (Farmer 1999).

Sorcery accusations are largely associated with untimely or unanticipated deaths, therefore the contest between these ways of thinking and biomedical understandings of disease and illness is important to examine. In this chapter, we argue that the explanatory power of biomedicine in PNG and Solomon Islands is hampered by several factors, not least the poor access to and resourcing of medical services. The reinvigoration of medical training and service provision is crucial to demonstrating the efficacy of biomedicine and improving health outcomes for PNG as well as combating the spread of competing understandings of illness and disease that give rise to maltreatment, social division, misogyny and violence.

This chapter draws heavily on the anthropological work of our friend Alice Street, whom we first met in Madang in 2009. Her insightful ethnographic studies of Modilon Hospital, the referral hospital for Madang Province (2009, 2010, 2011, 2014), have provided much of the grounding for the arguments we make in this chapter. However, we have our own experiences of Melanesian hospitals and the people who work in them, particularly doctors, whom Phillips has had particularly privileged access to as a senior colleague. Like Street, Cox is an anthropologist who has done fieldwork in Madang for his study of middle-class investors in 'fast money schemes' in PNG (Cox 2011, 2013; Cox and Macintyre 2014). Phillips is an emergency physician who since 2006 has worked

---

1   Here we use 'Melanesia' as a shorthand reference to PNG and Solomon Islands.

closely with Papua New Guinean and Solomon Islander doctors completing their training in emergency medicine through the University of Papua New Guinea. This has included the establishment of a Visiting Clinical Lecturer Program at Divine Word University (Atua and Phillips 2014; Phillips et al. 2012). Phillips has also done medical capacity development work in Kiribati and Myanmar (Phillips et al. 2014) and has conducted programmatic reviews of emergency departments (EDs) in East Timor (2009) and Solomon Islands (2014). The reflections in this chapter draw on these experiences and on a recent (July–August 2014) visit to PNG by both authors. We also thank our dear friend Dr Vincent Atua, director of the ED at Modilon General Hospital, Madang, for years of stimulating conversations about these issues and for his comments on an earlier draft of this chapter.

Emergency departments in Melanesia

Here we focus on hospital EDs as sites where the social meanings of sorcery are enacted and contested. In their role of providing biomedical services, EDs are important places for the treatment of victims of violence arising from sorcery accusations. Sometimes relatives of people who have died will come to EDs seeking a post-mortem medical diagnosis in order to resolve accusations of sorcery (cf. van Amstel and van der Geest 2004). EDs are also places where staff, patients and relatives publicly reproduce sorcery discourse and therefore indirectly legitimate violence. EDs are relatively recent spaces in hospitals around the world. Traditionally, they have been the domain of unsupervised junior doctors and often used as a place of last resort for underperforming medical and nursing staff. In PNG, emergency medicine is in its infancy (Aitken et al. 2003). Only 10 local emergency physicians have graduated through the specialist training program at the University of Papua New Guinea Medical School that commenced in 2002. Of those 10, only six remain working in the public health system in PNG. Solomon Islands has no emergency medicine specialists.

Emergency medicine concerns itself with the prevention and clinical care (diagnosis and management) of all acute and urgent health problems across the entire spectrum of illness and injury. Emergency medicine cares for all types of patients at every stage of life, and also incorporates pre-hospital care — the delivery of first aid and supervised transport to hospital for people who need urgent medical and nursing attention. Emergency care specialists prioritise clinical care according to urgency rather than type or severity of health problem (Hsia et al. 2010; Razzak and Kellermann 2002). Emergency medicine is a population-based discipline that reflects the demographics and health problems of a community when preventative and primary care systems are insufficient. All of these factors make EDs invaluable places from which to observe emergent trends both in health and society more generally.

In Melanesia, training in emergency medicine has largely been confined to doctors, despite the integral team-based nature of emergency care practice. Since the infancy of the emergency medicine specialist training program at the University of Papua New Guinea, Australasian emergency physicians have been involved as clinicians, teachers and peer-supporters of doctors from PNG, Solomon Islands and Vanuatu (Curry et al. 2004). Some of those doctors have spent time in Australian EDs to practise emergency medicine and experience advanced triage and other tools in a mature system as part of their specialist training. For nurses, training in emergency care has been much more ad hoc; confined to team-based short-course teaching and the efforts of a few dedicated nurses. One small program has involved nurses from the EDs of St Vincent's Hospital in Melbourne and the Port Moresby General Hospital visiting each other's environments as an educational exchange (Phillips 2013).

There are several notable exceptions, such as the new ED at the Port Moresby General Hospital but, generally, EDs in Melanesia are poorly designed and ill-equipped to provide core components of emergency care. Space for resuscitation is often cramped and crowded and basic necessities such as oxygen, suction and essential medicines are frequently missing. Rooms for acute care delivery are poorly lit, poorly ventilated and with little amenities. Areas for triage, waiting patients and patients requiring observation were never incorporated into past ED building designs, and so those functions are now delivered outside or in an ill-fitting space. Basic investigations such as X-rays and simple blood tests are often impossible to obtain in a timely manner, thereby substantially limiting diagnostic ability in emergency situations, quite apart from the issues regarding tests discussed in Street (2011) and later in this chapter. In the vast majority of EDs around the region, there are no clinicians with the essential skills and knowledge for emergency care.

Hospitals as spaces of contested meanings and practices

Anthropologists have argued that hospitals are not simply places governed by biomedical ideals. Rather, a range of beliefs and practices shape day-to-day behaviour within hospitals, including the interactions between patients, their relatives, doctors, nurses and hospital management. Hospitals in Melanesia may even play significant roles in negotiating compensation claims (van Amstel and van der Geest 2004). We endorse Zaman's insight that the hospital is not an isolated subculture or an 'island', rather it is a microcosm of the larger society in which it is situated. A hospital ward is therefore a mirror that reflects and reveals the core values and norms of the broader society. (Zaman 2005:18, cited in Street and Coleman 2012:7)

Christianity is constitutive of the public realm in PNG, Solomon Islands and other Pacific islands countries (Tomlinson and McDougall 2013). This extends to health services, which were often initiated by Christian missions. Hospitals in Melanesia are often run by churches, but even notionally secular government facilities are Christian in practice. Hospitals host interdenominational religious fellowships for their staff and are regularly visited by evangelists and other religious practitioners, who may preach to patients and certainly leave religious magazines and so forth in the hospital (Street 2011). However, this religious permeation of the hospital space sometimes meets limits. In Port Moresby a recent controversy over Pentecostal groups advising AIDS sufferers to abandon their medication in favour of faith healing has led to a ban on visitors praying with patients (Cochrane 2014; Eves 2008).

Street (2010, 2011) has shown how Christian practices of belief function in the PNG hospital setting, where patients attempt to demonstrate their moral worthiness as a means of accessing curative services. As Eves (2010:497) has noted, Christianity has a long pedigree of associating illness with immorality that underpins this logic of personal moral regeneration. In Madang — and more widely in Melanesia — many nurses feel free to proselytise to patients, or offer them specifically Christian moral exhortation and prayer. This pastoral role is not seen as incidental to their nursing responsibilities but is integrated into their biomedical practice, which is seen as 'God's work' (Street 2010:262). Rather, a number of nurses see themselves as active agents who are more directly involved with patients than doctors and who therefore can claim a unique efficacy in the curative process. According to Street (2011:7), the ward nurses she observed believed that their expertise included counselling patients about their illness, allaying fears of sorcery and persuading them to turn to God. This may not characterise all nurses in Melanesia, but certainly forms part of the context of biomedical practice in Madang and elsewhere, as the following example also illustrates.

Prayer and the demon-possessed girl

Prayer has long been a complementary accompaniment to biomedicine in Melanesia (and well beyond). Nevertheless, it seems that there are new trends within the formal health system that go beyond a complementary relationship, threatening to displace the logic and practice of biomedicine, and shifting the balance towards spiritual diagnostics and treatment. In some cases, the sick who seek out medical treatment may even be blamed for their lack of faith in God, who is thought to be able to cure all illnesses. This is particularly noticeable in places influenced by Pentecostal teachings on bodily health as contingent on the believer's faith (Barker 2003; Eves 2010).

Explicit Christian medical practice is less common among doctors. However, Phillips recently witnessed the treatment of a young girl in the Solomon Islands National Referral Hospital in Honiara who was assumed by doctors and nurses alike to be 'demon possessed'.

The 11-year-old schoolgirl had been rushed to the resuscitation room of the ED by her family in an agitated state. The junior doctor, 'Kathy', who was attending her described the girl's initial presentation as 'struggling' and reported her yelling at one stage 'Satan! Satan! Satan!'. Apparently the girl had gone to school in her normal, well state that morning, and suddenly became physically agitated and emotionally distressed with 'yelling and struggling'. Family had been called to collect the girl and had secured transport to get her to hospital where upon arrival she was ushered into the resuscitation room by the ED nurses. Kathy was rapidly on hand and with the nurses' help administered a dose of sedative medication by intramuscular injection. Nothing happened immediately, so the family continued to hold the struggling and distressed girl down on the ED bed so that another dose of commonly used sedative was injected.

When asked what she thought was going on, Kathy's immediate working diagnosis was 'satanic possession'. 'Could it be anything else?' Phillips asked; a common technique she uses when teaching or supervising junior staff back in Australia to trigger more critical thinking about the clinical presentation. Kathy's response was: 'Not really. I know it's difficult for outsiders to understand, but this is part of our belief system here in Solomon Islands. It's quite a common occurrence. I mean, I should consider mental or organic illness, but I really think this is demon possession.' McDougall (2013) has noted that the modern public culture of Solomon Islands is highly evangelical and Kathy's rendering of 'our belief' fits with this interpretation.

For Kathy and the other ED staff, the proof of supernatural origins of the girl's symptoms was the lack of immediate response to the biomedical treatment of the sedative medication. 'We gave the diazepam and haloperidol, and nothing happened.' The fact that the girl didn't immediately calm down after receiving Western medicine was clear reinforcement of a supernatural diagnosis, rather than a pharmacological understanding of the likely time of onset of these drugs when administered via an intramuscular pathway (which was likely to be delayed by 15–20 minutes or even longer).

Phillips asked Kathy what the treatment for 'satanic possession' was. 'Prayer' was the confident response. By this stage, the young schoolgirl was deeply asleep (as a result of the repeated doses of sedative that she had received) and her family gathered around her rubbing and massaging her limbs. A Melanesian Brother (Anglican lay brothers known in Solomon Islands and Vanuatu as *tasiu*: Taylor 2010, in press) had been summoned and had commenced reciting prayers at the head of the bed. He also sprayed water from his home-made spray bottle in a ritual bewildering to Phillips — he alternated between spraying water onto the girl's body and into his own mouth (cf. the 'water of life' described in Eves 2008 and 2010). All of this 'treatment' was carried out on one of the three trolleys available in the resuscitation room, while family members of critically ill patients and staff also in the room looked on, or gave support. Here the *tasiu* had replaced the doctor and nurses as the expert curative practitioner.

A few hours later, Phillips learnt that the girl had woken up calm and been discharged into the care of her family. The possibility of an alternative diagnosis such as mental illness, physical disease or her exposure to a harmful or traumatising event was never to be considered. This story is but one example of the overlapping domains of knowledge that operate within Melanesian hospitals where biomedical models often give way to other understandings of illness and curative processes that privilege supernatural agency. It can also been seen as evidence to support Denoon's (1989) observation that women are systematically underserviced in Melanesian hospitals.

Sik bilong marasin, sik bilong ples and white doctors

Cox recently asked 'Byron', a well-educated young Papua New Guinean academic, whether he believed in sorcery. Byron shifted in his seat and answered, 'Not really but sometimes when there are limits to scientific medicine; when the doctor doesn't know what is wrong with the sick person, then we look for other explanations'. Byron, who comes from a relatively affluent Pentecostal family and grew up entirely in Port Moresby, did believe in sorcery but as an explanation of last resort only to be deployed when biomedicine has tried everything and reached its limits. As another doctor from Madang told us:

> When I tell patients that I am unable to diagnose the cause of their illness or if I say that I'm not sure what it is. It is often a reflection of my own lack of knowledge, compounded with a lack of diagnostic and specialist support. The patients see me as a know-it-all — so if I can't diagnose or fix the sickness then their logical conclusion would be, 'If the doctor can't figure it out, then it must be sorcery related'. Typically patients

will say, 'Ok doctor, we know what the cause is' or *'em sik bilong ples'*. 'We just brought him to you to exclude a "white man's sickness" and if you say he hasn't got that then it's probably a "sorcery-related illness" and we will take him to a *glasman* [Tok Pisin: diviner]'.

It is not uncommon for doctors to be approached as expert witnesses to conduct autopsies with the purpose of adjudicating whether sorcery was the cause of death, again with the assumption that an identified medical diagnosis would rule out sorcery but that any failure of biomedical explanation would imply the use of sorcery. This does not always work. One Papua New Guinean doctor told us that he had returned to the village for a relative's funeral and took the opportunity to explain that his uncle had died of cancer, not sorcery. This expert advice was ignored, when several days after he had gone back to town some of his relatives attacked suspected sorcerers (also relatives), assaulting them and burning down their houses. The doctor was dismayed that his informed opinion had been set aside in favour of listening to a *glasman*, particularly when all the protagonists were relatives. He himself is seen as part of an educated and successful family and now feels that his reputation is in tatters and is paying reparations for the damage done by his cousins. He is also shocked at how easily family ties and respect for people were replaced by the fervid violence of sorcery accusations.

Taylor (in press), writing of Vanuatu, has made the argument that strenuous denunciation of black magic tends to reinforce beliefs in sorcery. A similar point is made by Piot (2010) in his account of the advance of Pentecostalism in West Africa. There the spread of militant Christianity intolerant of tradition and equating it with sorcery actually reaffirms the efficacy of sorcery by attributing it to the powerful agency of Satan. Similar patterns have been observed in the public life of PNG, particularly around the 2013 controversy over the removal of allegedly satanic carvings in the national parliament (Eves et al. 2014).

Taylor (in press) notes that contemporary Melanesian sorcery and Christianity emerge from the same system of thought (cf. Barker 2003). Christian ritual and practices of sorcery both mobilise supernatural powers for good or evil and the Christian *tasiu* has a counterpart in the *kleva* (Bislama: sorcerer). Both may access sacred power for curative results as Street's (2011) example of the *glasman* (see below) also indicates. Dundon (2007) also documents groups of charismatic Christian women 'prayer warriors' who identify sorcerers and perform healing rituals, often in health centres.

A typical point of view that we heard most recently in a conversation with 'David', a junior medical officer in Madang, also describes sorcery as a healing power. David articulates these domains as a temporal sequence: 'Patients are using sorcery [meaning traditional medicines] in the village [to heal themselves] but then when that treatment doesn't work, they go to the clinic but there are no drugs there, so they come to the hospital, so by that time they are very sick and there is not much we can do for them. So the hospital gets a reputation as a place where people die.'

Street describes a similar understanding of illness and injury among the patients and staff at Madang Hospital. There, sickness was often described in terms of severity, rather than as the manifestation of a particular illness identified through diagnostic processes (Street 2011). Patients distinguished between illness that is curable by biomedical means (Tok Pisin: *sik bilong marasin*) and that which biomedicine cannot cure because of its supernatural or traditional origins (*sik bilong ples*: 'village sickness'). Burton et al. (2013) note that *sik bilong ples* and *sanguma* (sorcery) are often used interchangeably. In the hospital, patients would seek out experts in countering sorcery — *glasman* who would prescribe remedies and even visit the patient in the ward. However, rather than *sik bilong marasin* implying a biomedical understanding of illness and its treatment, Street argues that this term denotes a racialised cultural domain (cf. Bashkow 2006; Cox 2015) wherein 'white' medicine can cure 'white' sickness but only Papua New Guinean cures can heal Papua New Guinean illnesses (Street 2010).[2] The racialised division of the origins of illness frequently has a moral valence (e.g. Dundon 2010). As we shall see below, this racial framework is also applied as a critique of hierarchical relationships between doctors and nurses (Street 2011).

Forgetting sorcery?

While patients may solicit the skills of the *glasman* to counter hostile sorcery, Street (2010) documents nurses who advise their patients to leave sorcery behind or put it out of their minds. This exemplifies proper Christian conduct in rejecting sorcery and is believed to assist in the curative process, not least by resolving troubling divisions with kin. Jealousy and other forms of broken relationships are believed to cause illness and even death and are certainly thought to provoke the use of sorcery by offended parties with the result that victims experience illness, injury or death (Strathern 1968). Street argues convincingly that the nurses' advice was not an epistemological rejection of sorcery beliefs but the marking out of a preferred moral course of action focused on turning to God for healing. Barker (2003:289) states that 'Healing becomes a matter of expressing a strong personal commitment to a distant deity rather than of making amends within the community'. However, Street's nurses appear to have integrated these two practices. While they advised patients to repair broken relationships, this was to be done with a clear focus on their own renewed relationship with God.

---

2   Eves (2010) describes a similar distinction between local and exogenous illnesses but notes that Lelet are pragmatic in searching for cures from various sources.

While the nursing staff Street worked with in 2003, and in subsequent visits, may have urged their patients to reject all thoughts of sorcery, this discourse seems to be intensifying. In recent short visits to the EDs at Port Moresby General Hospital, Madang Hospital and Goroka Hospital, Phillips observed a proliferation of sorcery discourse among hospital staff. Sometimes, as in the temporal sequence outlined above by David above, 'sorcery' was simply a reference to traditional healing practices, which might have a magical dimension but lack the malicious powers that Eves (2013) argues should define sorcery proper.

However, in several other cases, such as the demon-possessed girl in Honiara, hospital staff betrayed a willingness to accept supernatural agency as the primary explanation of illness and injury, without reference to biomedical causes. Even allowing for the ideological permeability of hospitals as social spaces, the explicit sidelining of biomedical knowledge by nursing staff is rather surprising. In effect, the curative powers of 'white' biomedicine have been dismissed as not applying to an expanding domain of *sik bilong ples*. Indeed, proclamations of supernatural agency or sorcery seem to be deployed quite carelessly and have become quite normalised. This may reflect the advance of revivalist Christian ideas of illness where God has the power to heal any illness (regardless of the *sik bilong marasin/sik bilong ples* distinction) or may send illness as a punishment for sin or a test of faith (Eves 2008).

One example concerns a middle-aged woman brought in to the ED in Madang Hospital by a male relative. She'd been brutally assaulted with a hammer and large piece of wood, and came shuffling in to the department led by her companion, her swollen face partially covered with a cloth. Once laid down on the resuscitation bed, the woman's injuries could be inspected; multiple open wounds over her head and face were a result of the hammer attack, as well as deformed and swollen elbows on both arms, which had been deliberately smashed. The piece of wood had been used over her torso and back, which was already showing signs of severe swelling and bruising.

As the ED nurse, 'Meredith', attended to her wounds, Phillips asked what had happened. 'She's been attacked because she is a sorcerer' was the explanation, without any further detail. The explanation of the reasons or history behind the attack was not required or sought by the ED staff, and the patient's history simply became 'attacked because of sorcery'. This was repeated each time the patient was referred to within the department, or even altered to 'the sorcerer who has been attacked'. After an X-ray had been done to diagnose the broken bones, Meredith proceeded to cut off all the woman's hair in order to properly clean the scalp wounds. Phillips expressed sympathy for the patient, as Meredith reiterated that 'she was a sorcerer'. In carrying out her duties as an

ED nurse, Meredith treated the patient dutifully but was seemingly oblivious to any further effects of apparently reconfirming the label of 'sorcerer', which had been the cause of horrific injuries to the woman.

Spiritual disorder

The second example of ED staff uncritically accepting the framing of illness or injury in terms of sorcery is of a small boy who had been referred to the Madang Hospital ED from a rural health clinic because of a gunshot injury. The attending clinician at the clinic (a nurse or health extension officer) had bandaged the boy's wounds in both his ankles and sent him and his mother on some transport in to town. Fortunately for the small boy, the gun and bullets used were almost certainly home-made, and his injuries not nearly as severe as initially feared, although a wound washout and removal of bullet shrapnel from the wounds was required in the operating theatre.

The referral letter stated 'shot in both ankles by sorcerers'. This was also the story repeated by the boy's mother, who provided some extra detail about how they were being chased by sorcerers and trying to hide in bushes, when the boy was shot in both ankles. Again, no further details were required or sought by the hospital ED staff, and the cause of injuries, as stated in the official referral letter, became the factual history of the patient's injuries: 'shot by sorcerers'. There was no need for any ED staff to question the legitimacy or delve into the story in any way; it was simply unquestionably accepted as fact, perhaps because of the practices of writing that Street (2011) has argued fail to close off diagnoses.

It is interesting to consider the absence of another possible framing of the violence against this boy and his mother in terms of *raskols*, PNG's notorious criminal gangs (Goddard 2005; Macintyre 2008). The threat of *raskol* violence is something of a national concern and certainly drives a burgeoning private security industry (Lusby 2014) and would seem to provide an adequate explanation of this boy's situation. However, the social disorder of raskolism has been transformed in this case into the spiritual disorder of sorcery. Roscoe documents moral panic over raskolism in East Sepik where raskols could use their 'ill-gotten gains' to 'alleviate the threat of retaliatory sorcery by buying off sorcerors' (Roscoe 1999:178). In this example, however, generalised moral panic over sorcery appears to have subsumed raskolism as the source of ubiquitous, malign violence (Kulick 1993).

Health systems in decline

Across Melanesia, health systems are routinely decried as in decline (Wiltshire and Mako 2014). For PNG, the devolution of responsibilities to provincial governments appears to have been disastrous for health services. For rural populations, primary health care has effectively been withdrawn, except in areas considered to be mining enclaves (but see Burton et al. 2013). This national decline in access to medical services also implies a corresponding decline in access to authoritative biomedical explanations of sickness and death, allowing *sik bilong ples* and sorcery-based explanations to hold sway.

The decline of biomedical knowledge and authority has also left space for the proliferation of pseudoscientific cures. These include the *Bio Disc*, a glass disc sold online and said to have the ability to cure AIDS, cancer and other illnesses. Bio Disc has been promoted and sold by a number of hospital staff in both PNG and Solomon Islands. Indeed, a senior medical specialist from Solomon Islands once assured us that he had cured a child of a stomach complaint by shining a torch through the Bio Disc onto the child's abdomen. This specialist sells Bio Disc products when doing clinical rounds in provincial hospitals, using his medical expertise to give credibility to a scam. This information was volunteered to us at a formal dinner in a Chinese restaurant in Honiara, where it was clear that the junior doctors around the table regarded this spruiking of pseudoscience as an unethical abuse of the man's position. They did not believe that there was any reasonable prospect of effective redress through official disciplinary systems, a perception borne out in other perhaps more serious examples of senior doctors who are regularly absent from their posts or neglect their professional responsibilities in other ways.

Medical training is under stress in PNG and Solomon Islands. Both undergraduate and postgraduate clinical teaching rely heavily on the apprenticeship model, whereby inexperienced trainees learn at the patient bedside, mentored and actively taught by experienced clinicians. Immediately before and after completing the medical degree, medical students and junior doctors are usually required to complete a structured, supervised and assessed hospital-based learning program with clear objectives and requirements. Often these programs are significantly compromised through lack of supervision and assessment; the workload of the few engaged supervisors being overwhelming.

In severely under-resourced hospital environments, where there are barely enough doctors for even basic service provision, the role of the competent, experienced doctor as a teacher is impossible. In many hospitals, junior doctors and students are left to their own devices. They make critical clinical decisions without supervision and often progress through their career without access to ongoing medical education opportunities. Those senior doctors who are engaged in teaching and training rapidly become burnt out, as demands for their skills exceed the limitations of their personal goodwill and energy. Professional frustrations compound this, where doctors are forced to work below their level of skill and training as a result of limited resources and inadequately supported health systems. The few hospitals that can support teaching and training are still vulnerable to precarious staffing situations, whereby the loss of one or two senior doctors can rapidly render the department or hospital into a survival mode of service provision over perceived 'extras' such as staff education and medical teaching.

Divine Word University is the site of health extension officer training through a four-year Rural Health bachelor degree. Phillips has worked with Divine Word University over several years to improve the standard of training for health extension officers, which has previously been perceived as insufficient. Modern methods of medical education have yet to be adopted into the curriculum or teaching program, relying instead on limited didactic practices. Clinical training suffers the same stress as that for medical students and doctors outlined above, compounded by the double duties of senior doctors in the Madang Hospital to supervise both University of Papua New Guinea and Divine Word University trainees. The end result is health extension officers with limited knowledge and inadequate clinical skills to meet the requirements of independent healthcare practice, let alone meet public expectations of a high standard of quality and safety.

The contestation of medical roles

Even as the resources for primary health care centres falter and medical training struggles, Street's ethnography demonstrates that the hierarchical ordering of biomedical expertise is under sustained resistance from nursing staff and even doctors themselves. Street (2011) documents the ways in which doctors come under criticism from nurses for ordering too many laboratory tests. Many doctors appear to have internalised these ways of working and prefer to focus on managing the expectations of nurses lest they be seen to be operating as 'white doctors'. This term of disparagement is used to decry doctors who seek to assert a hierarchy in the hospital workplace over the more egalitarian structure that is based on the pastoral roles adopted by nurses. 'White doctors' are thought to neglect their relationships with others and only act on behalf of themselves. Often conducting routine activities such as the issuing of instructions on patient care or diagnosis is sufficient to upset this order of relationships and provoke a reaction from the nurses.

If medical education, training and ongoing professional development continues to be under-resourced, then it is highly likely that doctors, health extension officers and nurses will lack the expert knowledge that is necessary to reassert the primacy of biomedical understandings of diagnosis. Curative practices that centre on this expertise and require a functioning hierarchy of roles in order to be effective are currently being undermined by Christian pastoral roles that privilege supernatural agency and so give credibility to sorcery as a cause of illness and injury. Sorcery accusations, then, are not only the effects of Christian ideology. They are the social outcomes of an impoverished system of biomedical service provision where the training of expert staff who are key to the production of effective health services is neglected.

Conclusion: The failure of biomedicine and the rise of sorcery

Burton et al. (2013), writing of an impoverished district in Morobe Province of PNG, have argued that sorcery is an effect of poverty that explains misfortune and illness but does so in an unsatisfactory manner that lowers expectations of health services and makes it unlikely that villagers will demand better services from government or their elected representatives. Although our experiences have been largely in urban centres and specifically hospitals, we agree with this analysis. Farmer (2010) makes a similar point, calling for more attention to be given to the structural causes of the poverty that causes illness.

In our view, the current resurgence of sorcery-related violence is best explained by reference to social inequality and poverty. However, the effects of poverty and inequality are manifold and include the shaping and reshaping of ideas of illness and injury. Like Farmer, we reject the interpretation of sorcery simply as a matter of cultural difference, of the persistence of Melanesian cosmologies of the body and society. Rather, we see the decline of medical services and training (not to mention the educational franchise) as a characteristic of modern Melanesian polities that are now marked by extreme inequality.

This is dismaying to us and to millions of Melanesians, many of whom turn to supernatural explanations of their situation, not least in various forms of revivalist Christianity.[3] As access to quality health services retracts across Melanesia, communities lose their collective memory of the efficacy of biomedicine, reducing it to simply another option alongside magical means, or even an inferior option when compared with the healing power of God.

---

3   Vaughan (2010), however, notes a more structural critique of poverty among PNG highlands' young people involved in a critical reflection process using Photovoice.

In re-establishing the efficacy of biomedicine in this context, EDs are crucial sites because of their role as the 'front door' of the biomedical system. It is imperative that ED staff receive excellent foundational medical and nursing education and that this be supported by ongoing professional development activities and skills training. In the experience of Phillips and many other foreign doctors who have worked in the region, there is a great hunger for this kind of training and support among doctors and nurses alike. We recognise that all of this is impossible in isolation and also requires a renewed political and bureaucratic commitment by the PNG and Solomon Islands governments and their partners to providing well-resourced healthcare systems.

References

Aitken, P., C. Annerud, M. Galvin, D. Symmons and C. Curry 2003. Emergency Medicine in Papua New Guinea: Beginning of a Specialty in a True Area of Need. *Emergency Medicine* 15:183–87.

Atua, V. and G. Phillips 2014. Integrating Global Health Training and Postgraduate Medical Education in Australia. Oral presentation, Australian Medical Association National Conference, Canberra, 23–25 May 2014.

Barker, J. 2003. Christian Bodies: Dialectics of Sickness and Salvation among the Maisin of Papua New Guinea. *Journal of Religious History* 27(3):272–92.

Bashkow, I. 2006. *The Meaning of Whitemen: Race and Modernity in the Orokaiva Cultural World*. Chicago: University of Chicago Press.

Burton, J. with T. Phillips and R. Lennie 2013. Failing to Articulate the Causes of Poverty: Witchcraft and Human Behaviour in the Bulolo District, Papua New Guinea. Paper presented at the Sorcery and Witchcraft-Related Killings in Melanesia: Culture, Law and Human Rights Perspectives Conference, The Australian National University, Canberra, 5–7 June 2013.

Chandler, J. 2013. It's 2013, and They're Burning 'Witches'. The Global Mail 15 February. www.theglobalmail.org/feature/its-2013-and-theyre-burning-witches/558/, viewed 22/8/2014.

Cochrane, L. 2014. From Journalist to Faith Healer in PNG. ABC Correspondents Report 27 July. www.abc.net.au/correspondents/content/2014/s4054427.htm, viewed 22 August 2014.

Cox, J. 2011. Prosperity, Nation and Consumption: Fast Money Schemes in Papua New Guinea. In M. Patterson and M. Macintyre (eds.) *Managing Modernity in the Western Pacific*. St Lucia: University of Queensland Press, 172–200.

Cox, J. 2013. The Magic of Money and the Magic of the State: Fast Money Schemes in Papua New Guinea. *Oceania* 83(3):175–91.

Cox, J. 2015. Israeli Technicians and the Postcolonial Racial Triangle in Papua New Guinea. *Oceania*. In Press.

Cox, J. and M. Macintyre 2014. Christian Marriage, Money Scams and Melanesian Social Imaginaries. *Oceania* 84(2):138–57.

Curry, C., C. Annerud, S. Jensen, D. Symmons, M. Lee and M. Sapuri 2004. The First Year of a Formal Emergency Medicine Training Program in Papua New Guinea. *Emergency Medicine* 16:343–47.

Denoon, D. 1989. Medical Care and Gender in Papua New Guinea. In M. Jolly and M. Macintyre (eds.) *Family and Gender in the Pacific: Domestic Contradictions and the Colonial Impact*. Cambridge: Cambridge University Press, 95-107.

Dundon, A. 2007. Warrior Women, the Holy Spirit and HIV/AIDS in Rural Papua New Guinea. *Oceania* 77(1):29–42.

Dundon, A. 2010. AIDS and 'Building a Wall' Around Christian Country in Rural Papua New Guinea. *The Australian Journal of Anthropology* 21(2): 171–87.

Eves, R. 2008. Moral Reform and Miraculous Cures: Christian Healing and AIDS in New Ireland, Papua New Guinea. In L. Butt and R. Eves (eds.) *Making Sense of AIDS: Culture, Sexuality, and Power in Melanesia*. Honolulu: University of Hawai'i Press, 206–23.

Eves, R. 2010. 'In God's Hands': Pentecostal Christianity, Morality and Illness in a Melanesian Society. *Journal of the Royal Anthropological Institute* (N.S.) 16(3):496–514.

Eves, R. 2013. Sorcery and Witchcraft in Papua New Guinea: Problems in Definition. *SSGM In Brief* 2013/12. Canberra: State, Society and Governance in Melanesia Program, The Australian National University.

Eves, R. and N. Haley, R.J. May, J. Cox, P. Gibbs, and F. Merlan and A. Rumsey 2014. Purging Parliament: A New Christian Politics in Papua New Guinea? *SSGM Discussion Paper* 2014/1. Canberra: State, Society and Governance in Melanesia Program, The Australian National University.

Farmer, P. 1999. *Infections and Inequalities: The Modern Plagues*. Los Angeles and London: University of California Press.

Farmer, P. 2010. The Consumption of the Poor: Tuberculosis in the Twenty-First Century. In H. Saussy (ed.) *Partner to the Poor: A Paul Farmer Reader*. Berkeley: University of California Press, 222–47.

Goddard, M. 2005. *The Unseen City: Anthropological Perspectives on Port Moresby, Papua New Guinea*. Canberra: Pandanus Books.

Hsia, R., J. Razzak, A.C. Tsai and J.M. Hirshon 2010. Placing Emergency Care on the Global Agenda. *Annals of Emergency Medicine* 56:142–49.

Jolly, M. and M. Macintyre. 1989. Introduction. In M. Jolly and M. Macintyre (eds.) *Family and Gender in the Pacific: Domestic Contradictions and the Colonial Impact*. Cambridge: Cambridge University Press, 1–18.

Kulick, D. 1993. Heroes from Hell: Representations of 'Raskols' in a Papua New Guinea Village. *Anthropology Today* 9:9-14.

Lusby, S. 2014. Preventing Violence at Home, Allowing Violence in the Workplace: A Case Study of Security Guards in Papua New Guinea. *SSGM In Brief* 2014/49. Canberra: State, Society and Governance in Melanesia Program, The Australian National University.

Macintyre, M. 2008. Police and Thieves, Gunmen and Drunks: Problems with Men and Problems with Society in Papua New Guinea. *The Australian Journal of Anthropology* 19(2):179–93.

McDougall, D. 2013. Evangelical Public Culture: Making Stranger-Citizens in Solomon Islands. In M. Tomlinson and D. McDougall (eds.) *Christian Politics in Oceania*. New York and Oxford: Berghahn, 122–45.

Phillips, G. 2013. Nursing Capacity Building for Emergency Care in PNG. *IEMSIG: Newsletter of the International Emergency Medicine Special Interest Group of ACEM* 9(2):19.

Phillips, G.A., J. Hendrie, V. Atua and C. Manineng 2012. Capacity Building in Emergency Care: An Example from Madang, Papua New Guinea. *Emergency Medicine Australasia* 24:547–52.

Phillips, G.A., Z.W. Soe, J.H.B. Kong and C. Curry 2014. Capacity Building for Emergency Care: Training the First Emergency Specialists in Myanmar. *Emergency Medicine Australasia* 26(6):618–26.

Piot, C. 2010. *Nostalgia for the Future: West Africa After the Cold War*. Chicago: University of Chicago Press.

Razzak, J.A. and A.L. Kellermann 2002. Emergency Medical Care in Developing Countries: Is It Worthwhile? *Bulletin of the World Health Organization* 80(11):900–5.

Roscoe, P. The Return of the Ambush: 'Raskolism' in Rural Yangoru, East Sepik Province. *Oceania* 69(3):171–83.

Strathern, A. 1968. Sickness and Frustration: Variations in Two New Guinea Highlands Societies. *Mankind* 6(11):545–51.

Street, A. 2009. Failed Recipients: Extracting Blood in a Papua New Guinean Hospital. *Body and Society* 15(2):193–215.

Street, A. 2010. Belief as Relational Action: Christianity and Cultural Change in Papua New Guinea. *Journal of the Royal Anthropological Institute* (N.S.) 16:260–78.

Street, A. 2011. Artefacts of Not-Knowing: The Medical Record, Diagnosis and the Production of Uncertainty in Papua New Guinean Biomedicine. *Social Studies of Science* 42:1–20.

Street, A. 2014. *Biomedicine in an Unstable Place: Infrastructure and Personhood in a Papua New Guinean Hospital*. Durham and London: Duke University Press.

Street, A. and S. Coleman 2012. Introduction: Real and Imagined Spaces. *Space and Culture* 15(1):4–17.

Taylor, J. 2010. The Troubled Histories of a Stranger God: Religious Crossing, Sacred Power and Anglican Colonialism in Vanuatu. *Comparative Studies in Society and History* 5(2):418–46.

Taylor, J.P. in press. Two Baskets Worn At Once: Christianity, Sorcery and Sacred Power in Vanuatu. In F. Magowan and C. Schwarz (eds.) *Conflicts and Convergences: Critical Perspectives on Christianity in Australia and the Pacific*. Leiden: Brill Publishers.

Tomlinson, M. and D. McDougall (eds) 2013. *Christian Politics in Oceania*. New York and Oxford: Berghahn.

Vaughan, C. 2010. 'When the Road Is Full of Potholes, I Wonder Why They Are Bringing Condoms?' Social Spaces for Understanding Young Papua New Guineans' Health-Related Knowledge and Health-Promoting Action. *AIDS Care: Psychological and Socio-Medical Aspects of AIDS/HIV*, 22(S2):1644–51.

van Amstel, H. and S. van der Geest 2004. Doctors and Retribution: The Hospitalisation of Compensation Claims in the Highlands of Papua New Guinea. *Social Science & Medicine* 59(10): 2087–94.

Wiltshire, C. and A. Mako 2014. *Financing PNG's Free Primary Healthcare Policy: User Fees, Funding and Performance.* Canberra and Port Moresby: Development Policy Centre and The National Research Institute.

3. Witchcraft, Sorcery, Violence: Matrilineal and Decolonial Reflections

Salmah Eva-Lina Lawrence

Introduction

In this chapter, a version of which was presented at the June 2013 conference Sorcery- and Witchcraft-Related Killings in Melanesia: Culture, Law, and Human Rights Perspectives, I discuss witchcraft and sorcery in the Milne Bay context, specific to communities in and around Alotau and the surrounding bay area, and some of the islands in the China Strait. I am also concerned with the law and human rights perspectives surrounding much of the discussion of the recent sorcery- and witchcraft-related violence in Papua New Guinea (PNG). I make an argument for decolonising both the discourse and the formulation and implementation of policy. I conclude with what is so obvious to us Papua New Guineans that it is taken for granted. And this fact is, that for most Papua New Guineans, the choice is not, and never will be, either culture or modernisation. It is both culture and modernisation. Policy formulation, therefore, has to be undertaken within this context.

It is refreshing and encouraging to see from the spread of papers in this book that many Melanesians have been given space to articulate their views. It has been more often the case that we are lectured about being basket cases in an 'arc of instability'. From the late 1990s, the 'arc of instability' has been used to describe a range of countries from East Timor to Fiji, encompassing PNG and Solomon Islands (Rumley 2006). These states are deemed to fall short of the liberal democratic model, lacking robust institutions, good governance and security for their populations. However, as Dobell (2007) argues, the term may have use in Canberra but has no value as an analytical tool and probably has more to do with what Rosewarne (1997:97) called 'Australia's pretensions as a superpower in the region'.

The chapters on PNG in this volume demonstrate an array of belief systems and ways in which accusers and perpetrators of violence relate to victims. However, the overall theme is that witchcraft and sorcery invariably lead to physical violence. Some questions are also raised on the different types of witchcraft and sorcery. In this paper, I challenge the notions that witchcraft and sorcery invariably lead to violence, that there is only one type of witchcraft and sorcery, and that what is labelled witchcraft and sorcery in English is entirely superstitious nonsense. I heard too from fellow Papua New Guineans at the June conference on the importance of our cultures to us and I also heard from them that a defence of culture is not a defence of violence, themes that I also touch upon.

This chapter is partially a reflection shaped by my lived experience as a woman from a matrilineal culture in PNG, a culture in which witchcraft and sorcery remain significant despite early Christianisation. A reflection that is shaped by a mutual embeddedness, me in my culture and my culture in me, an embeddedness that is not weakened by my Western education, nor by a career in senior management for a global business advisory firm in London and New York, nor by working for the United Nations in international development. Here I share thoughts about my culture and its traditions of matriliny and also about witchcraft and sorcery, and how these have shaped egalitarian gender relations in much of Milne Bay Province.

Despite early Christianisation, belief and practice of witchcraft continues to be prevalent in this primarily matrilineal province. Even outside the province, the flying witches of Milne Bay are legendary and Milne Bay itself has been described anecdotally as the witchcraft centre of PNG. In contrast to other chapters from PNG in this volume which speak of witchcraft and sorcery accusations that generate brutal violence on the accused, violence against women is much less in this province where witchcraft is highly articulated, and it is said to empower and contribute to the status of Milne Bay women. Addressing this paradox is a key theme of this chapter.

I will start with a discussion of matriliny and gender relations in Milne Bay, as these form a framework for understanding why violence is largely absent there. Then I will present some observations on witchcraft and sorcery as it unfolds in Milne Bay. I next present my arguments for decolonising the discourse and then I share some ideas about policy and practical responses before I finish with some reflections on culture.

Matriliny and gender relations in Milne Bay

Matriliny is often defined as a rule of descent and inheritance, but in Milne Bay it provides a basis for an identity interwoven with land and kinship relationships (Demian 2007; Lepowsky 1993). For the people of Milne Bay, matriliny is both a descent system and a way of organising social relations. The problem with translation into English is that one loses the depth of meaning inherent in our own languages because an equivalent value and practice does not exist in Anglocentric social systems. Matriliny is the closest term that only partially describes the way kinship is central to gender relations in Milne Bay.

Social relations shaped by matriliny demonstrate a predisposition towards egalitarian gender relations, or gender complementarity.[1] Indeed, since the 1870s, Europeans making their way through precolonial eastern Papua have noted the relatively high status of women (Wetherell and Abel 1998).

That gendered roles exist throughout Milne Bay is not contested, but I have suggested that egalitarianism and acceptance of difference is the basis of gender relations. When compared to United Nations' measures of equality, Milne Bay people in their traditional environments score very highly (Lawrence 2013). Milne Bay women exercise a great deal of autonomy. They have physical mobility, a key factor in power relations and they continue to travel, and to have freedom in marriage partners and in divorce. Abhorrence of physical violence and a respect for autonomy produced an environment in some of the islands where rape was unheard of (Lepowsky 1993). Women have access to economic power as they have access to land and are able to accumulate wealth (Demian 2007). (Milne Bay people traditionally did not own land; however, custodianship confers rights to determine or control usage.)[2] Women practised traditional contraception, spaced their children and enjoyed premarital sexual freedom (Lepani 2012). In other words, women control their own bodies. Across Milne Bay, male and female children are equally desired; there is recognition that matrilineages cannot be sustained without both males and females (Demian 2000). Women's influence included not only determining when to go to war, they also participated in generating peace through preventing war and bloodshed and they have not relinquished this power (Lepowsky 1993). This form of restorative justice, and a key feature of Milne Bay women's agency, continues to be initiated in the present day — women will remove their skirts in situations of conflict. This method is used in the islands of the Bwanabwana district and even in the urban environment of Alotau.[3]

Lest I be misconstrued as suggesting that Milne Bay people are singular social beings, let me be clear that violence did and does exist. I am here pre-empting charges of exceptionalism, especially as I have elsewhere positioned Milne Bay gender relations as indigenous best practice. My intent is not to create separateness from other Papua New Guineans. It is to demonstrate that the mainstream development model, in which the exceptionalism of European culture is implicit, and which thus seeks to bring gender equality to supposedly lesser developed peoples, is culturally and racially constructed because it

---

1   Gender as stipulated within Western feminism is not universal. This is recognised, particularly by Third Wave feminism, contemporary African-American, Latin American, African and other majority world feminists, who have argued that in many parts of the world gender roles are complementary. See, for example, Oyěwùmí (1997). Others, such as anthropologist Peggy Sanday (1981), have also explored non-adversarial gender relations.
2   Personal communication in May 2013 with Anne Dickson-Waiko clarified this point.
3   This method has been utilised in contemporary times by some women in my extended family.

denies that these lesser developed peoples, of whom I am one, could possibly have moral frameworks that promote women's status. The challenge for other Papua New Guineans is to identify similar models in their own cultures that correspond to a rights and responsibilities framework and the challenge for all of us is to continue to live as a pluralist nation-state. Let me also be clear that best practice for me does not imply a single universal model. For the people of Milne Bay, matriliny and gender relations are a practice that has contributed, and continues to contribute, to our survival. It will remain relevant for as long as it is useful for the people of Milne Bay. That it is best practice in Milne Bay does not automatically position it so for all of PNG.

Violence in Milne Bay includes precolonisation warfare, which was often triggered by witchcraft and sorcery allegations, and was rife among some communities, and domestic, family and sexual violence does exist (Macintyre 1983). Interaction through relatively early European contact has brought changes that include new structures for managing relationships, some of which I will demonstrate later (Macintyre 1995). Nonetheless, Milne Bay people continue to strongly assert their own identity and the social basis for egalitarian gender relations remains strong (Kaniku 1981). Some have also suggested that women's use of witchcraft is a factor in these egalitarian relations (Macintyre 1987).

Witchcraft and sorcery in Milne Bay

Witchcraft and sorcery in Milne Bay are part of the fabric of daily life in the sense that they are omnipresent. Few practitioners openly admit their involvement, perhaps due to the legacy of negative connotations conferred by Christianity and colonisation, and if they do, they are reluctant to divulge knowledge. But I have also met two women who have been entirely transparent about being practitioners. I will use the Suau language words *alawai* and *balau*, which approximate to witch and sorcerer, and operate as nouns and verbs. I say approximate because witch/witchcraft and sorcerer/sorcery have overwhelmingly negative connotations in European cultures but *alawai* and *balau* do not necessarily convey negative meanings in Milne Bay.

An *alawai* is usually, but not always, female. The activity attributed of *alawai* is attributed to many women, who in this matrilineal culture are said to pass their *alawai* skills on to their daughters. A *balau* is usually male, although it is known for men to pass their skills to daughters in the absence of sons. Both *alawai* and *balau* are said to fly; that is, they can leave their bodies and travel through space but not through time. Both exercise an array of functions that might include garden magic and protective magic.[4] *Alawai* cannibalise the dead; like *balau* they can kill the living. But they can also heal; their knowledge of herbs being essential to pregnancy, childbirth and contraception among other things. There is also a third category of persons who protect. This person does not seem to have a different designation in the Suau language; one of the men I interviewed, who defined himself as providing protection through sorcery, refused to be identified as either *alawai* or *balau*, nor was he able to offer a Suau word to designate his function. This is possibly because Suau, our common language, was not his native language. In other parts of Milne Bay, however, this third category of person is designated differently.[5]

Masigili, which translates as dark/darkness is also associated with *alawai* and *balau*, regardless of whether they heal or harm. There seems to be a reticence in attributing *alawai* or *balau* to named individuals, whereas one can imply their involvement by the less direct term *masigili*. Nonetheless, *alawai* are often associated with brightness, appearing at night in forms that emanate light. I suspect that missionaries who positioned their teachings as *mala*, meaning light, intended to create the binary of *masigili/mala*, darkness/light. *Alawai* and *balau* do not always need a physical medium like food by which to enter a person's body. Much fear is generated by the belief that they can affect a person by gaze, by touch, and through the non-physical body they use to fly. Illness and death, especially among young people, continues to be attributed frequently to *alawai* or *balau*, notwithstanding the early Christianisation of this part of PNG.[6]

In the course of researching this paper, I uncovered only one recent instance of what was classified by the courts as a witchcraft-related killing in Milne Bay Province.[7] In 2007, Sedoki Lota and Fred Abenko, both from Normanby Island, were charged with the murder of Marcia Kedarossi, whom they alleged killed their parents through witchcraft. According to court documents the accused were offered payment of cash and traditional money and wealth by a man from a neighbouring village, and this led to the attack on, and decapitation of, Marcia Kedarossi.[8] Witchcraft accusations aside, the court determined that this was clearly a premeditated murder for which the accused were to be paid by a third party and the accused received the death sentence.

---

4   Personal communication in May 2013 with Anne Dickson-Waiko, herself from Milne Bay, confirms that for communities in and around Ahioma, the range of practices includes gardening magic, healing and protective magic. See also Lepani (2012) on these practices in the Trobriand Islands.
5   See also Lepani (2012).
6   Following exploratory forays in the preceding decade, the London Missionary Society, the Anglicans and the Methodists all established missions on the mainland and islands of Milne Bay in 1891 (Wetherell 2012).
7   I spent one month in Milne Bay Province where I interviewed four practitioners and conducted two focus groups, at Alotau and at Kwato, about *alawai* and *balau* persons and activities. I also interviewed one policeman, three village councillors, and one female community worker.
8   *State v. Sedoki Lota & Fred Abenko* (Unreported, N3183, 2007, Sevua J).

Why, then, are cases of physical violence towards practitioners of witchcraft and sorcery less frequent in Milne Bay Province even when the practices are seen to be the underlying cause of disease and deaths? My earlier discussion on matriliny and gender has highlighted a sociality predisposed to gender egalitarianism, which unfolds as an aversion to physical violence, and includes a practice of restorative justice traditionally initiated by women through the removal of their skirts to protect, and to prevent war and bloodshed (Kaniku 1981). In the present, and on a practical level, conflict, witchcraft-related or otherwise, is managed through community mediation. Besides accused, accuser, and their kin, a mediation can involve the village councillor and the pastor, actors introduced through contact with Europeans.

I have been an observer at one such mediation which involved an extended family group that could be regarded as middle class: members are university educated and/or have professional qualifications; many are urban based; and they are strongly associated with the church and identify as Christian. After a spate of deaths of young to middle-aged people in this group, and some serious illnesses, an older woman was accused of causing this misfortune through witchcraft. She vigorously denied all accusations, going to the extent of shaming herself by removing her clothing during the community mediation. This woman was raised in a mission not a village. She and her husband, who was already deceased at the time of the accusations, were both professionals. The woman's nudity was, however, insufficient to quell the animosity and accusations directed at her. Physical violence was threated on her person as a future quid pro quo. But no physical violence was enacted on the day and has not been enacted in the intervening three years. Is this because this extended kinship group has a high degree of Western education, is it because they are Christianised, modernised? I cannot be certain but I speculate that as a female elder with significant control over kin and land, coupled with her extremely domineering personality, the accusation of witchcraft was a method by which the family group articulated latent hostilities which, once brought into the open, allowed members to get on with their lives.[9]

---

9   According to Patterson (1974), theories of sorcery and witchcraft can be broadly classified as anthropological or psychological, notwithstanding the disciplinary overlap. Where the latter tend towards the causal, anthropology orients to the functional/structural and causal. Social control is one such functional theory — those who are marginal or non-conformist are often foci for hostility and scapegoats of accusations. In this intra-group scenario, as data from Africa demonstrate, accuser and accused are known to each other. But evidence suggests this does not hold universally — the degree of hostility/strain/tension is not an accurate gauge of accusations and, Patterson highlights, is particularly problematic in the context of Melanesian data where peculiarities exist vis-à-vis whether the accusation is related to an illness or to a death, and whether it is intra- or inter-group. Nonetheless, in my case study, in which illness and death are coeval, the woman accused, a female elder with significant influence, is not marginal, but her controlling and domineering personality might be said to be non-conformist in an egalitarian society.

Drawing on consultations I had with a policeman, several village councillors, and a female community worker, the same kind of mediation at the village level is often successful in diffusing the potential for physical violence. One of the councillors with whom I spoke claimed the bulk of his time was spent in such mediations. Enabling participants to air their grievances allows for hostilities to be dispersed and thus, in parts of Milne Bay, this appears to mitigate the tendency to physical violence. However, I must stress that mediations are not public forums; there is no blatant naming and shaming, and public records are not made. Mediations remain private matters among the kinship groups involved.

My intention in using this particular case study is to demonstrate that Westernisation does not lead to relinquishing traditional ontologies and epistemologies. Indeed, the Eurocentric premise that science would eventually trump religion and magic continues to be proven erroneous with the rise of religious fundamentalism in the United States and elsewhere, and the continuing beliefs in, and practice of, magic including Wicca and Paganism in the Anglophone West. Although science has been positioned as that which makes European knowledge singular, Tambiah (1990) and Nader (1996a) argue that this categorisation is but another social construction essentialising the hegemon's superiority over those who utilise magic and religion. Since the placement of Western science as superior is a socially constructed rather than universal truth, it is, therefore, unsurprising that other ontologies and epistemologies, such as those of the people of Milne Bay, indeed of PNG, continue to thrive.

Why, then, in the one place in PNG where witchcraft is articulated in so much depth is there so little violence against women, or cases of violent witchcraft-related accusations and killings? There is a historical and cultural basis for the reduced levels of violence against women. In addition, a different trajectory to modernisation, which included relatively early exposure to introduced institutions of rule of law and church and new forms of managing conflict, has undoubtedly also had an impact.[10] This raises other questions not addressed by this chapter, such as how do different cultures respond to the modernising project and the experiences of modernity? How are other places in PNG with different gender dynamics and different experiences of modernity responding to the West's model of development? Analysing these distinctions may provide insights into why accusations of witchcraft or sorcery have generated horrific violence in some parts of PNG but not in other parts, such as Milne Bay.

---

10   In 1884, prevailing geopolitics led to the annexation of the south-eastern portion of the island of New Guinea to form British New Guinea, which in 1905 became the Territory of Papua (Murray 1912). Missionaries had been active in Milne Bay since 1847, but it was from 1891 that major bases were established on the mainland and in the islands of Milne Bay by the London Missionary Society, the Anglicans and the Methodists (Wetherell and Abel 1998; see also Wetherell 2012).

Which witchcraft? Decolonising the discourse

Decoloniality, like the postcolonial, challenges a Eurocentric view of the world. Where it differs is a focus on scholars and thinkers from the majority world, an insistence that social and economic development is not a linear progression, and a commitment to pluralism.[11] For me, the activism component of decoloniality unfolds through an emphasis on first looking within one's own culture for frameworks that correspond to, for example, human rights norms, then building on these frameworks as a means to bring about sustainable change.

I now turn to my reflections on the discourse of witchcraft and sorcery as it relates to PNG. When framed in relation to Christianity, witchcraft and sorcery assume negative connotations. Even in Patterson's (1974) pioneering efforts to classify Melanesian sorcery and witchcraft, in which she acknowledges that translation into English is problematic, she nevertheless opts to use a definition that is entirely negative, situated through its capacity to inflict harm. She qualifies that attending to this nuance is immaterial for the analysis she is undertaking, which is 'to explain the consequences these beliefs and the practices connected with them have for interpersonal and intergroup relations and for the individual ... [and] to determine the reasons for the differential stress placed on certain aspects of the phenomena in Melanesian societies' (Patterson 1974:140). Nonetheless, the oversimplification favouring a Eurocentric bias continues to inform many discussions of witchcraft and sorcery in Melanesia. Patterson (1974) does go on to acknowledge the different types of Melanesian magic and, in fact, makes reference to garden magic and sea magic, which are creative, productive and protective, not harmful. More recently, Lepani (2012) has provided a balanced presentation of the different applications of magic and its relationship to individual agency. It is clear that what is called magic is not always the malign force it is made out to be.

So which witchcraft are we talking about in this volume? My discussion has demonstrated that there are at least three types of practice in Milne Bay: harming, protecting and healing. In particular, the healing component has promoted gender egalitarianism as it has allowed women to have control over their bodies through regulating their fertility among other things. These bodies of knowledge, which are often dismissed in the West as being magical and therefore irrational, in fact constitute what UNESCO (2006) recognises as key resources that communities can utilise to combat destabilisation and marginalisation resulting from modernisation and globalisation. UNESCO (2005) protects these knowledges through conventions such as the Protection and

---

11   For more information on the Decolonial School see the special issue of *Cultural Studies*, Volume 21, Issue 2–3, 2007, Routledge.

Promotion of the Diversity of Cultural Expressions. Furthermore, in Milne Bay it is recognised that this knowledge constitutes aspects of a person's wealth. Indeed, women who practise these forms of knowledge are said to be *sibasiba*, or wise, so it is unsurprising that witchcraft contributes to the esteem given to women in Milne Bay.[12]

What is this knowledge exactly? It is knowledge of psychology — understanding and, at times, manipulating human fears, desires and weaknesses. It is knowledge of the environment and ecology — including knowing how to sustain oneself from the land and sea, indeed how to navigate by reading the environment.[13] It is knowledge of the body and of medicine — knowing what vines to use to set broken bones and what plants to treat dengue fever or aid childbirth.[14] There is now a wealth of evidence that demonstrates how indigenous peoples the world over have highly developed knowledges of their environments in pharmaceutics, botany, navigation, and resource and food management, knowledge which Western science is benefiting from (Nader 1996a). Indeed, the ability to observe, test and validate to create knowledge is not unique to science (Nader 1996a).[15] It is therefore, extremely problematic that magic or witchcraft and sorcery continue to be used to classify many different types of indigenous knowledges.

Tambiah's (1990) seminal work *Magic, Science, Religion, and the Scope of Rationality* draws on diverse disciplines to demonstrate that given its cultural construction, science is no more and no less rational than other cultural constructs such as magic and religion and that, ironically, its roots can be found in magic and religion. Nader (1996a), drawing on Tambiah, highlights how anthropologists from Edward Tylor, James Frazer and Bronislaw Malinowski are implicated in the construction of hierarchies essentialising the superiority of European science over reliance on magic and religion. So ingrained have these ideas become that

---

12   Anne Dickson-Waiko, personal communication May 2013, helped illuminate this point.
13   Over the course of my lifetime I have observed how people from Milne Bay plan and undertake activities for their livelihoods. Out in the islands (Kwato, Logeia) few people are employed in regular cash-generating employment. The source of food is still largely subsistence gardening and fishing. Ensuring a sufficient harvest to sustain the household requires knowledge that is not apparent to those of us whose provisions come from a supermarket. Likewise, navigating watercraft without the aid of machines means observing and knowing about winds, tides, stars and planetary positions, and a host of details such as the feel of the waves lapping at the sides of the craft. I know of many young men, and increasingly young women, from islands in the Bwanabwana district of Milne Bay, who possibly because of early exposure to such knowledge, are finding employment in the international maritime industry.
14   A man who lives at Divinai village demonstrated to me knowledge he had acquired from his grandfather regarding which vines were the most effective to set broken bones. Diseases such as malaria and dengue have obviously been present since before first contact with Europeans, and have been treated variously. Some of the remedies shared with me are similar to those in folk medicine in Thailand and Malaysia, according to friends from those countries.
15   Of this Eurocentric knowledge production, Nader (1996b:2) says '[a] style favoured by contrast includes some things, excludes others, and creates hierarchies privileging one form of knowledge over another … Contrast also tends to fix a positional superiority in the mind of the categorizer — the notion that one is superior by virtue of being in a position to create the categories'.

they continue to be used to justify interventions in the name of developing so-called 'primitive' peoples. While many are the critiques of magic and religion, scant in popular discourse are those that challenge the construction and ideology of science, natural and social, including those of the rule of Western law and human rights. These are ideologies that contribute to the construction of entire peoples as lacking, whether economically, jurisprudentially, and/or morally, and thus provide the basis for development interventions.[16] Is it not, however, a form of fundamentalism, this extremist insistence that Western knowledge and concepts are the only valid epistemologies and ontologies for the entirety of humanity?

To decolonise the discourse is first to frame it from the subaltern side of the colonial divide. Furthermore, as Epeli Hau'ofa (1994:156–7) reminds us, '[o]nly when we focus on what ordinary people are actually doing, rather than on what they should be doing, can we see the broader picture of reality'. When one looks beyond media headlines into the lives of ordinary Papua New Guineans, one finds no sharp increase in accusations of witchcraft- and sorcery-related violence. There have always been such accusations — perhaps social media has made them more visible. There is, however, an increase in brutal violence inflicted on the accused, and only in particular parts of the country. Absent too, from popular discourse, is a balanced approach that would also acknowledge the negative effects of Eurocentric modernity and its contemporary guise of development, and consideration of its impact upon civil unrest and criminal activity, and indeed upon gender violence. For example, while recognising that violence has been prevalent in gender relations in much of PNG since before colonisation, recent scholarship presented in *Engendering Violence in Papua New Guinea* (Jolly et al. 2012) also explores the links between modernity and gender violence, exposing the culpability of commodity economics and extractive industries as well as the introduction of Western justice and law.

Hau'ofa (1994) has written eloquently on colonial, postcolonial and neo-colonial Eurocentric relations of control, domination and subordination in Oceania. He too is cognisant that the international system, its norms and institutions, is one in which Pacific islanders have been forced to participate. It is not of our making and rarely reflects our cultural values of rights embedded in responsibilities (Hau'ofa 1994). (I should make clear that Hau'ofa does not speak of rights embedded in responsibilities. It has been argued that the more common perspective advanced by indigenous Pacific island scholars is that the concept of human rights does not inform our cultures.[17] I agree that direct comparison between the West and Melanesia, for example, exposes a lack vis-à-vis the West.

---

16 For a critique of the discourse of development see Escobar (1995). The role of law in the construction of societies that lack is outlined in Nader (2004–2005).
17 See, for example, Dickson-Waiko (2001).

However, when I situate myself in my culture, unconcerned with comparisons, I see that as a woman from a matrilineal society I have very clear rights, such as those regarding custodianship of land, but these rights are always embedded in responsibilities to my community. That they are not the same rights accorded by, and in, Western societies does not diminish that I do have rights in my society. It is for this reason that I speak of rights embedded within responsibilities.) Inspired by Hau'ofa, I am compelled to ask different questions — decolonial questions. For instance, in lieu of assuming that belief in witchcraft and sorcery is the cause of insecurity and fear, I ask too, what is it in the Eurocentric model of development that fuels this culture of insecurity and fear? Is it that it is a model that reinforces inequality and hierarchy and has reinforced patriarchy in many parts of PNG? Is it that it is a model that is predicated on individual rights without explicit corresponding responsibilities?[18] Is it that it is a model that Melanesians have had no part in designing, let alone influencing, such that the outcome of trying to implement it is akin to forcing a square peg into a round hole?

Other questions I am compelled to ask include if witchcraft and sorcery are a problem, should we not be also talking about these practices in places outside Melanesia, for example, Wiccan practices across Europe and the United States? Moreover, if sorcery and witchcraft are a negative force on economic and social development, then what of demand-sharing and the obligation to reciprocity and exchange that underlies social relations in PNG? Should one regulate kinship as well in the name of economic development?

In a different vein, like Grosfoguel (2008:1) I also ask, '[h]ow can we overcome Eurocentric modernity without throwing away the best of [it] as many Third World fundamentalists do?' And, like other decolonialists, I argue that an epistemic pluralism that embraces majority world perspectives can progress this debate precisely because decoloniality respects the many multiples of local particularities. (I prefer 'majority world' to designate what is often referred to as the developing world, in order to avoid the infantilisation implicit in the term 'developing'.) Scott (1996:71), however, is correct to highlight that '[i]f the sharing of knowledge were to be reduced to a skimming-off by Western specialists of indigenous empirical insights, and their mere insertion into existing Western paradigms, then it would be an impoverished and failed exchange that would ultimately contribute to undermining indigenous societies and cultures'. Decoloniality, therefore, embraces the best of Eurocentric knowledge production and the best of majority world knowledge, acknowledging difference without needing to control and dominate it.

---

18 I acknowledge that human rights discourse does emphasise responsibilities through the critique of neo-liberalism. The responsibilities that I focus on in Melanesian societies are actual lived responsibilities, to which we are socialised from birth, not an intellectual discourse.

These reflections stem from both a matrilineal and decolonial perspective. But regardless of either perspective, without any evidence of a causal link between witchcraft/sorcery and the breakdown of civil society and social relations in Milne Bay, the real issue for me becomes violence, whatever its source. And it is from this perspective that I address policy and practical measures in the next section.

Policy and practical measures

I would now like to share some thoughts on policy and practical measures and I present these from my assumption that violence, indeed growing violence, is the issue that needs to be addressed.

Ume Wainetti, national coordinator of the PNG Family and Sexual Violence Action Committee, gave a talk at The Australian National University shortly before the June 2013 conference Sorcery- and Witchcraft-Related Killings in Melanesia. Three points resonated. Firstly, a trip she had taken to the United States to learn about services that are provided to those who have suffered from family and sexual violence was, in her words, a waste of time. Not because the services were deficient but because PNG cannot hope to replicate that level or type of service in the near to medium-term; in other words, context is critical. Secondly, Ume spoke of how a basic understanding of human rights and the operation of the rule of law had enabled at least one woman in the highlands to break a cycle of violent payback through the use of court orders in lieu of tribal war. And thirdly, Ume has observed that younger Papua New Guineans understand their rights but that these rights are exercised in a vacuum free of responsibility. I shall address these points collectively.

Research on human rights and gender violence reveals that vernacularisation of human rights is necessary for local acceptance, for without context many will resist the fundamentalist insistence that rights can only be framed in one way (Merry 2006). Translation, however, does not lead to transformation. At the local level a rights framework will coexist with other moral frameworks, contingency dictating which framework will be leveraged by individuals, predicated to a large extent on which system is perceived to best deliver the desired outcomes. For example, a battered woman in the highlands of PNG, despite being aware of her human rights, may elect customary justice if she perceives it to be the system that will best deliver her the desired outcomes for that situation. While the paradox of contextualising the universal presents a number of dilemmas, it does enable incremental change, which can be more sustainable, at a local level. My experience as a board member for an international non-government organisation confirms this: WASH (water, sanitation and hygiene) messages are best crafted and delivered by locals in order to be taken seriously and integrated into the lives of households and communities. Another example is that of Tostan, a non-government organisation working in Senegal to give women a say in female genital cutting practices, which are illegal in Senegal. By engaging the community in debating moral frameworks of rights and responsibilities, communities are able to make their own collective decision about the practice.

Advocacy for human rights education must not only be framed in local terms — it needs to be explicit about the corollary of rights, which is responsibility. A fundamental issue in PNG over the discourse of human rights is the conflict between individual rights and collective responsibilities (Dickson-Waiko 2001). Milne Bay scholar Dickson-Waiko, questioning the ethics of insistence on individualism, informs us that in PNG the collective, by way of community and/or kinship relations, is so critical to the well-being of the human that 'if the appropriate relationships are not maintained the community itself may be destroyed and with it the individual members' (Dickson-Waiko 2001:51). The idea of the human, therefore, cannot be separated from the idea of the community.

Yet to make the argument, either for vernacularisation, or for the importance of the collective, often invites charges of relativism with the corresponding charge that this stance encourages female subordination in particular, and repression in general (Jolly 1996). However, both Jolly and Dickson-Waiko (2003) have demonstrated that women of Vanuatu and PNG, far from being trapped in rigid traditions, are proactive in debating and defining their contemporary rights vis-à-vis culture, modernisation, religion and the state. Indeed, this was evident as well at the June 2013 conference, whereby PNG activists Lily BeSoer and Clara Bal demonstrated through their work that patriarchal traditions of violence can be challenged without destroying the ontological Papua New Guinean human, embedded in social relations. It has also been evident in the way ordinary Papua New Guineans have participated in public events and on social media to protest against the violence that also motivated this conference. In the PNG context then, rights and responsibilities are equally important and Papua New Guineans are aware of the tensions that these generate and are actively negotiating the pressures.

Culture? Modernisation? Both?

I started with some words about culture and I will finish with the same.

Many people from the developing world, or the majority world as I prefer to call it, can tell you that there is considerable trauma in having one's culture or aspects of it essentialised as inferior and primitive, as the media reports have tended to do when reporting on witchcraft- and sorcery-related violence in PNG. We joke about it among ourselves but I suspect that the mainstream development model that demonises our cultures by constructing the idea that we are lacking morally and intellectually, actually creates many of the social tensions that plague PNG.[19] The adoption of aspects of Eurocentric modernity brings its own traumas but the process would be much less painful without the implicit racial and cultural hierarchies built into it.

We all know intuitively that any process of change brings its own stresses, whether a divorce at the household level or new technology at the organisational level. In fact, in my experience in international business, large, blue chip corporations would rarely undertake programs of change without giving due consideration to how the trauma of displacing one organisational culture for another is likely to unfold. There is recognition in the world of international business that cultural disruption can create fundamental organisational instability and that this is not a healthy situation over the long term. This acknowledgement is largely absent from mainstream development, although critiques from some scholars and practitioners have noted the lack of reflexivity in the model that rarely questions the racial and cultural hierarchies that are implicit within it.[20]

Back in 1996 Nader (1996b:7) noted that indigenous peoples were becoming much better informed, and a decade later Maori scholar Linda Tuhiwai Smith (2004:34) wrote 'we are still being colonized (and know it)'. What this means is that majority world peoples are cognisant of the myth of the white man's burden of refashioning the uncivilised rest, critiqued recently by Nader (2007) and Easterly (2006), and which underpins top-down development. To consider this myth from the bottom up is to identify another myth — that the rest desire to be like the West. The reality, however, is that some things are adopted (washing machines, air travel), others not (discarding customary land tenure), and yet others are adapted to local needs (Christianity). In fact, majority world peoples have always been aware of racial and cultural hierarchies, but are becoming less accepting, as Nader notes. Policymaking and implementation surrounding cultural issues such as witchcraft and sorcery, and introduced institutions such as rule of law and human rights also have to negotiate this terrain. Indeed, there are a growing number of us in the majority world for whom postcolonial rhetoric has done little to shift power relations between a minority world of developed nations and a majority world of emerging and developing states. This is leading us to adopt a decolonial stance that calls for expression of human rights through recognition that our peoples and cultures had, and continue to have, moral frameworks. And that it is by leveraging our own cultural models

---

19 While this is not the conclusion of this volume, it nonetheless touches on aspects of modernisation that impact upon gender violence (Jolly et al. 2012).
20 See, for example, Escobar (1995).

that, yes, include beliefs in what the West calls witchcraft and sorcery, in lieu of having foreign models imposed on us, which will enable us to better negotiate the transition to modernity on our terms. Only through this can we live up to Hau'ofa's exhortation that '[w]e must not allow anyone to belittle us again and take away our freedom' (Hau'ofa 1994:160).

Witchcraft and sorcery form part of the cultural terrain and indigenous knowledges of PNG. But culture is not a valid argument for the use of violence. Nor is violence a valid argument for the outright and totalitarian dismissal of all aspects of PNG cultures. If indeed violence were a valid argument for such, then what of Eurocentric modernisation, which from conquest to colonisation and Christianisation, through to globalisation and developmentalism, has been a project of organised violence through enslavement, genocide and territorial appropriation, and which continues to unfold as structural and epistemic violence in the international system?[21] The fact is that for most Papua New Guineans it is not, and never will be, either culture or modernisation. It is culture *and* modernisation. A linear approach to policymaking assumes that increasing modernisation will result in dissolution of cultural bonds. A non-linear approach, however, rejects the paradigm of (A OR B) or (A therefore B) to replace it with the paradigm of both (A AND B). This approach is crucial for the complexity, diversity and dynamism of a nation-state like PNG.

Conclusion

I have argued that a large part of the knowledges dismissed as witchcraft and sorcery constitute an aspect of both the cultural heritage and knowledge capital of PNG, and that in Milne Bay, this knowledge is highly correlated with gender egalitarianism. In fact, the paradox that Milne Bay presents — highly articulated forms of witchcraft and sorcery yet low levels of gender violence — suggests that factors beyond witchcraft and sorcery inform a large part of the brutal violence that has been directed at those accused in other parts of PNG. I have suggested that by approaching the issue from a decolonial perspective one is able to frame different questions to explore contributing factors to this violence. On the issue of policy, I have argued that the starting point be the lives and actions of ordinary people, rather than international and state rhetoric.

The late Epeli Hau'ofa had great faith in the ability and resilience of Pacific island peoples to adapt, saying '[t]he future lies in the hands of our own people, not of those who would prescribe for us, get us forever dependent and indebted because they can see no way out' (Hau'ofa 1994:159). For we Melanesians, it

---

21 For elaboration see Dussel (2000), Maldonado-Torres (2004), Mignolo (1995), and Quijano and Ennis (2000).

is necessary that we take responsibility for effecting the changes that provide for our contextual development. There are no easy answers. In the spirit of generating solutions that are appropriate for us, there needs to be more intra-Melanesian, indeed intra-Oceanic, debate that is driven by agendas we set. And we should be engaging more with others in the global south, with whom we share more than the experience of being colonised. We place similar value in our kinship systems and we may find that we are also more united in the concept of both rights and responsibilities than we are in the concept of just individual rights.[22] Like Hau'ofa, I am optimistic that our peoples, having thrived for millennia before European contact, and despite colonisation, continue to have the ability and resilience to negotiate change.

Acknowledgements

I am grateful for feedback received from Anne Dickson-Waiko, Katherine Lepani, Katerina Teaiwa and Margaret Jolly.

References

Demian, M. 2000. Longing for Completion: Toward an Aesthetics of Work in Suau. *Oceania* 71(2):94–109.

Demian, M. 2007. 'Land Doesn't Come from Your Mother, She Didn't Make It with Her Hands': Challenging Matriliny in Papua New Guinea. In H. Lim and A. Bottomley (eds.) *Feminist Perspectives on Land Law*. London: Routledge-Cavendish, 155–70.

Dickson-Waiko, A. 2001. Women, Individual Human Rights, Community Rights: Tensions within the Papua New Guinea State. In P. Grimshaw, K. Holmes and M. Lake (eds.) *Women's Rights and Human Rights: International Historical Perspectives*. Basingstoke: Palgrave, 49–70.

Dickson-Waiko, A. 2003. The Missing Rib: Mobilizing Church Women for Change in Papua New Guinea. *Oceania* 74(1/2):98–119.

Dobell, G. 2007. The 'Arc of Instability': The History of an Idea. In R. Huisken and M. Thatcher (eds.) *History as Policy: Framing the Debate on the Future of Australia's Defence Policy*. Canberra: ANU E Press, 85–104.

---

22   In many African societies, kinship is an important organising principle (see Oyěwùmí 1997).

Dussel, E.D. 2000. Europe, Modernity, and Eurocentrism [translated by J. Krauel and V.C. Tuma]. *Nepantla: Views from South* 1(3):465–78.

Easterly, W.R. 2006. *The White Man's Burden: Why the West's Efforts to Aid the Rest Have Done So Much Ill and So Little Good*. New York: Penguin Press.

Escobar, A. 1995. *Encountering Development: The Making and Unmaking of the Third World*. Princeton, NJ: Princeton University Press.

Grosfoguel, R. 2008. Transmodernity, Border Thinking, and Global Coloniality: Decolonizing Political Economy and Postcolonial Studies. *Eurozine* [online]. http://www.eurozine.com/pdf/2008-07-04-grosfoguel-en.pdf, viewed 17/6/2013.

Hau'ofa, E. 1994. Our Sea of Islands. *The Contemporary Pacific* 6(1):147–61.

Jolly, M. 1996. Woman Ikat Raet Long Human Raet O No? Women's Rights, Human Rights and Domestic Violence in Vanuatu. *Feminist Review* 52(Spring):169–90.

Jolly, M., C. Stewart and C. Brewer 2012. *Engendering Violence in Papua New Guinea*. Canberra: ANU E Press.

Kaniku, A. 1981. Milne Bay Women. In D. Denoon and R. Lacey (eds.) *Oral Tradition in Melanesia*. Port Moresby: University of Papua New Guinea and Institute of Papua New Guinea Studies, 188–203.

Lawrence, S.E. L. 2013. Gender and Development in Papua New Guinea: Matriliny and Indigenous Best Practice in Gender Relations. Masters thesis. Deakin University, Geelong, Australia.

Lepani, K. 2012. *Islands of Love, Islands of Risk: Culture and HIV in the Trobriands*. Nashville: Vanderbuilt University Press.

Lepowsky, M.A. 1993. *Fruit of the Motherland: Gender in an Egalitarian Society*. New York: Columbia University Press.

Macintyre, M. 1983. Changing Paths: An Historical Ethnography of the Traders of Tubetube. PhD thesis, The Australian National University, Canberra.

Macintyre, M. 1987. Flying Witches and Leaping Warriors: Supernatural Origins of Power and Matrilineal Authority in Tubetube Society. In M. Strathern (ed.) *Dealing With Inequality: Analysing Gender Relations in Melanesia and Beyond*. Cambridge and New York: Cambridge University Press, 207–28.

Macintyre, M. 1995. Violent Bodies and Vicious Exchanges: Personification and Objectification in the Massim. *Social Analysis* 37:29–43.

Maldonado-Torres, N. 2004. The Topology of Being and the Geopolitics of Knowledge. *City* 8(1):29–56.

Merry, S.E. 2006. *Human Rights and Gender Violence: Translating International Law into Local Justice*. Chicago: University of Chicago Press.

Mignolo, W. 1995. *The Darker Side of the Renaissance: Literacy, Territoriality, and Colonization*. Ann Arbor: University of Michigan Press.

Murray, H. 1912. *Papua or British New Guinea*. London: T. Fisher Unwin.

Nader, L. 1996a. *Naked Science: Anthropological Inquiry into Boundaries, Power, and Knowledge*. New York and London: Routledge.

Nader, L. 1996b. Introduction: Anthropological Inquiry into Boundaries, Power, and Knowledge. In L. Nader (ed.) *Naked Science: Anthropological Inquiry into Boundaries, Power, and Knowledge*. New York and London: Routledge, 1–25.

Nader, L. 2004–2005. Law and the Theory of Lack. *Hastings International and Comparative Law Review* 28(2):191–204.

Nader, L. 2007. Promise or Plunder? A Past and Future Look at Law and Development. *Global Jurist* 7(2). doi: 10.2202/1934-2640.1221.

Oyěwùmí, O.É. 1997. *The Invention of Women: Making an African Sense of Western Gender Discourses*. Minneapolis: University of Minnesota Press.

Patterson, M. 1974. Sorcery and Witchcraft in Melanesia. *Oceania* XLV(2): 132–60.

Quijano, A. and T.B.M. Ennis 2000. Coloniality of Power, Eurocentrism, and Latin America. *Nepantla: Views from South* 1(3):533–80.

Rosewarne, S. 1997. Australia's Changing Role in the South Pacific: Global Restructuring and the Assertion of Metropolitan State Authority. *Journal of Australian Political Economy* 40(Dec):80–116.

Rumley, D. 2006. Australia's Arc of Instability: Evolution, Causes and Policy Dilemmas. *The Otemon Journal of Australian Studies* 32:37–59.

Sanday, P.R. 1981. *Female Power and Male Dominance: On the Origins of Sexual Inequality*. Cambridge: Cambridge University Press.

Scott, C. 1996. Science for the West, Myth for the Rest? The Case of James Bay Cree Knowledge Construction. In L. Nader (ed.) *Naked Science: Anthropological Inquiry into Boundaries, Power, and Knowledge*. New York and London: Routledge, 69–86.

Smith, L.T. 2004. *Decolonizing Methodologies: Research and Indigenous Peoples.* London and New York: Zed Books.

Tambiah, S.J. 1990. *Magic, Science, Religion, and the Scope of Rationality.* Cambridge: Cambridge University Press.

UNESCO 2005. *Convention on the Protection and Promotion of the Diversity of Cultural Expressions 2005.* UNESCO. http://portal.unesco.org/en/ev.php-URL_ID=31038&URL_DO=DO_TOPIC&URL_SECTION=201.html, viewed 3/6/2013.

UNESCO 2006. *Traditional Knowledge.* UNESCO Bureau of Public Information. http://www.unesco.org/bpi/pdf/memobpi48_tradknowledge_en.pdf, viewed 3/6/2013.

Wetherell, D. 2012. Creating an Indigenous Christian Leadership in Papua. *The Journal of Pacific History* 47(2):163–85.

Wetherell, D. and C.W. Abel 1998. First Contact Mission Narratives from Eastern Papua New Guinea. *The Journal of Pacific History* 33(1):111–16.

4. Sorcery and Witchcraft as a Negative Force on Economic and Social Development in Solomon Islands

Lawrence Foana'ota

Introduction

The main focus of this chapter is on sorcery and witchcraft as a negative force on economic and social development in Solomon Islands. Throughout Solomon Islands, many people believe in different types of sorcery and witchcraft. For example, in the Marovo Lagoon, Western Province, the type of sorcery and witchcraft practised there is called *pela*; on Guadalcanal it is called *vele*; while in North Malaita it is called *arua*. These are just a few of the practices that still exist in these islands. This discussion will focus on these examples in order to understand their negative effects.

It is expected that by discussing these examples, some understanding can be achieved of the consequences of these beliefs today on the economy, society, and law and order in the islands. The information will also cover the way allegations of sorcery and witchcraft are dealt with at the community level.

The discussion will conclude by providing some concrete policy recommendations for the way forward in dealing with this practice that is causing much anger, fear, frustration and hindrance to the economic and social development in contemporary Solomon Islands society.

The information contained in this chapter was collected by me during informal conversations with people from the northern part of Malaita Island, my original home, and also from other language groups in the islands. Other sources of information came from newspapers, books and personal knowledge as well as experiences during field trips to other parts of the country while I was director of the Solomon Islands National Museum from 1972 until recently.

Like other countries in Melanesia — in particular Papua New Guinea, Fiji, New Caledonia and Vanuatu — the Solomon Islands population of more than 500,000 consists of people with a diverse and rich cultural and linguistic heritage. Within this cultural diversity and richness, there are good and bad practices which some people still maintain and apply widely in some communities today.

A common and widely known example of a bad cultural practice in Melanesian countries today is sorcery and witchcraft, including related killings. Generally, the forms of sorcery and witchcraft as a negative force, and any related killings, vary from country to country and island to island in Melanesia. This also applies to the views and reactions of the people including authorities in the communities, churches and governments in this region.

In the past, death or suffering and mishaps believed or suspected to be caused by sorcery and witchcraft were sometimes followed by the killing of the practitioner to prevent further similar incidents occurring. Today, cases of actual killings are rare, but other means of dealing with deaths or events suspected to relate to these practices do exist — for example, destruction of personal property, compensation demands and chasing away suspected persons.

In the northern part of Malaita Province, *arua* is the most commonly practised and feared kind of sorcery and witchcraft. In the past, if someone was believed to have caused the death of another person with the use of *arua*, that person must be killed either by the victim's relatives or a hired killer from another tribe. The hired killer would normally be paid with traditional shell money strings known as *tafuliae*. One shell money consists of 10 strings with lengths varying from 6 to 12 feet (Figure 1). In this part of Solomon Islands, the general belief is that 'all deaths are supposed to be caused by sorcery, [and] since a woman is often not related by blood ties to her husband's kinsmen, wives would frequently be suspected' (Hogbin 1939:53).

My great-grandmother, Thangotafia, was a victim of such sorcery- and witchcraft-related killing carried out in 1910 at Funoa, in Toabaita, North Malaita, by a hired killer from another tribe. He was paid for carrying out the mission with one of the 10 strings of shell money similar to those shown in Figure 1. She was killed by mistake while the real sorcerer or witch escaped unscathed. The instruction given to the hired killer was to go to Funoa hamlet where the suspected sorcerer was staying and look for a woman weaving a basket and not the one carrying a baby. Unfortunately, when he arrived at the scene it was my great-grandmother who was weaving, while the suspect was carrying my great-grandmother's baby. Thangotafia was shot with a rifle. This killing was carried out in retaliation for the death of a person in a neighbouring tribe. The death was believed to have been caused by sorcery and witchcraft known as *arua*. The relatives believed that the witch took remains of the deceased's food and fed it to the *arua*, which was in the form of a snake.

Figure 1: Shell money strings used as traditional currency.

Source: Photograph by Lawrence Foana'ota.

In 1967 at King George VI Secondary School, Honiara, the only government secondary school at that time, an incident happened that was believed to have been caused by witchcraft known as *vele* from Guadalcanal. This particular incident involved one of the students from Guadalcanal who went into the forest with others collecting bush materials for a new chapel building at the school. His recollection of what actually happened was that he met a *vele* man who used his magic to make him lose his sense of direction and wander away from his group, deeper into the forest. Since he knew how to cure the effects of this particular witchcraft, he was able to treat himself and regain his senses. It was already dark so he had to find his way back to the school. The school authority was alerted of the missing student and a search was mounted to find him. He finally arrived at the school past midnight, tired and worn out.[1]

Those who practice *vele* on Guadalcanal use it either to kill another person or for the user's own benefit. For example, in 2004 a woman from a community in the mountains near Marau on Guadalcanal had an encounter with a *vele* man while she was working in her garden. After he had applied all the necessary procedures, which included making her lose her memory so that she could not remember him, he told her that she had only a few days to live then allowed her to return to her family in the community. Fortunately, she recovered after a group of young men from a church visiting the area from Honiara prayed for her.[2]

During the ethnic tension from 1999 to 2003, several incidents occurred, especially in Honiara. One of these incidents happened in a church-administered college where boys and girls board at the school. According to information from some of the students, six of the boys entered one of the girls' dormitories at night and shaved off hair from the girls' private parts without the girls knowing what was happening until they woke up the next morning. These boys used *pela*, which is a type of witchcraft practice from Marovo, Western Province, to turn into rats and flying foxes before they entered the dormitories. When those who were involved became known to the church and school authorities they were immediately expelled.[3] *Pela* is also believed to be used by someone practising it to eat vital organs such as the heart or liver by simply looking with piercing eyes at someone's chest.

At the height of the conflict in 2001, my house was broken into at night. This was a scary incident because the intruder(s) used witchcraft to enter through a tiny window before entering the main bedroom. The door and windows of the main bedroom were securely locked, yet the intruder(s) managed to enter.

---

1 Witnessed by the author, who was also a student at the school.
2 Information provided by the members of the church group.
3 Students' own story about the incident. Church authorities were reluctant to speak about this incident.

This incident happened without my family being aware until the next morning when they woke up and realised the doors and windows were unlocked and some personal belongings were missing.

The family found some objects the intruder(s) used to enter the master bedroom. On an ironing board near the windows, they found lime and a midrib from a coconut leaf. When information about the incident was heard by some of the neighbours, they immediately said the intruder(s) may have used either *pela* or *vele* witchcraft practices from Western or Guadalcanal provinces.[4] Their conclusion was based on the fact that these two types of practices usually cause victims to fall into deep sleep when someone wants to steal or to do stupid things, such as the incident in the church college.

In an incident in 2012 a woman almost killed her husband and one of his relatives. One night the husband wanted to sleep with his wife and suddenly she pushed him flying into the air and he landed against the wall of their house. Before he fell unconscious he saw a rat entering his wife through her private parts. When he regained consciousness his wife told him she had received the *arua* from another woman and it was impossible to get rid of it from her body. The husband called the chiefs to investigate the wife's involvement in this practice. After the chiefs confirmed that she had the *arua*, the husband told her to go back to her family. Early this year two brothers and their families were sent from their homes due to suspicion of practising *arua* and have gone back to their father's original home in another part of Malaita.[5]

Anyone who practises any of these forms of sorcery and witchcraft is regarded as an outcast or a bad person; hated, feared and despised by members of their own families or other communities. Recently, reports have been received that some families' lives have been threatened, while others have been asked to leave or have been chased out of their homes and have gone to settle in other places or on other islands.

In some other cases, suspects' homes have been destroyed (Di'isango 2014; Figure 2) while others have paid compensation since they do not have anywhere else to migrate to and so they have been allowed to stay, but under close monitoring. These kinds of harsh reactions are directed mainly towards those practising *arua* and less towards those who practice either *pela* or *vele*.

---

4   Personal encounter and experience.
5   Wesley Foarorongo, personal communication 2013 and February 2014.

Figure 2: Home razed over sorcery claims.

Source: Photograph by Stephen Di'isango, *Solomon Star*, 6 August 2014.

Sometimes the practitioners are not welcomed into communities, especially when they have jealous minds, which may lead to killing someone who has a good permanent house, owns a business, has acquired a good education or has a major development project on his or her land. Their actions cause fear and division and affect relationships among members of families, communities and tribes.

The sudden deaths of politicians — recently, the member of parliament for Ngela Constituency — and deaths at different times of three brothers from the same family who had built permanent high-storey houses in Honiara between 2010 and 2013, as well as the death in 2013 of Delight Inomae's husband, who was a prominent SIBC radio announcer,[6] were the results of sorcery and witchcraft, according to relatives and family members' beliefs.

Delays in the implementation of a number of important projects have been attributed to the effects of sorcery and witchcraft. For instance, the Bina Harbour Development Project that was initiated 30 years ago in 1984, the Suava

---

6   Inomae Delight, personal communication, April 2013.

Bay Fisheries Project, and the Kadabina Industrial Park Project in which the government and landowners carried out the groundbreaking ceremonies in 2011–2012, are still to be developed before they can start operating.

Malaita Company, which was started in the late 1960s, operated a bus service along the north road of Malaita, and the Malaita Development Authority, which started in the 1980s, provided shipping services to different parts of the country using three passenger boats. Unfortunately, both companies have gone bankrupt.

People strongly believe that the delays and failures relating to these development projects and companies are caused by the effects of sorcery and witchcraft as a negative force.

During the colonial administration, 'charges of sorcery [were] officially ignored and around the early 1930s, a regulation on this subject was contemplated by the government but when the district officers furnished reports so many practical difficulties were raised that the matter was dropped' (Hogbin 1939:151).

This attitude continued until recently when a handful of government officials and a few individuals started talking about sorcery and witchcraft with members of the community.

Unlike Papua New Guinea, where discussion regarding sorcery and witchcraft is very strong at all levels, Solomon Islands seems to take a moderate approach to this issue. For example, in Papua New Guinea, the churches are very vocal about the need for a sorcery law. This is because the '[c]hurches in the country fear there will be more deaths in sorcery-related crimes if the government does not pass a sorcery act soon' (*Solomon Star* 2013a).

At the political level, the governor of Eastern Highlands Province, Papua New Guinea, was reported to say that repealing the country's *Sorcery Act 1971* is 'unlikely to stop gruesome sorcery-related killings' (*Solomon Star* 2013b). The first sorcery-related killing to reach a national court, in 2013, involved a 21-year-old who was sent to prison for 30 years after he was found guilty of killing his aunt for sorcery (*Solomon Star* 2013c).

In Solomon Islands the politicians and churches do not speak out against sorcery and witchcraft and the courts have not charged anyone for any antisocial behaviour such as fist fighting, chasing families from their homes or destroying properties. No cases have been brought before the courts even though people believe that some sudden deaths or other unnatural incidents in their communities are related to the effects of sorcery and witchcraft.[7]

---

7   Moses Manata; data on a fist fight between a suspect and relatives of a deceased, which happened in Auki, the capital of Malaita Province, on 14 May 2013. Police did not take any action against those involved.

The general belief in Solomon Islands is that the influence of Christianity has contributed positively to a reduction in the number of these cases and related killings in some places, while in others they have completely stopped. For instance, only the killings in retaliation to deaths were stopped, while the actual practices of witchcraft and sorcery continue, even though many Christian churches strongly condemn and oppose them. This seems to be the case in general throughout the communities in the islands.

Even though the majority of people are Christians, the present trend is that the number of those using negative forces and the deaths suspected to have been caused or associated with them has increased recently. In some instances, a number of those who claim to be Christians are also practising sorcery and witchcraft. Many of the practitioners are women but the number of men is also increasing.[8]

Today for instance, there are women and men who believe in God as well as in the power of using sorcery and witchcraft in meeting either their own or other family members' needs in any difficult situation. For example, if a family member is sick or a business is not gaining any profits, the first thing to do is pray for healing or revelation of the person or whatever forces may be causing the problems. When nothing happens, a priest, sorcerer or witch may be called upon to find out the causes or treat the effects with traditional or *kastom* medicine or offer a prayer. In return they will be paid or be given an offering, therefore benefiting economically from any services they provide.

Conclusion

In concluding these discussions, it is clear that sorcery and witchcraft is a negative force on economic and social development in parts of Solomon Islands contemporary society. Many Solomon Islanders believe that sorcery and witchcraft does exist and is rapidly increasing in the numbers of both mature and young people practising it.

All deaths and diseases are considered unnatural, so sorcery or witchcraft is always given as the main cause. Many people still believe that it exists and that practitioners always keep their practice secrets to themselves. If a sorcerer or witch has enemies he or she wishes to kill or make suffer, he or she would steal some of the victim's food remains or other items that may be associated with them, call up a creature from the spirit world with a spell and give it the fragments to eat. Anyone suspected of practising witchcraft will never admit this openly.

---

8   Information collected by the author between 2013 and July 2014.

When a death occurs, relatives of the deceased always ask the question, who was the dead person most unfriendly with when he or she was alive. If someone had argued with him or her recently, this person is almost certain to be blamed. If not, the relatives would consider someone who might be envious of the victim's wealth or social status in the community. It is clear that people believe in sorcery and witchcraft as the main cause of accidents, deaths, diseases and failures either in business undertakings or in work.

It is also clear that the kinds of actions victims of sorcery and witchcraft and their relatives usually take in responding to the negative effects it causes do not go to the extreme of killing a suspect, as in other parts of Melanesia. Even if someone is suspected, the kinds of actions taken against such a person usually involve the destruction of personal property and sometimes fist fighting, but not killing. There are confirmed cases of these kinds of actions taken as recently as January and early August 2014.

Among the Christian communities, the family members or relatives usually pray with the culprits and forgive them without giving anything in return for the loss of a life, although some still do not agree with the practice of forgiveness.

The government's view is that it is not a murder case if someone is suspected to have died from sorcery and witchcraft. This view may be influenced by the fact that it is hard to come up with admissible evidence in a court of law and so it is impossible to convict anyone suspected. As a result, the government and church authorities have not paid much serious attention to incidents that are related to sorcery and witchcraft as a negative force on the economy and social development in the country until now.

Since current information indicates the number of people practising sorcery and witchcraft and the cases of suspicious incidents are rapidly increasing across Solomon Islands, it is very important for the government to take serious note now and put in place legal mechanisms to address these practices.

In concluding these discussions, communities, organisations and government institutions at all levels in the country need to acknowledge that sorcery and witchcraft is a cultural phenomenon that needs to be dealt with according to the people's customs or traditional ways of dealing with it. This should include a nationwide education program that highlights the negative effects sorcery and witchcraft is causing on the economic and social development in the country.

Further research work should be carried out to document the diversity of practices and the best way to control or eliminate some of its negative impacts. Local authorities such as chiefs, elders, women and youth leaders are empowered by a legal system that would assist them if they knew that a person suspected could be legally imprisoned, and they might put themselves at risk in finding acceptable evidence.

Finally, the government should pass a law to address the superstitious beliefs that are having significant negative effects in the economic and social development of the country. Such law should have a provision whereby customary doctors who claim to be either fortune tellers or healers could be prosecuted. Any person who accuses others of practising sorcery and witchcraft should also be able to be punished under such a law in the future.

References

Di'isango, S. 2014. Home Razed over Sorcery Claims. *Solomon Star,* 6 August.

Hogbin, H.I. 1939. *Experiments in Civilization: The Effects of European Culture on a Native Community of the Solomon Islands*. London: Routledge and Kegan Paul.

Solomon Star 2013a. Churches: Sorcery Law Needed. *Solomon Star* Issue No. 5108, 5 March, p. 14.

Solomon Star 2013b. Governor on Sorcery. *Solomon Star* Issue No. 5150, 22 April, p. 14.

Solomon Star 2013c. Sorcery Killer Jailed for 30 Years in PNG. *Solomon Star* Issue No. 5152, 24 April, p. 14.

5. Huli Customary Beliefs and Tribal Laws about Witches and Witch Spirits

John Himugu

Introduction

While working as an ethnographic research officer at the Institute of Papua New Guinea Studies, I have carried out detailed research work on sorcery and witchcraft beliefs of the Huli people of Hela Province, as seen from their perspective. I was also on the Working Committee set up by the Constitutional and Law Reform Commission of Papua New Guinea in 2007 to look into sorcery-related killings in the country. I have travelled widely with the committee and met various ethnic groups like the Huli who believe sorcery and witchcraft are very real.

Many public commentators claim sorcery is an outdated belief that is hard to prove and must be outlawed. But sorcery and witchcraft matters are still very serious in Papua New Guinea, as the following media reports illustrate.

Legion Left Region — Matthew 8.28 (Walters 2006)
Walters comments on the reality and evilness of sorcery and witchcraft as mentioned in the above Bible verse, which claims 2,000 demons from hell entered human vessels, which they occupied as their homes and terrorised the inhabitants of a region. This highlights that the Bible, the acclaimed Book of Truth on spiritual matters, describes the existence of such body-possessing evil spirits.

Bribery, Corruption and Witchcraft Rampant: Dusava (*Post-Courier* 2007)
The former secretary for the Department of Foreign Affairs, Gabriel Dusava, comments on corruption and 'abuse, bribery, witchcraft and dirty personal attacks' during the 2007 national election campaign in his Yongoru Sausia Open Electorate. This proves the rich and powerful are also using sorcery and witchcraft.

Exorcise Your Inner Demons (*The National* 2007)
Citizen Nick Yambu describes how exorcism can be used to remove evil spirits from alleged witches or sorcerers, without resorting to violence or killings.

Two Milne Bay Men Sentenced to Death (Kelola 2007)
The National Court sentenced two men to death for killing a woman they believed was a witch. The men's actions were sanctioned by the village court leaders. This poses the question of whose law is right — tribal law or state law. There is a need to balance laws that complement each other; for example, the Land Disputes Settlement Act, Chapter 45, handles customary land matters based on custom.

Sanguma — Myth, Belief or Reality (*Weekend Courier* 2009)
The Papua New Guinea Constitutional and Law Reform Commission conducts a nationwide investigation into sorcery. This demonstrates we are still looking for answers and examining recommendations at the highest level.

The Ugly Face of Sorcery (Poiya 2010)
This article reports a family attacked over sorcery allegations. This incident shows one needs to know all there is to be known about sorcery and witchcraft in order to protect oneself from being falsely framed and accused of being a sorcerer or a witch.

Killing a Councillor (Tiamu 2011)
The killing of a councillor, in Munum village, near Lae city, demonstrates that not only the poor and the weak are targeted and killed.

Most sorcery- and witchcraft-related violence and killings in Papua New Guinea are carried out by those who believe the alleged sorcerers or witches have committed a crime but that there is no proper law for prosecution or punishment. A way forward is to come up with a home-grown law with the basic ideas drawn from customary laws on sorcery and witchcraft, which various ethnic groups across the country have been using for generations.

This chapter describes how one ethnic group has built a comprehensive knowledge base on witches and witch spirits and has used that knowledge to form their belief-based rules and trial procedures and effectively prosecuted and punished witches whose witch spirits hurt or kill people.

The Huli belief system

The Huli, numbering some 250,000 people, are divided into about 50 independent tribes called *walihaga* or moiety groups who frequently fight each other. They believe a human being is made up of the body (*dongone*), the mind (*mini*) and spirit (*dinini*), and it is possible to kill a person by killing any of those three components by using invisible forces.

5. Huli Customary Beliefs and Tribal Laws about Witches and Witch Spirits

The Huli further believe the world has vast energies of invisible spiritual and cosmic forces and it is possible for human beings to tap into and use those forces to do good or evil. One of their main weapons of defence or attack was the use of poisons (*tomia*), spells (*gamugamu*) or spirits (*dama*) for invoking spiritual powers and forces. These are generally called 'sorcery' in English.

The above three types of sorcery are further broken down and given very specific names. *Tomia* includes the use of any specifically named poisonous herbal, biological, chemical or gaseous substances, mainly to kill. *Gamugamu* includes the use of named spells, rituals and chants, which are recited mainly for invoking a specifically named invisible physical, spiritual or cosmic force to do good or evil. *Dama* includes the use of any specifically named body-possessing or non-body-possessing spirit, which is engaged by conducting a specifically named ritual by their human host (*dama mambo*) to do good or evil.

Of the three, the most dangerous form of sorcery in Huli involves the use of *dama*. These include the ancestral spirits (*homa dinini*), bush spirits (*tagira dama*) and domestic spirits (*andaga dama*). (The supreme spirit called *Datagaliwabe* is considered to be too high to associate with human beings and not used by the Huli, other than to acknowledge his powers to punish arrogant wrongdoers.)

The domestic spirits were further broken down into the guardian bystanders (*haga*); the mates or friends of individuals or clans (*nenege*); and the body-possessing spirits (*gamubiaga*), which travel with or live inside human beings.

The body-possessing spirits known to the Huli include *toro*, *yaboro*, *kebali* and *heyolabe*, who all had human hosts who were usually bachelors. The hosts could call them up to carry out specific tasks for a fee agreed to between the host, the spirit and the customer.

The fifth body-possessing spirit is called *polomo* (witch spirit), and persons who are possessed by this type of spirit are called *polomo he* (witches). In other places, both male and female persons can be possessed by witch spirits, but in Huli only females can be possessed by witch spirits.

This chapter is written about witches and witch spirits because most killings reported in the Papua New Guinea media are on the killing of witches. People who use other types of sorcery including poisons, spells, chants or the spirits mentioned above are usually regarded as free agents. They may kill upon request, usually for a fee, and the main culprits in such cases are those who pay them to do it, and not the sorcerers themselves.

In contrast, witch spirits hurt or kill people of their own accord, without the knowledge or consent of their human hosts or witches (*polomo he*), so witches are sometimes killed by the community in the name of public safety.

However, in Huli, witches are not killed, firstly because the Huli believe the evil witch spirit would escape unhurt while only the innocent human being is killed. Secondly, accusers can have their complaints heard by tribal leaders, and more recently by village courts, and be paid a fair compensation in accordance with their customary beliefs.

How the witch spirits spread into the Huli area

The witch spirits spread into the Huli area in the late 1950s when new road networks made it possible for women who were unwanted for being witches in their own communities to travel into the Huli area. Some Huli bachelors married the witches. But when local leaders saw that they had married witches, they studied the behaviour of the witches and their witch spirits, gained ideas from other ethnic groups, and made rules for tackling the problem.

It is said that you have to live with a witch in order to understand them properly. I personally saw a witch when I was about nine years old. One of our tribesman returned home with his two wives from another area. The first wife was a witch or had a witch spirit. Sometime later, he chased her out for threatening his second wife and her child. The witch came and lived with my mother for a time. I lived in another house nearby with my father.

Every night, as soon as the woman fell asleep, her witch spirit would fly out with three bursts of whistling sounds (*hoe/pili*) given off at around five minute intervals, or less when she was in a hurry. Then every morning just before dawn, the witch spirit would return with the same three bursts of whistling. The whistling would disappear near the house and the woman could be heard waking up.

Sometimes we would hear the witch spirit killing one of our chickens. We have seen many dead chickens before, but the ones killed by the witch spirit would stink straight away, despite the freezing cold climate.

If told about the dead chickens, she would say, 'We haven't had much to eat lately. Shouldn't happen again!'

If asked to say a prayer before going to bed, she would say, 'Aren't I a child of God too? Why is it that I cannot pray too?' and she would say a prayer that sounded very shallow and without much conviction or depth and abruptly end it with a quick 'Amen'.

Later she was accused of killing the daughter of her husband and his second wife. So she was sent back to her own home area. While there, she and another witch were accused of killing a man. They were brought to the Koroba District

Court and tried for murder by witchcraft. She admitted to the killing. When pressed to give her reason for the killing, she said 'What we got was our normal food. Nobody stops you humans from killing and eating chickens, so why be angry with us?' She was sent to jail and later died in prison.

Apart from this story, I can relate to many others I have seen or heard. When the sorcery- and witchcraft-related killings in Papua New Guinea were becoming a big issue, many people claimed that the sorcery and witchcraft beliefs were fictitious. But I thought it likely they had never seen a real witch or a sorcerer in their lives. So I carried out a research project on the sorcery and witchcraft beliefs among the Huli people of Hela Province to provide information on how sorcery and witchcraft matters are understood and handled. This chapter discusses witches and witch spirits from that project.

The four types of witch spirits

The Huli believe there are four types of witch spirits. The first type do not hurt or kill people or animals. The second type dig up graves only. The third type kills babies, the old and sick or those people who are about to die anyway. The fourth type can kill healthy people and can also form packs with other witch spirits to hurt or kill people.

It is believed one witch can have up to six or seven witch spirits. The more witch spirits she has, the deadlier she becomes. Huli believe there is no skill or craftiness in being a witch, but just plain evil.

The biggest sufferers are the witch's husband, children, relatives and neighbours, who in most cases live in constant fear, and remain at the mercy of her witch spirit or spirits.

How a normal person can become a witch

It was said in the legends that once upon a time there lived four brothers and a sister. One day an evil spirit led the sister to a cliff-face and pushed her off. When her spirit departed from her body with fright, the evil spirit took over her body and landed it safely on the ground. But when her own spirit wanted to return to the body, the evil spirit pushed it out and took ownership of the body. The sister returned home unhurt, but did things very strangely. Later her brothers found out that she had an evil spirit in her and had become a witch.

That is what was said in legends, but today there are about 10 known ways in which witch spirits can enter a normal human being and make them into a witch.

Like in the legend above, a senior witch can pick any girl or woman of her liking and make her climb up and jump off a tree. When her spirit departs from the body with fright, the witch spirit takes possession of the body and lands it safely on the ground. This exercise is repeated over and over until the senior witch is convinced that the trainee is now a fully fledged witch.

Accidental transfers can also happen if a normal woman was sleeping next to a witch and if the witch spirit returns in the morning and enters the other woman by mistake. It is also believed if a group of women and girls are chasing fish or other small bush game, and if a witch is with the chasing team, in the excitement the witch spirit can come out and enter any of the females waiting to catch the escaping animal at the far end of the hunting or fishing ground.

A witch can also have as many as six or seven witch spirits if the original witch spirit invites more witch spirits to join her and occupy the same host. It is also believed if a normal person becomes too friendly to a witch, one of her witch spirits can visit her friend from time to time, and one day it may decide to stay with her permanently and make her into a witch.

It is also believed if a married man killed a witch, the witch spirit can follow him home and make his wife into a witch. It is also believed that when a witch dies, the witch spirit, if it has not found a new host yet, will stay by the gravesite and wait for any suitable female who passes by and make her into a witch.

At other times, some women or girls may just want to become a witch and can ask a witch who has witch spirits to give them one. So the witch can easily ask one of her witch spirits to go and live with the new host on a trial basis, then later transfer to her permanently. This is usually the case with girls whose mothers and sisters are all witches.

Some girls can also be persuaded into believing it is wonderful to be a witch when others talk of their adventures and conquests as witches. This talk of wealth and adventure stirs her imagination and makes her want to become a witch like them. She may volunteer to go on trial runs with a witch spirit, which can later be transferred to her permanently. Living an isolated life in an isolated area can also make it possible for witch spirits to go and stay with a lonely woman and over a period of time make her into a witch.

The external signs of having a witch spirit

People in the community can find out if a woman or a girl is a witch by observing several external signs that a person may be a witch.

First, after nightfall and as soon as the witch falls asleep, her witch spirit flies out of the house in the form of a flying fox-like creature, giving off three piercing whistling sounds at regular intervals. The spirit returns just before dawn, making the same whistling sounds. This happens every night and every morning. It disappears when she goes to live elsewhere and returns when she returns.

Another sign is that people may see a dog or a cassowary coming, but when it gets closer, it turns out to be a woman, and not an animal. But after she has passed, the woman disappears and the animal is seen again. The same animal stays with the witch for life.

Furthermore, if a woman is a witch, and if she has sons, they might die in mysterious circumstances, such as by drowning in a shallow creek. Those still alive would look sick and unhealthy, until they too would all die, one by one. In the long term, the witch and all her close family members would have no sons left.

Women with witch spirits usually put on weight when the body of a person she is accused of killing is decaying in the grave. The witch also puts on weight if she takes part in a killing or digging out graves in the neighbourhood with other witches.

Finally, in the event that a witch spirit has entered a woman by mistake, the woman would have bad dreams of herself raiding fresh graves and coming away with body parts. If she keeps having this dream night after night, and if she tells her relatives about it, then her relatives observe her personal behaviour before they organise an expert to remove the witch spirit in her.

The internal signs of having a witch spirit

When the above-mentioned external signs indicate that the person may be a witch, relatives observe closely to see if she really is possessed by a witch and, if so, by what type of witch spirit or spirits.

Firstly, split personality problems are noticed when a woman says something while her witch spirit says something else at the same time over the same matter. This makes her fumble words, or deny having said the very thing she had just said a few seconds back.

When a woman is seen sitting on her own, talking or mumbling to herself, it is believed she is pleading with her witch spirit not to attack someone.

When asked tough questions, she gives evasive answers, or answers the questions indirectly. But when put under pressure with more and more tough questions, the witch usually gives contradicting answers. Experts can detect which answers are coming from herself and which answers are coming from her witch spirit.

When sharing and eating food, especially pork, a witch will eat all her pieces in what looks like a single gulp and sit there staring at others who are still eating their share. It is believed if you don't give her some extra pieces, then her witch spirit can attack anyone in the group at any moment. Witches also stare at beautiful-looking babies or those who are eating or carrying good food and will not take their eyes off them or respond even when you disturb them.

If she comes from a feast, the witch will bring home two separate bags of food, one for sharing with the family and a smaller one for herself. This practice is noticed mostly with the older generation of witches.

The witch spirit can attack the husband of her host at any time. This may happen if he talks to other women or if the witch feels her husband is drinking away all his money. In this case, her witch spirit can go and attack him in the club. His friends would think he has fainted, but he would see his wife coming and plead with her to stop the attack just before he falls down and passes out.

If a woman with a witch spirit is asked to babysit a boy and a girl, the boy would become sick, while the girl would not. If one of the children gets a cut, the woman will stare at the blood and go numb or absentminded for a while.

A woman who has a witch spirit can also appear from nowhere to the bed of a sick person who is about to die, even though no one had seen her coming in through the door. She can also appear from nowhere at the bedside of someone who has just died, or when someone is getting buried. Witches can appear or disappear without a trace at any other place. For example, her husband may see her coming, but when he looks up to talk to her, she disappears. This is because what he saw was her witch spirit, who is her lookalike and not her true self.

When the above personal characteristics are noticed, friends and relatives believe that the person has a witch spirit or spirits. So they learn when, why and how witch spirits hurt or kill other people and take appropriate measures to protect themselves and their families from possible attack.

Why, when and how witch spirits hurt or kill other people

The Huli believe witch spirits are evil by nature. Firstly, they use some human beings as a conduit to come into the human world. While living inside the body of their human host, they behave and act like hungry wolves and use every opportunity to snatch a desirable or vulnerable life and hurt or kill that person.

Why witch spirits hurt or kill other people

The main reason why witches kill is to satisfy their lust for good-looking bodies. If a witch sees a beautiful child or a man and likes what she sees, then her witch spirit may kill to satisfy her lust for the good-looking body.

Secondly, if a witch sees someone getting or eating good food, and if it ignites her greed or lust for good food, her witch spirit might strangle the person with the food.

Witches can also attack a person to avenge for any wrong committed against her host. For instance, the witch spirit can attack the ex-boyfriend of her host or his new girlfriend, or both.

The witch spirit of an angry witch can also attack or hurt an innocent child or bystander as a spillover effect of anger, even though the bystander has done nothing wrong.

A witch spirit can also team up and attack other people upon the request of another witch who needs her help to kill a person. This could be to help, for example, make a tree branch fall onto the victim. To do this, the witches who control the wind, rain and clouds would be brought in to assist by playing their parts in staging this type of accident-based killing.

Witch spirits can also kill those who are about to die anyway (*mo mbedogo*), from illnesses such as AIDS. But the issue here is the sign and symptoms of witch spirit attack. For instance, if a person was hit by a car and dies instantly, the fact that he was going to die anyway from AIDS is not considered — instead, his death will be officially recorded as having been hit and killed by a car.

Finally the Huli believe, in order for a person to live, he or she must have their mind (*mini*), spirit (*dinini*) and body (*dongone*) balanced and in union at all times. Otherwise, the witch spirit can detect and kill any person whose spirit is not in union with his body and mind (*pu he*).

Experts can tell if a person has died a natural death or a witch spirit-induced death. With their gathered evidence, they bring in and question the accused witch to discover her reason for attacking or killing the victim.

When witch spirits hurt or kill other people

For witch spirits, the desire to attack their victim is ignited only after the witch has made visual contact with the victim or a close relative of the victim. Just before the attack, a tree branch or a twig must be seen or heard getting snapped. A gun can be heard to be cocked, too. Straight after that noise, the witch spirit will attack and within seconds the victim will start to get sick and lose consciousness.

At other times, an animal such as a dog belonging to a particular witch will be sighted in an area just before an attack. But if the witch was watching someone eating food, for example, the attack will be sudden and the victim will clutch his or her throat as if suffering from suffocation or choking, and pass out.

How witch spirits hurt or kill other people

It is believed in most cases the witch spirit removes the spirit of the victim and holds it captive for some time, usually high up in the branches of a tree. If she does not get caught, the witch spirit uses any credible means available in nature to kill the physical body of the victim. The most common method is by staging what would look like an accident.

Here the wind and rain may be used, to make a tree or a branch fall on the victim, for example. Or the victim may be drowned in a river or lake. In all cases the death would look natural, but some uncertainty would remain. For instance, a closer examination would reveal that the tree branch had fallen in the wrong wind direction, or the water in which the victim drowned was very shallow. Experts who know about such things and observe the details can show whether the incidents or accidents were truly natural or induced by witch spirits.

In attacks over food, witch spirits can cause food or other objects to get stuck in the throat. This may appear natural, but the presence of the witch where the victim was, along with her looks, actions or comments she may make at the time of the incident would link her to that attack.

The most common method for attacking a healthy person is to induce what looks like a heart attack (locally known as removing the heart). First, one might see a strange animal such as a dog that belongs to a witch appearing from nowhere and staring at the victim. Then all of a sudden something hits the heart of the victim, and he falls down clutching at his chest and passes out. But if the victim is taken to the hospital, doctors find nothing wrong with him.

Sometimes while a witch is cuddling a baby, the baby may start to die in her hands from symptoms that look like strangulation, suffocation or sudden heart failure. The witch would hand the dying baby back to its mother and sneak away. The mother might think her baby was asleep, but when it does not wake up she would realise her baby was dying.

Signs and symptoms of a witch spirit attack

The first signs and symptoms of a witch spirit attack on the body of a healthy person appear as sudden heart attack, choking, suffocation or an acute malarial attack. The victim would usually put his hand on his neck or chest and pass out. But when the victim is taken to the hospital, doctors find nothing wrong with the person.

Secondly, if the body of the victim turns blue around the chest and below the armpit areas very quickly, this is also a sign of a possible witch spirit attack.

Medical examination of a person who has been attacked by a witch spirit often finds nothing wrong. But after the person dies, the post mortem may reveal foreign material stuck in the victim's throat. However, when and how that foreign object became lodged in the throat would be a mystery. This is also an indication of a possible witch spirit killing.

Some gifted people (including church elders) can tell if the victim has been attacked by a witch spirit and give the exact description of the witch along with details on when, where, why and how the victim was attacked. They may also advise the victim to make peace with the witch, who is often a close relative, in order to get well. This approach usually works.

When a person dies, if relatives want to know whether the person was killed by a witch spirit, they could pay a medium (*halaga biaga*) to call up the spirit of the dead relative to tell them if he or she had been killed by a witch spirit.

Relatives and leaders can also use the *toro* ritual to find out if a person has been killed by a witch spirit, and the reason for the killing. In this ritual, the bones of a dead person are placed on a stretcher. Sticks are placed on the rib bones. 'Yes' and 'no' questions are asked. If the answer is 'yes', the sticks move and float, but if the answer is 'no', the sticks do not move.

Sometimes the victim, before passing out, calls out that he is being attacked by a witch and names her. This type of attack is usually made on husbands or close relatives of the witches themselves.

Experts on witchcraft matters use the type of evidence mentioned above to frame appropriate questions that can force the witch spirit to give one answer while the witch woman gives a different answer. This happens because although witch spirits are sneaky, they are not as clever as human beings. For instance, if asked about her skill and ability to attack, the witch spirit would become boastful and give away more details on how she had carried out the attack, while the witch woman would remain silent, and even deny having said those things. The same person making contradictory statements at the same time is evidence that the witch is guilty, and if she is caught early, she can cure the victim within minutes.

Traditional first aid methods

It is believed in order to kill a person, the witch spirit first removes the spirit of the victim and holds it captive for some time. Then if she does not get caught, she comes back to kill the physical body of the victim, who would now be very sick. So only aggressive-looking men and boys are chosen to take care of the victim. Some men chop the ground around the victim with a bush knife or axe from time to time to prevent the witch spirit from getting too close to the victim's body. This keeps the victim alive while other men hunt for the accused witch and force her to come and make the victim well.

If the victim is a baby, a person could hold it up by the legs and run around the house like a madman. It is believed that shaking the body violently will frighten it, and force its spirit to return and make the baby recover.

Hunting down and threatening the witch with instant death if the victim dies always brings an instant cure. It is believed the witch spirit can release the captured spirit and let it return to its body. When that is done the victim recovers almost instantly.

Some traditional healers can cure a person attacked by witch spirits, but it is very rare. Those who have this skill may have spirits who know how to negotiate with witch spirits at the spirit-to-spirit level to let the victim live.

Some gifted church elders can pray for a person dying from witch spirit attack and cure him. Others with certain gifts, such as a *glasman*, can tell when, why and how a witch spirit had tried to hurt or kill a victim and advise the relatives to make amends with the suspected witch in order to make the victim well.

5. Huli Customary Beliefs and Tribal Laws about Witches and Witch Spirits

An effective method is to confront the alleged witch and force her to visit the sick person. When the witch arrives, she will pray or pretend to pray for the victim and recovery is immediate.

In earlier times, witches when caught out would say 'it's not me, maybe it is my sisters out there who may have done it, wait and let me ask them to return the spirit'. Today they usually say 'bring the sick here and let me pray for the poor thing', but in her prayer, one could hear her rebuking her witch spirit for doing a poor job and getting them both caught.

However, after a victim gets well, some witches will sue the victim and his or her relatives for defamation. The witches use the formal court system with police support and win their defamation cases most of the time. This is putting the witches in danger in the long run because if the tribal leaders refuse to hear any more witchcraft cases, the accusers can kill them on the spot without trial.

What it is like to be possessed by witch spirits

The Huli believe that persons who are possessed by witch spirits have no control over what their witch spirits do. They further believe being possessed by a witch spirit is a type of a mental or spiritual illness, and that relatives and the general community have an obligation to seek appropriate traditional or modern exorcism methods to free those who are possessed by evil witch spirits.

How to remove a witch spirit from a witch

The Huli use several methods to suppress or completely remove the evil powers of witch spirits from witches.

Firstly, if a woman who has an evil witch spirit tells everyone that she has an evil spirit in her, the witch spirit will become timid and not kill human beings. Eventually it will leave her completely and the woman will become a normal person again.

It is also believed that if the husband of a witch mixes his urine with tea or water and tricks the witch into drinking it, the witch spirit will leave her and she will become normal again.

The most effective method is the use of bones of giant humans or ogres found in caves.[1] Here the bones are crushed into powder and mixed with drinking

---

1 Some cheeky boys play bad jokes on each other by picking up ogre bones and putting them under the beds of their mates, who get attacked at night by the giant spirits.

water, and a witch is tricked into drinking the mixture. In the night, the fierce-looking ogre spirits come in her dreams and attack her violently. This attack would continue for several days and nights until there were no more ogre bone particles left in her system. It is believed keeping the body awake forces the witch spirit to return to the body every now and again, only to come face-to-face with an ogre spirit. This makes the witch spirit feel her host has become unsuitable to occupy and so the witch spirit leaves.

Church elders who have the gift of driving out evil spirits can drive out witch spirits. To do that, the elders pray for some time and when they feel the power of God is with them, they command the witch spirit to leave the woman. Sometimes the woman will faint or pass out, but when she gets up she is a normal woman again. First the witch herself must ask the church elders to get rid of the witch spirit in her body, otherwise the witch spirit will talk back and refuse to leave. Usually a dog or a cat can be seen leaving the churchyard. If the animal looks back, then an attack will take place later, but if the animal does not look back, there will be no more related problems.

How to kill a witch or a witch spirit

There are several ways to kill a witch or a witch spirit. The witch's own relatives often denounce her activities and give permission for any offended person to kill her. Also, angry relatives of any of her victims can kill the witch or the witch spirit without permission from anybody, using various methods.

In earlier times, there were men who knew chants that they recited and applied vision-cleansing ginger on the eyes of a selected bachelor. This enabled the bachelor to see the witch spirit at night. He would then hide by a graveside and shoot the witch spirit when it came to the grave. When shot, the host of the witch spirit, who could be several kilometres away, would be accidentally pierced by a piece of stick. It was believed if the killer took the bowstring off, the witch would die, if he left it on, she would live.

It was believed if you saw a bird or an animal by the grave of a person who had just been buried, and if you killed that animal, the witch who was the host of that witch spirit would have an accident at the same time and die.

An accused witch may be murdered by the relatives of a victim, or even by her own relatives who do not want to keep paying compensation for victims her witch spirit keeps hurting or killing. But in Huli, any killing of any human being, regardless of whether she is a witch or not, is regarded as murder. So there is no public killing of witches for being witches, but those who do kill alleged witches, do so with the knowledge that they could be tried for murder.

In Huli, some types of spirits are hired to kill or remove other types of spirits, but they are not hired to kill or remove witch spirits. However, they can pay a witch to provide information against another witch leading to her arrest and trial for an alleged crime.

Huli customary protective measures, rules and laws

The Huli believe it is the responsibility of all human beings who live in areas where there are witches to take appropriate measures to protect themselves and their families from any possible attack. Based on their knowledge of when, why and how witch spirits attack their victims, the Huli have developed various rules to follow or apply for protection.

During meal times, the witch must always be the first to be served food and the last person to get any extra left so that she will feel she is getting the largest portion of food. When sleeping, the witch must be made to sleep near a door or window so that her witch spirit can go out and come in freely and when returning in the morning not get into another person by mistake.

When chasing game animals, women and girls must avoid going out with any known witches, because her spirit could transfer into any one of them. Generally, no females should be left alone with a known witch because she might transfer her witch spirit to her. And a known witch must not be left in the company of other known witches, because they might form a deadly pack and make daring attacks.

Witches must be kept away from possible victims such as children or sick persons. If a known witch arrives into the room while you are looking after a sick person, you must threaten her with death if the patient dies, and chase her out, and if you see a known witch staring at a person, you must tell her to back off immediately.

The witch must be verbally warned of an imminent attack on herself if she stares at you. But if you have food or money that has caught her attention, you have to give her something, but at the same time you must threaten to attack her if anything happens to you later.

When a witch dies, her witch spirit, if it has not yet found a new host, waits by the graveside for the next female who comes by. So when a witch is about to die, only men and boys must take care of her until she dies. When she is being buried, women and girls are not allowed to her burial ceremony or to the burial site afterwards.

If you have a witch living with you or in the neighbourhood, you must always have your family meals before nightfall. This is because, at night, the witch spirit could be watching in the cover of darkness and could attack any of the family members it sees as the most vulnerable.

When you are in a crowd where witches may be present, you must never look sick or tired or else one of them might mark you out as a possible easy target.

When someone is buried, people must light lamps and stay beside the graveyard for at least eight days and nights to prevent witches from digging up the body.

The Huli try to avoid contact with witches or their witch spirits, so those who live in the vicinity of houses where witches live do not stay outdoors during the time the witch spirits usually go out or come in.

The Huli also believe that witch spirits avoid Christians and churches. So if you live in an area where there are many witches, it is best to become a Christian to prevent yourself from any possible attack.

The relatives of witches have a duty to inform neighbours or new visitors to take any of the above protective measures. Otherwise, the relatives of witches may also be held responsible or accountable for any witch attacks.

Putting an accused witch on trial

When a witch is accused of hurting or killing a person, the leaders first ask the accusers for evidence to show that the accused person is a witch. For example, whether she had been involved in an incident of a similar nature before, or if any visual contact had been made between the witch and the victim before the attack, or if any comments had been made by the accused witch before or after the attack.

If the leaders are satisfied with the evidence given by the accusers, and if they believe it is a strong case, they will bring in the accused witch and tell her about the allegations made against her, and ask her to clear her name. She could be supported at the trial by any interested person, including her friends and relatives.

Confirmation and confession by the witch

If an accused witch denies everything, it is easy to let her go free because the leaders know exactly how witches talk and react when they are telling the truth.

If there are still some doubts, another witch who is known as a witch leader in the region could be paid to provide information on who hurt or killed the victim. The accused witch usually defends herself by accusing the informer of other killings the informer herself had been involved in. Then if the accused witch is pressured further by the leaders, she will justify her actions by saying, 'such killings are normal for witches like them'.

The trial proper is held to finally convince the witch to admit her involvement in hurting or killing the victim and, if so, to give her reasons for the attack and cooperate with the leaders to make peace with the victim or his or her relatives. If the victim is still alive, she will ask the leaders to let her see the victim, and to let her pray for him or her. In such a case, it is certain that the victim will get well.

If the victim is dead, the witch will say, 'you have come too late'. And if the leaders ask her to show them the dead body, she will refuse. But other witches will take the leaders to a site and show them a dead frog, or a dead lizard or a grasshopper. It is believed in the eyes of the witch spirits, they see the body of the victim and not insects.[2]

If the witch claims the victim was already cooked and eaten, and if the leaders ask her to show them the *mumu* pit and the leaves and ferns they had used in the cooking, she will refuse. But other witches will lead them to a site where witch spirits are known for congregating. There they will show pieces of wild ferns (*yagua*) and wild ginger (*guayapugunu*) leaves.

Finally, when all the evidence has been pursued, the accused witch fully confesses and gives her reasons for the killing. She will further name all the other witches who had taken various parts of the body. When the leaders ask those named witches to come forward and admit or deny their involvement, most of them will directly or indirectly admit to having been involved. If asked to explain their actions, they will all say it is normal for them, just like good people share good food with family and friends.

Crime and accountability rules

The Huli believe that allowing oneself to be used as a conduit by evil spirits to cross the forbidden human–spirit barrier is a crime punishable by revenge killing, compensation payments, forced exorcism or exclusion from society.

The specific crimes committed by a witch are for allowing themselves to be used as a conduit by witch spirits to come into the human world and disturb human beings, for not getting rid of the witch spirit, for not living in seclusion, for not preventing the witch spirit from attacking a person, or for the social and economic loss suffered by the victim's relatives.

---

2 The Huli say when you are invited into the world of spirits by spirits, you have to leave your human beliefs and logics behind for the time being.

However, those who live in areas where there are witches but who do not take appropriate measures to protect themselves and their families can be accused of neglect.

Compensation payable to the witch and her relatives

Tribal leaders may order accusers to pay compensation to the accused witch for defamation if she is wrongfully accused. However, some witches can go to the police station and lodge a complaint for defamation against her accusers and the tribal leaders. The leaders cannot prove that she is a witch in the formal evidence-based court system, so the witches win the defamation cases every time. But in the long run, this could force some communities to kill the witches or chase them away without trial.

Normally, compensation for attacking or killing a known witch cannot be asked for too aggressively by her relatives. This is because the witch's relatives have failed to remove the witch spirit in her and prevent her from killing people in the first place. However, village leaders can still force her killers to pay some compensation and the killers can also be sent to jail for murder.

The killing of a bird or animal that represents a particular witch will also kill the witch. But compensation for this type of killing is not talked about openly because the witch had crossed the forbidden barrier. However, if those who killed the bird or animal boast openly about it, they can be asked to pay compensation for the death of the witch.

Compensation payable by the witch and her relatives

In Huli, any killing by a witch spirit is treated like every other normal killing. The leaders can bring the accused witch to stand trial and, if found guilty, the main form of punishment is to pay compensation.

The leaders usually order the guilty witch and her relatives to pay compensation based on custom, just like any other type of murder. But the amount set by the victim's relatives is renegotiated if the other party feels it is too high. This can go into second and third rounds of negotiation until it is finally resolved by the leaders whose job is to strike a balance acceptable to both parties. In the end, the leaders witness the transaction and close the matter.

However, witches are usually disowned by their own families, and are in no position to pay compensation. So the tribal leaders may order the witch to be sent to jail, to be exorcised, to live in seclusion, or to be ordered out of the area.

In the eyes of the community, most witches, once cornered, break down very easily and give themselves away. So most community members just feel sorry for them, and chase them away and tell them never to return.

Other penalties

Huli leaders talk mainly in terms of paying compensation and never about other penalties like the death penalty or revenge killing, exclusion from society, exorcism or imprisonment, even though these options are left to the affected individuals to decide and execute.

For instance, no decision is ever made to put a witch to death, but the Huli believe the witch spirit has already killed the human spirit of her host. So she and her relatives know the witch could be killed by the relatives of any of her victims in revenge killing, or by her own relatives who do not want to keep paying compensation to the relatives of her victims.

In some cases, the witch is poor and her relatives unable to pay the compensation set by the leaders. So the witch is told to live in seclusion from society or forced to go and live elsewhere.

Some witches are deemed to be very dangerous and exorcism the only option, but executing it is a problem. Some men whose wives and daughters were all witches often carried out traditional exorcism bravely on their own. These had to be well planned and well executed.

Today, church elders who have the gift of driving out evil spirits are the most preferred method to use for removing witch spirits from witches and making them into normal human beings again.

Case studies on accusation and trial

Most of the events described below took place in Port Moresby during the time of my research, and involved Huli people. The details were given by the Huli leaders who were involved in solving the matters.

Offended wife kills husband with sorcery — Hohola, Port Moresby, July 2008

A young wife helped fund her husband to upgrade his school marks and get into the army. While in the army, he had affairs with other women. The wife asked a woman friend who had spells to help her bring him back, but the spells failed. So her friend helped her find a Samarai sorcerer. The Samarai sorcerer failed, too. Her friend helped her find a Tolai sorcerer. The Tolai sorcerer failed, so they found a Koiari sorcerer.

Eventually the husband got sick and was about to die because the wife had not followed proper instructions. The leaders questioned the wife, who denied everything. Later one of the leaders told her that she might be killed over this matter, but no one would know her side of the story. So in self-pity she confessed to using sorcery. The Koari sorcerer was found and asked to remove his sorcery, but he just placed his hands on the victim and claimed other sorcerers had worked on him, too, so it was beyond his powers to cure the husband. The husband died.

The leaders and the police saved the wife and her friend from possible revenge killing by locking them up at the Boroko police cell. The leaders then ordered the wife to pay two-thirds of the compensation payable for normal murder. Her friend was ordered to pay the other third.

Her friend was held accountable for helping the wife. But the sorcerers could not be charged as they are free agents under Huli customary law on sorcery.

The matter was closed as a sorcery killing carried out by an aggrieved wife.

Witch wins a false accusation claim — Tokarara, Port Moresby, 2005

Two angry women were seen arguing with each other at the back of a flat in Tokarara. One of them stormed out of the gate. Suddenly a six-year-old healthy boy who was standing by the gate started to get dizzy and lay down. Within minutes, he had blood oozing from his mouth and ears. His father took him to Port Moresby General Hospital. The doctor said it looked like an acute malarial attack and put the boy on a life support machine.

One of the relatives, however, said it was a witch spirit attack because he claimed one of the women who was arguing at the back of the flat was a known witch. So the father and relatives went to the woman's house and threatened her with instant death if the boy died. The accused woman claimed they were threatening her without evidence. But in the end, she was forcefully taken to the hospital to 'look at the boy herself' they said.

As soon as the woman set her foot on the hospital steps the boy started to get well, so the woman claimed the boy was never sick and she had been accused for nothing. She later laid a formal complaint against the father at Gordons Police

Station. The father, who didn't want trouble, asked the police to negotiate for a fair compensation payment acceptable to her, and paid her 300 kina through police mediation.

The matter was closed as a win-win witchcraft case.

Mother kills her own son — Gerehu, Port Moresby, 2007

A seven-year-old healthy boy died suddenly. The body was placed in the morgue. The leaders questioned the boy's mother, who seemed unnaturally happy in front of all the other grieving relatives. The mother, who was a witch confessed, 'I ate him and it went down very well when washed down with a drink of coke'. Her husband and relatives did not take any action. So the leaders let the matter rest.

The matter was closed as witchcraft killing of a close family member.

Traditional exorcism on wife and two teenage daughters — Pori, Hela Province, 1980

A man (named) had a wife and two teenage daughters. They were becoming famous throughout the land for being aggressive witches. He knew one of them would get killed or they would one day turn on him. He planned to carry out an exorcism. So he collected a piece of ogre bone from a cave in the mountain and grounded it into fine powder.

He then killed and cooked a pig and invited his wife and daughters to a family feast in their garden by the forest. The drinking place was far away, but the father provided the drinking water fetched in fresh bamboo containers. The three thirsty witches drank the water with the ground-up bone powder without even noticing.

The women could not sleep at night because the giant attacked them each time they tried to go to sleep. The witch spirits may also have seen the giant spirit around the house, which frightened them. This attack went on for several days and nights, until no more bone particles were left inside their bodies. By that time, the witch spirits found the three women to be unsuitable hosts and left for good. The three witches became normal women again from then on.

Talking it Through

Christian exorcism: witch spirit leaves witch — Mount Kare, Hela Province, 1989

Two small boys lay unconscious at the Mount Kare alluvial mining clinic. Some said it was a witch spirit attack and caught the accused young woman who was a known witch. The men built a huge camp fire and heated up iron rods. Others sharpened their axes and bush knives. The woman was made to stand in the centre of a ring of fierce men. Someone brought the local pastor to pray for her parting soul.

But the pastor, who was new in the area, refused to pray for her soul. Instead, he asked her if she was a witch. She replied they were accusing her of being a witch. At that moment the pastor in a vision saw another woman who was her lookalike standing behind her. He also had another vision that the boys' spirits were held on a moss plant growing high up on a tall tree nearby.

The pastor said to the young woman, 'God's spirit shows me that you have a lookalike sister who is standing behind you right now. His spirit also shows me that the boys are not dead and their spirits are held up on the moss plant on that tree over there. The men are sharpening their axes and bush knives here, but not for slaughtering a cow, but since the boys are still alive, you have a decision to make.'

When she hesitated, the pastor said, 'it looks like you are innocent but your lookalike who is standing behind you may have something to say about it. You can choose to keep her with you and die or ask her to go and live.'

In reply, she said, 'I want her to go'.

Then the pastor said to her witch spirit, 'you heard her in the witness of all of us here that she wants you to go'. In reply the witch spirit in her said through the mouth of the witch, 'don't kill her, I will return the boys and go'.

The spirit left quickly. The two boys regained consciousness within an hour. And the young woman became a normal person. Many people started going to the pastor's small church.

This pastor has dealt with many other cases. When asked how he does it, he said, 'the possessed person is the one who makes the decision. We support the decision of the possessed person. One cannot just order a spirit out. They too have rights, and they always stand their ground.'

Conclusion

Most people do not have enough background information on witches and witch spirits, so they are not in a position to talk about this matter. That might be good, too, because one of the informers said such details should be left to selected leaders only because spirits really love us when they hear us talking about them. So not talking about them at all is the best way to keep them out of our lives.

On the other hand, this lack of information makes most people believe we are the only ones on Earth. But the fact is there are some of us who associate with external forces to do good or bad against other people. These invisible forces include sorcery and witchcraft.

It is believed the witchcraft-related violence and killings in Papua New Guinea are carried out by those who believe the alleged witches have committed a crime, but there is no proper law in place for prosecuting and punishing witches. So the solution is to provide a legal avenue for the accusers to prosecute and punish alleged witches instead of citizens taking the law into their own hands.

The problem in Papua New Guinea is that the criminal laws were adopted from the English Common Law, which has no section for those affected by the belief-based sorcery and witchcraft matters. The *Sorcery Act 1971* did not work simply because it was not drafted properly. For instance, the main culprits in witchcraft cases are the witch spirits, not the witches, and exorcism should have been used as the main form of punishment for convicted witches. While in sorcery cases, the main culprits are those who engage the sorcerers for a fee and not the sorcerers themselves, who are free agents.

Some say there are big differences between the belief systems of the various ethnic groups, but the basic formula will work anywhere because all spirits, such as witch spirits, show similar characteristics.

This chapter on Huli beliefs and tribal laws on witches and witch spirits shows how one ethnic group has developed and used belief-based customary laws for resolving witchcraft-related cases in their communities.

First, the Huli developed a detailed knowledge base on witches and witch spirits. Then using this knowledge, they framed their belief-based rules and trial procedures, and used these to bring to trial and prosecute and punish witches whose witch spirits hurt or killed other people.

This has effectively prevented accusers from injuring or killing alleged witches in their communities. This shows it is possible to understand, analyse and frame belief-based laws and use them effectively for prosecuting and punishing witches whose witch spirits commit a crime.

A suggested way forward is to draft a better home-grown law with the basic ideas drawn from the customary laws on sorcery and witchcraft, which the various ethnic groups in Papua New Guinea have been using effectively for generations. Input from known sorcerers, witches, traditional healers and the Bible could be considered and included.

Notes — The informants

Gane Abe Mbalo — Had taken part in many traditional rituals and ceremonies.

Ala Arapa — Had lived among many witches.

Pastor Dondoli — Had carried out exorcism on witches and settled disputes.

Joe Kayuria — Had his son attacked, then was sued by the witch for defamation.

Duliya Maeyago — Community leader who handled many witch-related cases.

Philip Pugulabe — Contact man who can find sorcerers, healers and gifted persons.

Ben Mindiria — A local preacher gifted in driving out bad spirits from persons, houses or areas.

Many others who told stories of personal encounters with witches.

References

Kelola, T. 2007. Two Milne Bay Men Sentenced to Death. *Post-Courier*, 4 October, p. 5.

National, The 2007. Exorcise Your Inner Demons (letter to the editor). *The National*, 5 September, p. 27.

Poiya, J. 2010. The Ugly Face of Sorcery. *Weekend Courier*, 6 February, p. 12.

Post-Courier 2007. Bribery, Corruption and Witchcraft Rampant: Dusava. *Post-Courier*, 4 June, p. 8.

Tiamu, E. 2011. Killing a Councillor. *The National*, 27 January, p. 6.

Walters, J. 2006. Legion Left Region — Mathew 8.28. *The National*, 9 November, p. 17.

Weekend Courier 2009. Sanguma — Myth, Belief or Reality. *Weekend Courier*, 12 December, p. 16.

6. Talking *Sanguma*: The Social Process of Discernment of Evil in Two Sepik Societies

Patrick F. Gesch

As with so many others, I was shocked to see the front page photo and read the newspaper article of the *Post-Courier*, 7 February 2013, captioned 'Burnt Alive'. We all read:

> A tragic and brutal sorcery-related murder took place in full view of hundreds of onlookers in a Mount Hagen City suburb in Western Highlands Province yesterday morning. The relatives of a six-year-old boy doused petrol on a woman whom they had suspected of killing the boy with sorcery and burnt her alive ... The victim, who was from Enga Province, was suspected of killing the six-year-old boy through sorcery after he died at the Mount Hagen general hospital on Tuesday. (Wama 2013)

We presume this is a case of highlands *sanguma*, and the story was followed up by many further reports of *sanguma* and calls from all over the world to stop this kind of action from occurring. This was murder; but it was promoted by the bystanders because they saw the burned woman as an evil *sanguma* killer. Does there need to be a special law for *sanguma*, or was parliament correct in repealing the *Sorcery Act 1971* about this time?

Sanguma is a term used widely in Papua New Guinea, and it appears that the term is called upon today more frequently than ever before. The word describes a practice of sorcery or witchcraft, as well as a person or group (college) who perform the practice. I wish to describe *sanguma* as it has been explained to me in East Sepik Province, which is contiguous with the highlands provinces, but a separate cultural zone ranging from the dominant Sepik River over the densely populated mountains to the coast. The Tok Pisin word *sanguma* is used in the Sepik and the highlands, and in other provinces of Papua New Guinea as well. There was an attempt to make the *Sorcery Act 1971* cover all of these things, but it is a matter of killing by religious instrumentation and I suspect there are as many religions as languages in Papua New Guinea, and the many languages and religions are very different from each other. The stories of how *sanguma* functions are very much differentiated from each other but share a hold on the religious *mysterium tremendum et fascinosum* ('might awesome mystery') of Rudolf Otto (1979). There seem to me some aspects of the Sepik accounts which clarify how *sanguma* functions in community reactions, and it is possible that some references to this term can be explained and even accepted by the outside world. An attempt to make a single sorcery law to cover all of Papua New Guinea would be presumptuous.

The term *sanguma* for East Sepik seems to me to be a statement of a religious nature. When it is invoked, it is a statement that says, 'There are issues of life-and-death seriousness behind this event. There are powers at work here which are not obvious, discontinuous from what can be observed and which need to be searched out for their meaning for villagers.' My impression is that '*Sanguma*!' as a call identifying an event means that a process of social discernment must follow, and in that discernment all the powers of society will be invoked, for the continuance of life for an individual as a social being is at stake.

Even though East Sepik does not rank as a highly reported area for *sanguma* stories in the national newspapers,[1] it is a matter of daily concern in most areas. The newspaper article quoted above includes the term 'murder' as a suitable description of the brutality that was witnessed. Although village people in East Sepik sometimes express themselves as sympathetic with highlands procedures, they can distinguish their own *sanguma* cases from murders. Without doubt, Sepik *sanguma* has a life-and-death seriousness about it and Sepik villagers think *sanguma* operators should be identified and killed as one way of eliminating them from the community. However, I believe that the seriousness of Sepik *sanguma* occurs as a discernment process — divination — without doubting the emphasis on the killing and the danger of *sanguma* from the village viewpoint (Gesch 1979). When the meaning of a person's sickness is given as that of a wholly useless and offending character, it sets in train a bad feeling that worries a villager to death.

The notion of discernment is that signs are posited or discovered and, from the social context, given a certain mindset; meaning is read from these signs in ways that can be full of bitter consequences. Without wanting to trivialise the matter, discernment can be compared to my mother's habit of reading teacup leaves. She would keep some leaves in the bottom of her cup and interpret pictures from the shapes visible. Then from her mindset and social context she would identify a course of action to follow. Continually, there is a call in the Sepik for identifying signs in cases of illness and death. Today it is possible to identify a murder as a clearly identified killing by another person,[2] or to identify a death by old age,

---

1   See Table 2, Gender and location of 156 accused and punished sorcerers reported by the media (2000–2006), in Zocca (2010:199). This information is drawn from Zocca and Urame (2008:74–91). East Sepik Province is not mentioned among the 156 reports, although two East Sepik Province victims appear in the original table.
2   It is still well remembered in Yamuk that around 1998 an ex-Defence man from the village took a gun and shot and killed a thief who stole money from a visiting carving buyer. No one called for *sanguma* talk in that case.

or an accidental killing, but someone might raise the *sanguma* possibility, even in such cases. This appears to be a lightening of the dictum that 'nobody dies a death from natural causes in Papua New Guinea'.[3]

In this chapter, I will discuss the *sanguma* discernment process from two localities in East Sepik Province that are familiar to me after many years in each place: East Yangoru (Negrie parish in particular) and Yamuk village in Pagwi District.[4] Each locality uses a discernment process to deal with *sanguma* and the ways of one village shed light on the ways of the other within the unified context of East Sepik. I will first illustrate what is meant by discernment in sorcery and witchcraft. From the discernment viewpoint, there is not a great difference to be observed between sorcery and witchcraft.

Sorcery is the main instrument of religious aggression in Yangoru. It consists of taking leavings of a person and sending them to a remotely located person with learned magical skills. The discernment process for this begins when a person gets sick in a troublesome way (the severity, suddenness, extended duration or features of the sickness) such that there seems to be a sign involved. *Sanguma* is specifically identified in Yangoru for certain kinds of victims, which I would render briefly as 'bush hysteria' for love-confounded young people. In the Yamuk area, *sanguma* is the ready recourse for identifying all kinds of troublesome sickness and deaths, and many such evils can become a subject of *sanguma*. I could not (these days) find much about how to learn to become a *sanguma* practitioner, but the myth of how it is done on someone is an essential part of village understanding.

It is not my wish to elide Yangoru with Yamuk. Both belong to the Ndu language family, which covers most of the 350,000[5] people of East Sepik Province. Speakers of both places recognise familiarities in the languages, but do not mutually comprehend each other. The East Yangoru village, Kiniambu, from which some of my experience is taken, is only 25 kilometres from Yamuk and there is some market exchange between the places. Yangoru shares the style of the mountain village culture made famous by Margaret Mead for the Arapesh language (Mead 1970). Although there are four electorates in Yangoru-Saussia, I will use Yangoru here as if it were a single entity, meaning East Yangoru (largely co-extensive with the Negrie parish area), where villages are closely contiguous.

---

3   Compare Mantovani (1998:104) further quoted in Zocca and Urame (2008:39).
4   I spent 10 years (1973–1983) in a parish and research appointment in Negrie parish, Yangoru, and since then have been continually in contact with Negrie neighbours in Madang and by return visits to Negrie. My association with Yamuk began in 1984, following contacts in Madang, and in returning for research periods and church building over the years. I confess that it took me 19 years to do something with the 54 sheets of corrugated iron that the parish priest had put in the village to get them turned into a church.
5   The population of East Sepik Province is 343,181, as reported on the National Research Institute website, www.nri.org.pg/research_divisions/cross_divisional_projects/11%20East%20Sepik%20Province.pdf, viewed 26/3/2014.

Yamuk is from the Sawos language area, the bush just off the Sepik River, and the villagers identify closely with the cultural world of Gaikorobi (Schindlbeck 1980). Since both places have recourse to a discernment process for *sanguma*, their practices shed much light on what is meant by *sanguma* as a word for religious aggression in East Sepik Province. I use two sets of examples from tolerably related areas to explain the discernment process.

The discernment process

How sorcery discernment works in Yangoru

I was beginning a Catholic mass in Kiniambu during one visit in 1977. A call came from the village nearby, and all the men immediately stood up, left the church and went down to the village, where they joined in discussions ranging over two full days. A senior member of the community had been taken with a sudden severe illness, in which it seemed he was about to die. There was a discussion during the two days of who might have sufficient hatred in his heart to be trying to kill the big man. Typically for Yangoru, the discussion would go by a procedure of identifying conflicts that the sick man was involved in, as identified by his supporters and family, and putting a coconut leaf rib (*nok*) into the stripped back of a sago palm leaf (*pangal*). A number of these sticks are put into a standing position, until those involved in the identified disputes come forward with counter arguments and remove a stick to indicate that the dispute was removed. The procedure continues until a consensus is formed about the sticks that remain standing as witness to lasting disputes with the sick man. In the Kiniambu case, a son-in-law was identified as having a dispute with the sick man, and admitted having taken leavings from a fish that the sick man had been eating, so that sorcery could be worked on this material. This is a way of doing sorcery identified as *tak* in Tok Ples (vernacular language), or *poison* in Tok Pisin (Melanesian pidgin). It takes place as a discernment process: who has enough hatred in his heart to want to make the sick man die? It is to be noted that an expert who can cause this magic is presumed in the action, but this expert is nowhere identified or sought out, because he is expected to be in some area remote from the discussion.

To make poison work, six agents are required and all of them taken together make for a juggling act in the discernment process. We take the sick person first, and second the person with hatred in his or her heart, who is the real killer in the process and who must find the cast-off materials to use in the magic. However, the community discussion is called when the sickness shows signs of being something beyond ordinary daily experience. Fourthly, a big man of the village has to weigh the consensus. Once a big man of the village said to me, 'Nobody dies in this village unless I say so. I am the only one who kills by poison in this village'. When I questioned him whether this might not be a dangerous acknowledgement, he said that of course he means he passes on a person's leavings together with 100 kina or shell money to the pertinent messenger to get the magic done in some other, remote village. It is the big man's job to form the consensus on the need for the killing. The messenger has a traditional name — *mowintuo*. He delivers the message, the materials and the valuables to a real magic-working person called a *yehwontuo*. Finally, this man sits in his house with a fire and a bowl of lime and brings religious knowledge to bear on the parcel of leavings, which is exposed to the magic. The victim gets sick and can be relieved or finally disposed of depending on the action of the *yehwontuo*. The magic man is moved by payments that come from the original community. This social discernment would not differ greatly for sorcery or for witchcraft.

Is *sanguma* real?

The above description emphasises the discernment aspect of the sorcery or *sanguma* process. Advantages in doing this are that it provides an alternative answer to the question, 'Is *sanguma* real?' It is real inasmuch as the sick person is struggling to clear his name in the village and to say that he should not be cast off to die at the wish of the people. It does not need to be real in the sense of using objects of aggression such as long sharp needles, torture or chemical poisons. Also, it is part of the argument: Will the death penalty solve *sanguma*? Whom could you convict in such a scenario since the actual practitioner of religious powers is remote and unidentified? The real killers are the ones with hatred or condemnation in their hearts, the purveyors of personal materials and the community sitting in judgement. Perhaps any death penalty should apply to the purveyors and the community, but we are dealing with a traditional justice system, and the sick person or the dead person or the ones whose houses have burned down are the offending people in the view of the *sanguma* discernment and discussion.[6]

Is *sanguma* a nonsense, non-scientific belief that might work just because people believe in it? Clearly a belief in the *sanguma* discussion process is something that is hard to shake loose when the whole community is forming a consensus about a person's value as a community member. To say that something is 'merely belief' seems miserably short as self-reflective knowledge. Belief can build a

---

6   It is not easy to be sympathetic with this viewpoint from a European perspective. For example, at the seashore I was reassured that I would not be taken by a shark (or crocodile): '*sapos i no gat rong long skin bilong yu*'. This means that if I do get taken, it is an indication that I am guilty of some village wrong. This is adding insult to injury with a vengeance.

tall building in a way that a hammer cannot. At the same time, this description supports the view that the older members of the community pass judgements on *sanguma*, but the young men take it into their own hands to work violence on suspects. This is just murder on the part of the vicious young men, something extra to the discernment work, and not part of the question: What is *sanguma*? It must be observed again, that in East Sepik the sorcerer or the *sanguma* person is not deeply involved in the discernment process, although he is completely necessary to the ideology that guides the discussion. *Sanguma* people and sorcerers are killed if villagers get the chance, and the killings are applauded, but the real focus is on the person with hatred or condemnation in his heart sufficient to want someone dead by direct religious means. The person who initiates any particular *sanguma* magic will suffer retaliation only when the family initiates revenge magic.

There are two bridging questions to get from discernment to highlands *sanguma* cases. One, does the *sanguma* in East Sepik ever make his own decision about killing or letting live? Two, does it help to kill someone identified as *sanguma*? Brief answers are: Yes, informants tell me the *sanguma* can take it on himself to presume the consensus of the community and do his work directly. Second, the college of *sanguma* is very important, and it would be a great risk to kill a *sanguma* because the group could retaliate on either yourself or any family member.

Before enlarging on these answers, I will describe Yamuk *sanguma* and Yangoru *sanguma* in more detail.

Yamuk *sanguma*

How the *sanguma* work in Yamuk

The power of *sanguma* in Yamuk belongs to the community. The *sanguma* person can secretly go to the *haus tambaran* (spirit house, a large and elegant construction dominating a village of the East Sepik) and address the *garamut* slit drum. This *garamut* is a large, wooden log carved with a trough down the middle. When struck with a solid stick it is used for solemn announcements throughout the village and for kilometres beyond. This drum has an ongoing intergenerational spirit name and many spears used to go into the middle trough at the time of war with an enemy or when men are trying to shoot and kill bush pigs. When a pig is killed, the men bring the blood back to the *haus tambaran* and sprinkle it in the house, over the *garamuts* and the beds where men sit to talk. The *garamut* thus gathers a historical memory of power and the living tradition of the village. This general collection of memory and things is called *kipnda*, the strategic memory of the village. The *sanguma* can draw on this history of spells, prayers and pig offerings to gain power for his own purposes. He does so by using words at this locality. This is the *sifuo kundi*, the powerful magical spell. In this sense some men say that everything in the *haus tambaran* is *sanguma* — the house posts, the ground, the drums, beds, stools and whatever is hanging from the roof. These things are witnesses to the power of historical activities and indicate the presence of spirits that may go around the village fires at night and gather the opinions and judgements of those with criticisms to make. ('*Samting bilong graun i save kirap na raun long paia bilong ol man long nait.*')

When someone is to die by the hand of *sanguma*, there will be signs at night: you might think you see some men in the shadows of the night; flying foxes might surprise you by forming a chain; or a certain frog or bird will call out as the mark of the *sanguma*. These shadows or signs might surround the house where a sick man lies. In the recent case of John Kangra,[7] he had a fever on and off for a whole week, and it seemed there were shadowy figures of men around the house and even inside the house watching the sick man on his bed in the presence of his family.

After John died, there was a quick examination in the nearby *haus tambaran*. Did anyone have disputes with him about the bush or ownership of land, the use of sago trees or in relationships with women? Some signs of this would be expected to appear. In this case a woven coconut leaf was thrown into the family house, and a coconut shell full of *Bougainvillea* flowers was found outside the house. This indicated to the family that a longstanding land dispute was at issue and this dispute was connected to a fellow villager. They could not say that the man with the dispute was a *sanguma*, but he could have hired a *sanguma* to kill John. Alternatively, it was admitted that the *sanguma* himself could have simply made the judgement that John should be killed for this long-running dispute. When it came time to discuss the issue in the *haus tambaran* after John's death, there was no calling of names. It was not necessary, because the land dispute existed from a long time ago, from the grandfather's time. This death was something the family would have to live with or they would have to retaliate with *sanguma*.

The explanation given by members of the community was that someone went to a *sanguma* with some money or a present and said it was about time John suffered or died. After the death the complainant would have had to visit the *sanguma* again to get his money back as a way of telling the *sanguma* that he had not really wished the death to take place. If the *sanguma* himself had not wanted to kill John, he would have tested John's goodwill by asking for a favour

---

7   I am not using real names of persons but pseudonyms throughout.

and then advising John to have an urgent discussion with the complainant. A *sanguma* gains a reputation by people going to him to ask him to make a sick person well, and by accepting money to inflict illness or to remove it. This is the politics of the *sanguma* discernment process.

The ideology known to everyone in the village is that a Yamuk *sanguma* works by going with his group to the offending party, such as John. The *sanguma* are senior men in Yamuk village or men or women from nearby villages. It is possible that they could be identified, and many times people tell me, 'That fellow is definitely a *sanguma*'. This accusation is of course dismissed by the fellow himself. The *sanguma* knock the victim out, generally expressed as 'killing' him, and then operate on him by removing some of his internal organs, parts of his major muscles, his penis or other meat. This meat will be kept and dried as a powerful agent of *sanguma* work. When the *sanguma* next wants to work, he will scrape this piece of meat with his teeth or breathe his spells over it. The *sanguma* will revive the man they have 'killed', and ask him if he recognises them. If he does recognise them and what they did, he will be knocked out again and revived until finally he does not know the *sanguma* who have terminated his life. The victim is then sent away with knowledge of the day and the circumstances under which he will finally die, but with no recognition of the *sanguma* men who have killed him. In the case of two brothers who had a longstanding dispute about some money, it was reported to me that the victim announced what was going to happen saying, 'I am going now. I will fight with my brother and I will die.'

Cases of *sanguma* from Yamuk

The name *sanguma* is connected with surprising and disturbing evil in the form of sickness or death, or misfortune such as house fires. But it is a word that can be further used for a range of worrisome matters.

At our tertiary institution, we had the sad experience of an apparently healthy village Torembi[8] student suddenly collapsing and dying on the sports field. After playing 15 minutes of a friendly soccer fixture, he took a five-minute break, and then ran back on to the field. There he collapsed and was pronounced dead at the hospital within an hour.[9] While the death of the young man is hard to come to terms with, the ready explanation or comment for his death is just as hard to come to terms with. Staff of our tertiary institution remarked, 'Clearly this was a case of *sanguma*'. If we take a loose idea of a *sanguma* to be a person with exceptional powers causing death or injury to another person in the context of social dispute, it is hard to see where the evidence of this appears

---

8   Torembi is a village near Yamuk, three-and-a-half hours walk away, largely sharing the same culture.
9   An Australian medical doctor told me that such sudden deaths of sports players are known in Australia also.

so obvious to some. Yet most times at morning tea our college staff discuss the well-being of people around us, and lecturers comment that some cases are 'clearly a case of *sanguma*'.

The word for *sanguma* in Torembi is *kuragua*. I once drove a young friend from Torembi downtown in Wewak. He left the car to go about his business, but jumped back in the car within a minute. In front of us was someone I considered to be a gentle old man of Torembi village, occasionally involved in church affairs. The young friend said that he was a well-known *sanguma* man and he was scared at seeing him.[10] On another occasion, an old catechist of the church from former times had gained a reputation as a carver of Christian images. He was accused of being a *sanguma*. At the end of an enclosure for an initiation ceremony, the old man had his wife follow him, and together they limped around the enclosure before the eyes of everyone, as if they were following a trail on the ground, the wife emitting the call of a '*sanguma* bird'. The old catechist explained to me that everyone, including his son, was pointing to him as a *sanguma* but that was obvious nonsense, so he was acting out his supposed evil ways of pursuing victims. Those around me were not convinced; they claimed they had evidence that he had taken money to do his nefarious deeds.

One summer I went to Yamuk village on the hunt for evidence of *sanguma* in its social context. I kept asking men in the men's house for evidence. The evidence was always fresh and current. For example: 'Last night we were late coming back to the village when we heard someone running through the dense bush. It was not a pig. Don't you think we know the difference between a person running through the bush and a pig running through the bush? This was the sound of some *sanguma* people.' As we were sitting in the men's house at 11 am that day, a loud cry went up from nearby, 'Willie has collapsed. He is throwing up and they are carrying him to his house.' Men turned to me and said, 'You wanted evidence. There, you have it now.' For the next few hours healing men performed various rituals for Willie, a strong and otherwise healthy adult, married with a family, as we sat in his house. Finally, a one-centimetre-long spear was taken out of what Willie had ejected into a coconut shell, and buried in the bush near the toilet. Willie started to improve in health after that. I was told that I now had all the evidence I could possibly ask for.

At one time I entered a *hausman* (small open house for men's gatherings) in the village of Yamuk and was surprised to hear two adult men shouting at their father that he was a *sanguma* and that he had better stop his evil deeds.

---

10   To have a reputation as a *sanguma* in Yamuk does not mean that the person is likely to be a social outcast. Of the men in Yamuk who have been identified to me as 'leading *sanguma*', some were truly strong and effective church leaders in my estimation; others were village councillors. Such people do put in a word of defence for the *sanguma* process, saying 'Beware of getting rid of *sanguma* altogether. How do we deal with really bad troublemakers living among us otherwise?'

The father appeared unmoved by these hostile public recriminations from his family. I was told that the meaning of this was that a *sanguma* does his work of killing people with the help of fellow *sanguma*. One gets his colleague to kill the undesirable person, but in retaliation and payment, one of the junior members of the first group will have to die also. So, to be part of a group sheltering a *sanguma* was to be in a dangerous position — you kill this offending person for me, and then I will have to kill someone from your place or family to repay this.

Below is a collection of examples of the use of *sanguma* in Yamuk in other contexts.

- A young man of Yamuk was drinking beer with his friends in a Wewak settlement. Three shadowy persons called him below the house and told him to go with them. They appeared hazy but he kept talking with them and later when he asked others about what he had done, they said they had not seen anyone with him. Clearly these had been *sanguma* men and he was frightened because they were jealous of his success.
- Another young man had great pain in his groin. He was cured by magical spells, according to his friends, but somebody discerned the meaning of this to be that he was initiating a train of *sanguma* action for his family, and he was in fact the son of John Kangra, mentioned above, who died soon afterwards.
- After drinking alcohol continuously for days, a young villager went into his house and started cutting his own clothing and throwing it outside the house, a sign of going away for a long time. A few hours later he died in a fight after suffering a blow that did not seem lethal proportionate to the force used. These matters were taken as signs of *sanguma*. Whether the youth had a sufficiently bad reputation to deserve elimination was left to individual judgements.
- An older man was found to have a broken shoulder and neck bones after he died. This was an indication that he had been taken by *sanguma*, operated on, and then revived to wait his inevitable death.
- There is a set of stories about the playfulness of *sanguma*, which is one way of insisting that *sanguma* are powerful people with special spiritual powers. My judgement is that the stories are fables to entertain, but they are told as true accounts. A young man walking with his father was carrying a bundle of firewood. It became too heavy to carry and he had to put it down. Then he realised his father was no longer with him, but appeared to him as a little man coming out of the firewood bundle. Using a special kind of lime powder, *sanguma* can disappear or reappear in the form of another person. They can make themselves into small creatures, in the manner of one person outdoing another person, or just for a joke. The playfulness in these stories seems

at odds with the killing or injuring intent of *sanguma*, but nevertheless demonstrates powers beyond normal human powers.

In all these cases villagers follow an ideology of looking for signs in evil things that they are experiencing and identifying their causes in the religious powers of specially trained, skilled persons. When these powerful people cause harm, this meaning can be uncovered by community discussion looking for a history of past social offences. These *sanguma* might have objects inside their bodies to assist them in their powers and communication. They do not inherit these things in a biological sense but pick them up during training. Their decisions to act are informed by community discussions among men and women that might go on at firesides anywhere, and then in consultation with their colleagues they take the action of inflicting pain and trouble.

The social discernment of evil in Yamuk

The process of discernment in Yamuk is a public one, as for the Yangoru procedure. Men are summoned by the *garamut* drum to gather in the *haus tambaran*. Speeches are made with the help of three bundles of long *tanget* leaves. The speaker beats the mouth of the *garamut* (in other Sepik communities a speaker's chair is used as a table for beating) and sets the scene for the discussion. Anyone can speak in reply, beating the *garamut* and then laying down the three bundles of *tanget* leaves one by one as he talks, before gathering them up again to repeat the action.[11] There is an effort to gather evidence, the history of arguments, points of view and reasons for actions. Sometimes the speeches can become very angry displays of opposition. Comments made about the proceedings show that the men believe that *sanguma* persons are actually sitting with the other villagers in the *haus tambaran*, watching the formation of opinion about what has been done, or about the personality of the one who is sick or has already died. The *sanguma* are also watching for evidence or reports of payments that have gone in any direction.

As was said earlier, it is fairly common for villagers to make a statement like, 'Sengi is a *sanguma*. He is one of the strongest *sanguma* in the village.' If you ask such a man, he will say, 'Nonsense. We have no *sanguma* in our village. If you go to Slai village, yes, there are *sanguma* there, and many of them are women.' Such charges are common. It is apparently hard to gather a body of feeling in the village that Sengi must surely be a *sanguma*. People in town settlements say they do not like village life because *sanguma* are a threat to good living; they would like to see them all removed. Then they will say, 'After you live in the village for some months and you don't do anything wrong, then you will find you

---

11 My observation is that the beating with the leaves is not very rhythmical, and not used to highlight points so much as a nervous thing to do with the hands.

can continue to live peacefully at home'. To turn to someone and identify that person as a *sanguma* has the difficulty already mentioned, of rousing the wrath of the college of *sanguma*. They work together, coming from nearby villages to form their decisions and do their work at any place, employing mysterious powers of invisibility or of seeing all things. This is the myth of how *sanguma* persons work in Yamuk and this is the basis of intense feelings of fear, revenge and uncertainty.

When I am pursuing the topic of *sanguma*, I ask: What is a *sanguma*? How do they function? What do they want? How do you deal with them? After I have collected a set of narratives like those given above, my research assistant repeatedly comments, 'They are hiding it from you'. While I believe my assistant wants to hear names, dates and cases from village life in order to pursue local politics with other villagers, I think that I am trying to gain clarity on the general nature and structure of *sanguma* action. What is an answer that would satisfy me?

Before I turn to that discussion let me add the case of Yangoru *sanguma* as a way of discernment that sheds light on the *sanguma* concept.

Yangoru *sanguma*

Sanguma in Yangoru is termed *maientuo* (a witch man). The action is related in its function to sorcery, called *tak* in vernacular and *poison* in Tok Pisin.[12] Both these operations are a part of the sickness of any person seriously ill in the village. It was often something of a puzzle to me that I would sit in a church council meeting of a Sunday and hear people say that Christians should denounce the bad old ways and affirm the good traditions of the ancestors. Definitely *sanguma* and sorcery were part of the bad old ways. Then everyone would rise from the meeting to go home because back in the village there was talk of *tok poison* going on. The leaders had to be present, and there was no way they could refrain from talking. In village meetings the church leaders would talk about disputes in the village involving a sick person in some way. I understand that there are bad ways of talking about people involved in disputes and better ways. So the Christian leaders' duty was to keep the village discussion running in a good way. But from a certain viewpoint it can be said that talking *tok poison* is the essence of what sorcery is all about. This is because it is the discernment process where the villagers talk about the offences of an individual, guess at his motives

---

12   I give the two words from the Yangoru vernacular, *maientuo* and *tak*, but they are not shared in the Yamuk vernacular or in other East Sepik language groups. Therefore I have chosen to remain with the Tok Pisin word *sanguma*, which is somehow understood all over Papua New Guinea. The reason I give the Yangoru vernacular at all is to emphasise that these are separate traditional concepts.

and his future trajectory and what would be appropriate to chasten such a person. Whoever has indulged in gossip will know the sweetness of character assassination that gets community backup.

It seems there was little attention paid to the witch or *sanguma* person in Yangoru. Philip Gibbs has given a recent account of witchcraft magic from the nearby and similar Arapesh language group, detailing materials to be used and the people who use them (Gibbs and Wailoni 2009), but this topic rarely surfaced for me when I was asking about *sanguma* matters in Yangoru. Who commits witchcraft and how? In my first 10 years of exposure to Yangoru, there were few incidents referring to actual known people with special powers of sorcery and none involving those doing witchcraft. One day high school boys came back from Yangoru to Negrie nearby to report that a 200-litre drum was set in the middle of Yangoru, filled with small packages of palm leaves representing sorcery materials wrapped up. The boys found it horrifying. Another time I was in the village shortly after a man had had his house inspected by self-appointed sorcery police, and they had found a small package of waste materials that could be used in sorcery. This man admitted that he had been uncovered and was penitent, but said that he had been keeping this thing just in case it was needed against the person being stalked. On another occasion I was introduced to a 45-year-old, cleanly shaven man sitting with the men at a hamlet in the village. This was John M and he had been a sorcerer living alone on a remote mountain ridge, making money from those who wanted him to perform magic to harm people. He also received money for removing the spells. John said he did not want to be a sorcerer anymore and had turned to the church. The community had accepted him back.[13] Apart from these three incidents demonstrating real sorcery, it was said that the sorcerers were always men from distant communities, faceless and remote, not liable to be tortured, interrogated or murdered as *sanguma*.

The appearance of sorcery symptoms in Yangoru seems to me a form of hysteria or catatonia, as Sigmund Freud used the expression.[14] One afternoon a schoolboy about 15 years old was brought to me. He was helplessly, unceasingly crying. He had previously been identified as having had sexual relations with a young girl in our dormitory area at the school. My guess is that that afternoon, while collecting firewood, he had had a terrifying encounter with a small group of men in the bush to remind him of this, and was reduced to hysteria. He was helped by an old man in a nearby community who had skills in this area. On another occasion, a 25-year-old school teacher with a public, troubled relationship with

---

13   Recent news is that John has returned to his old way of life. The performance of magic was too much a part of his personality to give up, and he needed the money.
14   This is not to be taken as a psychiatric diagnosis, but as a literary reference. The articles of Micale (1993), and Owens and Dein (2006) warn us of historical difficulties with these terms, which are not to be interpreted here in a clinical way.

her presumed partner, walked back to our school and sat in her house. She was motionless, and I personally witnessed a sewing needle stabbed into her arm without her flinching. On a further occasion, a strong young man described how he had met men in the bush who had apparently worked some spell on him. After that he wanted to return every day to see them, even though he made signs to indicate that in five days he must die. The elements of these stories are repeated in further cases. It seems to me that they refer to young people who are in a confused state with regard to sexual relationships, and *sanguma* becomes a form of planned social terror to give them a severe warning.

There remains to be uncovered or guessed at the story of who the *sanguma* person is in relation to the village or the afflicted person: how did this person get his or her powers, how did the act of *sanguma* or sorcery take place, and how can the victim be helped to shake off the effects of *sanguma*? I doubt that this aetiological explanation is necessary for my understanding of what is going on.

What is 'understanding *sanguma*' in this situation? What mindset can I employ to be able to follow the conversation and anticipate the turns that the story takes? Even if the story is wickedly evil or nonsense for the lack of verifiable evidence from some viewpoint, the story continues, and whole communities continue to use this idiom for sickness and social disruption. What comes closest to an understanding for me?

The problem of explanation of *sanguma* for two mindsets

At the death of our university student, I was interested in a set of biological connections that could be seen as causative on a level leading to death of the bodily system. Some community and family members related the death to a presumed social dispute, and proceeded to uncover who had a sufficient dispute with the student's family as to set in motion special powers that would cause his death. A pathologist was hired from Lae and a post-mortem conducted. The pathologist found 80 per cent occlusion of the arteries. The student was known to have been drinking distilled alcohol continuously for three days before the game. But this was not enough and some statements I heard clearly identified the person likely to have employed *sanguma* in this case. Was there evidence to satisfy me about this extra step? Yes, there was circumstantial evidence to look for — a person employing *sanguma* has to give a payment to make the bodily affliction take place by religious powers. Further payments might be made to make the sickness worse, or to provoke a response from the sick person and his family, or to end the life of the person. The *sanguma* associate with other *sanguma* people in a group. The members of this group accept money to do their magic. When word of their accepting money gets out to the public, people can begin to identify *sanguma* with hard evidence.

Talking about *sanguma*

The problem is: how do we talk about *sanguma* usefully in Papua New Guinea? *Sanguma* is one of many Tok Pisin words that are polyvalent, meaning something different in the different cultures of the country; other examples being *kandere* and other family connections like *brata, papa, mama, bikpela*. These words need to be defined on the basis of cultural expectations and performance, not just as static relationships. Not only do we know from recent Melanesian Institute publications that *sanguma* means something different in the highlands and on the coast (see, for example, Bartle 2005; Gabutu 2012; Kuman 2011; Schwarz 2011; Zocca 2009; Zocca and Urame 2008), but there is an obvious cultural divide between Papua New Guinean villagers and overseas missionaries or educators about what the word means. The simple answer is to say that *sanguma* is an application of remotely working mechanics; or nonsense belief; or worse, that it is sin or causes sin and not a fit topic of conversation for reasonable people. But if we presume all the people who take part in the *sanguma* conversation are reasonable people, then what kind of explanation is fitting and reliable for this topic? At first my answer to this might seem to reveal my original, Australian-type prejudices. An answer for me needs to cover all the evidence and be attuned to what the evidence is; it needs to predict the behaviour of participants; it needs to be repeatable in different places and times and with different people; and it needs to be a heuristic model able to accommodate future evidence. In other words, it needs to be scientific. Social science depends on social evidence and it is admitted on all sides that evidence has to be found which is convincing to the cultural group and their interlocutors. Let me now flesh out a mindset that is useful in discussing *sanguma* from two different viewpoints — an Australian-type mentality and a village one — where a mindset refers to an enquiring attitude looking for specific types of evidence and being satisfied with certain types of explanation.

What is *sanguma* in Yangoru? What is *sanguma* in Yamuk? They are both signs of social disruption, disputes and even mortal hatred between community members. My earlier question, can a *sanguma* initiate a killing by himself, does not make much sense in Yangoru, where the *sanguma* is not present to deal with on this matter, or to receive instructions from community discussion. But the question is more pertinent in Yamuk, where *sanguma* actions are initiated by a person with a serious concern going to a 'known' *sanguma* person and talking about what upsets him, doing so with the giving of a gift. One then leaves the matter for the *sanguma* person to discuss with his fellow *sanguma*. They might decide to afflict the person who gives the offence. As noted earlier, if the person with the complaint sees that the offender gets sick, or even dies, then he acts to hide the trail of evidence leading to himself. If his money has caused the death of someone, then he should go back to the *sanguma* and get his money back so that the evidence is removed. After that he can give the *sanguma* twice the amount to express his happiness at the death that has taken place. Not to remove his complaint money would invite retaliation from the *sanguma* college, who would want to exact a balancing death for the one that took place. In this case, a member of the community is initiating the work of the *sanguma*, but it is left to the *sanguma* college to make a judgement and to take action.

To use the term *sanguma* is thus to summon the community to investigate and reveal what is going wrong in social relationships, or to find out whether a person can be healed, why another person has died, why these 10 houses have burned to the ground or why the crocodiles have led to the disappearance of community members. People are looking for signs, they want to know what the signs mean, and there is a considerable level of fear about being killed by mysterious religious powers in the hands of some men or women. In Yamuk, even the *sanguma* are involved in the process of social discernment in the community.

The way forward

In the course of writing this chapter, examples of *sanguma* have come to light in the national newspapers from the broader Momase area, the north coast of Papua New Guinea. Madang, long known as the beautiful province, the peaceful province, has now produced a series of anti-*sanguma* movements, which entail mass murders (Mark 2014a). The Black Jesus movement of Steven Tari involved sexual rituals and cannibalism, leading to the brutal killing of Tari by his own villagers (Marks 2013; Matbob 2010).[15] In the western end of the province at Tangu, an anti-*sanguma* movement led to many killings (Gumar 2012). More recently, the people in the mountains above Gusap, in the Nahu Rawa local level government area, have concluded an initiation *hausman* with the pursuit and killing of *sanguma* (Mark 2014b). There are said to be about 300 *sanguma* waiting for identification. An eyewitness says that, at the time of writing, the killing of *sanguma* or *hausman* persons has become vicious and brutal with many being slaughtered on both sides, and dead bodies have become unremarkable, as decapitated people die like animals in the bush.

---

15   The term *sanguma* is not used of this movement. The Black Jesus movement has some derivations from the earlier cargo cult movement of Yali that Peter Lawrence (1964) wrote about. But these days Black Jesus belongs to the context of sinister village movements and monstrous killing.

Considering situations like this — socially complex movements of murderous and monstrous seriousness, akin to tribal fighting — the idea of *sanguma* and how to tackle the question on a national, legal level becomes very much moot. Is there anything at all in common between Madang *sanguma*, and that of East Sepik or of Simbu and Southern Highlands provinces?

In Madang, the community longs for the government to take the situation seriously. A mediation team came and went with no follow-up. Everyone wants identified *sanguma* people to be eliminated from the communities. Can this be done with a discernment process, or by a trial by torture seeking confessions, or by simple 'surrender'[16] ceremonies? The polymorphism of *sanguma* advises against any uniform national policy for the problem. Local communities require follow-up from the government and police when things start getting out of hand. Given the right understanding of the various *sanguma* processes, I would have to come down on the side of education and progressive experience to work against the *sanguma* religious reaction. If you cannot tolerate the religious dimension in life, then it will be difficult to allow any traditional interpretation to hold sway. But villagers recognise grudgingly that penicillin, as well as magical spells, is very good for horrible sores. Education does get things done in the long term even though it is as irrelevant as government in the short-term. The short-term answer is reconciliation and retributive justice, as in Bougainville. The long-term answer to *sanguma* is better health services, better education and effective government.

References

Bartle, N. 2005. Death, Witchcraft and the Spirit World in the Highlands of Papua New Guinea: Developing a Contextual Theology in Melanesia. *Point* No. 29. Goroka: Melanesian Institute.

Gabutu, G. 2012. Sorcery and Magic according to the Motu, Koita and Koiari Peoples of Port Moresby. *Catalyst* 42(2):146–59.

Gesch, P. 1979. Magic as a Process of Social Discernment. In N. Habel (ed.) *Powers, Plumes and Piglets*. Adelaide: AASR, 137–48.

---

16 Surrender, given sometimes in Tok Pisin as *salenda*, appears frequently in the newspapers when youths are pictured before homemade guns lying on the ground and implements for distilling alcohol. Communities clean themselves up regularly. Some of these troublesome implements are removed, replacements are found, but in some sections of the community progress is made, while in others a surrender is just part of the tension of modern life. A Gusap *sanguma* who hands over his implements of herbs and tree barks with a confession will be allowed to go free. Whoever runs away will be pursued and killed.

Gibbs, P. and J.J. Wailoni 2009. Sorcery and a Christian Response in the East Sepik. In F. Zocca (ed.) *Sanguma* in Paradise: Sorcery, Witchcraft and Christianity in Papua New Guinea. *Point* No. 33. Goroka: Melanesian Institute, 55–96.

Gumar, P. 2012. Eradicating Sorcery Backfires on Villagers. *The National*, 13 July, p. 65.

Kuman, G. 2011. Sorcery, Witchcraft and Development in Papua New Guinea. *Catalyst* 41(1):19–37.

Lawrence, P. 1964. *Road Belong Cargo*. Melbourne: Melbourne University Press.

Mantovani 1998. Challenges of the Bible to Christian Life in PNG Today. *Catalyst* 28(2):102–16.

Mark, D. 2014a. Community Living in Fear. *The National*, 27 March.

Mark, D. 2014b. Mass Arrests. *The National*, 22 April, p. 1.

Marks, K. 2013. Hacked, Slashed and Castrated: How 'Cannibal' Cult Leader 'Black Jesus' Steven Tari Met His Death. *The Independent*, 2 September. www.independent.co.uk/news/world/australasia/hacked-slashed-and-castrated-how-cannibal-cult-leader-black-jesus-steven-tari-met-his-death-8795240.html, viewed 13/5/2014.

Matbob, P. 2010. Black Jesus Behind Bars; but Says He Did Nothing Wrong. *Islands Business* December 2010, p. 29.

Mead, M. 1970 [1938]. *The Mountain Arapesh*. 5 volumes. Garden City, New York: Natural History Press.

Micale, M.S. 1993. On the 'Disappearance' of Hysteria: A Study in the Clinical Deconstruction of a Diagnosis. *Isis* 84(3):496–526. http://www.jstor.org/stable/235644, viewed 24/5/2013.

Otto, R. 1979 [1917]. *The Idea of the Holy*. London: Oxford University Press.

Owens, C. and S. Dein 2006. Conversion Disorder: The Modern Hysteria. *Advances in Psychiatric Treatment* 12:152–57. http://apt.rcpsych.org/content/12/2/152.full, viewed 24/4/2013.

Schindlbeck, M. 1980. *Sago bei den Sawos (Mittelsepik, Papua New Guinea). Untersuchungen über die Bedeutung von Sago in Wirtschaft, Sozialordnung und Religion*. Basel: Ethnologisches Seminar der Universität und Museum für Völkerkunde.

Schwarz, N. 2011. Thinking Critically about Sorcery and Witchcraft: A Handbook for Christians in Papua New Guinea. *Occasional Paper* No. 14. Goroka: Melanesian Institute.

Wama, R. 2013. Burnt Alive! *Post-Courier,* 7 February, p. 1.

Zocca, F. (ed.) 2009. *Sanguma* in Paradise: Sorcery, Witchcraft and Christianity in Papua New Guinea. *Point* No. 33. Goroka: Melanesian Institute.

Zocca, F. 2010. Gender and Accusations of Malevolent Sorcery and Witchcraft in Papua New Guinea. *Catalyst* 40(2):192–206.

Zocca, F. and J. Urame (eds.) 2008. Sorcery, Witchcraft and Christianity in Melanesia. *Melanesian Mission Studies* No. 5. Goroka: Melanesian Institute.

7. The *Haus Man* Cleansing at Nahu Rawa

Patrick F. Gesch and Jonathan Julius

On 22 April 2014 the front page headlines of *The National* read, 'Mass arrests — A group of 120 men and 69 juveniles have appeared in court over the alleged killings of eight people at a village in Madang last Monday' (Mark 2014b). One of the juveniles was 10 years old. The story went on to say that the provincial police commander, Sylvester Kalaut, had gone with a team of police officers to Sakiko settlement in the Ramu River valley, and from there, after a marathon court hearing by a Madang magistrate, had taken those arraigned to Madang's prison. The magistrate reported that the group had voluntarily surrendered after a raid on Sakiko settlement, for which they had prepared themselves by rubbing the brains and heart meat of previous victims over their own bodies.

Police commander Kalaut said that seven men had been killed and then a three-year-old boy had been snatched from his mother's arms and also killed. One of the victims was from Jiwaka in the highlands and a strong retaliation for him was expected. One fear was said to be that these killings were related to cult practices, such as those that occurred with the Black Jesus of Amele up to 2013 (Matbob 2010; see also Marks 2013), or with the *sanguma*-finding cult of Tangu in western Madang (Gumar 2012). The evidence of this ritual, given in the newspaper report was that, 'People were slashed from the legs up and had their heads cut off'. The group doing the killings was identifying itself as *haus man* (the men's house as an initiation enclosure). They had killed these eight victims because they labelled them sorcerers for the newspaper, but in the local area the victims were termed by the Tok Pisin name, *sanguma*. The villages from which these men and youths came were given as Niniko, Gomumu and Ranara.

The beginnings of *haus man*

Gesch interviewed a local resident about these events. He is a teacher from Sepik,[1] not long graduated but about 30 years of age, a fellow with an impressive physical appearance that helps to give him status in the community. He came to Niniko Primary School at the beginning of 2011 and won the confidence of the

---

[1] The Sepik teacher referred to in the text is Jonathan Julius, who initiated the report on the Nahu Rawa killings after personally witnessing many things. Gesch has since then worked with Julius to draw up this report and to incorporate the developments as Julius is made aware of them. The writing was a collaborative work.

local people. In August 2012 some men from the local villages came to him and asked him to write formal complaints about members of their families having been killed by *sanguma* from 1990 to 2010. They said they would use these reports as their complaints to the police. Following their instructions he also listed the names of the dead, numbering up to 100. The teacher was sufficiently sympathetic with the evils of *sanguma* to want to help this group, who were the beginnings of the *haus man* faction in the troubles that followed.

One weekday in 2013, the teacher took a run down to Gusap township, which is about 15 kilometres distant in the Ramu River valley, and then returned slowly to the mountain school. As he arrived at Tapimi village, he had the strange experience of hearing a pig cry out in the valley basin below, as if it was being killed, but crying in such a way that the cry came from every side. Passing through Tapimi hamlet he saw men and women were already running about bringing their belongings to the bush and garden houses. On arriving at Gomumu village he was told some men had fought each other and those from Tapimi had fled to Gomumu. In the daytime, Asumu Gausa, a woman of Gomumu, had been killed by *sanguma*. It was suspected that her spirit was put inside a pig and killed, which was the cause of the strange pig cry. On the weekend the situation had deteriorated and 17 houses had been burned and domestic animals killed at Tapimi, the place of Ronuwe, who was the chief suspect for the killing of Asumu. Duma Gausa, her younger brother, led the raid on the suspects' houses.

The following Sunday morning, in front of the Lutheran church, an assault was made on Ronuwe, as a group of men tried to kill him. Witnesses said that bush knives and tomahawks were swung directly and forcefully at his skull, but he was able to smile and remain standing. One report says they even tried to shoot him with cartridges, but the plastic cartridges bubbled up before they could be used. Nevertheless, Ronuwe was badly injured and they threw him back into his own village. The Gomumu village councillor, Dowena Gausa, older brother of Asumu, took him to a house and cared for him. The informant states that he inspected the body and could see no wounds remaining from the attack except under the soles of his feet. They took him down to Gusap health centre, and *haus man* members followed him with the intent of killing him. He was transferred to Lae but another attempt on his life was made so he was transferred to Goroka, where he recovered.

Haus man deals out justice to the *sanguma*

In October 2012 , a well-known *sanguma* man from Numbaia village, Peter Binaru, came to the village Gomumu, in a manner which local people took to be ominous. It was he who had sat with Asumu when she was sick, and in a casual manner had touched her, by which it was said that he had taken her spirit, so that she could be killed elsewhere by *sanguma*.

Peter Binaru came to pursue the dispute started in Gomumu. He went under a high post house with his group of supporters, and waited for the *haus man* people to gather so they could resolve the matter. As the *haus man* men approached the house, one of Binaru's men shot an arrow into the *haus man* group wounding a man, Tau, on his shoulder. Enraged, the *haus man* group set the house on fire. Binaru and his supporters went upstairs, waiting desperately for a chance to escape the fire and the *haus man* attackers. In the heat of the battle, Binaru was killed, sliced up and dumped before a toilet. Binaru's grade 6 son, Sauke, was also killed and cast out into a field. Everyone was forbidden to cry for Binaru and his son. That evening a very dark cloud came into the valley and lightning lit up the whole darkened area as a threatening sign.

After this, killing continued on both sides and the teachers from elsewhere were sent to Madang for their own safety. Bodies were lying unburied in the bush around the villages. Peter Binaru's sons kidnapped a 12-year-old boy and a woman who were related to Duma and sent them across the Ramu valley to Kafe near Kainantu. The kidnappers' motives were to put demands on the *haus man*. By the beginning of 2014, only the woman had been released and sent back to Gomumu.

The teachers tried to return to duties in 2013. They did not believe the description of the events that said there was a cult going on. They could see nothing like ritual activities. It was more like tribal fighting, and *haus man* was simply the small building for initiations[2] where Duma's supporters gathered. At the end of the second term of the school year, the teachers had lined up the students for parade one morning early, when suddenly they all ran away into the bush. There had been a report of finding a body on the road, covered in many cuts. A teacher photographed the body, which was turned over for him to witness the many cuts. Duma and his men came to the teacher's house to see the photographs that evening and to blow on him and bespell him so that he could sleep peacefully after what he had witnessed. The teacher's family were not at ease, and could smell a strong smell of blood everywhere.

The sliced-up man was Yakasi, a brother of Ronuwe, the *sanguma* man who was said to have killed Asumu by *sanguma* practice. Presumably Yakasi was also a *sanguma*. Duma, at this visit to the Sepik teacher, indicated clearly that he himself was the one who had killed Yakasi. The ruling dictum is that to kill a *sanguma* you have to be a *sanguma*, or know *sanguma* ways.

---

2   This initiation is highlighted by the penile dorsal slit ritual common to much of Madang.

Some time after this my informant was invited to go on a pig hunt. Perhaps 'pig hunt' was a euphemism, because they told him to bring his camera, and they went about in the gardens destroying food when they found no one to kill.

There is a scaled-up fear of *sanguma* practices among the general population of Madang. Warfare and killing in anger have their reasons, but *sanguma* ritual seems beyond reason. In opposition to the claim about the use of ritual, my informant does not acknowledge any ritual practice as claimed in the newspaper article of April 2014. He remembers the occasion of Dorothy Mark's first article (Mark 2014a), when 106 men went to find a couple of suspected *sanguma*. They were saying, 'My bush knife must see blood'. So after one man was killed, everyone cut him further to put blood on their knives. The first man photographed apparently died in the course of a knife attack, not at the end of proceedings. Others were diced into small pieces and their flesh dispersed to the winds. This was warfare, not religious ritual and the methods of dealing with this are evil but more straightforward.

Government mediation begins

In April 2013 the government sent six police officers into Tauta station to investigate the *haus man* movement. The first mediation between the groups took place under the leadership of a Lutheran pastor at Ranara station. Police said they would return with their report, but they have not done so, and this has remained one of the enduring complaints of the local villagers, that there was no follow-up on government action. In preparation for the coming of the police mediators, the Sepik teacher and his teacher colleagues had been asked to make some banners with the local youth, so they prepared signs that read, 'Nahu Rawa youth say "no" to sanguma practices'. By November 2013 the community was saying to the teachers, 'The government has neglected us entirely. You teachers are the last service we have from outside. You cannot leave now.'

Once again at the beginning of 2014 the teachers tried to restart the school. For three weeks no student put in an appearance. At the beginning of the fourth week, there was an assembly, but that very day a girl was found killed at Duma's house. After that the children did not come again. They knew that *haus man* would 'move' now. They were meeting at a place called Yuriengo. Generally there were the three sides to the dispute: the *haus man*, the *sanguma* and about four or five men who tried to remain neutral. When the *haus man* moved, they went to Pisiko and killed four people. This story was covered by *The National* in late February 2014 (Mark 2014a). Duma managed to kill a few more, and the *sanguma* retaliated by killing a member of the *haus man*. The *sanguma* group brought the body of a boy to Serengo village, but *haus man* intervened at the funeral and killed three more, putting their bodies in the toilets. Killings on every side followed, and even some neutral men were killed now. By the time the first article (Mark 2014a) went to press 60 men were said to have died in this spate of killings.

Finding and killing *sanguma*

Who are these *sanguma* who are labelled as killers, and yet seem to suffer the brunt of revenge killing by the community?

According to the local understanding, the way to tell a *sanguma* is as follows: Someone accused is asked to produce their vital arsenal of *kawar* (ginger) or tree barks. If they do so, and show true repentance for their evil deeds of witchcraft, they are approved to return to the community. Anyone compromising in this surrender or trying to run away is obviously guilty, to be pursued and killed. There are said to be about 300 *sanguma* men in the larger area. Gomumu can declare there are 10 *sanguma* in their village, and each one must have two or three sons who follow his ways.

On reviewing the course of events, my informant feels that it started with the *sanguma* killing the woman, Asumu, then *haus man* paying back the killing on the *sanguma* person, Binaru, in Gomumu. Other village people said, 'That's good, come and do the same for us'. When asked to reflect on the group identity of the people called *sanguma*, the teacher denied any systematic connection with language differences or village location. The *sanguma* people from the mountain stayed together at Sakiko settlement in the Ramu River plains, which has now been burned to the ground. They are probably best referred to as '*sanguma* suspects'. They represent people from as many as 15 villages. According to my informant, perhaps the best identification of the *sanguma* people is that they are recent migrants to their villages. They were adopted into the village some generations ago, but now find themselves very much short of land, so they have resolved to remove the original landowners by *sanguma* magic. The *sanguma* can at times be referred to as *bastard pikinini* (illegitimate children of the village) as they try to gain ground and emerge as leaders in the community. They confuse the story of landownership in the local areas.

What the people want most of all is for the government to be consistent in their mediation efforts. There is a protest against religious forms of killing. There is the *sanguma* side of the argument largely unheard by the outside world. Obviously a large campaign of reconciliation and retributive justice, as for Bougainville, is necessary at this time.[3]

---

3   For this, see the experiences and prescriptions given in Howley (2002).

References

Gumar, P. 2012. Eradicating Sorcery Backfires on Villagers. *The National*, 13 July, p. 65.

Howley, P. 2002. *Breaking Spears and Mending Hearts: Peacemakers and Restorative Justice in Bougainville*. Annandale NSW: The Federation Press.

Mark, D. 2014a. Community Living in Fear. *The National*, 27 March.

Mark, D. 2014b. Mass Arrests. *The National*, 22 April, p. 1.

Marks, K. 2013. Hacked, Slashed and Castrated: How 'Cannibal' Cult Leader 'Black Jesus' Steven Tari Met His Death. *The Independent*, 2 September. www.independent.co.uk/news/world/australasia/hacked-slashed-and-castrated-how-cannibal-cult-leader-black-jesus-steven-tari-met-his-death-8795240.html, viewed 13/5/2014.

Matbob, P. 2010. Black Jesus Behind Bars; but Says He Did Nothing Wrong. *Islands Business*, December, p. 29.

8. 'The Land Will Eat You': Land and Sorcery in North Efate, Vanuatu

Siobhan McDonnell

Introduction

In Vanuatu the word 'sorcery' is most closely associated with the use of *blak majik* (black magic) known as *nakaemas* in Bislama, although there is a diversity of practices consistent with the extreme linguistic and cultural diversity found across the archipelago. *Nakaemas* is defined in this chapter consistent with contemporary usage in North Efate, not as the broader practice of magic that is sometimes associated with discussions of sorcery or witchcraft in the academic literature, but as nefarious practices of poisoning and other magical practices that cause bodily harm and untimely deaths.[1] Recent accounts of *nakaemas* in North Efate include incidences of poisoning, bodily possession, transformations of people into dogs and devils, control of bodies and minds and ultimately *nakaemas*-related deaths. Many accusations of *nakaemas* in North Efate occur in the context of land disputes and are made with reference to a broader cosmology of sacred power, or what I refer to here as the *kastom* power of place.[2]

Since Vanuatu became independent in 1980 almost 10 per cent of the total land area — previously held as customary land — has been leased (Scott et al. 2012). In this chapter I consider how narratives of *nakaemas* are shaped by land disputes and the commodification of custom land in North Efate through leasing. Local narratives of *nakaemas* reveal the sacred *kastom* power associated with place, and the terror of *nakaemas* that accompanies the conflict and jealousy associated with land disputes and land leasing. I attempt to gather these various, sometimes contradictory or overlapping, narratives around land leasing in some form as an example of the 'divergent modes of conceptualizing the moral and sacred' that 'coalesce as part of the experience of modernity in Vanuatu' (Taylor in press *b*:15).[3] Collected into an interwoven whole it becomes evident that

---

1   This is similar to the definition used by William Rodman (1993:217) in discussion of *mateana* in Ambae. Increasingly vernacular understanding of *nakaemas* are informed by a circular feedback mechanism between local discussion, discussion in media, and discussion in the policy–legal space, such as in the context of the Vanuatu Land Reform Commission.
2   See also Taylor's discussion of sacred power (Taylor in press *b*).
3   In writing this paper I have entered into an undertaking that details such as specific names and places will not be included. I apologise if this leads to frustration among readers who are hoping for a more specific account of some of these events. For me this undertaking means that pseudonyms alone will not suffice to

these narratives represent a salient critique of current leasing practices in North Efate in which powerful men, whom I have termed elsewhere the 'masters of modernity' in homage to Margaret Rodman's earlier description of the 'masters of tradition', lease land that belongs to other men or tribal groups (McDonnell 2013; Rodman 1987).

Finally, this chapter considers some of the reasons for the limited efficacy of the current formal criminal legal system in addressing the accusations of *nakaemas* that often accompany land-related disputes. It suggests that a better strategy may be to support existing customary institutions to manage land disputes so as to place accusations and threats of *nakaemas* into the broader social contexts of the relationships in which they occur. In relation to the *nakaemas* accusations that accompany land disputes, I will explore the implications of the new land reforms in Vanuatu that devolve power to customary institutions.

North Efate

Narratives of *nakaemas* power as linked to landscapes and powerful men are explored here in the context of North Efate. Efate Island is the central island of Vanuatu in the Y-shaped archipelago (Figure 1) and hosts the capital city Port Vila and a population of 78,721 people (VNSO 2009:2). The land area of Efate Island is 899.5 square kilometres. Statistics from 2010 suggest that 56.5 per cent or 121.5 kilometres of coastal Efate is under lease (Scott et al. 2012).

North Efate (sometimes termed North-West Efate) is a region that stretches along the coastline of Efate Island roughly from Tuktuk Point in the south to Samoa Point in the north. From a mountainous volcanic inland the landscape quickly descends steep escarpments to the coast and finally through reefs to the deep waters of Havannah Harbour. Since the mid-2000s people in North Efate have experienced the voracious leasing of large areas of coastal customary land. Much of this land was subsequently subdivided and resold as small blocks of coastal beachfront estates to expatriate investors (mainly Australians and New Zealanders) as locations for houses.[4] Some of the blocks of subdivided land have

---

protect the identities of the people involved. I have generalised relationships also. I am conscious of people in North Efate's concerns of how they and others are represented. I wish to avoid further inflaming any fears by giving particular details of any of these narratives of *nakaemas*. This is a difficult ethical landscape. I take these undertakings seriously as a researcher, as an adopted member of some of the families involved, and as someone who has at times become woven into these narratives in particular ways.

4 The attractiveness of North Efate as a location was greatly enhanced by the establishment of a tar-sealed ring road that changed travelling times from Port Vila from around one hour on sometimes impassable dirt roads to just over 25 minutes. The ring road was completed in April 2011 and sponsored by the United States of America through the Millennium Challenge Corporation. In the mid to late 2000s the North Efate region also hosted three *Survivor* television series including the most well known *Survivor: Vanuatu, Island of Fire* (Lindstrom 2007), which lent the landscape an international recognition that it had not previously had.

become commercial developments and the coastal estate of Havannah Harbour is now the location of Vanuatu's only five-star resort aptly named 'The Havannah' as well as numerous smaller resorts and a scattering of restaurants. One business, Havannah Eco Lodge, is owned by a local Lelepa Island man.

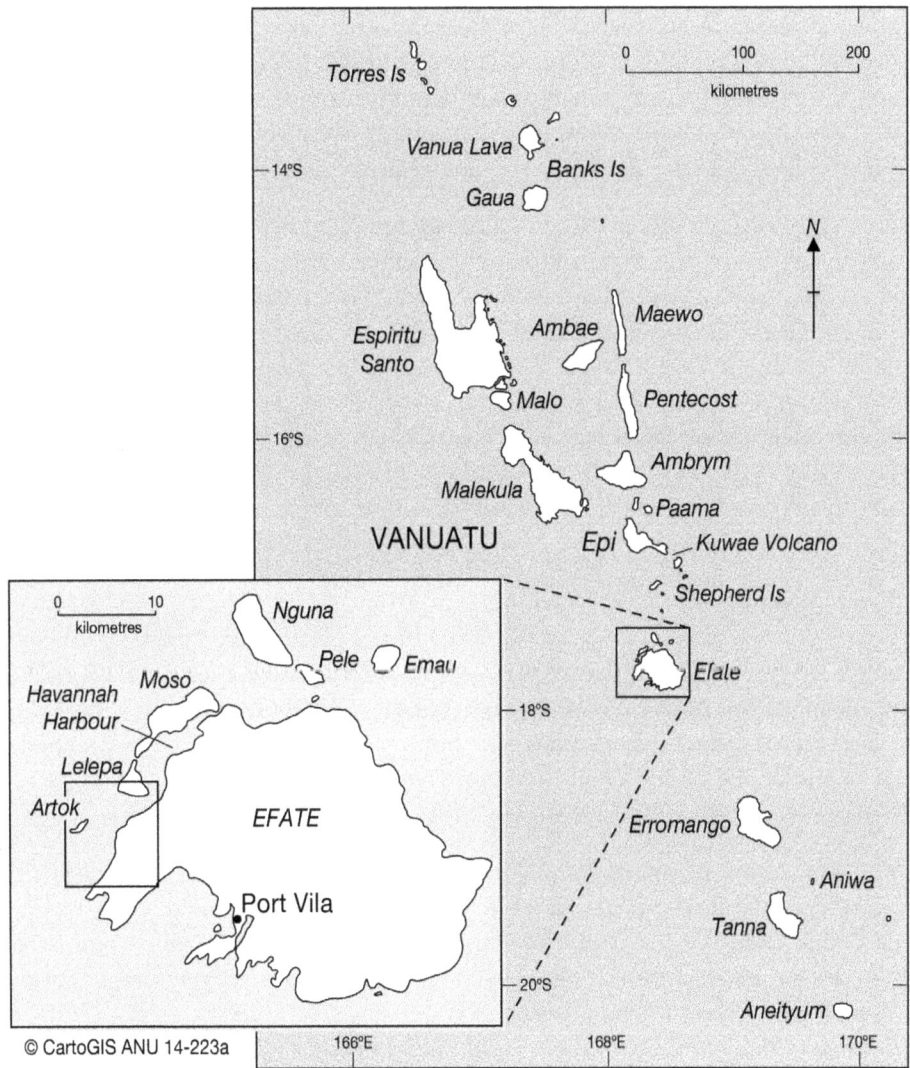

Figure 1: Efate Island, Vanuatu.

Source: CartoGIS, College of Asia & the Pacific, The Australian National University.

In North Efate, land deals through the 2000s saw the large-scale purchasing of leases by largely expatriate but locally based investors from locally powerful men who I have termed the 'masters of modernity'. From the 'custom owner' side, the men engaged in land sales are either chiefs or are heavily influenced by chiefs. In general, they are men who are confident in public forums, have numerous connections to investors, are able to manage complicated cross-cultural transactions (between ni-Vanuatu and expatriate communities) and usually have exceptional English language skills. This combination of status and skills enables them to manipulate land sales across the region. In this sense they are the 'masters of modernity' harnessing asymmetries of information; the sheer knowledge they are able to access, relative to other community members.

Available leasing data in North Efate shows that there are currently around 140 leases across the region along the coastline from Tuktuk Point to Samoa Point, Lelepa Island and the whole of Artok (Hat) Island. Of the 56 leases that are signed off by individuals, 45 leases (80 per cent) list the lessor as a local chief. Leasing by individuals in North Efate is overwhelmingly the providence of chiefs. The leasing data also indicates that chiefs play a major role in many of the lease transactions that have occurred in North Efate. Of the 129 leases, 70 leases (55 per cent) list a chief as the first name on the lease instrument and all others named as lessors (with one exception of one woman's name) are men, powerful in other ways.

The central *kastom* site in North Efate is Artok Island, which is the location of a mass grave of at least 60 bodies and the burial place of the famous paramount chief, Roi Mata. The island of Artok, the old *kastom* village of Mangasi (the residence of Roi Mata) and Feles Cave (the place of Roi Mata's death) on Lelepa Island are all sites of importance in the *kastom* narrative of North Efate. Together these sites make up the Chief Roi Mata's Domain World Heritage site (Figure 2), which was inscribed by UNESCO in 2008 (Wilson et al. 2011).

The population of North Efate lives mostly in the village of Mangaliliu and on Lelepa Island, although increasingly housing is also located along the ring road that circles the island and cuts along the coastline. The recent census records the population of Lelepa as 387 people (VNSO 2009:4) and around 91 households (VNSO 2009:7). While it is not possible to extract the population figures of Mangaliliu from the overall Shefa census data, current estimates put the population at around 550 people.

My fieldwork in North Efate was conducted over a four-year period. During this time I had many conversations with local people about *nakaemas* and attended numerous burials and *'ded'* ceremonies associated with the deaths of powerful men in the area. Many of the men who died during this period were friends, informants and close colleagues of mine. I also participated in a number

8. 'The Land Will Eat You'

of *kastom* and church-based rituals designed variously around clearing the *nakaemas* spirits from the landscape, or naming the supposed perpetrator of acts of *nakaemas*.

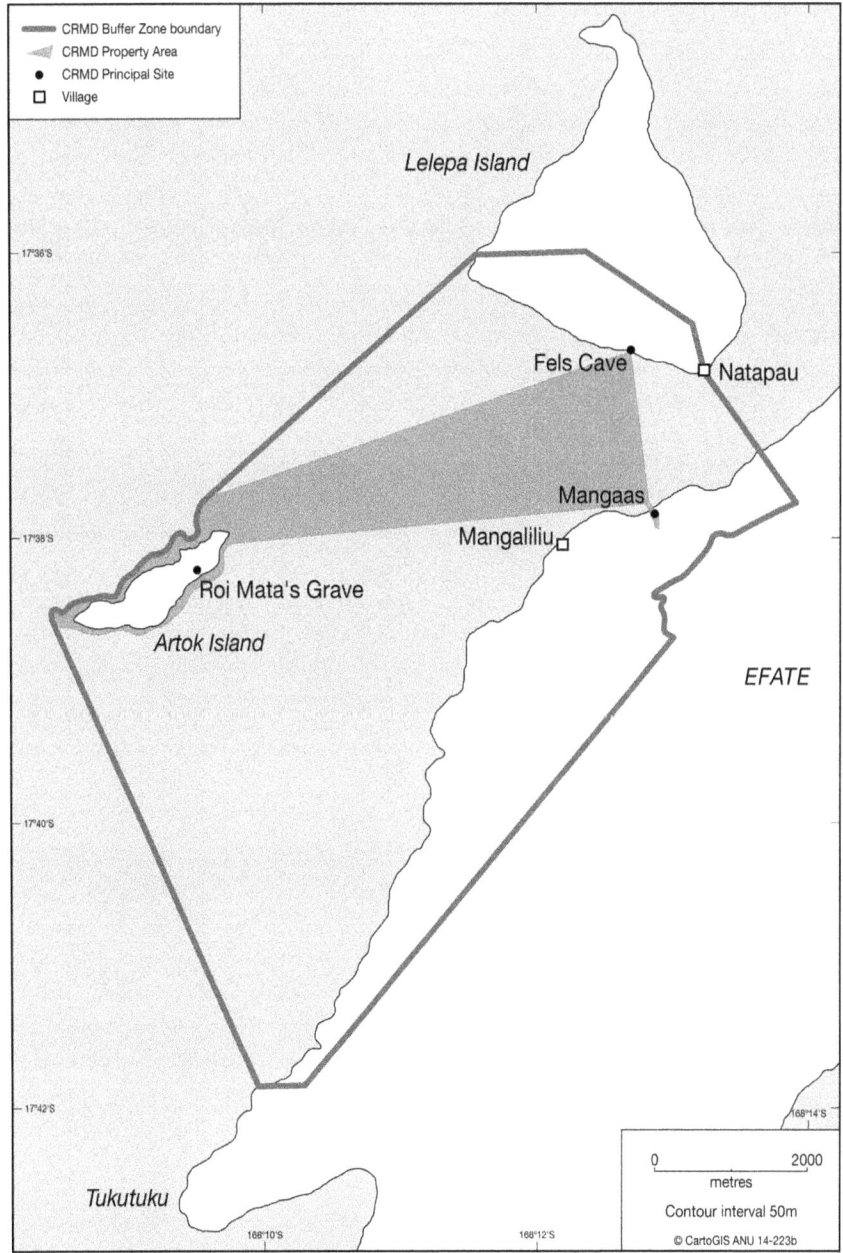

Figure 2: Chief Roi Mata's Domain World (CRMD) Heritage site, Vanuatu.

Source: CartoGIS, College of Asia & the Pacific, The Australian National University.

Talking it Through

Kastom, place and power

Links between identity and place are foundational to ni-Vanuatu. In his consideration of the word *'kastom'*, Taylor is clear that place (*ples*) is a defining narrative in sociality for the Sia Raga in North Pentecost (Taylor 2008:10–11). Throughout Vanuatu, being is tied to landscape and encapsulated in place. By contrast, a man without land is not a man in the sense of the sociality of place. This informs the idea of the contemporary Bislama use of *'man ples'*; the person or group who has land rights over a place. These rights correspond to rights to use and work the land or allocate land to others, to grow gardens and maintain houses, and to look after and visit sacred ancestral sites. *Kastom* and place also function as important political narratives used in the construction of the indigenous self. In contemporary use, *kastom* is increasingly a 'matter of selective perpetuation from past to present to future, of distinguishing good from bad *kastom* between those practices thought worthy of continuity or revival and those which should be left to expire' (Jolly 2012:123). *Kastom* narratives are a conscious and selective representation of key aspects of emplaced self.

In North Efate narratives of *nakaemas* are representative of this broader practice of the selective perpetuation of some *kastom* practices over others. The influence of missionaries in North Efate led to the destruction of many sacred *kastom* objects. Ellen Facey describes the mission project of Peter Milne, a Scottish Presbyterian: 'the voices of chiefs and the images of dead chiefs, the slit drums, had been burnt, and, in many instances, sacred stones and conch shells had been delivered up to Milne by chiefs or their sacred men' (Facey 1981:304). Missionaries regarded the practice of *nakaemas* as immoral, a description that continues to resonate in contemporary discussions. In conversation in North Efate *nakaemas* is often referred to as the *'rabis saed blong kastom'* (the rubbish side of *kastom* practices).[5] As a descriptor this operates within reference to deeper temporal understandings of the time before missionaries as *taem blong tu dak* — the time of heathen 'darkness' in contrast to Christian 'light' and the construction of moral narratives around the use of sacred power (Taylor in press *b*:13). Accordingly, for the Christian population of North Efate, the practice of *nakaemas* was until recently regarded as no longer practised and to have 'died out'. Many of the narratives associated with *nakaemas*, and discussed below, assume that a local man has paid a *nakaemas* practitioner living in Port Vila from

---

5   See also a discussion of the immorality of sorcery as influenced by Christianity such that it is representative of 'bad' *kastom* in Rodman (1993:221) and also the discussion of evangelical church crusades against *kastom* in Taylor (in press *b*). However, different denominations have approached the integration of *kastom* practices into the church in different ways. The approaches of the different denominations to *kastom* have also changed markedly over time and in response to the 'renaissance' in *kastom* that took place before independence in Vanuatu.

another island more closely associated with *nakaemas*. The assumptions in these accounts is that *nakaemas* services are accessed from 'outside' and are no longer found in North Efate.

The broad historical narrative of 'sorcery' in Vanuatu is that it is a secretly guarded *kastom* power closely connected to powerful men and embedded in specific places (Facey 1981; Rio 2002; Rodman, 1993; Tonkinson 1981). The practice of *nakaemas* in Vanuatu was historically the purview of powerful men who as 'leaders were considered either to have extensive supernatural powers themselves, or had magic men working for them who were able to manipulate these powers on their behalf' (Forsyth 2006:4). Powerful men used the threat of *nakaemas* to encourage obedience and as punishment of those who disregarded rules or flouted acceptable social behaviour.

Much of the terror associated with the practice of *nakaemas* in contemporary Vanuatu is that it is viewed as less controlled and more easily accessible in many places, particularly in urban areas. It is no longer viewed as a power regulated by powerful men. This has led to claims that *nakaemas* is 'out of control because people could no longer appreciate the agency of the sorcery act as an expression of power, since it was no longer seen as the tool of the socially constitutive high men of the hierarchy' (Rio 2002:131). Fear of *nakaemas* in contemporary Vanuatu is the fear of an unrestrained power, a power no longer bound by *kastom* governance structures, a power no longer linked to place. Responding to the report into the 2007 *nakaemas*-related riots involving the Ambrym and Tanna communities living in Port Vila and resulting in three deaths, Tannese spokesman Chief Jacob Kapare explained the violence as being caused by a breakdown in the *kastom* management of sorcery:

> every Island in Vanuatu is rich with their individual black magic/sorcery powers to kill people within their systems ... Normally this is supposed to happen within a network, an agreement between the *nakamals* but today it has shot out of control. (Joshua 2011a)

Without appropriate *kastom* governance structures there is nothing to manage or mitigate the fear that provokes the desperate search for narratives to explain why deaths have occurred. Increasingly, narratives of *nakaemas* are associated with conflict around access to the cash economy (Taylor in press *a*). Anthropological literature in Melanesia stresses that unequal access to cash and market commodities and narratives of 'development' can give rise to jealousy and result in the practice of sorcery (Lattas 1993; Rio 2002). The practices and fears associated with sorcery also look different in urban and rural areas. In an urban context, Taylor writes that in Santo township interlocutors describe 'the growing threat of *nakaemas* ... with the mixed nature of life in town amid increasingly hard economic conditions and a growing culture of jealousy'

(Taylor in press *a*:4). In urban areas *nakaemas* is seen as more accessible, 'fears are growing that it is becoming "commercialised" and the demand for *kastom* "hitmen" may be growing as sorcery is use[d] outside its respective boundaries and for the wrong purposes' (Joshua 2011b). By contrast, in rural areas of Vanuatu allegations around the practice of *nakaemas* are often closely related to land disputes, as will be explored later in this chapter.

Place and power in North Efate

I begin my discussion of *nakaemas* and land by considering contemporary understandings in North Efate of the way in which power is embedded in place. *Kastom* narratives of power in the landscape of North Efate take two broad forms. First, there is ancestral sacred power associated with place per se. Second, there is power associated with place of which one kind, *nakaemas,* has historically been harnessed by powerful men as part of a chiefly hierarchy. Embedded *nakaemas* that operates within a social structure was described by Mary Douglas as a controlled power 'exerted on behalf of the social structure; they protect society from malefactors against whom their danger is directed. Their use must be approved by all good men' (Douglas 2003:100). These powers can be contrasted with those that are dangerous to society; 'those who use them are malefactors, their victims are innocent … these are witches and sorcerers' (ibid.). Writing of the Maring in Papua New Guinea, LiPuma distinguishes between these different forms of power in a similar way, noting that: '[a]ncestors attack those who have abridged community norms, whereas sorcerers attack for their own malevolent purposes' (LiPuma 1994:152). While historically both of these forms of power have operated as social sanctions, narratives of *nakaemas* increasingly distinguish between the power of place which attacks those who have not adhered to the correct practices in *kastom* and the marauding dangers of commodified *nakaemas*. The *kastom* power of place recognises the agency of place; it is closely associated with *kastom* understandings of the ways of the place and the idea of ancestral power as a social sanction. The ancestral power of place is contrasted in this chapter with accusations or threats of *nakaemas* by an individual associated with a land dispute. Discussion of the sacred power of place is distinct from accessing commodified sacred power by paying a *nakaemas* practitioner. Ideas of commodified *nakaemas* are discussed locally in North Efate as purchased from outside the area, most readily from Port Vila, so as to fulfil a personal vendetta.

A key element of place in Vanuatu is the power of ancestral and spiritual beings within the landscape. The divine narratives of place are stories describing the actions and movements of ancestral figures within the landscape. In North Efate anthropological and local historicities describe the matrilineal relationships (termed *naflak)* linking people to place as originating from the important historical figure of Roi Mata (Ballard 2014). Considered to have lived in the 1600s, Roi Mata was described as the 'paramount chief of all chiefs of Efate', who developed the *naflak* 'totemic' systems on Efate (Guiart 1964:97). It is the narrative of Roi Mata and the associated *naflak* groupings that continue to link people to place across Efate and in the Shepherd Islands.

In Vanuatu *kastom* narratives of place are supplemented by the diurnal (and nocturnal) presence of visiting ancestors and spiritual beings who personify place. In this sense:

> the physical world is inhabited by ancestral and other spiritual essences. Both human-made objects — houses, canoes, carvings, textiles — and the natural environment — hills, animals, rocks, waterfalls — do not merely represent but *are in fact* the repositories or embodiment of what in English are sometimes described by terms such as 'ghosts' or 'spirits'. (Taylor in press *b*:9)

Part of the coastline of Havannah Harbour is, for example, inhabited by small 'dwarf' people named *sengalengale* who interfere with washing, knock over objects and steal food from houses and gardens. These little people become increasingly disturbed as their place is developed by housing that forms part of luxury residential subdivisions or hotels that increasingly mark the coastline of Havannah Harbour. Place in this context is embodied by the ancestral figures of the historical or recent past and by spiritual beings and devilish figures that inhabit the landscape. It is this personification of place that enables the land to have agency.

Key places in the landscape of North Efate also represent the spiritual path between the living and the dead. In North Efate, Tuktuk Point marked the junction in the journey after death to the spirit world; after death people believed that '[t]he spirit journeyed under the sea to Point Tukituki' (Facey 1981:305). As well as physical locations that mark pathways to the spiritual realm, different locations in the contemporary landscape of North Efate are identified with changing weather; calling on ancestral power for support in war, fighting, or disputes; good luck or other activities; and collecting luck for fishing. Increasingly, ceremonies are held at Mangasi in the compound of Roi Mata to ask for ancestral help, protection, power and guidance. There is also a location which is widely understood as being the place where a person (overwhelmingly thought of as a man) can go to harness the *kastom* power associated with *nakaemas*, to call the power to him.[6]

---

6 This is similar to Tonkinson's (1981) conception of sacred power in Ambrym as something that could be harnessed by sorcerers to bring about a range of effects.

Historically in North Efate there was a finely calibrated balance between the practice of *nakaemas* power and the authority of men within the chiefly structure who were able to control or guide the use of the power. Hierarchical chiefly structures consisted of a chief or *nawota* (in Lelepa language) supported by a number of other men who also held titled positions. These included a *munawae*, termed a *kleva* in Bislama (literally 'clever' in English), a sacred man holding a hereditary title 'who could perform extraordinary feats by virtue of his ritual knowledge and personal relationship to the world of spirits and gods' (Facey 1981:300). All chiefly dominions included spirits who dwelt in 'particular caves, a hole in a rock or a tree, or in the sea' (Facey 1981:305); the *munawae* or *nawota* was responsible for going to the place of the spirit and leaving a food offering so as to guarantee a plentiful harvest or success in warfare.

Recognition of the power and authority of chief came from the close relationship between a *nawota* and their *munawa*e (Facey 1981:310). For example, the holder of the 'Roi Mata' chiefly title had a *munuwae* whose title was 'Marikurai' (Guiart 1964). The contemporaneous inhabitation of a place by the living and the dead meant that the role of a *munawae* was that of a mediator with the ancestral spirit world. Unexplained sicknesses were sent by the ancestors and:

> thus sacred men visited them in spirit and would find the sick person's spirit bound by the ancestors. He [the sick man] would die unless he admitted the misdeed of which they accused him and rectified the situation. (Facey 1981:305)

The role of the *munuwae* was to save people from unexplained sickness and to protect them from being taken by ancestors or *nakaemas*. In this sense, *munuwae* act as mediums between ancestral beings and contemporary inhabitants of a landscape.

In contemporary Vanuatu *kleva* are healers who use a combination of *kastom* plant-based medicine, Western medicine and other esoteric healing practices (Taylor in press b). *Kleva* are also known for their powers in divining the cause of *nakaemas* or the name of the *nakaemas* practitioner.[7] They also possess the skills to 'clear' an area of malevolent ancestral beings, protect people or bring an end to a curse or other form of *nakaemas* power. *Kleva* are the personified embodiment of what Taylor describes as the 'Janus faced' relationship between the sacred power of Christianity and sorcery with their combined powers of 'black' and 'white' magic (ibid:6–7). Skilful practitioners will draw on the narratives of Christianity in order to justify and defend what may otherwise be

---

7   See, for example, Rio's discussion of the role of a *vanten ngea vanten hanglam rohle* in Ambrym (Rio 2002:137).

considered the dangerous and immoral use of *kastom* powers. These justifications of acts with reference to Christianity allay fears and enable the practice of skills that might otherwise be associated with *kastom* practices and 'black' magic.[8]

In North Efate today there is no one who claims to perform the specific role of a *kleva*, although there are some people who claim to have general 'healing' powers. Accordingly, there has been no clear pathway for mitigating the fear of *nakaemas* associated with recent deaths, which has resulted in communities engaging on separate occasions over the past four years healers from the Seventh-day Adventist Church; numerous other islands including Pentecost, Malekula and Epi; and a famed healer from Pango village. These delegations have held numerous faith healing, praying and 'clearing' ceremonies. There has also been a number of directives from various groups to cut down sacred banyan trees on the island, and to pull up all red flowers as these are 'a symbol of the devil' (McDonnell, field notes, North Efate 2011). So far these delegations have, in the minds of many community members, failed to address the practices and fear of *nakaemas*. During this period a number of people left their homes and relocated to Port Vila out of fear of powers that are out of control. The enigma for people in North Efate is that just as they maintain they no longer have 'black magic' *nakaemas* practitioners within the place, they have lost the 'Janus faced' powers to resolve issues of *nakaemas* historically embodied in the role of a *kleva*.

The power associated with place continues to be closely bound to the authority of chiefs in North Efate, just as it was in the past. Facey writes of the historical practice of one form of 'investiture' of chiefly titles, or what is now commonly referred to as ordination:

> The central element of the rite was the 'pulling up' of the sacred spirit from the predecessor and the instillation of it within his successor. This involved transferral of a potentially fatal power and so it had to be performed by other chiefs within a sacred enclosure of coconut fronds constructed especially for the occasion. If non-chiefs approached this area they could be killed by the force of the sacred spirit. (Facey 1981:300)

Ancestral beings have agency and continue to affect the course of peoples' lives and their claims to chiefly authority over land. Echoing Facey's account, one Lelepa man described to me the process for his chiefly anointment, termed *patnanu*, which involves a current chiefly titleholder passing the sacred *kastom* power held by a chief to another man. The *kastom* ceremony necessitates a

---

8 Without the careful deployment of Christian narratives, people performing the role of a *kleva* can become a target for *nakaemas*-related violence. See, for example, the discussion by Taylor (in press a).

complicated and particular placement of coconut (*nanu*) fronds underneath the current titleholder, in order to assume his chiefly position and appropriate his power. The Lelepa man described what occurred as this ceremony took place:

> At the time when I passed the coconut leaves underneath I turned the leaves. I had not meant to turn them but the spirits of the ancestors are alive today. When I pushed the leaves, another man was there, the power of the chief moved all about. The spirits of the ancestors made their work. (Translated from fieldwork notes, 2012)

Thus ancestral spirits subverted the chiefly anointment ceremony and stole the sacred power from the supposed successor, passing it to another man who today retains the chiefly title. In this narrative the agency of the ancestors of the place intervened to promote the interests of one man over another. Ancestors are very much alive. Place is embodied by ancestral beings that are essential to recognition of sacred power and authority in the landscape. As a result, authority means, among other things, being able to harness and channel the sacred *kastom* power of place.

Where the power of a place is defined in terms of *nakaemas*, chiefly authority is linked to a capacity to harness this power. Writing on North Ambrym, an island renowned for being the home of many *nakaemas* practitioners, Patterson writes of how this place is described as 'the Mother of Darkness', renowned for the practice of *nakaemas* among people from other islands (Patterson 2002).[9] Chiefly authority in this landscape thus requires claims of authority related to *nakaemas* or Christianity, or both held together in careful tension (Tonkinson 1981). By contrast, expatriates cannot really be part of the web of sociality that marks *kastom* and embeds people in place and therefore cannot hold or manage the power of *nakaemas*. Dousset (Chapter 9, this volume) raises this point in his discussion of *nakaemas*, noting that people suspected of sorcery 'are not complete foreigners, not unknown people, but are often (if not always) relatively close kin (or potentially close kin), people one has fed and protected'. This is particularly true of rural areas where one often sees the competing interests that mark intra-family or community disputes over claims to land. Here accusations of *nakaemas* mean that key agents take part in a narrative dance, alternately as victim or perpetrator, a type of musical chairs that reflects the pressures of conflict and competition (Dousset, Chapter 9 this volume). In rural Efate and other rural areas of Vanuatu this dance entails the choreographed performance of narrative claims and counterclaims to land and to chiefly authority over landscapes.

---

9 See also the discussion by Rio of how this has informed ideas on Ambrym about the darkness that lurks in villages (Rio 2002:137).

Nowhere does the fraught and political nature of opposing narratives of *kastom* and place become more transparent than in the legal entanglements related to opposing claims over land. Here the narratives of emplaced self are fought over by a handful of powerful men vying for authority over a landscape. It is men who are always the agents of these *kastom* narratives of place as it is the men who speak in court and in *nakamals* (often defined as men's houses or chief's houses). By disallowing the voices of women in these spaces the construction of *kastom* and place is overwhelmingly the domain of men. And it is around these contested claims over land that allegations of *nakaemas* often occur. I will return to this theme in my discussion of *nakamals* as customary institutions in the final section of this chapter.

Nakaemas and land leasing

Over the past four-year period accounts of *nakaemas* in North Efate have included incidences of poisoning, bodily possession, transformation of people into dogs and devils, control of bodies and minds and ultimately *nakaemas*-related deaths. *Nakaemas* accusations must be interpreted in the context of social relationships and as a response to tensions within social groups. *Nakaemas* accusations cannot be interpreted in and of themselves, but are more properly viewed as an ongoing process of circumspection that takes place around specific sources of tension, one of which relates to dealings over land. The tapestry of narratives of *nakaemas* is woven over time; with each death comes a new set of explanations and accusations which must be carefully considered and analysed before a conclusion is reached. With each subsequent otherwise unexplained death the process is repeated. My field notes following the death of a close colleague and friend I had been involved in caring for shows an example of this narrative weaving:

> The Council of Chiefs have held a meeting with a *kleva* from Tanna. She explained the reasons for the black magic and named … [the man] responsible for his death. The *nakaemas* narrative gains strength, people comment repeatedly 'those white people tried everything to save him but the poison was too strong'. His brother sits next to the grave each night to ward off the marauding spirits. The generator is kept running all through the night so that the grave can be lit. Other people have also been involved in guarding and protecting the grave. This will continue until the one month is over. (McDonnell, field notes 2011)

Temporally a narrative becomes woven from a series of events that may have taken place before and after the most immediate circumstances of a death. Together these competing and contested narratives in North Efate weave a complex critique of land leasing in the region and of the failure of powerful men, as the masters of modernity, to observe the appropriate protocols in the *kastom* management of place (McDonnell 2013; McDonnell thesis forthcoming).

Accusations of *nakaemas* around the recent deaths on Lelepa Island form around three intertwined narratives. The first narrative relates the deaths to a conflict within a family, a decision made within the family by two brothers that affected the life of a third brother, from which he was then felt to have wanted revenge and engaged a *nakaemas* practitioner from 'outside'.[10] This narrative is linked to accusations related directly to a specific family conflict, albeit one involving proper *naflak* relationships to place. One version of this family conflict echoes one of the *kastom* accounts of the death of Roi Mata, by poisoning at the hands of his brother. The circularity of local historicities mean that meanings in the present are inscribed with understanding from the past.

The other two narratives link *nakaemas* directly to the involvement of powerful men in disputes over land. Changes to the practice of sorcery in Melanesia have focused on the implications of modernity for access to and use of sorcery. The efflorescence of sorcery across Melanesia has often been linked to the inequalities associated with the incorporation of people into the cash and commodity economy (Eves 2000:454; LiPuma 1994; Taylor in press *b*). In this context unequal access to cash and market commodities can give rise to conflict, competition and jealousy and result in the practice of sorcery (see Dousset, Chapter 9 this volume; Taylor in press *b*). Land leasing in Vanuatu offers one of the main mechanisms by which local people can access reasonably large amounts of cash income, although these are often small relative to the value of the land that has been leased (see McDonnell, thesis forthcoming). The close proximity of North Efate to Port Vila has meant that, locally, people recognise the possibility of accessing a practitioner and purchasing commodified *nakaemas* services. In this account the actions of the five dead men individually and the role that they each played in facilitating land sales and developments or, as in the case of one of them, in opposing land developments in the area against the wishes of his immediate family members, has resulted in claims and counterclaims of *nakaemas*. This is a complicated account of the contested authority of some of these men as chiefs over landscapes. Importantly, each of these men was individually involved in a major land dispute in the area.

The conflict and jealousy surrounding land disputes and lease making in North Efate is increasingly associated with the fear that a disgruntled party may resort to *nakaemas*. As one Lelepa man describes:

---

10   Dousset (Chapter 9, this volume) defines sorcery as emanating from relations at the 'periphery' including 'nephews, cousins, in-laws' rather than 'parents or children or brothers'. By contrast, this account of *nakaemas* relates to a 'core' domestic unit, the relationship of brothers.

If I make a problem with another Lelepa man about land that man will go and find a *nakaemas* practitioner from another place to come and kill me. All men on the island are really frightened of *nakaemas* when there is a land problem. (McDonnell field notes, 2013)

In North Efate, masters of modernity are viewed as being more able to access *nakaemas* practitioners than others because of their greater access to cash (in part due to leasing land) and their larger networks in Port Vila. Increasingly, masters of modernity are also perceived as using the threat of *nakaemas* as a strategy to defend their leasing of land belonging to others. Threats of *nakaemas* create compliance among broader groups of disenfranchised custom owners or community members with the land dealings undertaken by masters of modernity. Many men that I have interviewed who have had their land 'stolen' and sold by a chief or powerful man report being frightened of challenging the authority of the man involved, of the ongoing social tensions that this would create, and of their deep and unassailable terror of *nakaemas*. Such fear means that land sales by these masters of modernity are often unchallenged in law or *kastom* proceedings, an issue that I will return to below.

The final narrative about the recent deaths in North Efate relates to the actions of the members of the same family in leasing Artok Island. Rights over the island are contested between two family groups. All of the men from the one family who signed as representatives of their family on the lease instrument are now dead. More than a land dispute, these are competing claims of authority as the rightful chief over a place. And not just any place but the central *kastom* place within the broader landscape, the burial site of Chief Roi Mata.

Kastom power resides in key places within the landscape, so if these places are disturbed, ancestors and spirits of the place may seek retribution. People in North Efate talk about the *kastom* curse invoked when a powerful man steals the land of other people or tribal groups. This occurs when powerful men: (1) claim rights that are not theirs in *kastom* over land; (2) claim land that is not theirs; or (3) engage in leasing land over which they have no right. In each of these cases *kastom* dictates that men who engage in these practices run the risk of being cursed: '*graon hemi kaekae yu*' ('the land will eat you'). The embodied landscape has agency and is able to curse the living who do not correctly follow the path established in the *kastom* management of place.

Within North Efate the agency of the landscape resides in key *kastom* sites, and its capacity to injure informs claims and accusations of *nakaemas*. The landscape is suffused with stories around deaths where men have been engaged in land dealings. These narratives are essential in rival claims over chiefly titles and corresponding landscapes. Deaths and sicknesses are explained as derived from men who have claimed authority over landscapes, or have dealt in land by leasing it, over which they have no 'rightful' ancestral claim. Together these claims represent a challenge to the authority of masters of modernity who have acted in a way that has abrogated their responsibilities in *kastom*. Consequently, many of the narratives that are now told about a recent series of deaths in North Efate represent a critique of land leasing and in particular the leasing of key *kastom* sites, the most centrally important of which is the burial site of Chief Roi Mata on Artok Island. *Nakaemas* is crucial in these narratives through the idea that people evoke their more legitimate claims to place by calling on the *kastom* power of the place; by literally speaking a *kastom* curse against another enabled by the right in *kastom* to a place; or by engaging a *nakaemas* practitioner because of their anger over another man's claim over their place.

The illusion that legislation is the answer

The increasing incidence of extreme acts of violence justified with reference to accusations of 'sorcery', particularly in Papua New Guinea, has prompted a new round of debate about the need to create legislative responses to accusations and attacks based on sorcery in Melanesia. Writing on biodiversity and traditional knowledge in the Pacific, Forsyth (2014:1) notes wryly the call for legislation to be 'a common response to almost every development issue in the region'. Like Forsyth, I remain concerned with the illusion of the power of the law to 'solve' the complex social dynamics associated with accusations and counter accusations of *nakaemas* when linked to land disputes. Caution also needs to be exercised in considering legislative models for the criminal prosecution of *nakaemas* accusations or violence as distinct from the context in which they evolve. This separation of *nakaemas* from context could easily result in punishments of 'offences' that do little to address the underlying causes of tensions — as is often the case with land disputes.

Legal pluralism offers insights into the dominance of the formal state legal system, with its colonial legacy, over customary institutions of law and governance in Vanuatu. Legal pluralism is defined as the 'situation in which two or more legal systems coexist in the same field' (Merry 1988:870). The hierarchical relationship between the formal state legal system and customary institutions means that the plurality of customary institutions are offered only limited legal recognition within the formal state-based institutional arrangements (Forsyth 2009; McDonnell 2013). The exception to this characterisation is the area of land law where recent amendments to the Constitution of Vanuatu and new legislative reforms have created a situation of legal pluralism, discussed in greater detail below.

In Vanuatu law the crime of sorcery remains an offence in the Penal Code, which is notoriously difficult to prosecute. A Vanuatu Law Reform Commission presentation identifies some of the problems associated with prosecution, offering the commentary of a police inspector:

> The prosecution in the Penal Code is not sufficient for the police to work with. There are no elements for sorcery so it is hard to prove it. If sorcery is defined it will help guide us as to what we want to prove in court. Most cases in sorcery are thrown out by the courts because there is not enough evidence. (Kanas 2013)

In spite of the identification of the problems with prosecution, the framing of this Vanuatu Law Reform Commission process seems oriented to further consideration of how 'law' and more specifically criminal law can be altered to address the problems of sorcery. Speaking of the Law Reform Commission process, then Minister for Justice, Ralph Regenvanu, stated that the process was designed to 'learn from what they [Papua New Guineans] are doing and amend our Penal Code to deal better with sorcery' (Joshua 2011b). This framing of how law can address the problems of sorcery fails to consider that at base the failure to successfully prosecute is a problem of the culture of law.[11]

The secular, post-enlightenment 'rational' culture of the Anglo common law system as adopted in Vanuatu's criminal law creates a normative framework aligned to procedural and evidential proof. As a result the current criminal system that operates in Vanuatu is unable to successfully prosecute the threat, accusation and act of *nakaemas* because of the difficulty of 'accommodating a ni-Vanuatu social reality into a western legal framework' (Forsyth 2006:12). Questions of 'guilt' or 'innocence' are also often extremely difficult to resolve even for the accused person themselves. William Rodman writes that 'the ambiguities of sorcery belief in Ambae blur questions of innocence and guilt in such a way that the accused person often is unsure whether he or she is at fault in causing sickness or death' (Rodman 1993:232). The cultural logic embedded in the normative Anglo common law framework adopted in Vanuatu is inadequate to accommodating the aetiological understanding of *nakaemas* as an act of violence.[12] At heart this is a schism in cultural logic.

Other obstacles exist to the use of formal state-based legal systems to manage issues related to *nakaemas*. Pragmatically, access to the formal state-based criminal justice system is extremely limited in Vanuatu, particularly for populations not located close to the capital of Port Vila or the other main urban centre, Luganville. In Vanuatu beyond urban areas the state and its institutional

---

11 For a discussion of the problems of 'the culture of the law' with respect to land law in Vanuatu see McDonnell (2013).
12 For a discussion of the 'cultural power' of law see McDonnell (2013).

apparatus remain a peripheral concept recognised for the provision of occasional services (roads, schools and health clinics), although the state rarely has a monopoly on service provision.

The reality of everyday lives is that governmentality in Vanuatu consists of the fabric of institutions available to people in their locality. Villages in rural areas are self-governed by local customary institutions, and to a lesser extent by church-based institutions. Practically, this is a foundational reason why customary institutions and chiefly structures are central to any proposed strategies to address accusations of *nakaemas*, particularly with reference to land disputes. This is not to suggest that these institutions are without tensions around leadership, authority and legitimacy. Within villages there is rarely a unified 'community' perspective on many issues. Nor is it designed to present a romanticised view of the operation of what are often referred to as 'traditional' or '*kastom*' governance structures. It is instead a recognition that the rules that govern peoples lives are usually dictated by chiefs, or local leaders and church representatives (almost always men), before they are enforced by institutions of the state. In reality extensive decision-making occurs, particularly by chiefs and local leaders, about whether to engage the formal state-based criminal legal system, for example, through contacting local police posts. Even the most serious of criminal offences such as *nakaemas*-related violence may be dealt with by localised customary (*kastom*) processes that operate well beyond the ambit, or even knowledge, of the state. Decisions by local male leadership have important implications for the operation of 'justice' and in particular in the prosecution of gender-based violence, and violence against children, at a local village level (Tor and Toka 2004:58). Where violence is perpetrated by a powerful local man it will often go unchallenged. The state remains removed from this decision-making, often strategically engaged at the behest of and for the purposes of local leaders and chiefs, and the formal criminal justice system operates as an extension of this relationship.

A further problem is that many people describe being frightened of pursuing land disputes through formal state-based institutions because of *nakaemas* concerns. These accusations influence how people are choosing to access formal legal arrangements designed to resolve land disputes, as one Malekula woman explains:

> Now when there is such an increasing number of disputes about land, all families where they think they have rights inside the dispute want to exercise their rights but they are very frightened of the other party to the dispute because of *nakaemas*. If one party decides to push forward with a strong case in [Western] law then everyone will say to those

people you need to be really careful that someone does not poison you. You need to be careful where you walk and study carefully everything around you ... With all land cases people are really afraid of *nakaemas*.

Not only does being a party to a land dispute mean that you live in fear of *nakaemas*, if you exercise your rights through the state-based formal legal system you may also be put at further risk. Families who are weighing up their choices over whether to take a case to court will make an assessment of whether the other party has any serious *nakaemas* practitioners for fear that these practitioners will use *nakaemas* against family members who have engaged in formal legal proceedings over the land. In a recent case before the Supreme Court, Justice Spear granted an urgent restraining order against a family in south-east Malekula who were fighting a land dispute against another family. During the dispute a senior family member died and the death was attributed to sorcery.[13] The judge, appreciating that the claimants were 'fearful for their lives', granted restraining orders against four family members, which shows some flexibility in the formal legal system and the possibility of using restraining orders in future situations.[14] It is unlikely that these fears are associated only with formal court proceedings, but in the fieldwork that I have undertaken people seem most concerned about the potential for instigating *nakaemas* acts when pursuing land disputes through formal legal courts as opposed to customary or church-based institutions.

In this chapter I have argued that throughout rural Vanuatu land disputes create major tensions within communities and often between or within families and that these disputes are increasingly linked with fear of, and accusations around, *nakaemas*. Appropriately dealing with these *nakaemas* accusations requires a consideration of the broader social relationships and land-related tensions that inform the accusations. This approach seems to suggest that there may be a role for customary or church-based institutions that are more able to focus on the holistic context of *nakaemas* accusations, rather than depending on formal criminal legal proceedings. This more holistic approach may be better able to deal with the conflict associated with land-related *nakaemas* accusations, rather than separating the accusation and supposed evidence of *nakaemas* from the context in which it is situated. While a discussion of the role of churches is beyond the scope of this chapter, I will focus now on the new land reforms in Vanuatu and the role of customary institutions in managing land disputes.

In February 2014 a new land reform package came o effect in Vanuatu. The new land legislation is supported by two constitutional amendments. Together these changes represent an attempt to enable legal pluralism such that customary

---

13   *Johnny v. Savoire* [2011] VUSC 331.
14   See Spears J, *Johnny v. Savoire* [2011] VUSC 331.

rather than formal state courts can resolve who the customary owner groups are for an area of land. The newly amended Article 78(3) of the constitution now states that 'the final and substantive decisions reached by customary institutions or procedures ... after being recorded in writing, are binding in law and are not subject to any appeal or any review by any Court of law'. As Minister Regenvanu explains: 'The new laws bring determination of custom owners back to customary institutions, it removes the power from courts and the government to determine who the custom owners are and puts it back under rules of custom'.[15] These customary institutions are defined in the legislation as *nakamals* or custom area land tribunals.[16] The new *Customary Land Management Act* creates new processes for identifying custom owner groups and managing disputes about custom ownership in accordance with the rules of customary law. It is customary law that guides the management of land disputes. It is possible that people appearing before these institutions may describe *nakaemas*-related fears as part of their broader concerns associated with land disputes. There is potentially more scope for consideration of these issues than in a formal state-based context where issues of land are seen as matters related to property law, distinct and separate from issues of sorcery under the Penal Code. In practical terms it may be important for the state to formally acknowledge that customary institutions may deal with *nakaemas* issues as part of land-related tensions. This could involve creating formal links between customary institutions, policing and the state-based legal system so as to allow, for example, customary institutions to request restraining orders be put in place. It may also involve creating links between customary institutions and church-based groups who offer services for dealing with *nakaemas*.

Pathways forward in dealing with issues related to *nakaemas* and land disputes must also recognise that customary institutions need strengthening in many areas of Vanuatu. This approach must consider ways of strengthening customary institutions so as to better manage community conflict. This *kastom gavanas* (governance) work must be slow and careful, but if managed properly it may offer communities more lasting solutions for the tensions associated with land disputes.

Finally, and perhaps most importantly, discussion around the operation of customary institutions can sometimes involve a reification of these institutions and can fail to acknowledge that the institutions are mostly dominated by

---

15   Ralph Regenvanu, personal communication 2 March 2014.
16   The *Customary Land Management Act* defines *nakamal* as 'a customary institution that operates as the seat of governance for a particular area. Members of a nakamal include all men, women and children who come under the governance jurisdiction of that nakamal. A nakamal may be related to a single custom owner group or extended family group, or may be related to a number of custom owner groups or extended family groups living in a village or larger area. The vernacular language terms for the customary institutions termed "nakamal" in this Act are different in different localities across Vanuatu and include *Farea* in parts of Efate, *Gamal* in parts of Malekula, *Naumel* in Motalava and *Jaranmoli* in parts of Santo.'

powerful men, or masters of modernity (McDonnell 2013). With respect to land leasing it is these powerful men in North Efate who are leasing land belonging to others. Fear of challenging the authority of powerful men is partly engendered by threats of *nakaemas*, which in turn reduces the opposition to the land leasing that these men have participated in. It is also likely that these fears may prevent people from speaking out during a land dispute heard by a customary institution. Discussion of customary institutions as a mechanism for resolving land disputes and associated accusations of *nakaemas* must recognise these tensions.

Conclusion

This chapter is I hope the beginning of a discussion of the narratives of *nakaemas* that are associated with land disputes in rural areas in Vanuatu. In the context of recent land leasing that has taken place in North Efate, I have described how *kastom* ideas of place and power are central to the critiques of powerful men engaged in leasing land. When a powerful man leases the land of other people or tribal groups by (1) claiming rights that are not his in *kastom* over land, (2) claiming land that is not his, or (3) leasing land over which he has no right, *kastom* dictates that 'the land will eat you'. Together these critiques of land leasing by powerful men represent a challenge to the authority of masters of modernity who have acted in ways that have abrogated their responsibilities in *kastom*. *Nakaemas* is crucial in these narratives through the idea that people evoke their more legitimate claims to place by calling on the *kastom* power of the place, by literally speaking a *kastom* curse against another enabled by the right in *kastom* to a place, or by engaging a *nakaemas* practitioner because of their anger over another man's claim over their place. A further intricacy in the narratives of *nakaemas* and land leasing is that the masters of modernity are increasingly using the fear of *nakaemas* as a strategy to stop opposition where they lease land belonging to others.

Nakaemas 'spreads an aura of everyday terror' that is actual and undeniable in many parts of Vanuatu (Taylor in press *a*:2). Attempts to redress this terror must acknowledge that *nakaemas* threats, accusations and acts are embedded in social relations and tensions between social groups. I remained concerned that the approach of prosecution under criminal law fails to recognise, or offer any resolution, for the underlying tensions in which the accusations, threats or acts of *nakaemas* take place. Even were it legally possible to generate prosecutions under the Penal Code, this does little to address the underlying source of tensions, as is the case with land disputes. A more appropriate solution may be to consider better ways to support existing customary institutions that manage land disputes. Where accusations of *nakaemas* arise in land dispute hearings it may be helpful to create avenues for mediation or reconciliation beyond what is already available to customary institutions in legislation, including formal links with church-based institutions, trained *kastom* healers or the police. In the context of North Efate these pathways are not established and many people continue to live in daily and night-time terror of *nakaemas*. This terror is divisive and continues to create ruptures between families. Is it any surprise then that this terror can sometimes be responded to with acts of violence?

References

Ballard, C. 2014. Oceanic Historicities. *The Contemporary Pacific* 26(1):96–124.

Douglas, M. 2003. *Purity and Danger: An Analysis of Concepts of Pollution and Taboo*. Routledge: New York.

Eves, R. 2000. Sorcery's the Curse: Modernity, Envy and the Flow of Sociality in a Melanesian Society. *Journal of the Royal Anthropological Institute* 6(3):453–68.

Facey, E.E. 1981. Hereditary Chiefship in Nguna. In M.R. Allen (ed.) *Vanuatu: Politics, Economics and Ritual in Island Melanesia*. Sydney: Academic Press, 295–315.

Forsyth, M. 2006. Sorcery and the Criminal Law in Vanuatu. *Lawasia Journal* 1:1–27.

Forsyth, M. 2009. *A Bird that Flies with Two Wings: The Kastom and State Justice Systems in Vanuatu*. Canberra: ANU E Press.

Forsyth, M. 2014. Navigating the Mythscape of Biodiversity and Associated Traditional Knowledge in Pacific Island Countries. Paper presented at Traditional Knowledge Book Symposium, Griffith University, Brisbane, 28 March.

Guiart, J. 1964. Marriage Regulations and Kinship in the South Central New Hebrides. *Ethnology* 3(1):96–106.

Jolly, M. 2012. Material and Immaterial Relations: Gender, Rank and Christianity in Vanuatu. In L. Dousset and S. Tcherkézoff (eds.) *The Scope Of Anthropology: Maurice Godelier's Work in Context*. New York: Berghahn Books, 110–54.

Joshua, J. 2011a. Sorcery is Public's Biggest Fear, Says Chief. *Vanuatu Daily Post*, 28 January.

Joshua, J. 2011b. Vanuatu Can Learn from PNG's Sorcery Act: Regenvanu. *Vanuatu Daily Post*, 10 August.

Kanas, B. 2013. Sorcery in Vanuatu: Presentation of the Vanuatu Law Reform Commission. Paper presented at the Sorcery and Witchcraft-Related Killings in Melanesia: Culture, Law and Human Rights Perspectives Conference, The Australian National University, Canberra, 5–7 June 2013.

Lattas, A. 1993. Sorcery and Colonialism: Illness, Dreams and Death as Political Languages in West New Britain. *Man* (N.S.) 28:51–77.

Lindstrom, L. 2007. Survivor Vanuatu: Myths of Matriarchy Revisited. *The Contemporary Pacific* 19(1):162–74.

LiPuma, E. 1994. Sorcery and Evidence of Change in Maring Justice. *Ethnology* 33(2):147–63.

McDonnell, S. 2013. Exploring the Cultural Power of Land Law in Vanuatu: Law as a Performamce That Creates Meaning and Identities. *Intersections: Gender and Sexuality in Asia and the Pacific* December (33).

Merry, S.E. 1988. Legal Pluralism. *Law and Society Review* 22(5):869–96.

Patterson, M. 2002. Leading Lights in the 'Mother of Darkness': Perspectives on Leadership and Value in North Ambrym, Vanuatu. *Oceania* 73(2):126–42.

Rio, K. 2002. The Sorcerer as an Absented Third Person: Formations of Fear and Anger in Vanuatu. *Social Analysis* 46(3):129–54.

Rodman, M. 1987. *Masters of Tradition: Consequences of Customary Land Tenure in Longana, Vanuatu*. Vancouver: University of British Columbia Press.

Rodman, W. 1993. Sorcery and the Silencing of Chiefs: 'Words on the Wind' in Postindependence Ambae. *Journal of Anthropological Research* 49(3):217–35.

Scott, S., M. Stefanova, A. Naupa and K. Vurobaravu 2012. *Vanuatu National Leasing Profile: A Preliminary Analysis*. Washington DC: The World Bank.

Taylor, J.P. 2008. *The Other Side: Ways of Being and Place in Vanuatu*. Honolulu: University of Hawai'i Press.

Taylor, J.P. in press *a*. Intimate Enemies: Sorcery, Violence, and the Moral Economy of Agency in Vanuatu.

Taylor, J.P. in press *b*. Two Baskets Worn At Once: Christianity, Sorcery and Sacred Power in Vanuatu. In F. Magowan and C. Schwarz (eds.) *Conflicts and Convergences: Critical Perspectives on Christianity in Australia and the Pacific*. Leiden: Brill Publishers.

Tonkinson, R. 1981. Church and *Kastom* in Southeast Ambrym in Vanuatu: Politics, Economics and Ritual in Island Melanesia. In M.R. Allen (ed.) *Vanuatu: Politics, Economics and Ritual in Island Melanesia*. Sydney: Academic Press, 237–67.

Tor, R. and A. Toka 2004. *Gender,* Kastom *& Domestic Violence: A Research on the Historical Trend, Extent and Impact of Domestic Violence in Vanuatu*. Port Vila: Department of Women's Affairs.

VNSO (Vanuatu National Statistics Office) 2009. *2009 National Census of Population and Housing: Summary Release*. Port Vila: VNSO.

Wilson, M., C. Ballard and D. Kalotiti 2011. Chief Roi Mata's Domain: Challenges for a World Heritage Property in Vanuatu. *Historic Environment* 23(2):5–11.

9. Sorcery, Poison and Politics: Strategies of Self-Positioning in South Malekula, Vanuatu

Laurent Dousset

Sorcery and (black) magic are far from being limited to non-Western worlds. In the industrialised world there has also been a recrudescence in beliefs and practices that relate to a supernatural world, state of consciousness or capacity to act, often labelled 'modern occultism'.[1] Taking for granted that researchers agree on the definition of sorcery — a problem whose answer is far from obvious — we must, however, admit that the study of these widespread phenomena is subjected to differing and sometimes conflicting layers of analyses summarised by two general perspectives. The first integrates these beliefs and practices into their local historical, material and social contexts of emergence and persistence. Here sorcery is seen as the consequence — and less frequently the cause — of disruptive social conditions. Because this perspective does not account for the widespread existence of sorcery, the second perspective concedes sorcery a place among all those phenomena that seem to be inherently human and are suggestive of universalism. The former approach is peculiar to ethnography and cultural or legal studies and is occasionally tinged with what could be called 'scientific moralism' in that sorcery is depicted in terms of notions such as crisis, disruption or stress. The latter finds adepts among psychoanalysts and philosophers — and, to some extent, anthropologists — and occasionally espouses a degree of ethnocentrism, because it is a difficult task to develop a generally applicable explanation without including a particular perspective, at least that of the analyst. Rarely, however, are these perspectives combined, and too often they remain echoes of conflicting points of (world) view and epistemologies rather than integrated analyses.

Delpech-Ramey's paper is a good example illustrating the opposition of worldviews the two approaches embody:

> For Adorno, *any* contemporary fascination with the occult must be read as a symptom of the deadlock of the Enlightenment. Such a fascination indicates ... the failure of Enlightenment to liberate us fully from magic and is a sign of the ongoing crisis caused by that incomplete liberation. (Delpech-Ramey 2010:9)

---

[1] See, for example, Owen (2004).

Sorcery and liberation from it are, for Adorno (2005), the consequences of unfinished historical processes. Delpech-Ramey, espousing the second perspective mentioned above, therefore rejects the latter's conclusions and turns to the more universalistic explanations of Deleuze and Guattari (1983, 1987). Because identities and collectivities are inherently relational and constantly in a 'state of becoming', they cannot be 'the subject of straightforward modes of representation, whether in ontological or political discourse' (Delpech-Ramey 2010:10). 'What Deleuze and Guattari see in the sorcerer', Depeche-Ramey (2010:13) continues, 'is a particularly condensed ability to "go beyond" the normal place of development'. In other words, sorcery is a place where boundaries become permeable and where institutions are restructured, where distinctions such as that between animality and humanity become precarious for a reconfiguration of human and social institutions.

> Not only do Deleuze and Guattari discuss sorcery specifically in connection with problems of group formation and trans-individual processes; Deleuze's earliest writings on occult themes also show that, at least in his mind, esoteric insights and occult powers are not ultimately the tools of the renegade or the means of escape from the perplexities of human institutions, but in fact *have their ultimate significance precisely in the creative rehabilitation of political institutions*. (Delpech-Ramey 2010:16; emphasis added)

The mention of Delpech-Ramey, Adorno, Deleuze and Guattari is of course not fortuitous here since, once their positions are combined, they reflect the perspective developed in this chapter. Following Adorno and others, sorcery in Melanesia and in particular Vanuatu will be considered as the consequence of specific historical conditions. But it will also be understood as a universal means of shifting borders and differences when institutions and representations are questioned.

Anthropologists have on many occasions attempted to combine the observation that sorcery is a widespread phenomenon across many societies with the analysis of its local and historical conditions of emergence. The papers in the volume edited by Zelenietz and Lindenbaum (1981), for example, illustrate how closely sorcery is tied to the general problem of 'power' and to the transformations it undergoes in particular contexts. Sorcery and the presumed recrudescence of it in Melanesia, as Lindenbaum (1981:119) told us in the early 1980s, is best tackled through an anthropology of legitimacy and control. Such an approach could combine the analysis of the general spectrum of sorcery and of its particularistic manifestations (e.g. Zelenietz 1981).

Here I would like to further explore this anthropology of legitimacy and attempt to combine it with Deleuze and Guattari's (1983, 1987) suggestion that sorcery embodies the permeability of constant becoming and changing. Despite the distressing situations sorcery often engenders in communities, my aim is to escape the scientific moralism mentioned above and engage local ethnography in more general and constructive considerations. I suggest that sorcery is a place where belonging and being are reconfigured and therefore where notions of the 'person', the 'group', 'ethnicity' or 'power' are redefined and adapted to changing historical and material conditions. I thus consider that the particular local conditions trigger and frame the processes of social reconfiguration, but that it is in and through sorcery that the cognitive and social schema of such change can take place, because sorcery is inherently a means of shifting borders. The supernatural points to a not-yet-redefined humanity, and sorcery is a vehicle through which the uncertain contours of humanity are simultaneously expressed and resolved. These hypotheses will be illustrated using the ethnography of recent sorcery accusations in the south of Malekula, one of the main islands in the archipelago of Vanuatu.

An ethnographic account

Let me start with an ethnographic case recorded in 2011 in Vanuatu. Explanations of the social and historical background will follow after the account. A few years ago, when John came back to his village on Malekula Island after living in Port Vila, the capital, for a few years, he claims he became the victim of sorcery attempts. Two elderly men, close brothers of a politically important chief from a nearby hamlet, were the primary suspects. 'Two men', John says, 'who I thought were close to me as well, whom my family had fed and dressed when they were in need. Two men I trusted.'[2] The story unfolds like a play.

Act 1: One day, the two old men invited John to drink kava made from bushes in their garden and prepared by themselves. Kava is a drink made from the roots of a pepper tree. It has sedative and anaesthetic properties. In many communities throughout Vanuatu, kava drinking, usually taking place at sunset, has become an important social time for collective gatherings. John is used to drinking kava every evening. But somehow he felt this invitation was a set-up. He hesitated and finally decided not to join the group. His doubts were confirmed the next day. He says that the two old men were angry that he had not come. They reproached him because they had had to throw away the kava they had prepared. This seemed to have confirmed his suspicions, since 'no one', John says, 'throws away kava just because someone doesn't show up! Something must have been wrong with this kava.'

---

2   The quotations are translated from Bislama, the pidgin of Vanuatu.

Act 2: John and his family, like other families in the village, have several gardens. One of these is on the other side of the peninsula, too far away to get there, work and come back the same day. It was in the middle of this garden, which grows yam, taro and cacao, that one day John discovered a plant he had never put into the ground. 'It was a sign', he says. 'Someone had buried something in my garden and planted this shrub on top of it to hide the traces.' Not knowing what to do, he ran home worried. But on arriving in his hamlet, he immediately decided to return to the garden and burn it. While walking up the hill determined to destroy the garden, he felt a strange presence. He stopped, turned around and saw one of the two old men mentioned earlier waiting, hidden behind some trees. Seeing that John had stopped, the old man came forward and said 'days are long, but life is short', John recalls.

Act 3: 'One day, the two old men prepared poison from toxic plants', John explains with assurance. The poison was intended to harm him. 'But one of the two men forgot to wash his hands after preparing it', John claims. In the evening, when drinking kava, he inadvertently dipped one of his fingers into the liquid, poisoned himself and died. The inhabitants of the surrounding hamlets were quick to accuse John of sorcery. Many public meetings took place in which John tried to demonstrate his innocence and convince the community of it. The situation became intolerable and highly conflictual. Only one solution seemed to remain: to leave the village again with his wife and kids and go back to town. The victim had become the suspected aggressor.

However, this would have meant accepting the accusations and leaving as the culprit. This is when John had the idea of calling a Marist priest from another island, a man reputed and feared for his powers. 'You have to pay the priest', John says, 'but when he is here, when he preaches and you are carrying poison with you, you immediately die, so powerful is he.' The priest came and organised a public meeting during which John had to swear on the bible that he possessed no poison and that he had not killed the old man. He publicly and in front of the priest proclaimed his innocence. The same ceremony was repeated during Sunday mass at the mission. 'At this moment', John says, 'many other inhabitants began to fear the consequences of the priest's power. Dozens of them went up to the altar and deposited leaves and cloth in which they had hidden poison.'

Final Act: Before leaving, the priest told John: 'In one year exactly, to the day, something will happen and you will understand who the true culprit is, who has poisoned whom.' 'One year later to the day', John says, 'the other old man, the one who had survived, offered me a cursed apple.' But John did not trust him and refused it, and because he had handled it wrongly, the second old man died as well. According to custom, the body was rolled in mats and buried. But it poured with rain for hours and hours and the tomb filled with water, freeing the corpse so that it floated to the surface. Several times the old man's family tried to weigh down the floating body so that it would sink. But the old man kept floating. It was only after many hours that the corpse finally sank under the weight of dirt and mud. 'This was the sign', John says, 'the sign of the deserved punishment'. And John was washed and freed of all accusations and suspicions. It was *he* who had been the victim.

Let me start the analysis with some general comments. The first point that needs to be made concerns the distinction between sorcery and poisoning. The ethnography shows that sorcery and poisoning follow similar processes and that they are intimately linked to each other in Vanuatu. In the symbolic and rhetoric landscape of south Malekula, both express a specific relationship to the body and the penetration thereof, both aim at destruction and both have an identical relationship with the imaginary that accompanies cannibalism. Moreover, the sorcerer is thought to manipulate poison, and poison is primarily the weapon of a sorcerer. Poisoning does not necessarily have to happen through direct ingestion alone, but can be done from a distance by means of the sorcerer's diverse powers. Hence, while poison is not the only means of action available to the sorcerer, it is certainly a favourite element of his repertoire. Furthermore, people who are accused of dealing in poisons are immediately considered to be sorcerers. In fact, in contrast to Rio (2002), who presents the prototypical form of sorcery in Vanuatu as a process in which the body is emptied and the still living person sent home to die later, I believe poisoning to be the ideal typical and most tangible form of sorcery because it best reflects the articulation of proximity and distance that sorcery seems to be all about in the cases I have encountered. This chapter will hopefully make this point clear. Therefore, sorcery and poisoning are here interchangeable words.

The second general point concerns some of the Christian, and more generally Western, elements reflected in John's recollections. A Marist priest is called and the revelation happens in church, during mass. The punishment endured by the floating body during long-lasting rain and floods, undoubtedly recalling Noah's story, points to Christian and more generally Western (the 'poisoned apple') themes of interpretation that have been studied by Eriksen (2008), for example. That there is a degree of syncretism in contemporary sorcery is beyond doubt, but also beyond the scope of this chapter. Here we will rather deal with the conditions of emergence and expression of sorcery accusations as reflecting changing configurations of being. Having established these two preliminary points, let me now turn to depicting the historical and cultural background to John's account.

Talking it Through

Sorcery as a consequence of historical conditions

John and his family live in an area of great historical disturbances. The peninsula of Port Sandwich, located in the south-east of Malekula Island, was once split between three clans, according to one version of local history: the Pnoamb, the Lambru and the Bangu. Each clan (people call them 'tribes') occupied and owned a territory extending across the peninsula and parallel to that of its neighbouring group, thus providing each of them with access to both the coast with its marine resources and the inland hills where gardens were cultivated. Although the villages are now exclusively situated along the coast, they were formerly also established in the hinterland, in the hills, and families seem to have practised some degree of movement between the inland hamlets and those along the coast.

Groups of brothers, the eldest of these often playing the role of head of the clan, distributed plots of land to individual families for their gardens. All of these families still have today several gardens at unequal distances from the hamlets in cleared and burned forest areas. People mainly grow taro, yams and bananas; now also tomatoes, cabbage, cassava, peanuts, lettuce and even strawberries. The soil is fertile, especially when winds carry volcanic ashes from eruptions on nearby islands. But the soil is also shallow and rotation of the gardens is a necessity. The pressure on land is thus not evaluated only in terms of the surface immediately accessible but includes the capacity to access land in coming years.

These clans, like other groups in southern Malekula such as the people of Southwest Bay studied by Deacon (1934), are characterised by a strong patrilineal ideology. Each patrilineal clan, sometimes divided into lineages, consisted of several hamlets that were the owners of an identifiable and bounded territory. These various hamlets were associated with a main village established by the clan's ancestor. This central hamlet, the heart of the clan, hosted the ritual site (called *nasara*) in which an important element was the men's house (*batu*). The *batu* housed the clan's sacred objects, for example, the skulls of deceased ancestors that had not yet undergone the second funerals (cf. Guideri and Pellizzi 1981; Huchet 1976; Servy et al. 2012). The men's house was divided into several sectors reflecting the religious and political ranks or grades of the men. The young initiates slept at the entrance, while the bottom of the *batu* could only be occupied by *namals*, the most senior and advanced ritual chiefs. *Namals* were considered to be almost spiritual beings able to transcend 'natural' and 'human' boundaries. They were also feared sorcerers and, for some at least, renowned cannibals, so people say. It is important to note that clan chiefs or elders — the landowners — were not necessarily also ritual and ranked chiefs, *namals*. The latter could be (and some say that they even were systematically) people from other groups and tribes, foreigners gaining access to power through the sacrifice and redistribution of pigs.

As already alluded to, inhabitants of the peninsula espouse several versions of the local history (see Dousset n.d. b). Most likely however, before the strong presence of the colonial powers, the peninsula was inhabited and owned by the three clans mentioned. They were linked through close religious, political and kinship ties. The kinship terminology and marriage rules were oblique and are thus evidence for the existence of these three groups and their organic interrelationship, since oblique marriages necessitate triangular relationships between groups (Dousset n.d. a).

The first white settlers arrived in Port Sandwich in 1884 and missionaries in 1890. These events severely disrupted the political and demographic situation of the peninsula. In the political domain, this was because missionaries struggled against the graded chiefs, who exercised their power in the religious sphere and used sorcery and cannibalism as a means to consolidate their authority. As might have been expected, the missionaries and settlers favoured negotiations with clan chiefs, who were the landowners and had authority in everyday affairs. The arrival of white settlers also had important demographic consequences, since their usurpation of land — often in return for a handful of tobacco or a gun — and the presence of new tools and goods as well as Christianity and the hope for pacification had significant effects on migration. Linguistic and ethnographic data, as well as ethnohistorical narratives and myths, reflects previous strong migratory pressures that increased significantly with the arrival of the Marists. Many groups from the interior of Malekula Island gradually moved to the coastal regions of the peninsula.

The period between 1884 and 1920 was hence a period of considerable disruption, conflict and adjustment between Melanesian groups who had to learn to live together and between Melanesians and white settlers. The situation culminated in 1920 with a new era, when the French colonial delegation was installed in Port Sandwich and when mass baptisms of the local population were organised. The strong foreign presence increasingly undermined all forms of indigenous power, not just that of the graded chiefs and *namals* as in former times, and resulted in the weakening of the authority of clan chiefs and landowners. The Melanesian hierarchies were being levelled out.

Like the later events of 1980, the year of Vanuatu's independence, the arrival of the French administration in 1920 is described by locals as having led to substantial change. Tensions and conflicts between families and clans were replaced by what they describe as a period of new social construction, with a sense of belonging to a new collective project. Port Sandwich was the new France in the New Hebrides, with its school, hospital and administrative services. It was a time, people stress, when everyone had work, when roads were built and kept clean, when the centre of the village was lit at night, when order reigned and when sorcery and cannibalism had disappeared. Port Sandwich was to become a new society in which former hierarchies had disappeared. Under the control of the French administration, the Melanesians became equal among themselves. What appears to be a situation idealised by the vast majority of the approximately 1,500 inhabitants of Port Sandwich (at least by the population that had actually experienced the presence of the French authorities before 1980) abruptly changed at the time of independence. Here we must again make a historical detour to better understand how, in the eyes of the population, this idealised society ended with independence, despite the colonisers leaving and handing back at least part of the land to the Melanesians.

The movement for the independence of Vanuatu was led by two important Melanesian figures, Father Walter Lini, anglophone and Presbyterian, and Father Gérard Leymang, francophone and Marist. Walter Lini was the main leader, and he and his friend Gérard Leymang both occupied in turn the position of prime minister, preparing for independence and drafting the future constitution of the independent state. Together, they led the National Party. However, shortly before independence, the two friends separated and adopted deeply contrasting perspectives. Lini announced his 'one country, one language, one religion' slogan, implying that the national language was to be Bislama, the pidgin of Vanuatu, and the national religion Protestantism. Leymang could not accept this statement and created his own party, the Union of Communities of the New Hebrides (UCNH), which later became the Union of Moderate Parties. It attracted mainly francophone Catholics. Lini, meanwhile, founded the Vanua'aku party with predominantly anglophone Protestants as members. The fundamental difference between these two parties was both simple and a source of conflict — the Vanua'aku party and Walter Lini demanded immediate independence, while the UCNH and Gérard Leymang wanted autonomy first and independence only at a later stage.

Let me now return to Port Sandwich. The UCNH party was well established in the peninsula. Indeed, Father Leymang was born in Port Sandwich, where his family still lives today. The peninsula had thus become the bastion of autonomy and was seen by Lini and his people as a place of betrayal of and rebellion against independence. On the day of independence, Papuan and Ni-Vanuatu troops, assisted by an Australian infrastructure, came to plunder the facilities of Port Sandwich and arrested the vast majority of its adult male population, some of whom were to be imprisoned for several months on Santo Island. In the eyes of the inhabitants of Port Sandwich, independence had thus become a nightmare and reminded them of humiliation and denigration and the loss of all benefits and privileges. Independence had become the word for all evil and eventually stigmatised the nascent state itself and its dysfunctions. Expensive education and health services, corruption and poverty were, and for some still are, seen as the consequences of a badly prepared independence movement. More importantly, however, the apparent equality among Melanesians that had been instituted by the French colonial power was crumbling. Internal hierarchies again emerged, with some clans and their leaders claiming to be the original inhabitants and landowners, descendants of the three original clans, and reducing others to being 'man-come', foreigners and invaders. There was again a big upsurge in accusations of sorcery.

Questions concerning the re-emergence of sorcery

With the arrival of missionaries and plantations owned by white settlers, other groups gradually, but massively, migrated towards the peninsula and settled in the area, as I mentioned earlier. While three *nasara* (a clan's ritual place including semi-buried stones that symbolise the clan's ancestors) seem to have existed on the peninsula before the missionaries arrived, today more than 20 are claimed to be there. Demographic pressure became a problem and landownership a disputed concept. The pacification of intergroup conflicts and the levelling of indigenous hierarchies by the colonial administration, as well as intermarriages, exchanges and the shared experience of colonial history that followed the migration of many groups to the coast, blurred the peripheries of the clans and was at the origin of a more uniform social landscape. The issue became crucial after independence, with the necessity and desire to identify traditional landowners once again. The question was and still is today: which families are the descendants of the peninsula's 'original' inhabitants, and what are their social and spatial boundaries?

These discussions and conflicts are accompanied by an increase in the perception of sorcery attempts. The reasons for this are the new means of accumulating wealth and of displaying it, which have consequences on the control of social values, as Eves (2000) has also shown for the Lelet. But the apparent increase in sorcery is also a result of the previously blurred peripheries of clans and domestic units during the colonial period. The haziness of these peripheries had to some extent been a useful means for establishing a oneness against other more distant Melanesian groups and white settlers. In the postcolonial context, however, internal divisions and boundaries have to be re-established and in some cases reconstructed. This is so because the demographic pressure on land is considered too high, but also because there is an increasing attitude of segregation and differentiation between people who consider themselves to be locals and who therefore consider others to be foreigners. Accusations of sorcery are among the tangible expressions of the attempts — and the rejections thereof — to re-establish social entities and hierarchies. In this context, one may ask whether it is not indeed in John's interest to be a victim of sorcery attempts? Does this not confirm him and his clan as arousing jealousy and thus as being 'authentic', descendants of one of the three original clans? Otherwise why would people try to eradicate him and his family? Let us attempt to answer these questions in more detail.

After independence, it is said, there was an impressive increase in cases of poisoning and sorcery in general — or at least in accusations of sorcery — in south Malekula, as elsewhere in Vanuatu and in many postcolonial situations. Some researchers link the phenomenon to a context of political insecurity and instability in which authority and its forms are questioned, in which new and old systems of power confront each other and in which new kinds of economic inequality emerge. For these researchers, sorcery is predominantly a thing of modernity. Because of its intrinsic link to the state, nation building and the emergence of a capitalist economy, many authors have analysed the complex relationship between sorcery, state governance and legislation (for example, and of course first and foremost, Comaroff and Comaroff 1993, and Geschiere 1988 for Africa; for Vanuatu, Forsyth 2006; Rio 2010; Rodman 1993 etc.).

Others have had more universalistic or cross-cultural approaches and seen in sorcery the necessary process of identifying the intentionality of social disruption in general (e.g. Clément 2003) and a way to perceive and interact with the invisible (Bonhomme 2005), or a means of deflecting grief on the death of a loved one towards an external figure (Stephen 1999). Still others, but again in a cross-cultural spirit, see in sorcery and magic a kind of religious behaviour, a form of communication promoting or protecting cooperative social relationships, in the case of sorcery, through threat and fear (e.g. Palmer et al. 2010).

In these latter approaches, sorcery is not tied to modernity as such but is a quasi-universal and not necessarily historically situated phenomenon because, as Bonhomme (2005:271) writes for Africa, 'modernity and tradition designate … not so much heterogeneous temporalities as different scales that coexist and are interconnected' (my translation). We have indeed seen above that sorcery was a means to regulate power even before the arrival of the colonial powers and the state and that it was a means in the hands of the *namals*, the ritual chiefs.

In most of these studies, be it from a historical, political and legal perspective or from a cognitive, psychoanalytical and cross-cultural one, sorcery is seen as a correlative of unstable and disruptive situations or as producing such situations, if not both at the same time. I would like to suggest that we could also turn the problem upside down. Accusations of sorcery are of course stressful and sometimes result in harm and even executions. What I would like to explore is how what seems to matter in the cases I have analysed is the answers to the following question: how come those who are suspected of sorcery are not complete foreigners, not unknown people, but are often (if not always) relatively close kin (or potentially close kin), people one has fed and protected, as John says, or people one could marry? How come the danger of sorcery comes from the immediate periphery?

One of the central points made here has been aptly put by Bloch (1998) and relates to the notions of commensality and consubstantiality,[3] even though I would like to go somewhat further. He writes:

> the Zafimaniry are as obsessed by the theme of poisoning as they are by the theme of domestic oneness. In reality, for them, the two are different sides of the same coin. (Bloch 1998:144)

Geschiere (1995:18) and Bonhomme (2005:259) have made similar statements for Africa. For the former, even in modern contexts, sorcery remains linked to the intimacy of the family. For the latter, sorcery articulates explanations of misfortune and the expression of conflicts within the lineage group. Sorcery is something local, not necessarily global. And it is so local that it seems to be intimately tied to values (see Eves 2000), the family or domestic unit and changes therein.

Inquiring into what are, among the Zafimaniry, the vehicles for the strong domestic unit ideology, Bloch (1998:135) defines *commensality* as the action of eating together and as one of the most powerful operators of social process. He talks of food as being a social conductor whose purpose is to reinforce or establish a shared substance. By recalling Durkheim's notion of organic solidarity, he explains how sharing food from the same animal or eating and drinking from the same bowl[4] is among the strongest social conductors. 'In many cultures', he writes, 'the sharing of meat is a sign of supreme closeness … which makes meat eating particularly suitable for feasts and celebrations' (ibid.).[5] Sharing food expresses and causes bodily unification, quite similar to that of kinship and marriage (Bloch 1998:137). We may also recall here the work of Lévi-Strauss (1968), among many others, on the relationship between eating and sexuality.

---

3   Also see Pitt-Rivers (1973) and Dousset (2005, 2013) for use of the notion of 'consubstantiality' in other but comparable contexts.
4   As opposed to eating separate pieces of different origins, which would be mechanical solidarity.
5   Also see Bonhomme (2005:261, note 4) for Gabon, who writes that sorcery is based on animal predation with the victim being the meat for the sorcerer who is represented as a panther.

Eating the same food unites bodies, eating different food distances bodies, Bloch explains, and Zafimaniry families strive to be continually unified by biology or kinship and as commensal units.

Although important, this is obviously a very general statement. Indeed, we may recall the work of Carsten (1997) who explains that for Malays being one family or kinship group cannot be envisaged in terms that do not, in part, refer to the act of eating what has been cooked on one hearth (quoted in Bloch 1998:139). Or I might add an example from the Australian Western Desert where the word designating the adopting mother also means the one who maintains the hearth on which food is cooked. Joining a family is about becoming consubstantial to the latter through the consumption of its food (Dousset 2011).

The relationship between eating and belonging has been widely documented and discussed. What is relevant for our concern here is that, like sexual relations or marriage, sharing food is an act that belongs to the mapping of social space through the redefinition of who sits in the inner circle, and for what reason, and who is outside; it is about the definition of proximity and distance, of self and stranger. Commensality, Bloch (1998:146) writes, is 'a means by which the domestic house unit can be adventurously expanded' (see also Munn 1986:13).

But this is not without risks, because 'the better a food is a conductor that creates bodily closeness, the better it is a medium for poison' (Bloch 1998:145). Interestingly, among the Zafimaniry, Bloch cites the drinking and sharing of rum (and we can think of kava as a similar medium in Vanuatu, as John's story testifies) as being the best conductor and thus also the best vehicle for poisoning, because it is a medium of and for social equality. Differences and shame or restraint are temporarily neutralised. Here I quote Bloch for the last time:

> the risks involved in eating are normally neutralized by eating with those one knows well. If one has to, or wants to, eat with distant others, however, it is normal that the fear of poisoning should increase, and, as a result, the willingness to overcome that fear becomes proof of a commitment that is continually being bargained about in the process of establishing moral social links. (Bloch 1998:147)

What can we learn from this? First, poison takes the same path as the social processes that confirm, reinforce or expand the domestic unit, those with whom one shares relatedness through commensality. This recalls another account I was given in the field, in which a man explained to me that sorcery 'arrives always from where you don't expect it, from family you trust and who share food or kava with you'. Sorcery is the invisible agent for the refusal of sameness and for both the usage *and* denial of the powers of commensality. It is the 'obscure underside of kinship' (Bonhomme 2005:265).

Second, when poison, or sorcery in general, comes into play, the boundaries — how permeable they are — of the circle of social confidence, of 'natural' trust, are questioned and remodelled. This happens when 'almost outsiders' are to be made members of the domestic oneness, when the boundaries are either expanded or retracted. I can again quote the same man, a self-declared magician and healer, when he added that 'the danger comes from your family ... but not your actual parents or children or brothers; it comes from nephews, cousins, in-laws ... who have been convinced and paid to do it'. These are people who are not unambiguously part of one's inner circle. They are those with whom oneness does not flow automatically, so to speak, but has to be acquired through sexuality, marriage and reciprocity. They are at the periphery; they *are* the periphery. Just like food, they themselves work as connectors to other lineages and domestic groups. They are potentially the obscure underside of kinship just as poison is the obscure underside of food. No wonder, one is tempted to state bluntly, there is a recrudescence in accusations of sorcery in postcolonial Port Sandwich with the boundaries, and therefore the peripheries, of social circles being reconstructed, remodelled and questioned.

The 'traditional' sorcerer, clan politics and humanity

There is another point that needs to be made, briefly at least, that was also addressed by Forsyth (2006): the 'generalisation' of sorcery and its subsequent loss of public legitimacy. In the south of Malekula, as was mentioned earlier, there were two parallel power structures that seem to have overlapped but only to a certain extent. The first was situated in the clan itself and in its chief. He was the guardian of the land and of the kin group's continuity. While it was not impossible for this kind of chief to also be a magician or even a sorcerer, the latter would not usually be part of his repertoire. The second power structure, on the other hand, resided in the system of graded chiefs, a process in which men and women could take part through the organisation of rituals that included the sacrifice of large amounts of pigs (see Guérard 1994). Ritual after ritual and grade after grade, these chiefs would move further away from being merely humans and progressively become spirit-like beings. As already mentioned, the highest of these grades, just before becoming an actual spirit, was that of the *namal*. *Namals* were feared for their magical powers and for their capacity to take on, like any sorcerer, a morphology different from that of the human being. They were also said to have been allowed to practise or to have practised cannibalism. A *namal*, or for that matter any graded chief, does not also have to be a local clan chief. Many are indeed reported to have been individual migrants from other groups who were adopted into local clans. Thus, while they were seen to be able to cross the borders between humanity and the supernatural, they were also at the periphery of the social group which had adopted them: foreigners but not unknown, people who married in, people with whom one shares things, in particular food, but not without some fear and hesitation, people who may eat those who feed them. The last *namal* of the Port Sandwich peninsula, who was killed by the French authorities in the 1920s, is said to have made extensive use of his cannibalistic rights and demanded the sacrifice of the other clans' masculine descendants. He thus directly interfered, through the sacrifice of the boys and sorcery, in other clans' capacity to reproduce themselves as a social unit.

Still today in Port Sandwich, the image of the sorcerer points towards features and capacities that, like those of the *namals* who no longer exist in Port Sandwich, sit on the blurred periphery of humanity. Indeed, people's accounts make it possible to paint a picture of the presumed sorcerer defined by three main characteristics: a changing morphology, unsocial attitudes, and destructive means of action.

Morphology

The sorcerer is considered to be a recognisable human. He may indeed be living in the midst of others. However, because of his ability to communicate with natural species and spirits and to handle dangerous human and non-human substances, his morphology is not permanent. He can even turn into an invisible creature. He may appear as a shark, as a bat, or as an insect flying in the twilight. The sorcerer has a changing morphology, he travels and works at night or in the dark and is not effortlessly noticeable: the shark coming from the depths that suddenly attacks at the surface, or the insect or bat that stings or bites humans in the evening or at night to inject its fatal substances. His behaviour is the opposite to that expected from humans whose movements are supposed to be predictable and visible.

Social attitude

In most accounts, the sorcerer is thought to be socially disinterested, if not dissocialised. He may not necessarily act of his own initiative, but may do so on behalf of another person who rewards him for his services. He thus has no compassion and is a ruthless professional. While those who may ask for the sorcerer's services are known kinsmen, the sorcerer himself remains voluntarily outside kinship. This is either because he no longer obeys the obligations associated with kinship or has become emotionally distanced, or because he is a foreigner who has forgotten or not yet been included into the local family or marital history. The sorcerer withdraws into the hills, into the bush, living on his own, eating little or not at all, respecting sexual abstinence, and avoiding contact with other human beings.

Means of action

The sorcerer has various modes of action to harm and destroy, but two modes are prototypical: body-draining is the typical form of sorcery according to Rio (2002), who worked on the island of Ambrym. Direct or remote poisoning is, in my opinion, the prototypical form of sorcery in Malekula, even though both types of action are thought to have existed formerly on the two islands. When body-draining, the sorcerer attracts his victim, kills them in one way or another (usually through poisoning or strangulation), empties the body and fills it up with plants. He then sews it back together and sends the victim home to die, alive but with no memory of what has happened.

Poisoning may take several forms. It can be done remotely or by physical ingestion of toxic substances. Potions are composed of plant substances and human parts: bones, blood or guts. The poison is thought to burn and destroy the body from the inside. In both cases, whether it takes place from a distance or through actual ingestion, penetration of the body is required. This penetration has to be undertaken through the use of powerful and dangerous substances, including those that are prohibited and even taboo, such as the blood and liquids of corpses. Conversely, non-sorcerers value cooked food eaten in common. Eating together, sharing a meal or kava are highly valued and define what it is to be a human being.

These images and elements that define the sorcerer, and for that matter also the *namals*, stand at the periphery of humanity or even reflect the opposite of the ideal typical conception of a human. The sorcerer is unpredictable, morphologically unstable, a known foreigner, a loner and a dissocialised individual valuing sexual abstinence, destruction and contagion. The ideal typical human being, on the other hand, is expected to be predictable and morphologically stable, to be a kinsman living collectively and socially and valuing abundance, reproduction, constructive attitudes and consubstantiality.

Conclusion

There are theories or suggestions that attempt to explain sorcery as a universal phenomenon. These approaches are often cognitive or psychoanalytical. And there are approaches that frame sorcery as a product of local cultural systems and historical conditions. This chapter has attempted to combine a cross-cultural with a contextual approach.

The cross-cultural aspects are those that link sorcery to the attempts of social groups to reproduce themselves in time and space through commensality. Sorcery, and in particular poison, as well as cannibalism, makes use of the same channels as humanity and its endeavour to become consubstantial, but has exactly the opposite ambition: to blur and weaken this commensality by eating or destroying those who eat and live together. If sorcery is the place where boundaries and institutions are reshaped, where being is redefined, it is not so surprising that sorcerers are in many cultures reported to also have cannibalistic and antisocial attitudes, as Needham (1978) has already pointed out.

John's story could have been looked at from various perspectives, such as through the Christian symbolism deployed. From the local historical perspective, I have approached the particular situation through the idea that sorcery is intimately tied to three elements. First, the definition and transformation of what is locally a social unit of commensality and how its boundaries are or have been shaped and reshaped by historical processes. Second, the idea that accusations and counter-accusations of sorcery are obviously embedded in local politics, in particular those politics which involve discussions on 'authenticity' and the primacy of culture and landownership, and those aspects of self-positioning that define belonging expressed through mutual trust or lack of it. Third, in certain contexts, being in danger of becoming the victim of sorcery provides proof of someone else's jealousy and one's own importance and rightfulness in the context of the abovementioned historical processes.

However, from the cross-cultural perspective, as Delpech-Ramey (2010) explains when discussing Guattari and Deleuze, sorcery is the condensed ability to 'go beyond' the normal place of development. It is the sign of and the means for shifting boundaries and institutions in general. It is the place where distinctions and similarities between animality and humanity are redefined and where the legitimacy of power is questioned. It is suggested that these are the universal aspects of sorcery. The local historical aspects are only those from which and on which sorcery works and acts.

References

Adorno, T. 2005. *Minima Moralia: Reflections on a Damaged Life* [Minima Moralia: Reflexionen aus dem Beschädigten Leben]. London: Verso.

Bloch, M. 1998. Commensality and Poisoning. *Social Research* 66(1):133–49.

Bonhomme, J. 2005. Voir Par-Derrière. Sorcellerie, Initiation et Perception au Gabon. *Social Anthropology* 13(3):259–73.

Clément, F. 2003. L'esprit Ensorcelé. *Terrain* 41:121–36.

Comaroff, J. and J.L. Comaroff (eds.) 1993. *Modernity and its Malcontents: Ritual and Power in Postcolonial Africa*. Chicago: Chicago University Press.

Deacon, A.B. 1934. *Malekula: A Vanishing People in the New Hebrides*. London: George Routledge & Sons.

Deleuze, G. and F. Guattari 1983. *Anti-Oedipus* [L'anti-Oedipe]. Minneapolis: University of Minnesota Press [1972].

Deleuze, G. and F. Guattari 1987. *A Thousand Plateaus* [Mille Plateaux]. Minneapolis: University of Minnesota Press [1980].

Delpech-Ramey, J. 2010. Deleuze, Guattari, and the 'Politics of Sorcery'. *SubStance* 39(1):8–23.

Dousset, L. 2005. Structure and Substance: Combining 'Classic' and 'Modern' Kinship Studies in the Australian Western Desert. *TAJA: The Australian Journal of Anthropology* 16(1):18–30.

Dousset, L. 2011. *Australian Aboriginal Kinship: An Introductory Handbook with Particular Emphasis on the Western Desert*. Marseille: Pacific-Credo Publications.

Dousset, L. 2013. From Consanguinity to Consubstantiality: Julian Pitt-Rivers' 'The Kith and the Kin'. *Structure and Dynamics: eJournal of Anthropological and Related Sciences*. 6(1). http://www.escholarship.org/uc/item/4fr203tx.

Dousset, L. n.d. *a*. Parenté, Territoire et Démographie. In M. Jeudy-Ballini (ed.) *Mélanges*. Press unknown.

Dousset, L. n.d. *b*. Rupture et Continuité dans le Sud de Malekula. In E. Nolet and P. Lindenmann (eds). *Logiques Locales, Logiques Nationales en Mélanésie*. Paris: Société des Océanistes.

Eriksen, A. 2008. *Gender, Christianity and Change in Vanuatu: An Analysis of Social Movements in North Ambrym*. Burlington: Ashgate.

Eves, R. 2000. Sorcery's the Curse: Modernity, Envy and the Flow of Sociality in a Melanesian Society. *Journal of the Royal Anthropological Institute* 6(3):453–68.

Forsyth, M. 2006. Sorcery and the Criminal Law in Vanuatu. *Lawasia Journal* 1:1–27.

Geschiere, P. 1988. Sorcery and the State: Popular Modes of Action among the Maka of Southeast Cameroon. *Critique of Anthropology* 8:35–63.

Geschiere, P. 1995. *Sorcellerie et Politique en Afrique. La Viande des Autres*. Paris: Karthala.

Guerard, C. 1994. Mana et Pouvoir dans les Sociétés à Hiérarchie de Grades (Vanuatu). *Archives des Science Sociales des Religions* 85:153–74.

Guideri, R. and F. Pellizzi 1981. Shadows: Nineteen Tableaux on the Cult of the Dead in Malekula, Eastern Melanesia. *RES: Anthropology and Aesthetics* 2:5–69.

Huchet, C. 1976. Fête Funéraire à Lendombwey (Centre-Sud Malekula) 'Netemstamp' (Septembre 1974). *Journal de la Société des Océanistes* 32(53):293–8.

Lévi-Strauss, C. 1968. *Mythologiques III. L'origine des Manières de Table*. Paris: Plon.

Lindenbaum, S. 1981. Images of the Sorcerer in Papua New Guinea. In M. Zelenietz and S. Lindenbaum (eds.) *Sorcery and Social Change in Melanesia. Social Analysis* No. 8 (Special Issue). Adelaide: University of Adelaide, 119–28.

Munn, N.D. 1986. *The Fame of Gawa: A Symbolic Study of Value Transformation in a Massim (Papua New Guinea) Society*. Cambridge: Cambridge University Press.

Needham, R. 1978. *Primordial Characters*. Charlottesville: University of Virginia Press.

Owen, A. 2004. *The Place of Enchantment: British Occultism and the Culture of the Modern*. Chicago: Chicago University Press.

Palmer, C.T., L.B. Steadman, C. Cassidy and K. Coe 2010. The Importance of Magic to Social Relationships. *Zygon* 45(2):317–37.

Pitt-Rivers, J. 1973. The Kith and the Kin. In J.R. Goody (ed.) *The Character of Kinship*. Cambridge: Cambridge University Press, 89–105.

Rio, K. 2002. The Sorcerer as an Absented Third Person: Formations of Fear and Anger in Vanuatu. *Social Analysis* 46(3):129–54.

Rio, K. 2010. Handling Sorcery in a State System of Law: Magic, Violence and *Kastom* in Vanuatu. *Oceania* 80(2):183–97.

Rodman, W. 1993. Sorcery and the Silencing of Chiefs: 'Words on the Wind' in Postindependence Ambae. *Journal of Anthropological Research* 49(3):217–35.

Servy, A., M. Abong and L. Dousset 2012. *Funérailles à Malekula, Vanuatu. Catalogue Augmenté et Documenté de L'exposition Photographique 'Georges Liotard (1974)'*. Marseille: CREDO and VKS.

Stephen, M. 1999. Witchcraft, Grief and the Ambivalence of Emotions. *American Ethnologist* 26(3):711–37.

Zelenietz, M. 1981. Sorcery and Social Change: An Introduction. In M. Zelenietz and S. Lindenbaum (eds). *Sorcery and Social Change in Melanesia. Social Analysis* No. 8 (Special Issue). Adelaide: University of Adelaide, 3–14.

Zelenietz, M. and S. Lindenbaum (eds.) 1981. *Sorcery and Social Change in Melanesia. Social Analysis* No. 8 (Special Issue). Adelaide: University of Adelaide.

Part 2: Legal Dimensions to the Belief in Witchcraft and Sorcery

10. The Courts, the Churches, the Witches and their Killers

Christine Stewart

Introduction

This chapter discusses the approaches of the formal legal system of Papua New Guinea (PNG) to cases of witch-killing, from colonial times to the present. The title is based on that of a movie from more than 20 years ago, entitled *The Cook, the Thief, His Wife and Her Lover*, a movie I saw accidentally and found totally gruesome and unappealing. But this adaptation of the title seemed apt, because there are some very gruesome aspects to witch-killing in PNG today (Forsyth 2013).

Sorcerer versus witch, victim versus killer

First, some matters of terminology and categorisation. What is the difference between a sorcerer and a witch? It is difficult to generalise across the many and varied cultures of PNG (Reay 1976; see also Stephen 1987). Practitioners may be differentiated in various ways; for example, sorcerers are usually but not always male, witches may or may not always be female. Different means may be employed to achieve the desired end, which could be injury, damage or death or, conversely, to produce a positive outcome such as love requited or a successful harvest. Skills may be acquired in different ways — learned from a relative, or through possession by some form of malicious spirit creature. They may be used for good or bad, sometimes only against enemies or strangers, sometimes only against other members of the practitioner's social group, sometimes against anyone.

The general consensus among those who write on the topic in relation to PNG today is that a sorcerer is usually a male who possesses skills which have been learned, often from a male relative, and which may be used for good or bad, but are often only used for good, whereas malevolent sorcery may or should only be used against enemies. A witch, on the other hand, may be either a male or female who has been possessed by some form of evil spirit creature, and who uses evil magic against anyone, because he or she is not in full control (Gibbs 2012).

These are very generalised definitions, which may not hold true in all societies or at all times. In this chapter, I have used the terms interchangeably as fits the context. I will also be talking only of bad or 'black' magic.

A more problematic question is who is the killer, who is the victim? The term 'witch-killing' can be understood in two opposed ways: the killing (or other harm) that is done *by* practitioners of sorcery; and the killing *of* sorcerers and witches by individuals or communities (Zocca 2009).

Witch-killing in Europe

PNG's formal legal system, derived from that of Europe in general and England in particular, has by various means tried to tackle both issues. It is relevant and revealing therefore to consider the history of witch-killing in Europe, where the condemnation of sorcery and witchcraft has a long history, stretching from the fourth to the eighteenth century (Bailey 2008; see also Briggs 1996). The early Christians believed that Christ came partly to overcome superstition and demonic pagan magic. From the sixth to the early eleventh century, magic was paganism except for healing practices. If Christianity approved it, it was not magic, it was something inspired by natural forces or divine power. Harsh punishments were imposed upon magic and its practitioners, but states at that time were fluid and lacked the powers to enforce their laws.

However, during the high medieval period of the eleventh and twelfth centuries, states stabilised, bureaucracies expanded, Roman law was reintroduced and combined with existing systems, canon and church law became more highly developed and the views of the educated elites diverged from those of the grassroots. The ruling classes started identifying and punishing marginal groups, including practitioners of magic. Earlier accusatorial procedures had placed the burden of proof on the accuser, which made it hard to prove the covert practices of magic. Despite trial by ordeal, the accuser was in a difficult position: if he failed to prove his case, he himself was often subject to prosecution.

Then in the twelfth and thirteenth centuries, churches became more organised and bureaucratic. Intellectual revival began, schools and then universities were founded, and legal and intellectual structures for understanding magic were developed. The inquisitorial system was introduced to investigate heresy. This placed the burden of proof onto the tribunal, which could act on accusation or even mere suspicion. Sorcery and witchcraft were classed as heresy, and witch trials became more common. They were conducted mainly by secular courts, required strict standards of proof, and usually involved torture, derived from Roman law, to extract confessions.

By the fourteenth and fifteenth centuries, concerns about magical practices were growing. This period saw the beginnings of the earliest real witch trials. The Renaissance of the fifteenth and sixteenth centuries brought new understandings of magic based on the rediscovered texts of antiquity. Protestantism in England reconceived how divine power operated and brought new reliance of spells and more intense fear of witches and demonic attack. This saw the era of massive witch-hunts, although it should be emphasised that these were aberrant social movements, rather than the norm. Gradually, belief in magic and witchcraft faded, particularly among the ruling classes, and legal sanctions against witchcraft were repealed by the eighteenth century. Nevertheless, beliefs and practices still persisted, mainly among the grassroots population, and the Christian churches, in England at least, still oppose witchcraft.

Witch-killing in the colony

This then was the background to the laws introduced into the colonies of PNG. Like their European Christian ancestors before them, the first colonists were greatly troubled by the widespread[1] evidence of sorcery beliefs and practices they found in PNG (Barker 2007; Dalton 2007; Sack 1974). Because they believed that their civilising mission would be largely achieved by the introduction of the Western legal system, they sought to prevent the practice of sorcery by the law. But from the outset, they had difficulty trying to prohibit something that they believed did not exist.[2]

An early attempt to resolve the situation was made by the first administrator of what was then British New Guinea, at the end of the nineteenth century. He tried to justify the anti-sorcery provisions that were written into the *Native Regulations*,[3] by prefacing the sorcery offences with the statement that

> Sorcery is only deceit, but the lies of the Sorcerer frighten many people and cause great trouble, therefore the Sorcerer must be punished.[4]

---

1 The cases discussed in this chapter come from all provinces except East Sepik, Manus and New Ireland. However, this is not to say that sorcery is not practised in these provinces.
2 The problem was later confronted by the framers of the *Sorcery Act* 1971, when the original elegantly brief Bill had to be expanded greatly to ensure that judges and magistrates were not to be taken as actually believing in the sorcery discussed in cases that came before them.
3 I use this as a compendium term for the *Native Regulations* made in British New Guinea beginning 1888, then in Papua under the *Native Regulation Act* 1908–1967 (Papua), and in New Guinea under the *Native Administration Regulations* made under the *Native Administration Act* (New Guinea) (Chapter 315). Daily village life in both territories was governed in minute detail by means of these regulations, which were constantly being varied and updated and the colonising enterprise expanded.
4 *Native Regulations* 1922 (Papua), R 87.

The *Native Administration Regulations* of New Guinea were not made until 1924, several years after Australia assumed the administration of what was then the Mandated Territory. The regulations omitted the original homily, but otherwise were similar in both territories, for example:

Any native who —

(a) practices or pretends to practice sorcery; or

(b) threatens any person with sorcery whether practised by himself or any other person; or

(c) procures or attempts to procure any other person to practise or pretend to practise or assist in sorcery; or

(d) is found in possession of implements or "charms" used in sorcery; or accepts payment or presents in the shape of food or otherwise when the obvious intention of making such payments or presents is to propitiate a Sorcerer,

shall on conviction be liable ...[5]

Sir Hubert Murray, who was the second administrator of Papua until his death in 1940, went further than a mere imposition of the beliefs of Western society. He studied Papuan societies in quite some detail, and noted that although twentieth-century Europeans do not accept that sorcery is a reality, nevertheless the Papuans do, and feel no guilt for killing a sorcerer. As well as malicious sorcery, Papuans also believe in 'good' sorcery, such as for prosperous gardening, hunting and fishing, and to manage the weather. Murray thought that people were frightened to give out information on sorcerers, for fear of retaliation from the sorcerer (although he may have overlooked the fact that they may also have been motivated by a fear that they would not be believed). As far as management by the introduced formal law system went, he realised that the six-month penalty in the regulations was quite insufficient as a substitute for private vengeance, and wondered whether the suppression of payback killings and tribal warfare had actually promoted the use of sorcery (Murray 1912:203–6).

The law and the killing of witches

The real crime

The *Native Regulations*, which applied to indigenous inhabitants only, prohibited the practice of sorcery by an alleged sorcerer. The more serious

---

5   *Native Regulations* 1939 (Papua) Section 80(2).

(and in the colonists' view, more real?) matter of killing the sorcerer already fell squarely within the ambit of the *Criminal Code*. Witch-killing was clearly murder in the eyes of the law. Various strategies were attempted by defence counsel to mitigate the murder charges against witch-killers. The first attempt was one of insanity, on the basis that a primitive belief in sorcery indicated a state of natural mental infirmity, but this was rejected.[6] A few years later the courts[7] decided that a belief in sorcery is not a reasonable belief, so there can be no defence of mistake of fact within the meaning of the Criminal Code. Nor was a witch-killing an act of self-defence or defence in aid. These defences only operate in situations of assault, and it was held that a sorcery attack does not constitute an assault. A few years later, the case of *R v. K.J. & Anor*[8] suggested that a defence of provocation could succeed, but only if the killing occurred in the heat of passion.

The mitigation factor

Clearly though, to treat witch-killers as ordinary murderers when they were operating under a different belief system was unjust. Many cases of witch-killing arose in remote areas, barely touched by education or mission. How could these people be made to understand what this alien law says? Writing in 1930, Justice Gore of the Papua Central Court opined that

> The native becomes a criminal only because of the law which somebody, of whom he has never heard, has imposed upon him. In justice the Court cannot award any punishment at all ... In order that punishment should deter through the terror it inspires the delinquent must know that he is doing wrong ... It is through the attitude of the Courts in their treatment of the criminal sanctions in relation to native crime that the necessary adjustment is made between the sanctions provided and the social condition existing. (Gore 1932:20–21)

Thus the colonial courts came to treat a genuine belief in sorcery not as a defence against the charge but as a special factor to be considered in mitigation of sentence after the accused has been convicted of his crime. In 1963, the *Native Customs (Recognition) Ordinance*[9] was enacted, and permitted custom to be taken into account in criminal cases, again not as a defence but only to determine the reasonableness of a belief or state of mind, or when considering sentence. The ordinance confirmed that a belief in sorcery operated in mitigation of sentence, once the witch-killer was found guilty. This tactic was supposed to relate the foreign criminal law to the circumstances of its adopted home (O'Regan 1974:77).

---

6 *R v. Womeni-Nanagawo* [1963] PNGLR 72.
7 *R v. Manga-Kitai* [1967–68] PNGLR 1; *R v. Ferapo-Meata* (Unreported, SC419, March 1967, Clarkson J).
8 *R v. K.J. & Anor* [1973] PNGLR 93.
9 Now renamed the *Customs Recognition Act*.

The *Sorcery Ordinance* 1971

Meanwhile, in 1971, the *Sorcery Ordinance*[10] was passed. Its language drew heavily on that of the *Native Regulations* cited above. Its main aim was to give jurisdiction to the formal courts to prosecute acts of sorcery, along the lines already provided in the *Native Regulations*, which were due to be repealed at Independence. But it also included a provision that enabled a defence of provocation to a charge of murder for killing a witch. This defence has the effect of reducing a charge of murder to one of manslaughter, and it is this factor that has troubled so many recently, prompting the repeal of the *Sorcery Act* 1971 in 2013.

The prosecution of sorcery

The *Sorcery Ordinance* was mainly aimed at working towards stamping out sorcery practices by legal action in the formal courts. It contained a lengthy preamble to justify itself, as follows:

> There is a widespread belief throughout the country that there is such a thing as sorcery … and because of this belief many evil things can be done and many people are frightened … it is necessary for the law to distinguish between evil sorcery and innocent sorcery … a person who uses or pretends or tries to use sorcery to do … evil things should … be punished just as if sorcery and the powers of sorcerers were real.

The original Bill was drafted in only five clauses. But magistrates, lawyers and judges wanted protection from accusations that by trying a sorcery case, they would be taken to believe in sorcery themselves. So the final version (Section 5) provided that nothing in the law either recognised or denied the existence or effectiveness of sorcery.

But there was a bigger problem with trying to deal with sorcery in the formal court system. It is a basic principle of the law that sorcerers should be brought to justice and not killed by self-help, but subsequent cases[11] have shown how hard it is to use the processes of the introduced law, particularly the evidentiary requirements, to convict a witch or sorcerer for killing by supernatural powers. This set the stage for continued acts of witch-killing, so long as sorcery beliefs persisted.

In 1974, when village courts were established to adjudicate on custom, they too were given powers to prosecute crimes of sorcery, comprising:

  (i) practising or pretending to practise sorcery; or

---

10 Renamed the *Sorcery Act* after Independence.
11 *State v. Noah Magou* [1981] PNGLR 1; *State v. Dickson Miritok* (Unreported, N3466, 2007, Kandakasi J).

(ii) threatening any person with sorcery practised by another; or

(iii) procuring or attempting to procure a person to practise or pretend to practise, or to assist in, sorcery; or

(iv) the possession of implements or charms used in practising sorcery; or

(v) paying or offering to pay a person to perform acts of sorcery.[12]

Village courts did not need to follow strict rules of evidence and procedure, which made it easier to prove sorcery in a village court than in the state courts using the *Sorcery Ordinance*.

Custom and the killing of witches

In the colonial period, customary belief in sorcery was more or less automatically accepted by the courts. However, the administration and the expatriate judges were sure that education and the influence of Christianity would eventually stamp out such beliefs, and believed there was already evidence of this process. Witch-killing cases at this time were decided on the basis that the degree of sophistication, or lack of it, affected the sentence.[13]

After Independence though, the suspicion started growing that sorcery practices may not be dying out. The Law Reform Commission in 1977 noted that sorcery may be increasing, and thought that this might be 'as a result of the uncertainties involved in modern development or underdevelopment' (LRCPNG 1977). In 1981, the Supreme Court (PNG's highest court of appeal) observed that education and sophistication had not stamped out sorcery beliefs.[14]

At this stage, enter Acting Justice Bernard Narokobi, the first chairman of the Law Reform Commission at the time of Independence. He had had a large input into the Constitutional Planning Committee Report, and wrote extensively of his dream of an indigenous jurisprudence which would combine the best of Melanesian custom, human rights principles and Christian belief (Narokobi 1977, 1980, 1982, 1989a, 1989b). He was an acting judge of the National Court in 1980–81, and tried in many ways to encourage his brethren on the bench to work towards devising a legal system which incorporated due respect for custom.

---

12   Regulation 3(p), *Village Courts Regulation* 1974.
13   For example, *Queen v. Asis & Bitimur* (Unreported SC559, 1970, Clarkson J); *Wanosa & Ors v. The Queen* [1971–72] PNGLR 90; *Secretary for Law v. Ulao Amantasi & Ors* [1975] PNGLR 134.
14   *Agoara Kebo v. State* (Unreported, SC198, 1981, Kidu CJ Kapi Miles J).

Acting Justice Narokobi dealt with several cases of witch-killing. In *Luku Wapulae's Case*,[15] five men killed a woman sorceress at Porgera, in Enga Province in the highlands. But they expressed no remorse, as they believed she had killed many people and it was an act of honour to rid the community of such a threat to the wellbeing of all. The judge drew an analogy with the way the nation through its laws and its health system declares war on germs that are responsible for sickness and disease. If at the local level sorcerers are believed to be responsible for deaths, he said, it was not difficult to see that the community would want to defend itself from this disease. He devised a defence of 'diminished responsibility', based on a Law Reform Commission recommendation, and ordered a three-month gaol sentence and a compensation payment of pigs. Then the following month, he tried to use custom to change the imported law by giving weight to the evidence of dreams that had led the accused to kill a suspected witch.[16]

But the Supreme Court wasn't interested in considerations of customs and their underlying philosophy. It held that to award compensation, even in an area as remote as that in which the killing took place, was unconstitutional; that there was no such thing as a defence of 'diminished responsibility'; and that the sentence for 'payback' killing was far too light.[17] Narokobi's attempts at law reform were unsuccessful.

Victim or perpetrator?

In a steady line of cases from the decolonisation era onward the defence has argued that the killers were acting in the belief that they were defending the community.[18] Sometimes, the whole community gathered and agreed that in order to save the people, the sorcerer should be put to death. One judge acknowledged this explicitly in 2006, when he said:

> To act on behalf of the community to commit a serious crime [such] as the one under consideration takes or requires so much courage on the part of actors as was the case of the two accused.[19]

---

15   *State v. Luku Wapulae* (Unreported, N233, 1980, Narokobi AJ).
16   *State v. Yale Gesie* (Unreported, N254, 1980, Narokobi AJ).
17   *Acting Public Prosecutor v. Uname Aumane & Ors* [1980] PNGLR 510. This case is critiqued in depth in Zorn (2006).
18   *Wanosa & Ors v. The Queen* [1971–72] PNGLR 90; *Secretary for Law v. Ulao Amantasi & Ors* [1975] PNGLR 134; *State v. Luku Wapulae* (Unreported, N233, 1980, Narokobi AJ); *State v. Aigal* [1990] PNGLR 318; *State v. Boat Yokum & Ors* (Unreported, N2337, 2002, Injia J); *State v. Saweno Visare & Ragu Maioi* (Unreported Unnumbered), CR.NO.1455 of 2005, 15 June 2006, Lenalia J.
19   *State v. Saweno Visare & Ragu Maioi* (Unreported Unnumbered), CR.NO.1455 of 2005, 15 June 2006, Lenalia J.

In this case, the accused had already pleaded guilty to wilful murder by complicity, but referred to their belief that they were defending the community, which prompted the judge's reflections on the matter. Nevertheless, he imposed a 15-year sentence in accordance with the Supreme Court's sentencing tariffs.

Custom or human rights?

This defence raises an interesting philosophical problem, one that the common law system was ill-equipped to handle: what is more important, protecting the individual or protecting the community? The usual way in which the postcolonial courts have countered the custom and community defence argument has been by reference to the individual human rights enshrined in the constitution, in cases almost to the present time.[20] Rights most commonly upheld are the right to life, the right to freedom from torture, the right to the protection of the law and a fair trial, and the test that witch-killing is repugnant to the general principles of humanity. While these rights continue to be raised in aid of mitigation of sentence, they have, over the past decade, been accompanied by reference to judicial opinion that witch-killing is also contrary to the beliefs and precepts of Christianity.

Christianity and the killing of witches

The preamble to the Constitution states that 'We, the people of Papua New Guinea … pledge ourselves to guard and pass on to those who come after us our noble traditions and the Christian principles that are ours now'. These days, this is often taken to mean that 'Papua New Guinea is a Christian nation'.

The courts have always incorporated references to Christian principles into their decisions. This stems from the earliest days of the colony, when the missions were viewed as part of the 'civilising' process that would see sorcery beliefs die out. But this theory did not hold true. In 1983, Chief Justice Kidu noted in *State v. Aiaka Karavea*[21] that while courts had once presumed a conflict between the belief in sorcery and the introduced law, nowadays even the best-educated people believe in sorcery. In other words, it has become a question not of custom or Christianity, but custom *and* Christianity. The early hopes of the colonial administration, that Christianity would replace sorcery, had been

---

20 *Acting Public Prosecutor v. Uname Aumane & Ors* [1980] PNGLR 510; *State v. Yale Gesie* (Unreported, N254, 1980, Narokobi AJ); *State v. Aiaka Karavea and Lelehua Karavea* (Unreported, National Court, N452, 1983, Kidu CJ); *State v. Aigal* [1990] PNGLR 318; *State v. Muare Kiage* (Unreported, N918, 1990, Brunton J); *State v. Siune Arnold* (Unreported, N1658, 1997, Batari AJ); *State v. Urari Siviri* (Unreported, N2747, 2004, Batari J); *State v. Maraka Jackson* (Unreported, National Court, N3237, 2006, Kandakasi J); *Irai Thomas v. State* (Unreported, Supreme Court, SC867, 2007, Kandakasi, Lenalia and David JJ).
21 *State v. Aiaka Karavea and Lelehua Karavea* (Unreported, National Court, N452, 1983, Kidu CJ).

confounded. *Siviri's Case*[22] in 2004 evidenced a melding of sorcery and Christian beliefs, when a suspected witch was killed in church grounds in the presence of the pastor. Rather than overcoming and supplanting customary beliefs and practices, it seemed that Christian doctrine had been incorporated into them.

But the courts, by now almost entirely consisting of PNG judges, have resisted this suggestion. More than 10 years ago, in 2002, Justice Injia (later to become chief justice) declared that:

> belief in the power of witchcraft and belief in the power of the Christian God cannot exist side by side. One belief system has to give way to the other.[23]

He thought that witch-killing is pure payback and included in his sentence an order for intensive Christian training of the witch-killers. Another judge took into account the fact that the accused was a Christian pastor, and refused to allow any belief in sorcery to mitigate sentence.[24] Yet another judge denied the belief outright, saying, 'There is no such thing as sorcery. It only exists in the mind of a person and does not exist in fact.'[25]

But despite the arguments of defence of the community, and the incorporation of much of Christian doctrine into the ever-changing precepts of custom, the judges were clearly getting tired of witch-killing. They started questioning the 'mitigation factor'. With increased education, mission influence and sophistication, why should a belief in sorcery still be a special factor in mitigation?[26] And in fact, not long ago the Supreme Court decided that it was no longer automatically a 'special' mitigating factor. Henceforth mitigation of sentence would depend on the facts of each case.[27] Finally in 2007, in a particularly nasty case of witch torture and killing, the death penalty was imposed.[28] And as recently as 2013, a newspaper report claimed that a man in Enga Province had been sentenced to 30 years in jail for killing his aunt on suspicion of sorcery. The killing was described as 'senseless, barbaric and brutal' (*The National* 2013). The judges had come to appeal not to customary principles and human rights, but to those principles expounded as 'Christian principles'.

---

22 *State v. Urari Siviri* (Unreported, N2747, 2004, Batari J).
23 *State v. Boat Yokum & Ors* (Unreported, N2337, 2002, Injia J).
24 *State v. Baipu* (Unreported, N2451, 2003, Jalina J).
25 *State v. Prodie Akoi & Steven Akoi* (Unreported, N2584, 2004, Kandakasi J).
26 *State v. Urari Siviri* (Unreported, N2747, 2004, Batari J); see also *State v. Prodie Akoi & Steven Akoi* (Unreported, N2584, 2004, Kandakasi J); *State v. Maraka Jackson* (Unreported, National Court, N3237, 2006, Kandakasi J).
27 *Irai Thomas v. State* (Unreported, Supreme Court, SC867, 2007, Kandakasi, Lenalia and David JJ).
28 *State v. Sedoki Lota & Fred Abenko* (Unreported, N3183, 2007, Sevua J).

To sum up

From early Christian times, the law in European states was directed at prosecuting sorcerers and witches. This trend was exported in the English common law to colonial PNG, where laws were made to prosecute acts of sorcery, although it proved difficult to prosecute sorcerers successfully under the introduced legal system, so self-help was actually encouraged.

The introduced law also prosecuted witch-killers as murderers, although a genuine belief in sorcery was a special factor in mitigation of sentence. But this introduced legal system focused on the rights and responsibilities of the individual and ignored customary principles of responsibility to the general community, where to kill a witch was viewed as protecting the community.

It was initially assumed that with education and modernisation, sorcery beliefs would die out, but after Independence, sorcery beliefs did not diminish with greater education, and co-existed with Christianity. However, the courts refused to accept that the two belief systems could co-exist, and prosecuted witch-killers even more strongly. Recently, the Supreme Court rejected the automatic special mitigation factor, sentences became heavier, and the National Court imposed a death sentence.

It is interesting to contrast this line of reasoning with that of Western European societies of the past two millennia, in which torture and killing of witches were carried out in the name of Christianity. In PNG, Christianity has been set in contradistinction to customary beliefs. But despite more than a century of attempts by the law and Christianity in PNG to deal with witch-killing, neither has managed to deal completely with the underlying question: Who are the criminals? The sorcerers? The diviners? The accusers? The torturers? The killers? The whole community? (Zocca 2009).

Nevertheless, it is possible that this latest trend in judicial opinion can indicate a way forward, not through specific legal action but through the deployment of Christian doctrine, preaching and prayer. Already there are some signs that this strategy is being used to good effect. Further judicial support along these lines is to be encouraged.

References

Bailey, M.D. 2008. The Age of Magicians. *Magic, Ritual and Witchcraft* 3(1):1–28.

Barker, J. (ed.) 2007. *The Anthropology of Morality in Melanesia and Beyond*. Aldershot, England: Ashgate.

Briggs, R. 1996. *Witches and Neighbours: The Social and Cultural Context of European Witchcraft*. London: HarperCollins.

Burridge, K. 1995. *Mambu: A Melanesian Millennium*. Princeton, NJ: Princeton University Press.

Dalton, D. 2007. When Is It Moral To Be a Sorcerer? In J. Barker (ed.) *The Anthropology of Morality in Melanesia and Beyond*. Aldershot, England: Ashgate, 39–55.

Forsyth, M. 2013. Witchcraft and Sorcery-Related Killings in Melanesia: The Legal Issues. *SSGM In Brief* 2013/1. Canberra: State, Society and Governance in Melanesia Program, The Australian National University.

Gibbs, P. 2012. Engendered Violence and Witch-Killing in Simbu. In M. Jolly, C. Stewart and C. Brewer (eds.) *Engendering Violence in Papua New Guinea*. Canberra: ANU E Press, 107–35.

Gore, R.T. 1932. The Punishment of Crime among Natives. *Territory of Papua Annual Report 1930–1931*. Canberra: Parliament of Australia, 20–22.

LRCPNG (Law Reform Commission of Papua New Guinea) 1977. Sorcery. *Occasional Paper* No. 4. Waigani: LRCPNG.

Murray, H. 1912. *Papua or British New Guinea*. London: T. Fisher Unwin.

Narokobi, B. 1977. Adaptation of Western Law in Papua New Guinea. *Melanesian Law Journal* 5(1):52–69.

Narokobi, B. 1980. *The Melanesian Way: Total Cosmic Vision of Life*. Boroko: Institute of Papua New Guinea Studies.

Narokobi, B. 1982. History and Movement in Law Reform in Papua New Guinea. In D. Weisbrot, A. Paliwala and A. Sawyerr (eds.). *Law and Social Change in Papua New Guinea*. Sydney: Butterworths, 13–24.

Narokobi, B. 1989a. *Lo Bilong Yumi Yet: Law and Custom in Melanesia*. Suva: Institute of Pacific Studies of the University of the South Pacific and The Melanesian Institute for Pastoral and Socio-Economic Service.

Narokobi, B. 1989b. Law and Custom in Melanesia. *Pacific Perspectives* 14(1):17–26.

National, The 2013. Killer Gets 30-Year Term. *The National* online, 22 April. www.thenational.com.pg/?q=node/48739.

O'Regan, R.S. 1974. Sorcery and Homicide in Papua New Guinea. *Australian Law Journal* 48:76–82.

Reay, M. 1976. The Politics of a Witch-Killing. *Oceania* 47(1):1–20.

Sack, P.G. 1974. Crime or Punishment: The Role of the Sorcerer in Traditional Tolai Law (New Britain). *Anthropos* 69(3/4):401–8.

Stephen, M. (ed.) 1987. *Sorcerer and Witch in Melanesia*. Melbourne: Melbourne University Press.

Zocca, F. (ed.) 2009. *Sanguma* in Paradise: Sorcery, Witchcraft and Christianity in Papua New Guinea. *Point* No. 33. Goroka: Melanesian Institute.

Zorn, J.G. 2006. Women and Witchcraft: Positivist, Prelapsarian, and Post-Modern Judicial Interpretations in PNG. In A. Whiting and C. Evans (eds.) *Mixed Blessings: Laws, Religions, and Women's Rights in the Asia-Pacific Region*. Leiden: Martinus Nijhoff, 61–99.

11. The Western Legal Response to Sorcery in Colonial Papua New Guinea

Mel Keenan

Introduction

In July 2013 the national parliament of Papua New Guinea (PNG) repealed that country's Sorcery Act, as one prong of a strategy aimed at bringing an end to the appalling sorcery-related violence throughout the country. Dating back to 1971, some years before independence, the Act's roots lie in the period of PNG's torpor as an Australian colony. This chapter takes the long historical view of the notoriously a-historical common law, in order to provide some examination of the response of colonial administrators working within an imported common law framework to crimes arising from the pervasive belief in sorcery throughout PNG.[1]

The Western legal 'response' to sorcery denotes the entire panoply of modern law making and law enforcing in colonial PNG: policymaking, the legislative process, law enforcement and judicial decision-making. At its core is how did the Western criminal justice system deal with the genuinely held belief that sorcerers could from afar be the cause of a wide range of results — including consequent self-protective or retaliatory violence — all of which were potentially punishable under the colonists' law? This requires the consideration in an introductory way of the common law's historical response to sorcery or witchcraft allegations, and the manner in which two leading colonial administrators in PNG, Sir William MacGregor and Sir Hubert Murray, used the common law to deal with contemporary sorcery-related crime. The failure to acknowledge that history, coupled with assumptions about the universal applicability of the common law, imposed on PNG a legal regime which at the one time gave statutory recognition to sorcery practices, while signally failing to provide effective protection from its aftermath. Arguably, this 'worst of both worlds' result exacerbated the recent upsurge in sorcery-related violence in PNG, and led to the Sorcery Act's repeal.

---

1   The material in this chapter is the result of research undertaken towards a thesis of the same title for the degree of Doctor of Philosophy in law from Monash University, Melbourne, under the supervision of Guy Powles and Melissa Castan.

An immediate issue is the intertwining of the processes of colonialism with that of the introduction of Western law to PNG: of course the latter could not have occurred without the former. However, I argue that theories of colonialism based on the proposition that the demands of capitalism necessarily entailed imperialist expansion, as capitalists in the metropolis sought increased resources and wider markets (see, for example, Blaut 1989) do not sufficiently explain the colonisation of PNG — although the South Pacific certainly was divided up as part of the imperial scramble of the late nineteenth century. Rather, the creation by the British of the rather odd entity, the Western Pacific High Commission, and the eventual extension of British 'Protection' over south-east New Guinea is better characterised as a policy of extending British sovereignty over her own subjects, inspired to some extent by the criminal activities of Australians — especially Queenslanders — kidnapping Pacific islanders to work on sugar plantations.[2] To this extent, the common law actually 'arrived' in PNG before any structures of colonial administration.

The first grandchild of the British Empire

Occurring in a colony of first Great Britain and then Australia, sorcery in PNG was dealt with as a criminal offence under colonial ordinances and regulations. Colonial administrators did make some efforts to establish how sorcery operated to maintain social equilibrium within tribal groups. Thus, Sir Hubert Murray in the early twentieth century referred to Bronislaw Malinowski's pioneering anthropological work among the Trobriand Islanders which highlighted the 'qualitative difference between the then-prevailing concept of law … and the native bilateral view of law as deserving obedience as one part of a larger, personally beneficial chain of binding relationships' (Donovan 2008:73–5).

I suggest that one lens through which the conduct of colonial administration might be viewed is the unusual way in which PNG became part of the British Empire. Supposedly concerned by the increasing German presence in the south-west Pacific, on 4 April 1883 Queensland Premier Thomas McIlwraith ordered the police magistrate on Thursday Island to formally annex New Guinea and adjacent islands in the name of the British government. The Colonial Office was unamused, and this unilateral action was disallowed on the basis that a colonial government had no authority to annex other colonies. However, when Imperial

---

2   The Western Pacific Order in Council of 1877 established the High Commission for the Western Pacific and gave the High Commissioner's Court jurisdiction over British subjects in the area. Article 24 of the order gave the high commissioner power to make regulations for the government of British subjects or 'for securing the maintenance (as far as regards the conduct of British subjects) of friendly relations between British subjects and those authorities and persons subject to them' (Angelo et al. 1989:31).

Germany claimed the north-eastern part of New Guinea as Kaiser-Wilhelmsland in the following year, the Union Jack was quickly hoisted in Port Moresby over the new crown colony of British New Guinea.

Subsequent to this brief flurry of activity, PNG held little interest for the vast majority of Australians, even after British New Guinea became the Australian Territory of Papua in 1906. This meant that administrators on the ground had considerable latitude in defining 'native policy'. This was particularly the case with Sir Hubert Murray, administrator of Papua from 1906 until his death in 1940. A trained lawyer, Murray was also chief judicial officer of the territory. However, despite the fact that he took pains to employ contemporary anthropological theories — especially the functionalism of Malinowski and his disciples — Murray was ultimately a public servant who wanted to maintain order, and the paternalistic practices introduced by him that had been groundbreaking at the time of World War I were woefully obsolete by the time of World War II.

After World War II, and under increasing international scrutiny, the real locus of power shifted from the administrator in Port Moresby to the minister in Canberra, particularly the exacting Paul Hasluck. As the British Empire was 'handed back' one territory at a time, Australia's lingering presence in PNG became ever more anachronistic, leading the Whitlam Labor government to thrust independence on the territory in 1975, the last act of colonial arrogance.[3]

Throughout this period the common law played a vital role in the 'pacification' and 'civilisation' of Papua New Guineans. Other than headhunting and cannibalism, sorcery practices were perhaps the most abhorrent to the colonisers' sensibilities — easily forgetting that only a few hundred years before, the common law in England and its American colonies had dealt with almost identical issues. As a question of public order, sorcery was prohibited under some of the earliest native regulations put in place by administrator Sir William MacGregor in the 1890s.[4] Nonetheless, even if the colonisers were unaware of regional varieties in belief, the ubiquity of sorcery practices meant that judicial officers had to take it into consideration in sentencing, and that a belief in its practice could be used as a provocation defence. The continuing strength and extent of the belief in the efficacy of sorcery was attested to by the passage of the Sorcery Act in 1971, shortly before independence, and the series of reports produced by the

---

3   See Nelson (1982:211). On the phases of Australian policy, see Hudson (1974:x) and Legge (1956).
4   MacGregor's biographer, the historian Roger Joyce, felt that MacGregor could have shown more sympathy and understanding towards native society, by reference perhaps to the anthropological work being undertaken by Charles Seligman in the Torres Strait in the 1890s (Joyce 1971:143). However, given that the Cambridge University expedition of which Seligman was a part didn't arrive on Thursday Island until April 1898, this is unfair to MacGregor.

PNG Law Reform Commission in the late 1970s.[5] Despite this official response — or perhaps partly because of it — sorcery-related crime remains a seemingly intractable problem in contemporary PNG.

The historical response of the common law

In dealing with criminal sanctions for the practice of sorcery, colonial legal authorities in PNG operated within a framework which had been applied to similarly alleged practices over a period of hundreds of years, as common law practice evolved. This evolution had taken place with a background of legislation in Christian Europe, which criminalised the practice of witchcraft, especially that of *maleficium*, or the deliberate inflicting of harm on persons and property. In the historical context, leading British anthropologist Keith Thomas (2004:48) restricted the term 'witchcraft' to mean:

> the employment (or presumed employment) of some supernatural means of doing harm to other people in a way that was generally disapproved of by the mass of society.

As will be seen, it was this concept of inflicting harm that was at the core of the common law response to alleged witchcraft.

Ultimately, belief in the Christian duty to eradicate witches within Europe was based on passages in the Old Testament, which, it has been argued, were in turn based on the earlier Laws of Hammurabi, dating back to before 1750 BC (Wright 2009:200–201). So there is a considerable lineage here. Still, despite these biblical injunctions, the early church paid little attention to the question of witchcraft, with St Augustine in the fifth century declaring that witchcraft and satanic power were impossible, as God alone had the power to suspend the laws of nature. However, church attitudes hardened in the wake of the popularity and strength of medieval heresies, so that by 1484 a Papal Bull recognised the existence of witches, and the ensuing Inquisitors' handbook, *Malleus Maleficarum* — the *Hammer of the Witches* — became the textbook for European witch trials for centuries. It was the *Malleus* that imprinted on the popular European imagination the image of the witch not only as the village practitioner of malevolent magic, but as the cohort of the devil flying through the night to worship Satan at Sabbaths.

The roots of the English legislative response to witchcraft lie in the ferment of the Reformation: whereas the medieval Catholic Church had provided 'magic'

---

5   These were Sorcery, *Occasional Paper* No. 4, October 1977; Sorcery among the Tolai People, *Occasional Paper* No. 8, April 1978; Sorcery among the East Sepiks, *Occasional Paper* No. 10, October 1978; and The Effects of Sorcery in Kilenge, West New Britain Province, *Occasional Paper* No. 11, August 1979.

of its own in the form of ritual blessings to ward off evil, the Reformation did away with these unbiblical practices. It is unsurprising then that the first Act criminalising witchcraft came in the course of the Henrician Reformation. The Witchcraft Act of 1542 defined witchcraft as a capital offence, and forbade:

> the use, devise practice or exercise … of any Invocations or conjurations of Spirits witchcrafts enchantments or sorceries to the intent to find money or treasure or to waste consume or destroy any person in his bodily members, or to provoke any person to unlawful love, or for any other unlawful intent or purpose.

The wording clearly shows that the Act was directed at *maleficium*, encompassing allegations such as causing people or livestock to sicken and die, destroying crops by summoning bad weather, and 'turning' butter or spoiling food. All of these were of vital import to small agrarian communities, living close to subsistence level, particularly in times of social upheaval. They also denote the intimate personal and economic relationships which often characterised accused and accuser in English witchcraft trials: women were disproportionately accused of witchcraft, and none more so than socially dislocated widows and spinsters whose poverty made them a drain on the welfare of their neighbours and the sparse resources of their communities.[6]

In 1603, the Stuart James VI came to the English throne from a Scottish realm in which both the practice of witchcraft and consulting with witches were capital offences. The ensuing Witchcraft Act of 1604 no longer focused on the malicious intent of the accused, but on the pact with evil spirits and devils, a felony punishable by death. As the witchcraft legislation did not include any specific ways of proving the *maleficium*, courts relied upon contemporary criminal procedure. Witchcraft was known as a *crimen exceptum*, or a category of grave offence which, of its very nature, was not amenable to finding evidence. It was therefore to be expected that its prosecution would not be possible with reference to existing principles of proof, normal standards of interrogation or court procedure (Larner 2002:205).

Relying on the Jacobean Act, in Essex during the English Civil War of the 1640s, puritan 'witchfinders' Matthew Hopkins and John Sterne used evidence-finding practices which in the twenty-first century might be described as 'enhanced interrogation techniques', such as sleep deprivation, to purportedly discern the 'marks' of a witch as a preliminary to trial. In doing so, in only 14 months they led to the arrest of nearly 300 men and women and effectively caused the deaths of 230, either by way of judicial execution, or in crowded local prisons in which disease was rife (Gaskill 2005). However, the Essex witch hunts were

---

6 Throughout England, issues of community responsibility, gender roles and poverty 'combined explosively with popular beliefs about the supernatural to create a tragedy' (Timmons 2006:304).

an exception to the general rule in England of findings of innocence due to a lack of credible evidence, and they can be attributed largely to the unique and explosive combination of social upheaval and the strength of local Puritanism, a combination which would again prove to be deadly in the Salem witch trials of colonial New England some 50 years later (Hoffer 1997:81).

However, by making witchcraft a felony, the witchcraft Acts had removed it from the remit of the ecclesiastical courts and given it to those of the common law; placing witchcraft trials in the hands of the common lawyers actually contributed to the professionalisation of roles of judge and prosecutor, thereby delineating the common lawyers as experts in assessing the evidence of witchcraft. The very success of the Essex witchfinders' reliance upon 'evidence' of the accused as witches contained within it the seeds of the destruction of the witchcraft trial. In stressing the reality of the discernible signs of witchcraft, the witchfinders effectively set the evidentiary boundaries for subsequent prosecutions, and it became necessary to show clear proof of a demonic pact. By the end of the seventeenth century, this 'increasingly taxing exercise in persuasion and proof' had become impossible. Accordingly, all of the 39 witchcraft indictments filed at the English Home Circuit — the populous counties of Essex, Hertfordshire, Kent, Surrey and Sussex — between 1660 and 1701 resulted in acquittals (Gaskill 2008:61).

The final English Witchcraft Act of 1736 demonstrated the change in mindset that characterised the early eighteenth century. Although there had been a decline in indictments prior to 1736, this was due to the fact that, as trials became somewhat of a legal embarrassment, judges increasingly dismissed them outright or dealt with them informally, so that the Jacobean Act was a dead letter long before its repeal (Davies 1999:8). Rather than punishing supposed *maleficium* or pacts with the devil, the 1736 Act aimed to prevent and punish 'any Pretences' to witchcraft, pursuant to which 'ignorant Persons are frequently deluded and defrauded', so that it was an offence to:

> pretend to exercise or use any kind of Witchcraft, Sorcery, Inchantment, or Conjuration, or undertake to tell Fortunes, or pretend, from his or her Skill or Knowledge in any occult or crafty Science, to discover where or in what manner any Goods or Chattels, supposed to have been stolen or lost, may be found.

The witch trial therefore played an important role in the construction of legal modernity. Between the Acts of 1542 and 1736, common lawyers forced those who alleged the statutory crime of witchcraft to prove the unprovable by way of inductive reasoning based on credible evidence. In relying on evidence of witch marks or a satanic compact that was to be admitted in court, the witchfinders' attempt to prove the irrational by way of rationality doomed the very notion of a witch trial. Once this process started, its momentum could not be stopped, and ultimately the law of evidence not only confronted witchcraft, but effectively vanquished it; as the founder of Methodism John Wesley lamented, the non-believers had 'hooted witchcraft out of the world' (Trevor-Roper 1967:96).

The reason for this trip through the centuries — or millennia if we go back to Hammurabi — has been to show that in England the common law vanquished the unprovable crime of witchcraft by the application of logic and the development of rules of evidence. However, it was a process that took many hundreds of years, and which undoubtedly was hastened by a decline of religious intensity among the educated classes. Nonetheless, if colonial administrators had been prepared to acknowledge this incremental process, they may have brought to PNG a more nuanced approach to applying the common law to sorcery beliefs.

The colonial response

The tone throughout the colonial period for dealing with crimes committed by Papua New Guineans had been set by perhaps the first application of British law when, in 1884, the special commissioner for what was then a British Protectorate, Sir Peter Scratchley, refused to sentence to death a payback murderer who had voluntarily turned himself in and offered compensation payment. Scratchley did not sentence him to death, because to do so in the wake of his voluntary submission would have been revenge rather than justice. Instead, he recommended to the Colonial Office that the culprit be detained at Port Moresby for 10–12 months and then returned to his home island.

Scratchley was not to oversee the establishment of the crown colony, as he contracted malaria and died at sea en route to Australia in December 1885. John Douglas — erstwhile premier of Queensland — then acted in the position of administrator until 4 September 1888, when British New Guinea was finally annexed as a crown colony and Dr William Macgregor, government medical officer for Fiji and deputy commissioner for the western Pacific, was appointed administrator.

As the first administrator of British New Guinea, MacGregor was adamant that a paternal form of justice was the most suitable for people 'in the act of stepping out of savagery and barbarism into civilisation' (Joyce 1971:120). Sorcery practices were the ubiquitous evil, as MacGregor acknowledged the pre-eminent belief among Papua New Guineans that death was caused by sorcery rather than by natural causes, a belief which led to a large number of murders or acts of violence, in vengeance against suspected sorcerers: indeed, he felt that the only commonality among the myriad indigenous tribes was this belief in sorcery. In the 1890s, MacGregor's chief judicial officer noted that where the motive for a murder led it to be justified among the natives — such as in sorcery-related crimes — it should not stop the court from reaching a verdict of guilty, but it would be reasonable for it to lessen the sentence. This remained the leitmotiv of criminal practice in PNG — criminal trials were conducted with the full array of royal justice; guilty verdicts sternly pronounced, but sentences a fraction of those that 'civilised Europeans' would have received.

MacGregor thus set about to cut the belief in sorcery at its roots, using the law as one of his main weapons. The Colonial Office had instructed him to introduce a judicial system that was as summary and simple as was possible, and the laws of Queensland were adopted for British New Guinea 'insofar as the same are applicable to the circumstances of the Possession and not repugnant to any provision in its constitution'.[7] They were soon complemented with a separate *Native Affairs Ordinance 1889* for the colony written in simple English and translated into Motuan, the language of the people of the Port Moresby district. Although the Letters Patent establishing the colony required the advice of nominated executive and legislative councils, the ideas for most ordinances were MacGregor's own, and his particular solution to combat sorcery practices lay in English, Fijian and West Indian precedents whereby the 'pretence' of holding such powers was made an offence (Joyce 1971:188). Thus, clause 80(1) of the *Native Regulation Board Ordinance 1893* provided:

> Sorcery is only deceit, but the lies of the Sorcerer frighten many people and cause great trouble, therefore the Sorcerer must be punished.[8]

In 1902 British New Guinea became the Australian Territory of Papua, and the 1893 ordinance was continued by the *Native Regulation Act 1908* of the Papuan administration of Sir Hubert Murray and remained largely in force until independence.[9] Murray's policies in the twentieth century can be viewed as a continuation of those of MacGregor — a 'benevolent tradition' of European development tempered by protective safeguards for the Papuans (Elkin 1940:28; Legge 1956:133–4). However, he was the first to realise that determining the appropriate legal response to an impugned custom required a thought-out policy, rather than simply responding to matters as they arose. Murray also

---

7   In June 1888 the Secretary of State for the Colonies, Lord Knutsford, had recommended extending Queensland law to Papua, but John Douglas disagreed, suggesting instead that a 'slight amplification and modification of the Ten Commandments would really be more suitable to the existing circumstances' (Sinclair 2009:50).

8   Eventually the Queensland Criminal Code of 1899 was adopted in Papua in 1903 and in New Guinea in 1921: ironically, even the practice of dissecting a body to ascertain whether the person had died from sorcery constituted an offence of interfering with a dead body under Section 236 of the code.

9   Section 6(1) of the *Papua Act 1905* (Commonwealth) stipulated that laws previously in force were to continue to operate until other provisions be made.

had the benefit of the legal anthropology of Bronislaw Malinowski, whose work among the Trobriand Islanders added momentum to the doctrine that law is social behaviour and not logical abstraction (Hoebel 1946:851).

There is a considerable corpus of material on Murray's reliance on anthropology, with some questioning whether he simply used it to bolster his own opinions and give an additional veneer of intellectual respectability to his administration.[10] Nonetheless, what is unarguable is that when the demands of anthropology and those of public order conflicted, public order always took precedence. Therefore, the determination of whether or not a traditional custom should be allowed to continue was always predicated upon to what extent it was viewed by the coloniser as congenial to the progress of the colonial project in Papua.[11] If, as Murray described it, the custom led to *disorder*, it had to be suppressed without equivocation. As the practice of sorcery was the exemplar of a custom that led to disorder, he rejected outright anthropological arguments for a policy response based on the centrality of sorcery beliefs to Papua New Guinean society:

> Take for instance the case of sorcery. We punish sorcery with six months' imprisonment, but only sorcery which is practised with intent to kill or injure — 'black magic' in short; and we punish it because it creates disorder by encouraging retaliatory murders and other acts of violence on the part of the relations of the man who has been bewitched. (Murray 1929a:14)

Murray suggested that Papua New Guineans felt that the statutory punishment was too light to be effective, but countered that care ought to be exercised in imposing a heavy penalty for what was 'really an imaginary offence' (ibid.), and that it should instead be thought of as a form of deceit, as set out in the relevant regulation. Nonetheless, he conceded that the sorcerer believed in his power as unreservedly as did his victim, and his writings show that his abhorrence of sorcery practices was not solely due to the fact that they were a cause of the disorder of retaliatory violence. Murray also felt that by suppressing sorcery he was freeing indigenous Papuans from that genuine fear which he felt blighted their whole existence:

---

10   See especially Gray (1999:56) and Hudson (1974:14), who maintained that Murray was caught by 'the three prongs of social conditions, the administrative and anthropological theories of his time, and his own preconceptions about the objects of administration'.

11   In spreading Anglo-Australian concepts of law and order, Murray did note that some of the older Papuans might regret 'the more stirring days of their youth'. As the administration had stopped all the excitement attached to raiding etc., the colonisers had to do their best to 'convert the disappointed raider into a more or less industrious husbandman' (Murray 1929a:20).

> Sorcery … is very real to the native, who in many parts of the Territory, is hardly free for one moment from the fear of sorcery, from the cradle to the grave, throughout the whole of his demon haunted life. (Murray 1938:9)

Despite having fought in the Boer War, he maintained that he had never realised what fear 'really meant' until he saw it in the eyes of an indigenous Papuan terrified by the potential wrath of a sorcerer (Murray 1929b:14). Accordingly, there was a very humane dimension to Murray's determination to stamp out sorcery, rather than simply an unreflective opposition.

Indeed, Murray was not above using sorcery to further public policy ends. In the wake of a smallpox scare in 1912–1913, Murray let it be known that a very dangerous and powerful sorcerer had conjured up a very bad sickness. But, although the sorcerer was strong the government was stronger, and when he saw the mark from the government — that is, the smallpox injection — he would realise that he was powerless and would 'retire foiled and baffled'. The smallpox scar became hugely popular, not only medically, but socially, and to be without the mark 'was to confess one's self the veriest outsider' (Lattas 1996:153). Nonetheless, although Murray's administration aimed to implement policies which the colonisers perceived as in the best interests of indigenous Papuans, the methods remained essentially those of control, law and order, and petty discipline. Hank Nelson (1982:20) suggests that the tragedy of Murray's career was that he served for so long that policies which had been progressive at the beginning of his tenure had become discriminatory and damaging by the end of it.

As for the anthropologists, on one hand there was the view of the Papuan Government Anthropologist F.E. Williams that the enforcement of the law against sorcery had done much to check its most harmful manifestations. He argued that where there was corroborative evidence of sorcery practice or a guilty plea, punishment enough to 'teach him a lesson, to make it psychologically impossible for him to pose as a sorcerer again' (Williams 1935:25). In stark contrast, New Zealand social anthropologist Reo Fortune argued against the ineffectual nature of the legal-administrative approach in a letter to Murray in 1928:

> haphazard hitting a certain practice while the beliefs behind are strong and undisturbed … can only terrorise practices into greater and greater secrecy and underhandedness. It is not a worthy thing. (Gray 1999:61)

As the Sorcery Act was introduced towards the end of the colonial era, but at a time when PNG was still subject to the Commonwealth Department of External Territories, it might reasonably have been assumed that it was a prime example of the colonisers using the blunt instrument of legislation to deal with a complex social issue. However, the Sorcery Bill was in fact introduced in the PNG House of Assembly by one of the Papua New Guinean members: on the last day of the June 1970 meeting of the assembly, Sir Paul Lapun, then member of parliament for South Bougainville, presented a Sorcery Bill, based on his stated belief that 'the people of this country, know that sorcery does occur' (Johnson 1983:19).

The ensuing Sorcery Act basically reiterated the earlier colonial sanctions, making it an offence to directly or indirectly pretend to be, hold one's self out to be, or profess to be a sorcerer who sought to do harm. However, it deliberately hedged its bets on the reality or otherwise of evil sorcery, so that Section 5 of the Act provides that:

> Even though this Act may speak as if powers of sorcery really exist (which is necessary if the law is to deal adequately with all the legal problems of sorcery and the traditional belief in the powers of sorcerers), nevertheless nothing in this Act recognizes the existence or effectiveness of powers of sorcery in any factual sense except only for the purpose of, and of proceedings under or by virtue of, this Act, or denies the existence or effectiveness of such powers.

This ambivalence was reinforced by the Act's evidentiary provisions. Once it had been proved that a person had committed an act of sorcery, it was immaterial that that act was actually incapable of causing the result intended, if the sorcerer, the intended victim, or anyone else who was meant to be influenced by the sorcerer's act believed that it was capable of producing that result.[12]

Conclusion

In its 1978 paper on sorcery among the Tolai, the PNG Law Reform Commission concluded that although sorcery could not be abolished, it might nonetheless be necessary for the law to be 'tough on evil sorcery' to reduce the incidence of its practice (LRCPNG 1978:16). While the Sorcery Act obviously failed to do so, an examination of its colonial roots suggests that this may be in part due to the fact that it can be characterised as 'weak' or 'state' legal pluralism, as opposed to 'strong' or 'deep' legal pluralism.

The delineation between these two concepts has been the subject of considerable debate for the past three decades,[13] but Miranda Forsyth has summarised the divide by noting that strong legal pluralism involves 'the coexistence of legal orders with different sources of authority', whereas with weak legal pluralism

---

12   Reading together Section 18 and Schedule 2 to the Act.
13   For a detailed discussion see Benda-Beckmann (2002).

there are 'two or more bodies of norms that have the same source of authority' (Forsyth 2009:43). The centrality of the practice of sorcery to traditional Papua New Guinean society was recognised by colonial administrators; had they regarded it as harmless, although offensive to their own societal norms, they most likely would have let it be. However, the violence attendant upon these practices impinged upon public order and moved them squarely into the realm of the introduced criminal law with its prescribed processes and penalties. Thus, rather than create some means of recognising the law-nature of sorcery, the ubiquity of belief in it was acknowledged in the sentencing process, in that sentences were relatively light for murders which arose from the sincere belief that the victim was a sorcerer.[14]

It is arguable that this weak legal pluralism contributed to what would appear to be the ultimate inadequacy of the Sorcery Act — on one hand it gave belief in sorcery normative status by enshrining it in legislation aimed at preventing and punishing 'evil practices of sorcery and other similar evil practices'; on the other hand it operated on the assumption that sorcery could effectively be dealt with by Western processes of law enforcement, rules of evidence and judicial decision-making. One Australian judge concluded that this very ambiguity meant that many indigenous Papua New Guineans felt that where sorcery allegations arose they had to take the law into their own hands, and then accept the Western legal consequences.[15]

In writing on 'Sorcery and Magic', American anthropologist Leonard Glick (1973) was unfortunately very prescient when he suggested that more, rather than fewer, sorcery accusations would be part of social life in PNG, and argued that every effort should be made to understand them, in their own social contexts, as manifestations of conflict. Although legal decision-makers did not doubt the reality of sorcery to indigenous Papua New Guineans, they in no way shared the faith in its existence or its efficacy. Magistrates and prosecutors applied the adopted Criminal Code, scrupulously adhering to the principles of evidence. In doing so, they failed to realise that one of the key ways in which they could have spoken a common language in relying upon those principles was through an appreciation of the fact that the witchcraft trial had goaded the common law into rational modernity, centred on provable evidence.

In adopting effectively a weak pluralist approach to sorcery by assuming that its suppression could be brought about by the imported processes of the criminal law, the failure of the Sorcery Act as a deterrent perhaps became inevitable

---

14 F.P. Winter, William MacGregor's chief judicial officer, noted that whereas it would be 'pernicious' to allow customary motives for murder to influence a verdict, it was 'perfectly equitable to regard it as a sufficient palliation to warrant a commutation of the sentence' (Legge 1956:71).
15 Justice David Selby of the NSW Supreme Court spent 6 months as acting judge of the Supreme Court of Papua New Guinea in 1961–1962, hearing cases which often involved sorcery and murder (Selby 1964:29).

as the social stresses identified by Glick intensified in contemporary PNG. If, perhaps, Hubert Murray's sympathies had occasionally allowed for the insights of anthropological discoveries to outweigh the demands of public order, the colonial regime may have crafted a stronger legal pluralism, which could have made a more effective and nuanced legal response to the current scourge of sorcery-related crime.

References

Angelo, A.H., H. Kirifi and A. Fong Toy 1989. Law and Tokelau. *Pacific Studies* 12(3):29–52.

Blaut, J.M. 1989. Colonialism and the Rise of Capitalism. *Science & Society* 53(3):260–96.

Davies, O. 1999. Witchcraft: The Spell That Didn't Break. *History Today* 49(8):7–16.

Donovan, J.M. 2008. *Legal Anthropology: An Introduction*. Lanham, Maryland: Altamira Press.

Elkin, A.P. 1940. The Place of Sir Hubert Murray in Native Administration. *The Australian Quarterly* 12(3):23–35.

Forsyth, M. 2009. *A Bird That flies with Two Wings: Kastom and State Justice Systems in Vanuatu*. Canberra: ANU E Press.

Gaskill, M. 2005. *Witchfinders: A Seventeenth Century English Tragedy*. Cambridge, MA: Harvard University Press.

Gaskill, M. 2008. Witchcraft and Evidence in Early Modern England. *Past and Present* 198(1):33–70.

Glick, L. 1973. Sorcery and Magic. In I. Hogbin (ed.) *Anthropology in Papua New Guinea: Readings from the Encyclopaedia of Papua and New Guinea*. Melbourne: Melbourne University Press, 182–6.

Gray, G. 1999. 'Being Honest to My Science': Reo Fortune and JHP Murray, 1927–1930. *The Australian Journal of Anthropology* 10(1):56–76.

Hoebel, E.A. 1946. Law and Anthropology. *Virginia Law Review* 32(4):835–54.

Hoffer, P.C. 1997. *The Salem Witchcraft Trials: A Legal History*. Lawrence, Kansas: University Press of Kansas.

Hudson, W.J. (ed.) 1974. *New Guinea Empire: Australia's Colonial Experience*. Melbourne: Cassell.

Johnson, L.W. 1983. *Colonial Sunset: Australia and Papua New Guinea 1970–74*. St Lucia: University of Queensland Press.

Joyce, R.B. 1971. *Sir William MacGregor*. Melbourne: Oxford University Press.

Larner, C. 2002. The Crime of Witchcraft in Early Modern Europe. In D. Oldridge (ed.) *The Witchcraft Reader*. London: Routledge, 205–12.

Lattas, A. 1996. Humanitarianism and Australian Nationalism in Colonial Papua: Hubert Murray and the Project of Caring for the Self of the Coloniser and the Colonised. *Australian Journal of Anthropology* 7(2):141–65.

Legge, J. 1956. *Australian Colonial Policy: A Survey of Native Administration and European Development in Papua*. Sydney: Angus and Robertson.

LRCPNG (Law Reform Commission of Papua New Guinea) 1978. Sorcery among the Tolai People. *Occasional Paper* No. 8. Waigani: LRCPNG.

Murray, J.H. 1929a. *Native Administration in Papua*. Port Moresby: Government Printer.

Murray, J.H. 1929b. *The Response of the Natives of Papua to Western Civilization*. Port Moresby: Government Printer.

Murray, J.H. 1938. *The Machinery of Indirect Rule in Papua*. Port Moresby: Government Printer.

Nelson, H. 1982. *Taim Bilong Masta: The Australian Involvement with Papua New Guinea*. Sydney: Australian Broadcasting Commission.

Selby, D. 1964. *Itambu!* Sydney: Angus and Robertson.

Sinclair, J. 2009. *Gavamani: The Magisterial Service of British New Guinea*. Adelaide: Crawford House Press.

Thomas, K. 2004. The Relevance of Social Anthropology to the Historical Study of English Witchcraft. In M. Douglas (ed.) *Witchcraft Confessions and Accusations*. London: Routledge, 47–79.

Timmons, S. 2006. Witchcraft and Rebellion in Late Seventeenth Century Devon. *Journal of Early Modern History* 10(4):297–330.

Trevor-Roper, H.R. 1967. *The European Witch-Craze of the Sixteenth and Seventeenth Centuries*. Harmondsworth: Penguin.

von Benda-Beckmann, F. 2002. Who's Afraid of Legal Pluralism? *The Journal of Legal Pluralism and Unofficial Law* 47:37–82.

Williams, F.E. 1935. *The Blending of Cultures: An Essay on the Aims of Native Education*. Port Moresby: Government Printer.

Wright, D.P. 2009. *Inventing God's law: How the Covenant Code of the Bible Used and Revised the Laws of Hammurabi*. Oxford: Oxford University Press.

12. A Pluralist Response to the Regulation of Sorcery and Witchcraft in Melanesia

Miranda Forsyth

Introduction

This chapter focuses on the dimension of sorcery and witchcraft defined by Mary Patterson as 'the belief, and those practices associated with the belief, that one human being is capable of harming another by magical or supernatural means'.[1] Sorcery and witchcraft in Melanesia mean that misfortune, accidents, business failures, sickness and death are commonly believed to have been deliberately caused by certain individuals through the use of supernatural powers, rather than resulting from natural causes. In turn, this may lead to violent responses against those accused of sorcery or witchcraft, which can involve prolonged torture, public executions, riots, warfare, banishment of individuals and entire families, and burning of houses and other property damage (Chandler 2013). These responses differ enormously in type and scale around the region, and are at their most extreme in parts of Papua New Guinea (PNG). However, in many other areas of PNG and Melanesia in general, sorcery- and witchcraft-related concerns are dealt with through non-violent community mechanisms.

In light of the apparent rise in sorcery-related violence in PNG,[2] and particularly two horrific incidents in early 2013 that attracted extensive international attention (Chandler 2013), there have been calls from both inside and outside the country for the government to take action to address the problem. At the same time, the law reform commissions in both Vanuatu and Solomon Islands have identified sorcery and witchcraft as an area of considerable concern for their populations and as requiring a legal response (see McDonnell, Chapter 8 and Kanairara and Futaiasi, Chapter 15 this volume).

---

[1] M. Patterson 'Sorcery and Witchcraft in Melanesia' (1974:132), cited in Aleck (1990) (copy on file with author). The terms sorcery and witchcraft are problematic and misleading, neither being an appropriate term for the various forms the belief takes around the region. Although anthropologists draw distinctions between the two terms (see Eves 2013), they are used interchangeably in the region and also in this chapter.

[2] See the claims made in CLRC (2011:9). However, the absence of reliable statistics makes any definitive claims about increases or decreases problematic.

This chapter therefore explores some of the questions that sorcery and witchcraft raise for the criminal justice systems of Melanesia, and in particular what regulatory responses may be of assistance. These questions include: whether or not there is a role for the criminal justice system in regulating this area, whether there should be witchcraft- or sorcery-related offences in the state criminal justice system, whether sorcery- and witchcraft-related beliefs should be treated as a defence of any sort, how sorcery- and witchcraft-related violence should be punished, and whether allegations of sorcery or witchcraft practices should be an offence.[3]

This discussion needs to be seen in the light of two important contexts as far as PNG is concerned. The first is the extensive corpus of literature about the treatment of sorcery and witchcraft in the region since the colonial period, and the legislative framework that reflects/reflected those discussions, much of which has been helpfully discussed in this volume by Stewart (Chapter 10) and Keenan (Chapter 11). The immediate post-independence approach, embodied in the PNG *Sorcery Act 1971*, tried to find a middle road between dismissing the beliefs as irrelevant to the criminal law and allowing them to become a justification for violence. The second context is the recent response of the PNG government towards the issue, which is directly counter to this post-independence position. As discussed in detail below, it essentially entails dismissing the belief in sorcery as 'nonsense', repealing the Sorcery Act on the basis that its existence has contributed to the violence, both by supposedly sanctioning the belief in sorcery and in facilitating the lenient treatment of those who kill accused witches (Miae 2013a). Instead, the government's new approach regulates the issue solely through tough new criminal laws to penalise those who kill accused sorcerers.[4] It is a very 'rational', command-and-control approach to the issues without, however, the existing institutional capacity to back it up.

In response, this chapter proposes that rather than viewing the issue of regulation of sorcery as solely a state matter, as has been done both historically and recently, questions of regulation should be viewed through two broader paradigms. One is a pluralist paradigm that views the state criminal justice system as one of a number of systems of legal ordering (the other most common ones are customary orders and the church). The other is a responsive regulatory paradigm that sees the state criminal justice system as part of a broader regulatory framework in which it can both support, and be supported by, other regulatory actors, such as non-government organisations, civil society advocates, academic institutions and other government departments. Regulation is conceived of in this chapter as involving legal rules and standards, but also other social activities such as 'persuasion, influence, voluntary compliance and self-regulation' (Parker and

---

3   This chapter expands upon my previous consideration of these issues; see Forsyth (2006, 2010).
4   Section 229A, *PNG Criminal Code (Amendment) Act 2013*.

Braithwaite 2003; see also Braithwaite 2002:29). These two regulatory paradigms may be a way of overcoming some of the operational problems that existed with the previous legislative framework. This in turn leads to my overall argument that this framework should not be completely jettisoned, but rather should be re-evaluated through asking the questions outlined above, in the light of these two paradigms.

Although referring at times to Vanuatu and Solomon Islands, this chapter focuses on the situation in PNG. This is because it is in PNG that the law and order problems are the most extreme, and also where there is an emerging national conversation about how to deal with these problems. This conversation was stimulated by a number of coalescing events, including the highly publicised deaths of two women accused of witchcraft in early 2013. It has involved two conferences, one in Canberra in June 2013,[5] and one in Goroka in December 2013,[6] and a workshop in June 2014 in Port Moresby in which participants drafted a national action plan to overcome sorcery- and witchcraft-related violence (Forsyth 2014). Each event involved a minimum of 80 participants from a range of government departments and civil society, church and academic organisations. I was involved in the organisation of all three events and they have greatly informed the ideas and observations in this chapter.

The role of the criminal justice system

It is clear from both the chapters in this book, and the significant body of literature on the topic, that the negative social consequences arising from sorcery and witchcraft, while in some respects rooted in a traditional past, stem from a number of current underlying social problems. In particular, they reflect conflicts and tensions over land, jealousies arising from inequalities in wealth distribution and access to resources, intergenerational tensions and the effects of declining health and education services. These developments also have a very definite gender dimension to them, which is being increasingly highlighted by academics, activists and even recently by the PNG Permanent Representative to the United Nations (Aisi 2013). It was recognised as early as 1977 by the Law Reform Commission of PNG that:

> It is possible that the amount of sorcery is increasing as a result of the uncertainties involved in modern development or 'underdevelopment' in Papua New Guinea. In a society in which differences in status and

---

[5] Sorcery- and Witchcraft-Related Killings in Melanesia: Culture, Law and Human Rights Perspectives Conference, The Australian National University, Canberra, 5–7 June 2013.
[6] Sorcery and Witchcraft Accusations: Developing a National Response to Overcome the Violence Conference, Goroka, PNG, December 2013.

income are increasing and traditional obligations are no longer as strongly upheld as they used to be, people often act against those who get too far ahead in social status through sorcery. Many senior public servants who have died young are believed to be sorcerised by their work mates who are believed to be envious of the promotions of the former. (LRCPNG 1977)

This reality raises very important questions about the role of the criminal law in this field. Some scholars have suggested that because the negative social consequences of sorcery beliefs and practices are symptomatic of deeper underlying social tensions and problems, the state justice system should not regulate this area. This view sees the criminal law as only able to have a relatively superficial effect, and expresses concern that the intrusion of the state could make particular conflicts worse. Knut Rio, for example, argues that increasing involvement of the state in the regulation of sorcery activities in Vanuatu is 'producing a transformation of the concepts of guilt and blame evoked in sorcery accusations and is leading to more widespread aggression and violence against those accused'. He does not, however, substantiate his claim with quantitative evidence (Rio 2010:187). McDonnell (Chapter 8 this volume) similarly states that she is concerned that 'the approach of prosecution under criminal law fails to recognise, or offer any resolution, for the underlying tensions in which the accusations, threats or acts of *nakaemas* take place'. In a presentation in 2013 at the Canberra conference, Burton also argued that accusations of sorcery and witchcraft were '100%' related to the appalling levels of mortality in rural PNG, and that therefore the focus should be on building up health care, rather than focusing on the law. 'No deaths, no reason to accuse witches', he opined (Forsyth 2013). The conclusion of these (and other) scholars is therefore to stop focusing on a state criminal justice response, and instead address the range of underlying causes of the problems.

While these arguments have considerable merit and point to the delicacy with which the issues must be addressed and the need to broaden the focus, they do not mean that a criminal justice response is irrelevant. There are several reasons why the state criminal justice system is legitimately and necessarily involved in questions of both actual and threatened personal physical violence and destruction of property, such as is occasioned by accusations of sorcery and witchcraft. First, the state criminal justice system claims to have a monopoly on the use of force, and therefore its help is needed to deal with threats and use of violence as a matter of practice. Second, the state criminal justice systems in the three Melanesian states considered here are engaged in an ongoing project of developing legitimacy in the eyes of the populations through extending the rule of law, and this cannot be done by ignoring what is considered by many to be a major cause of threat and violence in a community. The criminal justice system is widely seen by much of the population in all three countries as needing to do 'something' in response to the problems caused by sorcery and witchcraft beliefs, although there are widely differing views about what that something is. For instance, the PNG Constitutional and Law Reform Commission report 2011 found that '[t]he majority view was that sorcery must continue to be given legal recognition — with a view to severely punish sorcery practitioners, including those who aid, abet and/or sponsor sorcerers' (CLRC 2011:52).

Third, addressing the underlying problems that are giving rise to the law and order problems is crucially important, but involves long-term solutions. Appropriate criminal justice responses can potentially provide an important mechanism to stop violence and fear in the short term, although this is heavily qualified by the extremely limited geographical reach of the criminal justice systems across the region and the dysfunctional character of a number of aspects of them. Finally, it is possible that positioning the negative social consequences arising from the belief in sorcery and witchcraft as requiring a regulatory response is one way to stimulate discussions about these issues at community and government levels. In PNG, Vanuatu and Solomon Islands there has been a reluctance to discuss the issues at a government level until very recently, and it has certainly been off the radar for most development and aid partners. Yet this in itself is problematic, as sorcery and witchcraft beliefs give rise to many realities that need to be taken into account in a broad range of development programs. Initiating forums for conversations in which new ideas can be injected can also be a powerful way to stimulate people to question entrenched beliefs and responses. Clearly, however, there is a need to ensure this is done in a way that does not involve what is seen as the imposition of foreign value systems, such as can occur with certain human rights narratives (Merry 2006; see also Evenhuis, Chapter 14 this volume).

So there are several good theoretical reasons for the state criminal justice system to become involved in this area, but also undeniable risks involved in so doing. The balance between these competing considerations will vary in the three countries. Certainly the much reduced levels of violence in Vanuatu and Solomon Islands means there is less justification for state regulation.

Responding to the violence related to sorcery and witchcraft raises a variety of interlinked issues and questions that do not have simple solutions. However, one potential way forward is based on the insight developed by legal pluralists over the past two decades, that despite the positivist claims made by the state, the reality in many postcolonial contexts is that often a number of different systems of legal ordering are at work (Merry 1988:870). Rather than focusing on which of these legal orders has authority, pluralists propose that it is more useful to consider questions of function, such as which forms of ordering or regulation have normative force among particular social groups (Benda-Beckmann 1985;

Forsyth 2009; Griffiths 1986; Twining 2008). Following such an approach, it is clear that in Melanesia many social groups are ordered or regulated by customary or community-level regulatory systems, or by church organisations. In some places other institutions, such as private security firms, are involved as well.

Recognition of this plurality is important for three reasons. First, it provides us with a number of options when we are considering what type of regulation may work best in a particular context, such as with sorcery- and witchcraft-related violence. We are no longer confined to considering state responses; we can also think about a range of non-state actors and institutions, meaning our responses can be more creative and possibly more widely implemented. Second, we need to be aware that focusing a regulatory strategy through just one legal order involves a very high risk that it may be undermined by the other legal orders. For example, creating mandatory jail sentences in state courts may mean that chiefs or local leaders work harder to ensure that such cases stay outside the state criminal justice system. Third, a pluralist approach starts addressing questions of regulatory response by asking about the current reality, rather than starting with assumptions about what ought to be.

Working out in which areas, and how, the state criminal justice system should be involved is extremely complicated. It is likely to require continuing discussions, testing and refinement of different regulatory approaches. The rest of this chapter aims to contribute to this process by highlighting a number of the issues that arise from the perspective of the criminal justice system. In order to ground the issues, it situates them by discussing the PNG *Sorcery Act 1971* and its recent repeal by the PNG government.

The *Sorcery Act 1971*

PNG's Sorcery Act dealt with the issue of sorcery and witchcraft in three principal ways. First, it created a series of offences that aimed to indirectly criminalise the practice of sorcery and witchcraft in a variety of ways, including through the creation of offences of purporting to be a sorcerer and possessing implements of forbidden sorcery (Sorcery Act Section 6; see section Sorcery- or witchcraft-related practices as an offence, below). The rationale for so doing was set out in the preamble to the Act:

> There is a widespread belief throughout the country that there is such a thing as sorcery and that sorcerers have extraordinary powers that can be used sometimes for good purposes but more often for bad ones, and because of this belief many evil things can be done and many people are frightened or do things that otherwise they might not do … There is no reason why a person who uses or pretends or tries to use sorcery to do,

or to try to do, evil things should not be punished just as if sorcery and the powers of sorcerers were real, since it is just as evil to do or to try to do evil things by sorcery as it would be to do them, or to try to do them, in any other way.

In fact, as discussed below, courts above the village court level rarely used these provisions in practice. Second, the Act created a partial defence for sorcery- and witchcraft-related murder, although this defence has been rarely used and almost never in the past two decades.[7] Third, the Act provided for the offence of falsely accusing another of performing sorcery or being a sorcerer, a provision that was also hardly ever used. The Sorcery Act therefore was for all intents and purposes a fairly defunct piece of legislation.

However, as noted above, in 2013 the widespread publicity given to the deaths of two women accused of witchcraft in PNG drew international and national attention to the problem of sorcery and witchcraft accusation-related violence, and the Sorcery Act was targeted as a contributing factor (Amnesty International 2013b; UNHCR and Refworld 2013). It was argued that the Act legitimised such murders by making sorcery a legally recognised phenomenon,[8] and it was seen as being responsible for the light treatment of perpetrators of sorcery-related violence (Miae 2013a). Prime Minister Peter O'Neill stated that he would repeal the law 'To stop this nonsense about witchcraft and all the other sorceries that are really barbaric' (Fox 2013). The government followed the repeal of the Act with the creation of a new provision in the *Criminal Code Act 1974* (Chapter 262). Section 229A of the Criminal Code Act provides that any person who intentionally kills another person on account of an accusation of sorcery is guilty of wilful murder, for which the penalty is death. In other words, a mandatory death penalty.

Apart from the extremely problematic extension of the death penalty,[9] this approach is consistent with that advocated by international non-government organisations such as Amnesty and a number of United Nations Special Rapporteur reports (Amnesty International 2013a; Heyns 2014; Manjoo 2013; UNHRC 2011). It essentially sees the state criminal justice system as being legitimately involved only when the conflicts have led to extreme violence, and as not having a role in managing the underlying conflicts involved. Such a response has the virtue of being straightforward, and consistent with international human rights instruments (minus the death penalty part), but is it likely to curb the violence in PNG?

---

7   See *Regina v. KJ* [1973] PNGLR 93 for a discussion of the defence.
8   Manjoo (2003:15) reports: 'The Sorcery Act is reportedly rarely used, but some argue that its mere existence helps perpetuate the belief in sorcery as a means of harming or killing another person'.
9   The death penalty has been technically available in PNG but has not been implemented since 1954. See Amnesty International (2004).

There are several interrelated reasons why this approach is not likely to have much effect. The main problem is that, notwithstanding the government's wish to do away with 'this nonsense', belief in sorcery and witchcraft remains firmly entrenched in PNG,[10] and it is giving rise to ongoing acts of violence and brutality. Moreover, these acts of brutality are often sanctioned by a sizeable proportion of the community and carried out with public approbation. As Father Pat Gesch noted, 'it seems that everyone wants to kill the *sangumas*'.[11] Recent research by Eves and Kelly-Hanku in Goroka, Eastern Highlands Province, found all except for one documented attack were 'sanctioned by most community members, who were unanimous that the community needed cleansing of witches' (Eves and Kelly-Hanku 2014). Given that, for the vast majority of the population the real 'evil' is being committed by the accused sorcerers,[12] it is almost inconceivable that the population will simply accept a government directive that they are to forget 'the nonsense' and to stop attacks on accused sorcerers. In order for the government to enforce this law effectively, in the absence of any other mechanism, it would therefore have to invest a tremendous amount of resources in arresting and prosecuting the perpetrators of the violence (who may often amount to large groups of people).[13] At present, PNG's criminal justice system, with around 5200 police officers (McLeod and Macintyre 2010) and 38 prosecutors[14] for a country of close to 7 million people, simply lacks the capacity.

Moreover, not only does the general population want to 'kill the *sangumas*', but so does much of the police force. In a 2014 documentary a senior officer in Kundiawa police force was reported as stating 'if we get rid of them [the sorcerers] then I think we'll have no … human rights abuses of anyone'. When he was asked how he proposes to get rid of them, he replied 'we kill them, we just go ahead and kill them' (Aljazeera 2014). Partly as a result of police complicity, there is a widespread perception of impunity with regard to sorcery accusation-related killings. Other factors that currently stop prosecutions from actually being made are a lack of police logistics, personnel and training, the absence of complaints, intimidation of witnesses, bribes paid to police to drop cases, and people being afraid of police retaliation if they complain that cases have not been pursued.[15]

Only preliminary and informal research has so far been carried out to learn the consequences of the new government measures. The overwhelming impression

---

10   Manjoo (2013:8) notes: 'The belief in sorcery and witchcraft is widespread across the country, with 90 per cent of the population believing in its existence'.
11   Email to author, 26 June 2014.
12   The CLRC report states, 'During the nationwide consultations, it became obvious that the majority of the people were concerned more about deaths occurring as a result of sorcery' (CLRC 2011:57).
13   See, for example, a recent media report on the arrest of 122 men and 69 juveniles (*Post-Courier* 2014).
14   Office of the Public Prosecutor, personal communication, 15 June 2014.
15   These factors were listed by participants in the Port Moresby workshop in June 2014.

from discussions at the two events in PNG is that the changes have generated widespread confusion for the population at large, and even for key government officials whose duty it is to enforce the law. For the most part, messages about the changes in the law have not filtered down to the local and provincial levels. For example, I met with a senior sergeant in charge of community policing in West New Britain who told me in June 2014 that she had been trying to find out for months now whether or not the Sorcery Act had been repealed, and no one had been able to tell her. Even where there has been awareness of the changes, there is considerable misunderstanding about what these changes entail. Anecdotal evidence suggests that a popular interpretation of the recent changes to the law is that the government has finally realised that it must act to stop sorcerers from their unspeakable acts of violence.

People working in communities in which accusations of sorcery and witchcraft are prevalent report the following questions arising: What is the law in this area? Who has responsibility and authority to do what? If a village has a problem and wants assistance, what forms of assistance are available? For example, Catholic Bishop Bal recently held some workshops in Dirima and Neregaima in Simbu Province to discuss the problems of sorcery- and witchcraft-related violence. He said that people afterwards asked him who they can call upon if there is a case in their village that they want to report, and how they can get law enforcement or mediation teams to come in. They also suggested the need for a mediation team in the area that can move as a group to different places when such incidents arise.[16]

So far I have argued that the problem of sorcery- and witchcraft-accusation violence cannot be simply responded to by treating the belief as 'nonsense' and refusing to engage with it except to prosecute those who murder accused witches and sorcerers. However, it is also clear that the previous approaches under the Sorcery Act were largely ineffectual, as indicated by the fact that they were rarely used. There is a clear tension in this area between trying to achieve the most from the potentially transformative power of the law, and the need to recognise not only the very real limits that the law has in Melanesia in general and particularly in PNG, but also the risks of its powers being misused or giving rise to unanticipated problematic consequences. The question that arises is therefore are there other criminal justice regulatory strategies that can be adopted?

As a possible way of moving forward, I want to look at the three areas addressed under the Sorcery Act, but to consider them in the light of two very different paradigms:

---

16   Interview of Bishop Anton Bal by Father Philip Gibbs, 4 May 2014. Interview kindly shared with the author by Father Gibbs.

- a pluralist paradigm: looking at the different systems of legal ordering (state and non-state) and at their relationships, and at the ways in which they can better support each other
- a holistic paradigm: viewing the criminal justice system as part of a broader regulatory framework and operating in conjunction with a range of other government departments, non-government organisations etc.

Further, while not a new paradigm as such, this chapter focuses on the violence that emerges as a result of an accusation of sorcery or witchcraft against an individual or individuals, rather than on the violence said to have been caused by the sorcerer or witch. It also takes as an aim the breaking of the link between sorcery and witchcraft beliefs and violence, rather than addressing other negative social drivers of the beliefs, such as underdevelopment and poor health outcomes.

Two paradigms and a new focus

This section will briefly explain the two paradigms and the new focus outlined above. The first suggested paradigm change is to turn from a positivist approach (there is only one legal system and that is the state) to a pluralist approach that recognises a number of different legal orders or systems at work in Melanesia. The second paradigm involves seeing the criminal justice system as part of a larger regulatory response, drawing on Braithwaite's (2006) concept of responsive regulation. This approach responds to the fact that the violence being expressed is symptomatic of a number of social and developmental issues that cannot be adequately addressed in a criminal justice framework. However, the criminal justice system can be viewed as playing several important roles *in conjunction with* a range of other service providers. Braithwaite (2006) argues that responsive regulation has potential for developing countries as it mobilises cheaper forms of social control than state command and control. In essence, it involves the state actively networking with non-state regulators to overcome its lack of capacity.[17] Using this paradigm positions the criminal justice system as part of, and supporting, a wider regulatory strategy. This was the clear direction advocated by participants at the Goroka conference, which was subsequently developed through the workshop in Port Moresby in June 2014 into a national action strategy. In the national strategy, the criminal justice system as a whole is tasked with two areas (legal and protection) of a five-pillared strategy that also includes advocacy and communication, health, care and counselling, and research (Forsyth 2014).

---

17   The application of the principles of responsive regulation to the problem of sorcery is an ongoing research interest for the author but for reasons of space not elaborated further here.

Finally, the focus on breaking the link between sorcery and witchcraft accusations and violence has been developed through the planning stages of, and discussions at, the conferences and workshop outlined in the introduction. It takes into account the pride in, and dependence upon, 'good' magic, such as for gardening, healing and other positive contributions to social life, and makes it clear that this is not the subject of regulatory control. Focusing on breaking the link between the accusation and the violence arguably provides a helpful focus for regulatory interventions, which otherwise could go off in a number of directions. It also aims to create some conceptual separation between the beliefs themselves, and the turn to violence. As such, it is a pragmatic response to the enormity of the challenge of transforming belief systems, and allows for the viewpoint that such transformations may be unnecessary, and indeed could be problematic in a range of ways. The focus on stopping violence is possibly also the easiest message to communicate to people at the grassroots level. However, it must be acknowledged that this focus is likely to require considerable public awareness and advocacy, as the reality is that for most of the population it is the violence committed by sorcerers that needs to be overcome. The separation between the beliefs themselves and violent responses is therefore a highly permeable one.

I turn now to the three main ways in which the Sorcery Act attempted to regulate sorcery and witchcraft, to see if viewing these areas through the two paradigms and with this new focus can suggest different courses of action.

Sorcery- or witchcraft-related practices as an offence

The first issue is whether or not any form of sorcery or witchcraft practice should be criminalised by the state legal system. I deal with this issue first because it is the most difficult, and also because the other issues discussed come back to it in one way or another. At first blush it seems that this issue can be avoided if the focus is on breaking the link between sorcery and witchcraft accusations and violence. However, taking such a narrow interpretation ignores the reality that the vast majority of the population believes that sorcerers and witches *do* need to be dealt with in some way. If a community is told that they are not to engage in violence against people they believe are sorcerers and witches, then their legitimate response is likely to be: well then, how will this problem (of the harm caused by the sorcerer or the witch) be dealt with?[18] The state is obliged to provide an answer to this question if it is to have strong

---

18   Although Clara Bal (Chapter 16 this volume) suggests that a community can decide not to turn to sorcery as an explanation for misfortune if the decision is taken as a community to do so.

grounds in directing people not to have recourse to violent responses. This was indirectly recognised by Justice Toliken in *State v. Latuve* [2013] PGNC 207, a case where the accused murdered a reputed sorcerer, who was widely suspected of having been responsible for the deaths of some 34 people in the village, the most recent of whom was the accused's brother. In sentencing the accused to 20 years imprisonment, the judge stated '[w]e live in a society where the law rules supreme. The state has institutions such as the police and the courts where people can take their grievances to for the lawful and just resolution of disputes'. At the moment, however, many in PNG are asking exactly where they *can* take such grievances. To rely on a rationale such as Justice Toliken advocates, the state is obliged to create such forums.

So we find ourselves back in the conundrum discussed in the first section, whereby the most likely consequence of non-state involvement is the community taking responsibility for the response. While in many areas of PNG, Vanuatu and Solomon Islands, the community response can be non-violent and restorative, in some places and in certain circumstances the response can be one of horrifying violence. Therefore, even with the focus on breaking the link between sorcery accusations and violence, this issue has to be addressed. First I will discuss how this issue has historically been addressed, and then consider how changing the paradigm can change the range of responses that are open.

As outlined above, the Sorcery Act criminalised certain types of sorcery and witchcraft practices, and similar provisions can be found in the legislation of most countries in the South Pacific islands region. The wording of the offences differs, and represents perhaps different approaches to overcoming issues of proof that are always going to be problematic for such cases:

PNG Sorcery Act

6. SORCERY GENERALLY.

(1) This section does not apply in cases where the sorcery involved is innocent sorcery only.

(2) A person who, directly or indirectly, pretends to be, holds himself out to be, or professes to be a sorcerer is guilty of an offence.

(3) A person who influences or attempts to influence the acts of another person by the use or threatened use of the powers or services of a sorcerer as such is guilty of an offence.

Penalty: On conviction on indictment–imprisonment for a term not exceeding two years.

On summary conviction—imprisonment for a term not exceeding one year.

Solomon Islands Penal Code Act

SORCERY

190. Any person who—

(a) performs any magic ritual in respect of which there is a general belief among any class of persons that harm may be caused to any person; or

(b) has in his possession, without lawful excuse, any article commonly associated by any class of persons with harmful magic,

is guilty of a misdemeanour, and shall be liable to imprisonment for two months or to a fine of forty dollars.

Vanuatu Penal Code Act

WITCHCRAFT

151. No person shall practise witchcraft or sorcery with intent to cause harm or detriment to any other person.

Penalty: Imprisonment for 2 years.

The reason for this is that while traditionally there are ways of 'proving' witchcraft and sorcery, the types of methods used — divinations, tracings, torture, dreams and so forth — all fall short of the standard required in state courts.[19] As a result, in most cases the wordings of the offences avoid the need to prove causation (that witchcraft or sorcery actually occurred) and rely on physical elements that can be proven, such as holding oneself out to be a sorcerer, or having in possession an item that a class of people would believe to be an implement of sorcery.[20]

So provisions can be worded in such a way that they capture at least certain types of problematic behaviour related to sorcery- and witchcraft-related beliefs, such as people who threaten to cause harm to others through sorcery, or those who profit from it by accepting payments to cause someone harm through sorcery. These types of formulations can be agnostic about the issue of whether or not witchcraft or sorcery practices have any actual effect. Rather, they target people who deliberately manipulate other people's fears of sorcery or witchcraft

---

19   These are discussed in this volume by Stewart (Chapter 10) and Keenan (Chapter 11).
20   However, the current wording in Vanuatu's provisions is problematic; see Forsyth (2006). For an extended discussion of the problems sorcery and witchcraft pose for questions of causation see Aleck (1990).

for malevolent and/or pecuniary reasons. And there is considerable anecdotal evidence that such people do exist, and that such threats are made on a regular basis, causing considerable fear in the targeted individuals.

For example, in *State v. Parara* (National Court 2008) a man was convicted after trial of the offence under Section 6(3) of the Sorcery Act: influencing the acts of another person by threatened use of the powers of a sorcerer. He told the victim, in whose family there had been a number of deaths, including the recent death of his son, that if the victim gave him a chicken, he could put a stop to the deaths in his family; thereby issuing a threat that if the complainant did not comply, there would be further deaths. The victim attempted to comply with the accused's demands by providing the accused with a pig; and because his actions were influenced by the offender's threat, the offender was convicted. Another example was reported in the *Post-Courier* in 2013 whereby a man was found guilty of practising sorcery at the Angoram market for a particular candidate who was contesting the by-election. The accused was apprehended by police, who found in his possession implements such as oil in small containers, tree bark and other substances in a Murik basket. During formal questioning he admitted being in possession of the implements and further admitted that he was assisting a particular candidate to win the by-election. He was sentenced by the Wewak District Court to 12 months imprisonment at the Boram jail (Nicholas 2013).

However, as noted above, the fact is there have been very few such prosecutions for sorcery or witchcraft practices in the higher state courts (see Auka et al., Chapter 13 and Evenhuis, Chapter 14 this volume), and the record is not clear in regard to the village courts, which is an area that needs considerably more research.[21] This leads to the conclusion that, in addition to problems of proof, there are other difficulties with using state courts to prosecute such matters. This includes problems of police and the general public being afraid of becoming involved in such cases for fear that they will become a target of sorcery and witchcraft; the physical difficulties in accessing state courts, particularly in the highlands of PNG; and a reluctance of prosecutors to bring such matters before the courts.

I now turn to considering whether looking at these issues through the two new paradigms can point a way out of this somewhat intractable problem. There are two possible options, which are not mutually exclusive.

21　The village courts secretariat reported at the Goroka conference that out of 35,000 cases reported and dealt with by the village courts since 2009, 700 were cases of sorcery. However, these figures were stated to be incomplete. Goddard notes that cases of sorcery are often not recorded as such by the village courts, which complicates the matter further. The reason for this is said to be 'a tacit concern to keep from officialdom any mention of a practice that the inconspicuous communities served by the court feared would bring them to the attention of the police or other intrusive authorities' (Goddard 2009:196; see also Goddard 1996).

The first option is to create a series of offences that cover the same sort of offences as the repealed Sorcery Act, but to embed this response within a broader, complementary, regulatory framework. The types of offences involving sorcery and witchcraft that can be dealt with in state courts in accordance with the rules of evidence are those involving threats of use of sorcery and witchcraft to cause harm, holding oneself out to be a sorcerer or witch with intention to cause harm, obtaining a financial advantage through use of sorcery- and witchcraft-related threats, and possessing implements known to be associated with sorcery with intention to cause harm. Having such provisions in the criminal justice system responds to the argument that the state should attempt to regulate people who overtly threaten others or who profit from others' beliefs in sorcery and witchcraft. However, it is likely that such laws will only be able to be used in a small number of cases, due to the generally surreptitious way in which sorcery is engaged with. There is also the larger problem of the lack of functionality of much of PNG's criminal justice system, meaning that there is a fundamental lack of capacity to implement the law. The undeniable reality of lack of capacity, which has contributed to the past ineffectuality of the law, may be met by complementing these new laws with a range of other regulatory initiatives, such as awareness-raising in villages about the criminalisation of such offences, training of police and prosecutors and paralegals about how to use the provisions, development of witness protection programs, capacity building for community leaders to start to break down environments of fear, and making reliable connections between community leaders and state criminal justice personnel. In other words, the limited state capacity may be supported by a broader regulatory response that engages the work of civil society advocates, church organisations, and international non-government organisations.

The second option is for the state to support and/or develop non-state channels (or hybrid structures such as village courts) in which accusations of sorcery and witchcraft can be vocalised and dealt with in a non-violent manner. Rules of evidence are not a constraint in such forums, meaning in particular that the discussions will not be artificially limited by state rules of relevance. The idea here would be to use existing institutions wherever possible as this would be an opportunity to build their capacity, and would also leverage important local legitimacy into the exercise. The village courts are one such obvious institution in PNG, and their *Manual 2004* already provides that they may deal with:

> Sorcery, including: practising or pretending to practice sorcery; or threatening any person with sorcery practiced by another; or procuring or attempting to procure a person to practice or pretend to practice, or to assist in, sorcery; or the possession of implements or charms used in practicing sorcery; or paying or offering to pay a person to perform acts of sorcery. (Goddard 2009:283)

In Vanuatu these institutions would include *nakamals* and possibly land tribunals (see McDonnell, Chapter 8 this volume) and in Solomon Islands, the local courts. The aim would be to further develop or strengthen mechanisms that would allow for accusations of sorcery and witchcraft to be discussed as early as possible before they escalate into violence, and to provide forums in which everyone has a chance to safely discuss their concerns and formulate a resolution. For example, it may involve community mediation in which the mediators (who may be local leaders, pastors or village court officials) deal in an open-minded way with witchcraft and sorcery allegations by asking the community to consider alternative explanations for the 'trigger' event giving rise to the accusations (e.g. obtaining doctors' certificates that clearly state the cause of death, and police accident reports). As Philip Gibbs's (Chapter 17) and Clara Bal's (Chapter 16) research suggests, and as is testified by those involved in the Human Rights Defenders Network,[22] in many cases of sorcery-related violence there is a proportion of the community who are uneasy with the violent response, but lack the leadership or support to stand up against it. Empowering individuals who are prepared to take a stand in a variety of ways, including by supporting them with information about the law, the importance of human rights, and relevant Christian doctrine, is crucial given the absence of the state in many communities. Consideration may also be given as to how to restore relations between the parties once accusations have been made and the matter resolved (such as reconciliation ceremonies, public apologies, prayer and, where appropriate, compensation).

One example of such a mechanism is the Catholic Church's five-point plan, discussed by Philip Gibbs (Chapter 17 this volume). Of course, such an approach means it is likely that a community may conclude that a person has indeed engaged in witchcraft or sorcery, and this raises questions about what sorts of responses will then be not only acceptable, but also avert violence in both the short and long term. Some options to be explored may involve exorcisms as discussed by John Himugu (Chapter 5 this volume), payments of compensation, prayer, exclusion from the sacraments or other aspects of community life, voluntary or involuntary temporary or permanent banishment, or other pragmatic responses.[23] While some of these options are unappealing from a human rights perspective, they are arguably preferable to the type of torture and murder that is occurring on a regular basis in parts of PNG.

---

22   https://www.facebook.com/HighlandsWomenHumanRightsDefendersMovement.
23   For example, it was reported in the *Post-Courier* in June 2014 that two women who had been accused of sorcery following the collapse of a young girl had been rescued by Defence Force soldiers from being tortured and nearly killed. However, after rescuing the women the joint security forces then observed the women perform a ritual to restore the young girl's heart and bring her back to life (Poiya 2014). This may have been a pragmatic decision on behalf of the security forces to restore peace in the community, or it may have reflected their shared beliefs that the women did have supernatural powers.

Another problem is that it may sometimes be difficult for community leaders such as village court officials to deal with these cases because of their closeness to the community, and also fears for their own safety. This was a point made by a spokesperson for the village court secretariat at the Goroka conference, and suggests that support from the district-level courts and police will often be crucial in backing up local initiatives.

A further point is that, given the gendered nature of many pockets of sorcery-related violence, any forum that deals with sorcery would need to specifically address issues of equal treatment for women, and work towards encouraging active participation by women, both as users of the system and also as administrators of it. However, considerable research is needed to determine how this may work in practice. Initially it is likely to hinge substantially upon the quality of local leadership that exists in particular locations. The types of questions that need to be explored include what the state criminal justice system can do to support such local leadership and conflict-management structures, and what can be done to build such structures where they do not currently exist. Examples include clear referral pathways, police providing security at community meetings, and paralegal training programs for community leaders. Another suggestion is to develop a network of external mediators who could be invited into communities by the community leaders to assist them in working through the issues and arriving at non-violent solutions. Outsiders can act as circuit-breakers to cycles of fear and violence, and this would be a way to empower those community members who do not support violence. External mediators could also connect the community into broader support networks, such as those that offer counselling and also the criminal justice system if that becomes necessary. Although the capacity of the state to create such a network is limited, this may be a role that could be filled at least on a temporary basis by a non-government organisation or even a church organisation.[24]

Another important avenue of inquiry is which mechanisms are currently successful at a local level to deal with these issues in non-violent ways, and whether and how they can be imported into new locations that have a history of violent responses. It is of relevance that in both Vanuatu and Solomon Islands, where the belief in sorcery and witchcraft is also very strong, there is much less recourse to violence than in PNG, and this is likely to be in large part attributable to the non-violent community-level mechanisms in use.[25]

---

24 The Melanesian Brotherhood performs this role to an extent in Solomon Islands.
25 For a description of the non-violent mechanisms used by the *kastom* system in Vanuatu, see Forsyth (2009).

Sorcery or witchcraft beliefs as a defence

The next major issue is whether a belief in sorcery or witchcraft should ever operate as a defence or mitigating factor in the commission of an offence such as homicide or assault. A defence is something that removes or excuses criminal liability, meaning that a person is either found not guilty (for a complete defence) or found guilty of a lesser crime (for a partial defence). A mitigating factor reduces a person's sentence but does not diminish their criminal responsibility.

The Sorcery Act (Section 20) provided a special partial defence for sorcery- and witchcraft-related killings, extending the doctrine of provocation to make it available where the act of sorcery provoked the attack. However, this defence has been used extremely rarely, in part because of the difficult requirement to show that the defendant acted 'in the heat of passion', as such killings are often planned.[26]

Independently of the Sorcery Act, the judiciary in PNG had until about a decade ago a tradition of taking belief in sorcery into account as a significant mitigating factor in sentencing, often reducing the sentence by up to a third. However, since around 2002 this tradition has been largely suspended and judges have been imposing heavier and heavier sentences. In 2002, in *State v. Boat Yokum & Ors.* (Unreported National Court Judgment – 2002) the judge stated:

> A strong punitive and deterrent sentence is required to punish the offenders and to send a clear message to their own community; who apparently seem to think that it is alright to kill a sorcerer or a reputed sorcerer for that matter; that it is wrong to kill another person including a sorcerer, reputed or not, and that they will be punished by the Courts, if they do.

This trend has continued. For example, in *State v. Wilson Okore* (2009), Justice Kirriwom imposed a penalty of 50 years imprisonment as a deterrent, noting that recently sorcery-related killings have escalated.[27]

The next question is whether a belief in sorcery *should* ever be a defence or a mitigating feature. A crucial starting point is whether or not to accept that a defendant may have a genuine belief that the victim has caused another harm or death through sorcery, or whether it is always to be regarded as a pretext or cover for other motivating factors. My analysis proceeds on the basis that it can be a genuine belief at times, and a pretext at other times, and it is therefore up

---

26 However, see Justice Narokobi's treatment of this requirement in *State v. Gesie and Guluwe* [1980] PGNC 20.
27 A number of sorcery-related murder cases in 2012 and 2013 have also involved judges stressing the need for long prison terms to send deterrent messages. See *State v. Mesuno* [2012] PGNC 80; *State v. Naba* [2013] PGNC 115; *State v. Latuve* [2013] PGNC 207.

to the courts to determine whether there is a genuine belief in any given case. In cases where it is used as a pretext there is no possible justification for it to be either a defence or a mitigating factor; on the contrary, it should be treated as an aggravating factor, which is how the courts are treating it at present.

However, the issue is perhaps less clear if the belief is accepted as genuine. In *State v. Mathias* [2011] PGNC 228 the court identified three types of sorcery killings. First, the prisoner kills because a family member, a close relative or a close friend has died. Second, the prisoner kills not only because a family member, a relative or a close friend has died but also because he is believed or rumoured to be at risk of being killed soon through sorcery. He kills to stop himself being killed. Third, the prisoner kills because of his belief in sorcery generally without any real threat to him, his family, relatives or friends. I will add a fourth category, where a person kills on the orders of a customary leader under a sense of customary obligation to do as commanded.

Clearly these different situations raise slightly different arguments. The case for a defence is certainly strongest where the person kills in the firm belief that this is the only way to stop being killed. It may be argued that not taking such beliefs into account, when they are truly the motivating factor, means that the criminal law is not adequately reflecting the cultural basis of the society it is regulating, and thus risks being seen as illegitimate and a foreign imposition, and unfair and overly harsh in individual cases.

On the other hand it can be argued — and this is the prevailing view of the judiciary — that the law must disregard the belief in all of these situations from a public policy perspective, as it may be seen as tantamount to encouraging vigilantism, payback killings, and giving a licence to attack suspected sorcerers. This approach would argue that citizens today are far more educated than in the past and are well aware of the limits of customary responses and that payback killings are unlawful in any context.

Finally, it is important to stress again the interrelation between the different questions under discussion. Thus the question about the availability of a defence for genuine cases of belief in sorcery and witchcraft in state courts is related to the provision of a mechanism to manage concerns about the use of sorcery and witchcraft. If a state is going to adopt the position that a genuine belief in sorcery will not be a defence or a mitigating factor, then to be fair it is obliged to point to a process or an institution that can provide real assistance to a person who is either tormented by fear that they will be subjected to an attack of sorcery, or filled with rage that a person they love has been killed by what they consider to have been sorcery. In other words, if the state is to say 'don't take the law into your own hands', then this needs to be matched by the providing or indicating of an alternative course of action.

Punishment for sorcery and witchcraft accusation-related violence

Turning now to the issue of punishment and deterrence, the above discussion has demonstrated that the claim that the Sorcery Act in PNG is responsible for 'light' treatment of sorcery- and witchcraft-related attacks by state courts is for the most part misplaced (Amnesty International 2004; CLRC 2011:58). What is clear, however, is that the imposition by courts of heavier and heavier sentences will not necessarily have any deterrent effect, or even impinge upon the public awareness, as is shown by the apparent lack of public appreciation of the fact that judges have been steadily imposing stiffer and stiffer penalties in such cases for the past 10 years. In the recent case of *State v. Latuve* [2013] PGNC 207, Acting Justice Toliken stated: 'Sorcery-belief induced killings have not diminished. If anything killings have become more horrendous as seen from recent public torture and killings such as the much publicized killing of a young mother in Mt. Hagen who was burned to death with a tyre around her neck'.

One of the areas this flags for further research is to ask what specific and general deterrent effects are produced in the Melanesian context by long jail terms — or by other sentences such as the death penalty laws. This is a pertinent question in relation to sorcery- and witchcraft-related killings, but also more broadly, and there is little to no data available on which to make any informed assessment. In discussing the new death penalty laws in PNG, Archbishop Young stated:

> The one thing missing from the debate was any evidence whatsoever that the death penalty will deter violent crime. This argument was repeated over and over again without any credible evidence in support. This is because there is none. My own conversations with men and women who have committed violent crime indicate that they are not thinking beyond the release of their anger or passion. Most either expect to get away with it (and usually do) or simply don't care about the consequences. Criminologists know that it is not the severity of punishment that deters crime but its certainty. Until Papua New Guinea can detect, arrest, convict, and successfully imprison offenders for the duration of their sentence, prospective criminals will assume that they have a good chance of getting away with it. (Social Concerns Notes 2013)

To add a restorative justice dimension to this discussion, a new way to frame discussions about deterrence may be to concentrate less on heavier sentences, and more on *effective* sentences. This can be done by having regard to the types of sentencing practices that are used by non-state local and customary mechanisms, such as public shaming, public apologies, compensation payments, and restorative payments such as requirements to rebuild someone's house, or supply food, or cover medical costs. This would facilitate the development of sentences that act both as deterrents and also on repairing the harm that has been done to the victim and restoring relationships in communities. Such solutions are likely to be able to be developed more meaningfully at a community level, but may require support from the state to ensure that they are enforced. A restorative justice approach also allows us to consider questions about what happens after a state court has dealt with a matter — how can victims and offenders be reintegrated back into communities? This requires local-level conflict management to work in cooperation with the state criminal justice system to try to prevent another cycle of violence, given the tensions likely to exist as described by Gibbs (Chapter 17 this volume).

Accusations of witchcraft or sorcery as criminal offences

The final issue to discuss is whether or not the state should provide for an offence of alleging or falsely accusing a person of being a witch or of performing sorcery. As with sorcery belief-induced murders, there are a number of types of sorcery-related accusations that must be considered. We can view these in three conceptual categories, although in reality they blur into each other. The first is where the accusation is used as a weapon in the context of a dispute, or an attempt to get land or power, or through jealousy, in circumstances where there is no genuine belief that the person really engaged in sorcery or witchcraft (ABC News 2014; Oxfam International PNG 2010:10). The second is where the person making the accusation is genuinely frightened and believes that the accused person is causing others misfortune, but in fact this belief is a mistaken one and there are alternative explanations for what has occurred. The third is where individuals actually are practising what they consider to be sorcery and intending to cause someone harm, influence events (e.g. an election), extract money from people, or scare people. It is important to think about these different categories as they all need to be approached in different ways. In the first two cases we need to think about regulating the accuser's behaviour, and in the third case the focus should be on the accused's behaviour.

As discussed above, the Sorcery Act provided for the offences of falsely accusing another of performing sorcery or of being a sorcerer. However, these provisions were used in only a handful of cases. It may be that because of the way the provisions were worded proof that the accusation of sorcery was false was required, and prosecutors and police may have been unsure of how to do this.

Despite the non-use of these provisions in the Sorcery Act, there have been numerous calls for the state to criminalise the making of false accusations of sorcery in recent times. For example, in 2013 the chairman of the Churches Medical Council of PNG called for the government to create a law that punished a person for accusing others of practising sorcery. He observed that women and elderly people were the main targets in sorcery-alleged killings (Miae 2013b). Those calling for such laws argue that allegations of sorcery are key triggers of social unrest and disorder throughout Melanesia. Criminalising the making of such an allegation for malicious purposes may cause people to think twice before making such allegations, and may stop such disorder from eventuating. These offences may also be used by the innocent to protect themselves and to clear their names. The Gor Community Base Laws discussed by Clara Bal (Chapter 16 this volume) demonstrates that the community in her study considered that stopping sorcery-related accusations was key in stopping the violence that results.

However, there are a number of arguments against having such laws. It could be argued that these allegations could be dealt with using the general laws of defamation and criminal defamation and do not require specific provisions. A counter response is that because a defence to defamation is that the defamatory statement was in fact true, this may require the court to adjudicate upon the question of whether or not the accused was really engaging in sorcery, the evidential problems with which have been outlined above. Moreover, as court proceedings work slowly, they are unlikely to be an adequate response to the incendiary social effects of sorcery and witchcraft allegations. A further problem may be that criminalising the making of accusations may make the accusations more covert and hence more difficult to engage with early, thus undermining the mediation/conflict resolution approach outlined above. There is also the problem that these laws have been ineffective in the past, again demonstrating the profound problems of lack of implementation and enforcement capacity in the criminal justice system.

I now turn to consider whether viewing this issue through the new approach outlined above is of assistance. One possible way to overcome at least some of the problems just described that springs from the proposed focus on breaking the link between accusation and violence is to have a provision that criminalises *incitement to violence* on the basis of sorcery-related accusations, rather than the accusations themselves. This would not stop community leaders from being able to discuss sorcery accusations publicly, but it would provide a clear message about the need to deal with the accusations in a non-violent manner. Ideally this could be complemented by other parts of a comprehensive regulatory strategy, such as the provision by health workers of explanations of causes of sickness and deaths (see Cox and Phillips, Chapter 2 this volume).

Further, if we adopt a pluralist approach it can also be considered whether there are appropriate non-state mechanisms that could work on stopping sorcery accusations from being made, such as church interventions or local community governance mechanisms like the Gor Community Base Laws. It is probable that those at the community or village level are far more likely to be able to distinguish between accusations based on malicious intent and those made through genuine fear, and they could adopt different strategies to deal with the different types of accusations. For the first type, it may be of use to refer to the prospect of being charged with a criminal offence if the accuser does not retract their accusation and apologise. Village courts are particularly well placed in this regard. This again illustrates the need to improve communications and referral mechanisms between community-level conflict management structures and the state, which again raises the critical problem of lack of state capacity.

Conclusion

In conclusion I want to step back slightly from the detailed discussions above and try to contextualise the issues within a broader jurisprudential framework. Although this chapter has dealt with specific questions, it also raises important questions relevant to the development of Melanesian legal systems generally. Some of these include: What role should customary norms and customary institutions play in the state criminal justice system? How can human rights be effectively incorporated into Melanesian regulatory systems in ways that are considered legitimate by the population as a whole? How can regulatory systems best deal with the limited reach of the state and the richness of local governance mechanisms, where such local mechanisms still have effective influence? Is the supposedly rational basis of Western legal systems appropriate in all contexts in Melanesia? These issues are bound up in the ongoing conversations about how to create new and unique jurisprudence that reflects Melanesian culture and beliefs and recognises customary norms and practices, which was a dream at independence and continues to be important among some parts of the community and those in the justice system (Narokobi 1986:215; Ntumy 1995:7).[28] There are also important criminological questions that sorcery- and witchcraft-related practices and beliefs raise, such as: What will be a deterrent to the types of attacks on women accused of sorcery that have been on the rise in PNG? Do heavier penalties have any effect? The criminal law can be an effective instrument to deal with social deviance in some contexts, but it is highly dependent upon the state having the capacity to implement and enforce it properly. In the absence of this capacity, the law itself and the institutions tasked with enforcing it can become as cruel and unjust as the behaviour it is trying to regulate. In recognition of these problems, this chapter has tried

---

28   The continuing interest in this is shown by the *Underlying Law Act 2000* (PNG) and the ongoing CLRC inquiry into the underlying law.

to identify ways in which the criminal justice system can intervene before accusations of sorcery and witchcraft lead to law and order problems, as well as assisting it in its role of punishing wrongdoers.

References

ABC News 2014. Local 'Power Plays' Behind Rise in Sorcery-Related Violence in PNG, Says Institute of National Affairs. ABC News online, 2 August. www.abc.net.au/news/2014-08-01/png-sorcery-violence-on-the-rise/5642190, viewed 5/8/2014.

Aisi, R.G. 2013. Address to the 57th Session of the UN Commission on the Status of Women. 11 March, New York. www.un.org/womenwatch/daw/csw/csw57/generaldiscussion/memberstates/png.pdf, viewed 5/8/2013.

Aleck, J. 1990. A 'Rational' Perspective on Law and Sorcery in Papua New Guinea. *Working Paper*. Canberra: Research School of Social Sciences, The Australian National University.

Aljazeera 2014. A War on Witches. 101 East. www.aljazeera.com/programmes/101east/2014/04/war-witches-20144299354589156.html, viewed 5/8/2014.

Amnesty International 2004. Papua New Guinea: The State as Killer? ASA34/001/2004. www.amnesty.org/en/library/asset/ASA34/001/2004/en/f0de00eb-d5e9-11dd-bb24-1fb85fe8fa05/asa340012004en.pdf, viewed 5/8/2014.

Amnesty International 2013a. Incredible Progress on Ending 'Sorcery' Murders in Papua New Guinea. 2 May. www.amnesty.org.au/iar/comments/31683/, viewed 5/8/2014.

Amnesty International 2013b. Papua New Guinea Must Act After Woman Burned Alive for 'Sorcery'. Amnesty International News online 8 February. amnesty.org/en/news/papua-new-guinea-must-act-after-woman-burned-alive-sorcery-2013-02-08, viewed 5/8/2013.

Braithwaite, J. 2002. *Restorative Justice and Responsive Regulation*. Oxford: Oxford University Press.

Braithwaite, J. 2006. Responsive Regulation and Developing Economies. *World Development* 34(5):884–98.

Chandler, J. 2013. It's 2013, and They're Burning 'Witches'. *The Global Mail* 15 February. <www.theglobalmail.org/feature/its-2013-and-theyre-burning-witches/558/>, viewed 5/8/2014.

CLRC (Constitutional and Law Reform Commission of Papua New Guinea) 2011. *Review of the Law on Sorcery and Sorcery Related Killings: Draft Report*. Port Moresby: CLRC.

Eves, R. 2013. Sorcery and Witchcraft in Papua New Guinea: Problems in Definition. *SSGM In Brief* 2013/12. Canberra: State, Society and Governance in Melanesia Program, The Australian National University.

Eves, R. and A. Kelly-Hanku 2014. Witch-Hunts in Papua New Guinea's Eastern Highlands Province: A Fieldwork Report. *SSGM In Brief* 2014/4. Canberra: State, Society and Governance in Melanesia Program, The Australian National University.

Forsyth, M. 2006. Sorcery and the Criminal Law in Vanuatu. *Lawasia Journal* 1:1–27.

Forsyth, M. 2009. *A Bird that Flies with Two Wings: The* Kastom *and State Justice Systems in Vanuatu*. Canberra: ANU E Press.

Forsyth, M. 2010. The Divorce or the Marriage of Morality and Law? The Defence of Necessity in Pacific Island Countries. *Criminal Law Forum* 21(1):121–57.

Forsyth, M. 2013. Summary of Main Themes Emerging from the Conference on Sorcery & Witchcraft-Related Killings in Melanesia, 5–7 June 2013, ANU, Canberra. Outrigger: Blog of the Pacific Institute. <pacificinstitute.anu.edu.au/outrigger/2013/06/18/summary-sorcery-witchcraft-related-killings-in-melanesia-5-7-june-2013/>, viewed 5/8/2014.

Forsyth, M. 2014. New Draft National Action Plan to Address Sorcery Accusation-Related Violence in Papua New Guinea. *SSGM In Brief* 2014/18. Canberra: State, Society and Governance in Melanesia Program, The Australian National University.

Fox, L. 2013. O'Neill Vows To Repeal PNG Sorcery Law. ABC News online, 12 April. www.abc.net.au/news/2013-04-11/an-png-police-unable-to-stop-violence/4623874, viewed 5/8/2014.

Goddard, M. 1996. The Snake Bone Case: Law, Custom and Justice in a Papua New Guinea Village Court. *Oceania* 67:50–63.

Goddard, M. 2009. *Substantial Justice: An Anthropology of Village Courts in Papua New Guinea*. New York: Berghahn Books.

Griffiths, J. 1986. What is Legal Pluralism? *Journal of Legal Pluralism and Unofficial Law* 18(24):1–55.

Heyns, C. 2014. Preliminary Observations on the Official Visit to Papua New Guinea by Mr Christof Heyns, United Nations Special Rapporteur on Extrajudicial, Summary or Arbitrary Executions, 3–14 March 2014. Press statement, Office of the High Commissioner for Human Rights. www.ohchr.org/EN/NewsEvents/Pages/DisplayNews.aspx?NewsID=14373&LangID=E, viewed 5/8/2014.

LRCPNG (Law Reform Commission of Papua New Guinea) 1977. Sorcery. *Occasional Paper* No. 4. Waigani: LRCPNG. www.paclii.org/pg/LRC/OP_04.htm, viewed 5/8/2014.

Manjoo, R. 2013. Report of the Special Rapporteur on Violence against Women, Its Causes and Consequences. 13/3/2013, A/HRC/23/49/Add.2.

McLeod, A. and M. Macintyre 2010. The Royal Papua New Guinea Constabulary. In V. Luker and S. Dinnen (eds.) *Civic Insecurity: Law, Order and HIV in Papua New Guinea*. Canberra: ANU E Press.

Merry, S.E. 1988. Legal Pluralism. *Law and Society Review* 22(5):869–96.

Merry, S.E. 2006. *Human Rights and Gender Violence: Translating International Law into Local Justice* Chicago: University of Chicago Press.

Miae, E. 2013a. PNG Law Reform Group Advises Repeal of Sorcery Act. Pacific Islands Report, Pacific Islands Development Program, East-West Center. First published in *The National*. http://pidp.eastwestcenter.org/pireport/2013/March/03-19-03.htm, viewed 5/8/2014.

Miae, E. 2013b. Churches: Sorcery Law Needed. *The National* 4 March.

Narokobi, B. 1986. In Search of a Melanesian Jurisprudence. In P. Sack and E. Minchin (eds.) *Legal Pluralism: Proceedings of the Canberra Law Workshop VII*. Canberra: Law Department, Research School of Social Sciences, The Australian National University.

Nicholas, I. 2013. Wewak District Court in PNG Condemns Man For Sorcery. Pacific Islands Report, Pacific Islands Development Program, East-West Center. First published in *The National*. www.pidp.org/pireport/2013/September/09-05-14.htm, viewed 5/8/2014.

Ntumy, M. 1995. The Dream of a Melanesian Jurisprudence: The Purpose and Limits of Law Reform. In J. Aleck and J. Rannells (eds.) *Custom at the Crossroads*. Port Moresby: University of Papua New Guinea.

Oxfam International Papua New Guinea 2010. *Sorcery Beliefs and Practices in Gumine: A Source of Conflict and Insecurity.* Oxfam International. archive.org/details/SorceryReportFINAL, viewed 5/8/2014.

Parker, C. and J. Braithwaite 2003. Regulation. In P. Cane and M. Tushnet (eds.) *The Oxford Handbook of Legal Studies.* Oxford: Oxford University Press, 119–45.

Poiya, J. 2014. Soldiers Rescue Women. *Post-Courier*, 3 June, p. 7.

Post-Courier 2014. Court Charges Men with Sorcery, Cult. *Post-Courier*, 23 April, p. 8.

Rio, K. 2010. Handling Sorcery in a State System of Law: Magic, Violence and *Kastom* in Vanuatu. *Oceania* 80(2):183–97.

Social Concerns Notes 2013. tokstret.com/2013/05/31/social-concerns-notes-may-2013/, viewed 5/8/2014.

Twining, W. 2008. *General Jurisprudence: Understanding Law from a Global Perspective.* Cambridge: Cambridge University Press.

UNHCR (United Nations High Commissioner for Refugees) and Refworld 2013. UN Urges Papua New Guinea to Take Action after Woman Burned Alive for Witchcraft. UN News Centre, 8 February. www.un.org/apps/news/story.asp?NewsID=44096#.Uh-ucLy8LqM, viewed 5/8/2014.

UNHRC (United Nations Human Rights Council) 2011. *Report of the Special Rapporteur on Torture and Other Cruel, Inhuman or Degrading Treatment or Punishment. Addendum: Mission to Papua New Guinea.* UN Doc A/HRC/16/52/Add.5.

von Benda-Beckmann, F. 1985. Some Comparative Generalizations about the Differential Use of State and Folk Institutions of Dispute Settlement. In A. Allott and G.R. Woodman (eds.) *People's Law and State Law: The Bellagio Papers.* Dordrecht, the Netherlands: Foris Publications, 187–206.

13. Sorcery- and Witchcraft-Related Killings in Papua New Guinea: The Criminal Justice System Response

Ravunamu Auka, Barbara Gore and Pealiwan Rebecca Koralyo

Introduction

The Office of the Public Prosecutor (OPP) in Papua New Guinea (PNG) is empowered by the constitution to undertake the prosecution function of the state in the National Court and in the Supreme Court of PNG. The prosecutors of the OPP are therefore responsible for the conduct of trials in the National Court and the defending of appeals in the Supreme Court. This role places the prosecutors in a position of responsibility for securing justice for both victims and persons accused of sorcery and for victims of sorcery-related killings. Most often victims of sorcery-related killings are persons accused or held in suspicion of practising sorcery.

This paper will outline the historical and more recent responses by the criminal justice system to sorcery- and witchcraft-related killings. Furthermore, through analysis of case studies an observable trend in the increasing number and increasing levels of violence in sorcery- and witchcraft-related killings in PNG will be discussed. Finally, we will discuss the perspectives from the prosecutors of the OPP on the future role of the criminal justice system in responding to sorcery- and witchcraft-related killings.

Sorcery in Papua New Guinea

The overwhelming majority of Papua New Guineans, regardless of age and gender, believe in the existence of sorcery. PNG is a diverse country comprising more than 800 ethnic groups; all have a system of beliefs that accounts for sorcery and its existence. Sorcery is believed by many as being part of PNG's unique and noble culture and a sacred tradition that is observed in many different ways by the different ethnic groups (Gibbs 2009; Oxfam 2010; Rangan 2009).

The courts have recognised this widespread belief in sorcery in PNG, as expressed by the late chief justice Sir Buri Kidu:

> There is no doubt that in this country the belief in sorcery is widespread and nobody really has to prove to the court that it exists. Belief in sorcery exists amongst some of the most backward of our people in the mountains of every province and also in the urban areas, including Port Moresby. Very well-educated people believe that sorcery exists and that there is power in people who practice evil sorcery to cause the death of other persons.[1]

The preamble to the constitution recognises Papua New Guinean ways under National Goal 5. This includes the recognition of cultural practices and rituals experienced in our communities and daily lives. Although there are customary rules that regulate the communities and separate ethnic groups, the constitution enables and empowers other legislation and creates law-making and law enforcement agencies to govern and maintain law and order in society. Acts of sorcery have been governed by separate legislation, but other laws in this country are also observed to maintain fairness and peace in societies, communities and the country as a whole.

The law

Sorcery Act 1971

The national parliament recently passed legislation to repeal the *Sorcery Act 1971*, and this has already taken effect. The Act made sorcery an offence, with the Act defining and recognising sorcery and the belief in sorcery that exists in PNG. Sorcery is defined in the Act (Section 1) as:

> 'sorcery' includes (without limiting the generality of that expression) what is known in various languages and parts of the country as witchcraft, magic, enchantment, puripuri, muramuradikana, vada, meamea, sanguma, or malira, whether or not connected with or related to the supernatural.

Sorcery itself as an offence was very difficult to prove in any court of law. This is largely because in order for one to answer to such an offence there must be evidence demonstrating that sorcery was practised by that person. Almost always the evidence in such cases is lacking because sorcery is a sacred practice

---

1 *State v. Aiaka Karavea & Anor* [1983] N452(M) (20 September 1983).

and no one wants to talk openly about it. Additionally, no physical or tangible evidence can be brought before the court because with sorcery everything involves the use of supernatural powers or a supernatural being. Even when witnesses can be brought in, their accounts can be illogical, improbable, and of rather impossible events, making it impossible to prove in court. Having said that, it strengthens the notion that sorcery is something associated with the supernatural, and the belief that it exists. It must be emphasised that the Sorcery Act itself, or indeed the belief in sorcery, does not, nor did not, in any way prevent law enforcement and prosecution in the area of sorcery-related killings or violence.

The Criminal Code

The Criminal Code Act is the legislation that prescribes the most serious of criminal offences in PNG. One of the primary functions of the OPP is to uphold and to enforce the Criminal Code in terms of attending to and representing the state in criminal trials in the National Court and appeals in the Supreme Court. The Criminal Code does not specifically prescribe sorcery as a crime; this offence was prescribed under the Sorcery Act. However, the Criminal Code does provide for offences that amount to sorcery- or witchcraft-related violence. Most often the charges laid against persons for killing suspected sorcerers are that of wilful murder or murder. The difference between these two offences is that a person charged with wilful murder, which involves an element of intention to kill, is liable to the death penalty, whereas a person charged with murder is liable to life imprisonment. The role of OPP prosecutors is to present evidence in court against persons charged with killing a suspected or known sorcerer, and to have the person charged with that offence and be dealt with according to the law by the courts in their administration of justice.

Often, persons charged with killing a suspected or known sorcerer have indicated that their reasons for killing that person was because of the deceased's practice of sorcery killing or causing illness to a close member of their family or their friends. Bearing in mind PNG's culture and traditions, prosecutors and courts have recognised the belief in sorcery and have conceded to it being a mitigating factor in sentencing. The Supreme Court of PNG has taken the belief of sorcery and the violence that results thereof into account in one its judgments:

> The belief in sorcery taken together with other factors in their favour only operates to reduce a life sentence to a term of years. It does not and should not operate to render a sentence equivalent to that usually imposed by judges here for murder, manslaughter, dangerous driving causing death, infanticide.[2]

---

2   *Agoara Kelo & Anor v. State* (1981) SC198.

This had become precedence and the practice in the PNG criminal justice system in its approach to sorcery-related killings. In recent times this view has changed and sorcery or the belief in it is now held to be an aggravating factor when determining a sentence.

Sorcery-related violence cases in the Papua New Guinea courts

Formal legal system process

The number of cases relating to sorcery- and witchcraft-related violence that come to the National Court of Justice in PNG is not as many as it should be. The figures are inaccurate and do not reflect the number of acts actually occurring. This is evidenced by the numerous reports in the media; however, only a few cases of sorcery-related violence have come to court and even fewer cases of a person being accused of being a sorcerer have come to court. The only reported case of a person being convicted of sorcery was in 2008 when a man was charged under the Sorcery Act for threatening another that he would use sorcery on that person. The National Court sentenced that man for only a year. This was for the threat of using sorcery.[3]

Sorcery-related violence can be prosecuted in our courts under charges of murder or wilful murder, grievous bodily harm, or even as unlawful assaults. Prosecutors do not determine the number of cases that come to the National Court, but it is all part of the criminal justice process. The process begins when an aggrieved person lays a complaint with the police; the police then investigate and if there is sufficient evidence they will arrest the perpetrator or perpetrators and charge them accordingly.

The matter then goes through the committal process in the district court; the equivalent of the district court here is the magistrates court. This court determines whether there is enough evidence for the offenders to stand trial in the National Court. If there is, the matter comes to the OPP.

Criminal matters before the National Court can proceed by way of a trial or a plea of guilty. In the instance of a trial the prosecutors acting for the state present all the evidence the state has against the alleged offender or offenders. This evidence is what was collected by the police in the initial investigation, and any other evidence that the prosecutor considers relevant and admissible.

---

3   *State v. Parara* [2008] PGNC 259; N3957 (22 February 2008).

After all the evidence is put before the court the offender represented by their counsel can make their defence. Counsel may present evidence in the court that the alleged offender was not the person who committed the act of violence against the known or suspected sorcerer. Then the court decides whether the offender is guilty or not. If the court finds that he is not guilty then the court will acquit him or her of the charges, but if the court finds the offender guilty and convicts then the court decides the penalty.

This penalty is the sentence the court gives and the offender is to serve this in custody or sometimes it can be partially suspended depending on certain factors such as age or medical condition. The penalties given to an offender vary according to aggravating or mitigating factors. The aggravating factors refer to those facts in the case that make the sorcery-related act of violence heinous and more serious, whereas mitigating factors are those considerations that make the act of violence one that can be looked at less harshly, given that certain facts such as expression of genuine remorse, the offender is young or has pleaded guilty. Other considerations like medical reports are also taken into account because these reports are independent expert opinions that indicate the weapons used and the extent of the injuries inflicted to determine the degree of aggravation. These matters are placed before the court in submissions made by both the prosecutor and the defence counsel. The court then in their discretion and administration of justice determines the sentence to be imposed.

Court data and analysis

We now analyse data collected from 26 reported National Court judgments taken from the Pacific Islands Legal Information Institute databases (PacLII),[4] in order to gain a perspective of the way in which sorcery- and witchcraft-related violence has been dealt with by the National Court of PNG. The statistical analysis that follows is not comprehensive but does provide an indication of what is before the courts and what the criminal court response has been to sorcery-related killings. It is noted that most cases of sorcery-related violence in the National Court end up as a plea of guilty, with only the sentence to be decided by the National Court.

It is common knowledge that there are many cases in the country of sorcery-related violence as reflected in the media or tales heard in our communities; however, in 32 years, from 1980 to 2012, the number of cases reported on PacLII was only 25 (see list at the end of the chapter).

---

4 Online legal database of all or most reported National Court judgments (www.paclii.org).

Charges and sentences of sorcery-related violence

A person is usually charged with wilful murder or murder in relation to the death of a victim who is often accused of being a sorcerer. Upon conviction this person is liable to death, life imprisonment or imprisonment of more than 25 years. The ultimate discretion lies with the presiding judge, who takes into account the circumstances of the case with the law to award the appropriate sentence. From 1980 to 2012, nine charges of wilful murder were made, and 10 charges of murder. The sentences for these charges are summarised in Figure 1.

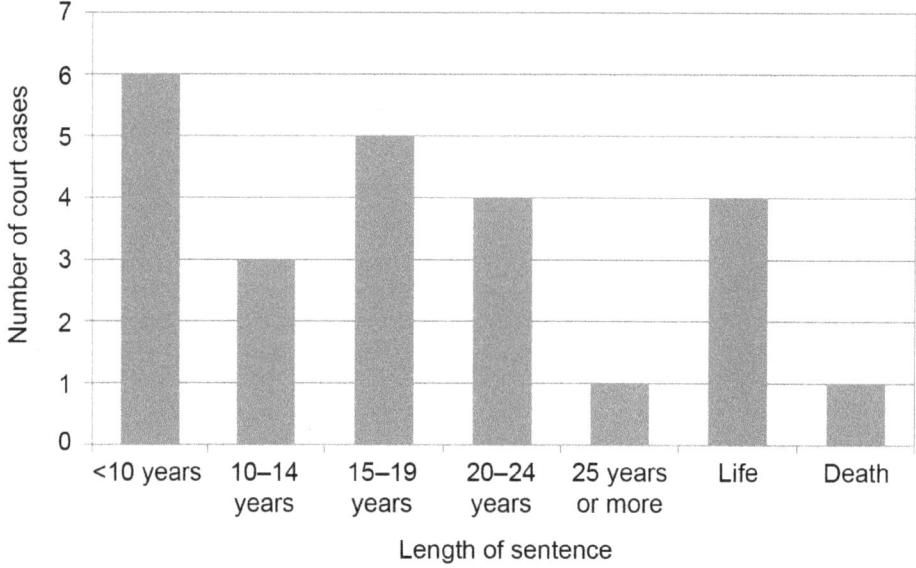

Figure 1: Sentences handed down in relation to the commission of sorcery-related violence offences, 1980–2012.

Source: Pacific Islands Legal Information Institute databases (www.paclii.org).

The most observable trend to note is that a person responsible for killing a known or suspected sorcerer will be charged with wilful murder or murder. The courts had earlier adapted to culture and traditions and saw sorcery as a major mitigating factor in sentencing. However, in recent times this view has changed and the courts are imposing harsher penalties on persons responsible for killing another person regardless of whether the victim was a known or suspected sorcerer.

For instance, in 2007 two people were sentenced to death, showing the serious approach taken by the courts in relation to sorcery-related violence. This can be contrasted with a case in 1980 where a sentence of six years was deemed appropriate given that sorcery-related killing was a special category of its own, meriting a lesser sentence than all other kinds of wilful murder offences that would normally attract a sentence of many years up to a maximum of life imprisonment.[5]

The case in 2007 was far more serious than the case in 1980. In his judgment the trial judge accepted that belief in the power of sorcery is common in many communities in PNG today and is a mitigating factor. However, it was his view that with the introduction of Christianity, western civilisation, and the establishment of government administration and authorities the courts should not continue to treat belief in sorcery as a bar to imposing the maximum penalty in a serious wilful murder case. The judge stressed that each case is different and the imposition of the death penalty depended on the factual circumstance of the case.[6] Therefore, in the 2007 case, a harsher penalty of death was warranted. This is an indication that the PNG courts will not tolerate sorcery-related violence. It is notable that after 2000 there have been more reported cases of sorcery-related violence and the sentences imposed by the courts have been harsher than in the 1990s, regardless of whether or not there is a plea of guilty.

Offenders and victims of sorcery-related violence

It is not often that a deed or offence is committed by an individual. From the 26 National Court cases examined, only 20 cases reported charges being laid for violence relating to sorcery, and of these 20 cases eight offences were committed by individuals and 12 offences were committed by groups. Most indications are that these offenders have a strong belief that the person they are killing is a sorcerer and it is in the common good of all that persons should take action to rid the community of this one person than to wait and see other people die.

This is the belief that drives offenders to brutally torture and kill another person suspected of sorcery. Even persons as young as 16 years are convicted of such offences because they are brought up and raised with this belief of sorcery and the harm it inflicts on another person and the community as a whole.[7] The following are quotes taken from judgments and sentencing decisions of persons being dealt with for wilful murder related to sorcery killings:

> In his sleep he had a dream. In that dream he saw the deceased [suspected sorcerer] come and carve out his son's eye with a knife. Shortly afterwards, the son developed swelling of his eye and died as a result of that swelling.[8]

---

5   *Public Prosecutor v. Apava Keru and Aia Moroi* [1985] PNGLR 78 at 80–1.
6   *State v. Lota* [2007] PGNC 167; N3183 (1 October 2007).
7   *State v. Tayamina* (Cr. No# 302 of 2010) (10 May 2013).
8   *State v. Gesie & Guluwe* [1980] PGNC 20; N254 (12 July 1980) at para 3.

The whole community believed that the deceased was a reputed sorcerer who was responsible for the death of some 53 people in the village previously. The whole community resolved it was time to put an end to their suffering by eliminating the deceased and called upon willing and able members of the community to carry out the decision.[9]

A strong punitive and deterrent sentence is required to punish the offenders and to send a clear message to their community; who apparently seem to think that it's alright to kill a sorcerer or a reputed sorcerer for that matter; that it is wrong to kill another person including a sorcerer, reputed or not, and that they will be punished by the Courts, if they do.[10]

Data from the National Court cases showed that the victims of sorcery-related violence were skewed towards men: 17 victims were men and 3 were women. One inference that can be drawn from this data is that when a suspected sorcerer who is killed is a male, the matter is pursued in the courts. Few of the cases involve women being killed simply because when they are believed to be sorcerers the matter rarely comes to the court. This could possibly mean that the death of a woman may be less significant or may go unnoticed in the community or may not be seen to warrant an action taken against the offenders. However, one must also bear in mind that in many societies in PNG a woman leaves her people to marry into her husband's family and lives in his community with his relatives. In these instances a woman is on her own, and her relatives are not there to enquire or assist when a woman is attacked after being suspected of sorcery. Also, in other societies, especially those that are matrilineal, women are accorded much respect and therefore there are fewer cases of such atrocities being committed against women and reported.

However, in PNG there are almost daily reports of women being tortured, burned, slashed with knives, beaten with iron rods, and killed because they are suspected of practising sorcery or witchcraft. These cases often do not come to the courts, OPP or the police, which is why no action in the formal legal system is taken against the persons who commit these acts of violence. This is an issue that all stakeholders in law enforcement and community development must seek to address. Media awareness of the law and its effective and efficient implementation could be a start in addressing this issue.

Geographical spread of sorcery cases

The geographical spread of sorcery-related violence cases throughout PNG, from the recorded National Court cases, is shown in Figure 2.

---

9   *State v. Yokum* [2002] PGNC 24; N2337 (4 December 2002) at para 2.
10 *State v. Siviri* [2004] PNGLR 12 (30 August 2004) at para 8.

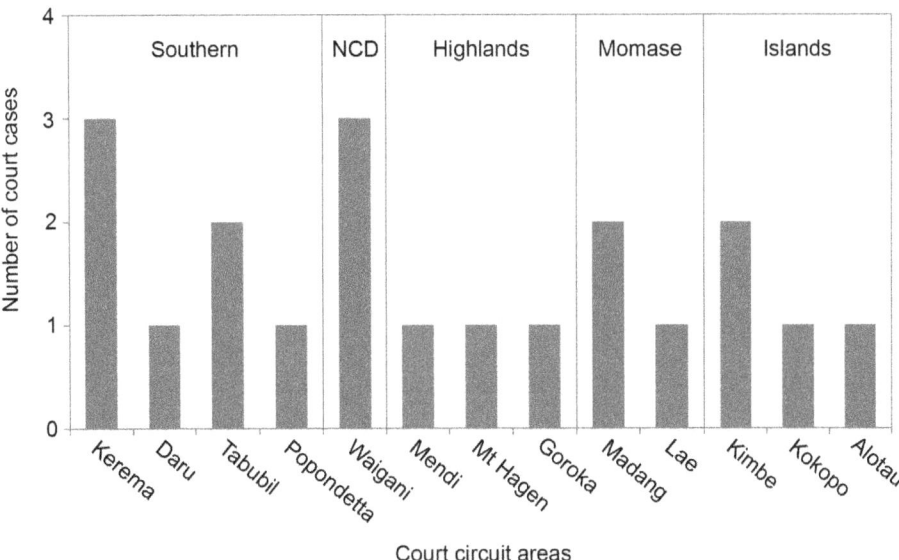

Figure 2: Geographical spread of sorcery-related violence cases in Papua New Guinea.

Note: NCD = National Capital District.

Source: Pacific Islands Legal Information Institute databases (www.paclii.org).

We can see from Figure 2 that sorcery-related violence cases are more prevalent in the coastal regions (Southern, Momase and Islands regions) than in the Highlands Region. The other inference that may be drawn is that prosecutions for sorcery-related killings are more likely to commence in the coastal or island regions of the country and not in the highlands.

Finally, it should be noted that in referring to the above statistics of court circuit areas, the Waigani circuit area is a composite in that this circuit deals not only with matters of persons from the National Capital District, but also all other PNG ethnic groups that live in the city. For this reason the Waigani circuit area would be likely to cover more cases of sorcery and sorcery-related violence being an urban centre comprising many ethnic groups.

Unexplained deaths

The issue of sorcery-related violence ultimately goes back to the existence of the belief in sorcery. Most people in PNG believe in sorcery with it being like a religion with a supernatural aura. Often people use sorcery as an excuse. Sorcery is used to account for unexplained deaths and unnatural events (Gibbs 2009).

When deaths occur it is often due to an illness, accident, or someone intentionally killing another person. The latter is done in instances of tribal warfare, retaliation or payback killing, or as a criminal act. However, when murder is not the cause of death, illness is a likely cause of unexplained death. Health facilities in PNG are not funded as they should be for illnesses to be treated properly.

Moreover, the lack of proper medical care in the country is apparent and the appalling state of its healthcare institutions gives rise to high mortality rates. One of the highest causes of death in the county is HIV/AIDS. This virus thrives in an infected person's body, resulting in imminent death. However, if access to proper health care is available for the infected person to get tested and treated then that person can live longer. Due to the lack of proper medical care this virus is causing many premature deaths of the working class in the country and thus is added to the average Papua New Guinean's mind as another unexplained death.

These unexplained deaths also result from fear of the unknown. People in the country do not all have access to good medical care for them to understand that a person looking sick and experiencing pain or other symptoms of an illness is basically just sick and requires medical attention. They are at times quick to point fingers and label it as an act of sorcery (Gibbs 2009:6).

Sometimes when deaths occur as accidents they are also held as acts of sorcery. In PNG the concept of accident is non-existent in that for every act there must be a possible reason, either physical or spiritual. For that reason often these deaths are not taken up in the courts of law, nor are enquiries made to ascertain the cause of the accident, but simply viewed as an act of sorcery because it occurred under supernatural or extraordinary circumstances. This habit of assumption has become a culture or norm in PNG society, with this largely attributable to a lack of understanding of health and medicine, fear of the unknown and the need for better health services to be provided to Papua New Guineans.

Recent amendments to the Criminal Code

On 28 May 2013 the PNG government enacted legislation amending the existing laws in the Criminal Code. These amendments were largely done in relation to the penalties to be imposed for wilful murder, rape and other crimes of atrocious nature with aggravating circumstances. The new amendments contain a separate provision on sorcery-related wilful murder. This provision states that any person found guilty of murdering a suspected sorcerer is liable to the death penalty. This is the government's stand against sorcery-related killings and shows that such acts will not be tolerated.

The OPP has usually treated sorcery-related killings as wilful murder and has charged accordingly, with the penalty for which the offender is liable to one of death. It awaits to be seen how, if at all, the recent amendments will impact on the prosecution, court and formal legal system response to sorcery-related killings.

Challenges for the criminal justice system

In PNG there are already laws in place that provide for acts of sorcery and sorcery-related violence. The laws in place do not in any way prevent law enforcement. Law enforcement can be utilised against persons responsible for acts of violence related to sorcery. For these reasons media and public awareness of these laws must be made. This all can be done, through proper funding and an increase in law enforcement capacity. In PNG the police are inadequately paid and infrastructure relating to their work needs either maintenance or restructure. With a police force in this situation, PNG cannot possibly contain sorcery-related violence, because the violence is usually a group attack and everyone in the community usually takes part. Police are often outnumbered and outgunned.

The other difficulty law enforcement faces is that of the costs and lengthy processes of the court. As explained earlier, the process to get a matter into court can be long, and at times witnesses move elsewhere and costs are incurred just to secure evidence before the court. This should not be the case, if our courts and law enforcers had adequate capacity and funding to deal with these cases. Costs can also be incurred by the investigations; these include medical bills, transport, and phone bills. Therefore, the way to justice is long and quite costly.

One of the fundamental things lacking in PNG is interagency communication between stakeholder groups. Stakeholder agencies such as law enforcers and other agencies, including non-government organisations, need to better communicate, in a coordinated way, to tell the public what their offices do and that there is help for those who have been victims of sorcery-related violence or that persons suspected of sorcery can be dealt with by law. Awareness is a key factor.

Conclusion

There are laws already in place that make unlawful acts of sorcery and witchcraft-related violence. It is up to PNG and its people to utilise these laws and involve law enforcers to have justice administered. This case analysis has shown that sorcery and the belief in it is indeed something the criminal justice system recognises and PNG's laws have been created to provide for this and to address the matter of sorcery-related violence. However, analysis of the data show that there are not many cases before the criminal courts of sorcery-related killings and even fewer of persons accused of practising sorcery. One possible explanation for this is the act of sorcery-related violence is perceived by the entire community as being an act of elimination of suffering and evil in their communities.

Another insight from the data is that where a woman is suspected of being a sorcerer and is subjected to acts of torture, violence or even death, these matters are rarely brought to court or followed up in any investigations to result in legal proceedings. This unfortunately is consistent with the widely held view that women are less influential in the PNG community than men.

There are evident challenges for law enforcement agencies, educators, health and caregiver agencies, and the country of PNG as a whole. It is undoubtedly people's lack of understanding and fear of the unknown that has made deaths of known or suspected sorcerers to be insignificant. Although sorcery-related violence may seem understandable in the PNG context, the international community views it as heinous, and PNG must realise that such deaths cannot be overlooked. To address this serious issue PNG must act now to maintain interagency communications, to attain appropriate funding for infrastructure and capacity building, and also work with the community to respect the culture but also instil knowledge and understanding of the laws and the appropriate actions to take. The people must know that these services are here and that offenders of the law can, and will, be dealt with by the courts of this land.

References

Constitutional and Law Reform Commission of Papua New Guinea 2011. CLRC Reference No. 7: Review of the Law on Sorcery and Sorcery Related Killings.

Gibbs, P. 2009. Sorcery and AIDS in Simbu, East Sepik, and Enga Provinces. *Occasional Paper* No. 2. Boroko: The National Research Institute.

Oxfam 2010. Oxfam Studies on Violence & Insecurity in the Southern Highlands, Simbu, and Eastern Highlands Province. Draft paper, International PNG Highlands Program.

Rangan, J. 2009. *Sorcery in Kokopo*. Office of Public Prosecutor and New Guinea Islands Regional Office.

Sorcery-related violence court cases, 1980–2012

Acting Public Prosecutor v. Uname Aumane [1980] PNGLR 510

State v. Gesie & Guluwe [1980] PGNC 20; N254 (12 July 1980)

State v. Karavea & Karavea [1983] N452(M) (20 September 1983)

State v. Kwayawako [1988] PNGLR 174

Kwayawako v. State [1990] PNGLR 6 (30 November 1989)

Roger Jumbo and Aidan Awatan v. State (1997) SC516

State v. Arnold [1997] N1658 (21 November 1997)

State v. Sambura [2002] PGNC 114; N2219 (18 April 2002)

State v. Yokum [2002] PGNC 24; N2337 (4 December 2002)

State v. Baipu [2003] PGNC 59; N2451 (30 July 2003)

State v. Siviri [2004] PNGLR 12 (30 August 2004)

State v. N'Danabet [2004] PGNC 56; N2728 (9 November 2004)

State v. Binape [2004] PGNC 57; N2727 (12 November 2004)

State v. Visari [2006] PGNC 61 (15 June 2006)

State v. Jackson [2006] PGNC 154; N3237 (24 October 2006)

State v. Mohavila [2006] PGNC 106; N3385 (25 October 2006)

Irai Thomas v. State SCR 8 of 2006 Unreported SC Judgment dated 26 Feb, 29 August 2007

State v. Miritok [2007] PGNC 164; N3466

State v. Lota [2007] PGNC 167; N3183 (1 October 2007)

State v. Parara [2008] PGNC 259; N3957 (22 February 2008)

State v. Martin [2008] PGNC 29; N3312 (12 March 2008)

State v. Wapsi [2009] PGNC 84; N3695 (24 July 2009)

State v. Mathias [2011] PGNC 228; N4670 (9 September 2011)

State v. Niruk [2012] PGNC 152; N4821 (3 October 2012)

State v. Tayamina (Cr. No# 302 of 2010) (10 May 2013)

14. Sorcery Violence in Bougainville Through the Lens of Human Rights Law: A Critical View

Mark Evenhuis[1]

> Colonial categorisations and ways of knowing the world are embedded in international law and continue to have powerful effects in this putatively 'postcolonial' era. (Pahuja 2004:245)

Introduction

Allegations of malevolent sorcery resulting in retaliatory violence and sometimes murder appear to be increasing on both mainland Papua New Guinea (PNG) and the Autonomous Region of Bougainville. This, coupled with increased media reporting of the issue, has spurred local civil society organisations, international human rights institutions and non-government organisations (NGOs) to demand that the governments of PNG and of Autonomous Bougainville take immediate action to address the issue.

Drawing on the postcolonial and critical legal methodology of Third World Approaches to International Law (TWAIL), this chapter interrogates the promise and limitations of relying upon the law, and language of human rights, to know about and respond to the emerging problem of sorcery accusation-related violence in Bougainville. I argue that human rights law inevitably conceptualises sorcery-related violence as a traditional practice productive of societal disorder, which demands state-led interventions involving law and cultural transformation. This conception of sorcery accusation-related violence replicates colonial forms of knowledge and is, as such, unable to comprehend the role of sorcery allegations as a misdirected attempt to reorder Bougainvillean society in the face of growing inequality and conflict.

The call for more law, punishment and cultural transformation in response to sorcery accusation-related violence risks restaging prior colonial interventions under the more palatable guise of human rights. I argue that this 'restaging' is

---

[1] Mark Evenhuis is a Senior Policy and Advocacy Adviser at Plan International Australia, and formerly worked in Bougainville and PNG as a human rights adviser and consultant. He has recently completed a Masters of Law and Development at the University of Melbourne. He wishes to thank Miranda Forsyth and Laura Vines for their input and editorial assistance.

enabled through the human rights discourse preoccupation with the eradication of putatively harmful 'traditional' practices in the present which obscures other forms of violence authored by the state — in both its current and colonial form — and corporate transnational actors; namely through their destabilisation of indigenous forms of dispute-settlement practices and the cultural, social and economic dislocations attendant to PNG's incorporation into the global economic order.

Looking outside the lens of human rights, I then develop alternative understandings of the meaning of sorcery accusation-related violence. In doing so, I draw attention to the key paradox sustaining human rights law's encounter with sorcery accusation-related violence through the case study of Bougainville: while the rise in this practice can in part be attributed to various governmental and economic interventions which have driven inequality and fuelled disorder within PNG and Bougainville societies, the rationale of human rights law typically prescribes only greater intervention based on law and cultural transformation — interventions which are blind to, and thereby risk perpetuating, the systemic causes of the violence itself. The ongoing propagation of this paradox is only possible through a discursive focus on immediate symptoms of violence and the concealment of its socio-economic and political precursors (Orford 2003). I then rely on this broadened understanding of sorcery accusation-related violence (and failed prior interventions) in order to discuss the potential for non-violent and community-focused responses to the immediate issue within Bougainville and, perhaps more importantly, to foreground the wider political and economic issues at play.

Finally, this chapter urges a fundamental rethinking of the use and power of human rights to understand and respond to issues such as sorcery violence. I discuss the radical potential of human rights as a language through which to articulate claims for a more just and less violent local and international economic order, as well as one possible means of redirecting increasingly internalised rage at growing inequality within Bougainvillean societies towards its largely external economic causes.

Part 1: Sorcery accusation-related violence in Bougainville — a brief overview

Media reporting and interviews conducted for the purpose of writing this chapter suggest that between 2010 and 2013 at least 30 individuals were murdered in Bougainville following accusations that they had harmed or killed others by practising sorcery. The true number of deaths, however, is likely much higher given that sorcery accusation-related killings are rarely covered in the media or reported to police, largely because many occur in remote areas far from government aid posts or police stations and are often 'hushed up' by community members who have led group attacks against alleged sorcerers.[2] Notably, a recent Bougainville-wide study conducted by the South African Medical Research Council on behalf of the United Nations found that '[h]alf of the men and a quarter of women [surveyed] had witnessed sorcery accusation-related violence' and that '[o]ne in five of the men had participated in such violence' (Jewkes et al. 2013:5). Many of these killings were carried out by groups of young men often under the protection of ex-combatants.[3] A majority of these murders occurred in Central Bougainville, an area that was at the heart of the Bougainville conflict.[4]

Allegations of sorcery often circulate after a community member has become sick or has died; in Bougainville, sorcery is often believed to be a cause of serious unexplained illness or of death (Hamnett and Connell 1981). Retribution motivated by suspicions of malevolent sorcery — particularly against those whose non-traditional wealth or status has elicited community jealousy — is a key immediate cause of sorcery-accusation related violence.[5]

While in PNG as a whole, older women are typically understood to be the key targets of sorcery accusation-related violence, especially in the highlands (Zocca 2010), this does not appear to be the case in Bougainville where there exists a diversity of cultural beliefs about which sex has the ability to perform sorcery (for instance, on Nissan Island, only men are believed capable of sorcery).[6] My research suggests that men in Bougainville are more likely to be accused of sorcery than women (a majority of the approximately 30 people murdered over the past four years were male) and that women are at most risk from harm after an immediate male family member had been accused.[7] So while sorcery accusation-related violence in Bougainville has gendered aspects — largely due to cultural beliefs about who can possess sorcery powers — this chapter does not characterise it as *primarily* a women's rights issue.

---

2   Interview with Informant 1, 23 April 2013.
3   The term 'ex-combatant' refers to those who took up arms during the Bougainville conflict.
4   Although Jewkes et al. (2013) suggest a majority of sorcery accusation-related violence occurred in South Bougainville.
5   Interview with Agnes Titus, sub-national co-ordinator, UN Women, Autonomous Region of Bougainville (AROB), 20 April 2013.
6   Interview with Agnes Titus, sub-national co-ordinator, UN Women, AROB, 20 April 2013.
7   Although UN Women in Bougainville anecdotally believe that the number of murders is currently evenly split between men and women. Interview with Agnes Titus, sub-national co-ordinator, UN Women, AROB, 20 April 2013.

Part 2: Viewing sorcery through the lens of human rights

As Luis Eslava (2014:3) reminds us, international law 'like photography, involves a way of observing the world, and a way of categorising what is worth looking at'. Its technologies of 'enframing' organise both how we perceive the world and 'our political responses to it' (Eslava 2014:3–4). Similarly, I want to interrogate how international human rights law designates sorcery accusation-related violence as necessitating our gaze, provides particular ways of knowing about sorcery accusation-related violence and prescribes state-led interventions drawn from this knowledge. Here, I want to consider how this manner of viewing non-state actor violence as ultimately demanding more pervasive state control replicates colonial understandings and interventions directed towards pacifying and reforming the colonised 'other'. I do this with a view to questioning the capacity of the solutions typically prescribed by human rights law to reduce sorcery accusation-related violence.

The application of human rights law to sorcery accusation-related violence

First, let us consider how human rights law applies to this form of non-state authored violence. Under international human rights law, where an individual accused of sorcery is murdered, this amounts to a breach of their fundamental right 'to life, liberty and security of person' (Article 3, UDHR). Where alleged sorcerers are punished through assault, torture or murder, this is a breach of their right not to be disciplined or deprived of their liberty 'except on such grounds and in accordance with such procedure as are established by law' (Article 9, ICCPR).

While sorcery-related violence is generally carried out by non-state actors, international human rights law imposes a duty on the PNG Government and Autonomous Bougainville Government (ABG) to 'exercise *due diligence* to prevent, punish, investigate or redress the harm caused by such acts by private persons or entities' (Human Rights Committee 2004:3, my emphasis). This positive obligation of 'due diligence' is concretised in Article 2 of the International Covenant on Civil and Political Rights (ICCPR)[8] which obliges state

---

[8] PNG acceded to the ICCPR on 21 July 2008. The oft-cited international law maxim of *pacta sunt servanda*, as elaborated under Article 26 of the Vienna Convention on the Law of Treaties, provides that once a state party has ratified a treaty, it must carry out its obligations under that instrument in good faith. Many of the human rights enshrined within ICCPR have been legislatively incorporated into the Constitution of the Independent State of Papua New Guinea (for example, see Division 3: Basic Rights). This obligation also binds the ABG by operation of Section 293 of the Constitution of the Autonomous Region of Bougainville.

parties, including PNG, 'to respect and to ensure to all individuals within its territory and subject to its jurisdiction the rights recognized in the Covenant'. This duty of 'due diligence' is underpinned by PNG and ABG's legal systems, which give the state a monopoly on both the use of force and the trial and punishment of people accused of wrongdoing.[9]

Sorcery-related violence as disorder in need of law

TWAIL theorist Antony Anghie observes that the human rights framework 'creates in the legal sphere a set of principles that appear to correspond with the project of the postcolonial state to expand into every sphere of society and establish itself as the single authoritative, universal and encompassing entity' (Anghie 2006:462). The human rights principle of 'due diligence' does just this through affirming the centrality of nation states to regulate violence and simultaneously demanding state intervention in the face of perceived disorder.

In the case of sorcery accusation-related violence in Bougainville, and PNG more broadly, this call for state-led intervention has been iterated by senior PNG leaders and by human rights institutions alike; in 2010 the perceived rise in sorcery- and witchcraft-related violence against women in PNG led the Committee on the Elimination of Discrimination against Women (CEDAW) in its concluding observations for PNG to call on the PNG government 'to prosecute and punish the perpetrators of such acts and to prevent their reoccurrence in the future' as well as 'to strengthen the enforcement of relevant legislation' (CEDAW 2010:6). The Human Rights Council's 2011 Report of the Working Group on the Universal Periodic Review for PNG also contained recommendations that it, among other things, 'accelerate its review of the law on sorcery and sorcery-related killings', 'strengthen the enforcement of relevant legislation' and 'prosecute and punish perpetrators of such crimes' (Human Rights Council 2011a:[78.21]). Similarly, international human rights NGOs such as Amnesty International have taken up the call for legal intervention and reform (Amnesty International 2013a, 2013b).

Such legal prescriptions are not new to PNG; in early Papua and New Guinea, the British and Australian colonial administration sought to curb perceived 'native' disorder — such as the practice and punishment of sorcery — and concentrate power in the hands of colonial authorities through the putative power of law (Murray 1913). Despite its disbelief in the existence of sorcery, from its early days the administration passed laws criminalising the practice of malevolent sorcery or the making of unfounded accusations against others of

---

9 Constitution of the Autonomous Region of Bougainville, Sections 115(3) and 148; and Section 37 of the Constitution of the Independent State of Papua New Guinea.

practising sorcery (Murray 1929). The *Sorcery Act 1971*, adopted by the PNG House of Assembly prior to independence, represented the continuation of this approach in the post-independence era.[10]

Through human rights' insistence that the PNG state have greater access to its moral interior in order to contain intra-community violence through the application of law and punishment, the state is invited to internalise the imperatives of the colonial 'civilising mission' that preceded it.[11] The recent repeal of the *Sorcery Act 1971* itself can be read as a state intervention intended to shift indigenous morality through law; at the behest of international institutions and international NGOs, in removing a rarely used law[12] which purportedly sustained a belief in sorcery or the legitimacy of punishing sorcerers, the PNG national government again attempted to transform (or civilise) the belief system of Papua New Guineans through legislation.

Yet, these colonial, state-led and human rights interventions have been largely ineffective. During the era of colonial rule, the administration had limited coercive capacity to quash sorcery or allegations of sorcery — colonisation in PNG always occurred 'on the cheap' through a modified form of indirect rule.[13] While the administration was not averse to the use of force to 'pacify' local people, its ability to enforce the law was always limited (Dorward 2003). So, colonial laws prohibiting sorcery or unfounded allegations of sorcery were more testimony perhaps to the colonists' somewhat magical belief that, in the absence of actual enforcement power, the administration could legislate morality and behaviour within the largely semi-autonomous field of indigenous self-regulation.

---

10   Mel Keenan (Chapter 11, this volume) gives an excellent and detailed overview of colonial attempts to control sorcery and sorcery accusation-related violence, content that I have touched on only briefly here.
11   By civilising mission I mean, as Anghie (2004:3) describes it, 'the grand project that has justified colonialism as a means of redeeming the backward, aberrant, violent, oppressed, undeveloped people of the non-European world by incorporating them into the universal civilization of Europe'.
12   Only 19 published cases (many unreported) have considered the application of the Sorcery Act since its introduction. The following cases related to charges for the act of sorcery: *State v. Magou* [1981] PNGLR 1 (31 January 1981), *State v. Obande* [1983] PGNC 15; N444 (10 November 1983), *State v. Parara* [2008] PGNC 259; N3957 (22 February 2008). The following considered a belief in sorcery in mitigation of sentence (many refused to take into account this belief as a special mitigating factor — largely due to perceived incompatibility with the repugnance provisions of the constitution of PNG): *State v. Wapulae* [1980] PGNC 9; N233 (4 June 1980), *State v. Gesie & Guluwe* [1980] PGNC 20; N254 (12 July 1980), *Kwayawako v. State* [1990] PNGLR 6 (30 November 1989), *State v. Sambura* [2002] PGNC 114; N2219 (18 April 2002), *State v. Gena* [2004] PGNC 142; N2649 (24 September 2004), *State v. N'Danabet* [2004] PGNC 56; N2728 (9 November 2004), *Baipu v. State* [2005] PGSC 19; SC796 (1 July 2005), *State v. Jackson* [2006] PGNC 154; N3237 (24 October 2006), *State v. Mohavila* [2006] PGNC 106; N3385 (25 October 2006), *State v. Lota* [2007] PGNC 167; N3183 (1 October 2007), *State v. Martin* [2008] PGNC 29; N3312 (12 March 2008), *State v. Niruk* [2012] PGNC 152; N4821 (3 October 2012), *State v. Tayamina (No.3)* [2013] PGNC 110; N5288 (10 May 2013). In the following, an act of sorcery was considered provocation for murder: *State v. Manipe* [1979] PGNC 8; N196 (1 June 1979), *State v. Gesie & Guluwe* [1980] PGNC 20; N254 (12 July 1980).
13   British Indirect Rule represented 'an Empire wide repertoire of the arts [and techniques] of governing and colonising peoples' which relied upon 'the ideological production of "native society" as a specific object of government' in order to advance the interests of empire (Silverstein 2012:42).

The gap between the PNG state's assumed constitutional and human rights-imposed mandate to regulate sorcery-related violence, and its actual ability to do so, continues into the present. In Bougainville, both regular and Community Auxiliary Police have stated that they lack the institutional capacity to prevent and investigate accusations of sorcery and resulting vigilante violence (Human Rights Council 2011b). Although, it is not uncommon for members of the community accused of sorcery to request to be locked inside police cells for their own protection. This is not always an effective solution; on at least one occasion in Arawa, armed ex-combatants forcibly removed alleged sorcerers from the police lockup and subsequently murdered them.[14] When the UN Special Rapporteur on Torture visited the Arawa Police station in 2010 he was advised that police had not been investigating alleged sorcery violence cases in the villages because 'there are too many cases in the communities' and 'not enough resources' (Human Rights Council 2011b:40). So despite the call for more law and punishment, police remain unable or unwilling to intervene to contain sorcery accusation-related violence.

Perhaps it is this widening gap between law and enforcement that has spurred the PNG government's recent reintroduction of the death penalty for crimes of extreme violence (Callick 2013). While symbolic of the PNG state's desire to assume control of both life and death (something which exceeds its grasp) it is highly unlikely that the imposition of the death penalty will be effective in reducing sorcery accusation-related violence, given its proven ineffectiveness in reducing violent crime in other jurisdictions (Cheatwood 1993). Rather than reducing sorcery and witchcraft accusation-related violence, every intervention based on more law and punishment merely widens the gap between 'law on the books' and the state's capacity to regulate violence in practice. Guided by the human rights obligations of 'due diligence' — in what could be described as a 'regulatory feedback loop' — the ever widening ungovernable juridical space between legislation and enforcement appears productive of a desire for more law and punishment. This fetishism of the law, within the context of reputedly growing disorder and societal fragmentation, 'lies in an enchanted displacement, in the notion that legal instruments have the capacity to orchestrate social harmony' and misses the point that 'law in practice … is a social product, not a prime mover in constructing social worlds' (Comaroff and Comaroff 2001:38).

Sorcery as 'native savagery' in need of transformation

Human rights literature and international media, in its recent discovery of sorcery and witchcraft violence, typically depicts it as a brutal, traditional

---

14 Interview with Informant 1, 23 April 2013.

practice directed against vulnerable, poor and isolated women (Amnesty International 2013b; Fox 2013a), irrespective of the reality that those murdered include men and women from different strata of PNG society. The framing of the issue and dissemination of imagery by NGOs has also played a key role in defining this violence and its victims in a similar manner (Fox 2013b). The Crying Meri exhibition by photographer Vlad Sokhin — sponsored by Amnesty International and the United Nations, exhibited throughout PNG and soon to become its own book — features individual portraits of disfigured and scarred bodies of female survivors of sorcery and witchcraft accusation-related violence and scenes of public torture. These photos have also been widely disseminated on the internet and used by Amnesty International in its fundraising efforts.

The focus on isolated female victims of sorcery accusation-related violence acts to heighten the perceived sense of brutality and moral outrage through drawing on gender norms that conceive women as victim-objects in need of the international community's protection and intervention. Because these women survivors are photographed either alone or unassisted as they are publicly tortured, this suggests that there is no one outside the frame, no friend or relative who might support them (Orford 2003), when this is often simply not the case. Overall, these internationalised discursive and photographic practices — which portray female subjects as victims of their tradition — 'reinforce ... stereotyped and racist representations of that culture and privileges the culture of the West' (Kapur 2005:99), while at the same time attempting to legitimise calls for the 'taming' or 'civilisation' of that culture.[15] While women are undoubtedly subject to much gendered discrimination and violence in PNG — and I do not wish to minimise that problem or undermine the valuable work of local activists to address it — I do wish to draw attention to the effects of this instrumentalisation and enframing of women's bodies and suffering.

International human rights institutions have also leveraged a characterisation of sorcery accusation-related violence as traditional barbarity to bolster their call for the cultural transformation of Papua New Guineans. For example, the United Nations 2011 Universal Period Review for PNG included several recommendations that PNG implement strategies for social and cultural transformation to prevent further killings (Human Rights Council 2011a). Such prescriptions, which single out and target violence perceived to have a basis in culture or tradition, expose the latent potential of human rights law to reproduce binary colonial differentiations between 'civilised' and 'uncivilised'. As anthropologist Sally Engle Merry points out:

---

15   For a detailed interrogation of the victim subject within international/postcolonial feminist legal politics and its colonial antecedents, see Kapur (2005:96–136). It is worth making the point that while sorcery accusation-related violence sometimes represents a form of gender-based violence against women, this is not always the case and depends on the particular cultural context and individual circumstances.

> Like colonialism, human rights discourse contains implicit assumptions about the nature of civilized and backward societies, often glossed as modern and traditional … The practice of human rights is burdened by a colonialist understanding of culture that smuggles nineteenth-century ideas of backwardness and savagery into the process, along with ideas of racial inferiority. Rather than using these clearly retrograde terms, however, human rights law focuses on culture as the target of critique, often understood as ancient tradition. (Merry 2006:226)

A view of sorcery as traditional backwardness replicates prior colonial understandings of sorcery in PNG. Before independence, the administration and expatriate missionaries alike generally characterised sorcery as an endemic form of 'native savagery' to which their ward was enslaved (Murray 1913, 1929). Such a view of sorcery as traditional backwardness — which is sustained by human rights discourse — demands that Papua New Guineans and Bougainvilleans be transformed through education about the ills of sorcery accusation-related violence; in its 2010 concluding observation, CEDAW recommended that sorcery-related violence be countered through 'awareness-raising and educational efforts' (CEDAW 2010:6).

The idea that Papua New Guineans must be tutored into civility replicates a colonial understanding of the colonised as children in need of education. The notion of 'colonialism as pedagogy' and the 'coloniser as educator' is central to the rationality of colonisation (Orford 2003). As Leela Gandhi asserts, the 'perception of the colonised culture as fundamentally childlike feeds into the logic of the colonial "civilising mission" which is fashioned, quite self-consciously, as a form of tutelage or a disinterested project concerned with bringing the colonised to maturity' (Gandhi 1998:32).

In colonial Papua and New Guinea, Sir Hubert Murray, lieutenant-governor from 1908 to 1940, sought to transform indigenous society through a paternalistic system of 'native administration' built on 'preserving the Papuan and raising him eventually to the highest civilisation of which he is capable' (Murray 1913:360; see also Beaver 1920; Elkin 1940; Lyng 1919). This pedagogical project included the liberation of the colonised from a belief in sorcery that supposedly so enslaved them (Murray 1929). So in prescribing cultural transformation or the modernisation of the harmful and traditional, human rights law invites the PNG nation-state to pick up the 'white man's burden' of the colonial administration that came before it. The futility of these paternalistic attempts to eradicate aspects of indigenous belief — deemed inconsistent with morality of the colonist or developmental state — is evident in reputedly rising sorcery accusation-related violence in present day PNG and Bougainville.

Part 3: Other ways of viewing sorcery-related violence

Looking through the traditionally narrow lens of human rights negates our ability to grasp the structural connection that exists between particularised and exceptional human rights abuses and the local and international order in which they are situated (Eslava 2014). It also obscures alternative ways of understanding such violence that may hold the key to more effective, just and durable means of responding to violence within society.

Through signifying sorcery practices as disorder or aberrant traditional practice, a comprehension of sorcery accusation-related violence as a form of indigenous social regulation or as a misdirected critique of growing inequality, are hidden. Through its tendency to draw our gaze to immediate crises and 'exotic' forms of 'traditional' violence and its demand for intervention, the traditional human rights response conceals the role of prior and ongoing legal and economic interventions in destabilising indigenous dispute resolution systems and societies. And by understanding sorcery as 'savage' violence, other forms of violence — including the economic and symbolic violence attendant to PNG and Bougainville's incorporation within the global economic order (and the processes of colonisation which preceded and enabled this process) — are conveniently masked.

Sorcery as regulation

A view of sorcery-related killing as a manifestation of indigenous or traditional disorder, which human rights discourse sustains, precludes an understanding of how such practices constitute a way of making meaning within and of attempting to reorder a society of growing inequality. Within pre-contact Bougainvillean societies, sorcery was often imposed and sanctioned by the village leadership as punishment for individuals who offended against local norms or failed to fulfil their customary obligations.[16] On Buka Island, for example, known sorcerers who held the status of chief were only permitted to practise sorcery to punish another where the local chiefs (including the sorcerer) had reached a unanimous decision approving its use. The fear of such punishment helped keep the peace as it encouraged obedience to prevailing societal norms.[17] The punishment of alleged sorcerers was also highly regulated; when a death was allegedly caused by sorcery, only the senior female chief had the authority to decide what

---

16 Interview with Helen Hakena, 23 April 2013.
17 In Buka, fear of sorcery also helped keep villages clean; villagers would take care to not leave *buai* spit or husks lying on the ground lest it be used in an act of sorcery against them (interview with Helen Hakena, 23 April 2013); see also LRCPNG (1978:18) and Schwarz (2011:34).

punishment should be imposed.[18] I do not wish to perpetuate a view that pre-contact Bougainville was a non-violent garden of Eden benignly regulated by fear of sorcery (Filer 1990). However, it is important to acknowledge that while violence was frequent in pre-contact Bougainville societies, 'when it occurred [unlike the present, it] was highly ritualised, with few deaths and complex, deeply rooted customary mechanisms for ensuring swift and lasting resolution' (Oliver 1991, cited in Kent and Barnett 2012:36).

While sorcery has its roots in Melanesia's ancient and diverse cultures, it is not a static, traditional belief that has endured despite the influences of Christianity, colonisation and development. Rather, the role of sorcery as a means of regulating and making meaning within society has changed through its encounter with post-contact life in PNG and Bougainville (Rio 2010; Schram 2010). Throughout Melanesia today, sincere belief in sorcery is often 'articulated through relations marked by fear, anger or jealousy' (Rio 2010:182) flowing from perceived inequalities in material wealth (see also Forsyth 2006). In Bougainville, accusations of sorcery are commonly made against financially successful individuals (who own a car and live in a permanent house, for instance) who are perceived to have failed to redistribute their prosperity appropriately, or against people who have achieved a high non-traditional status (for example, through private business or government employment).[19]

In this context, an allegation of sorcery, and the violence which sometimes accompanies it, often signifies an attempt to level perceived inequality in the community (Eves 2000)[20] through a misdirected attack provoked by this relationship of inequality.[21] I say 'misdirected' because, as will be discussed later

---

18   Interview with Helen Hakena, 23 April 2013.
19   Interview with Marilyn Havini of the Bougainville Women's Federation, 2 June 2013; interview with Helen Hakena, 23 April 2013; interview with Agnes Titus, sub-national co-ordinator, UN Women, AROB, 20 April 2013; interview with Informant 1, 23 April 2013. For example, in the recent sorcery-related killing in Bana, Helen Rumbali held the position of Bougainville Women's Federation president in the area, one of her sons was a member of parliament in the ABG, another son was the executive officer of the District Office and another was the chair of the local-level government. Another 'economic' aspect to the recent murder of Helen Rumbali was that, following her murder, claims worth more than US$125,000 were lodged with the ABG by people claiming they had helped the remaining family escape (Australia Network News 2013).
20   Although Eves is of the view that the explanation of envy alone is overly simplistic and that an understanding of allegations of sorcery based on wealth-based envy should be determined within their particular local context. I also note that this article focuses on the Lelet Plateau in New Ireland. In a similar vein, according to Rio (2010:186), sorcery allegations sometimes carry 'a certain moral legitimacy against those who have success in business or other activities which privatise income and profit'.
21   Jealousy about non-traditional prosperity may give rise to allegations of sorcery for the reason that such forms of wealth cannot be accommodated or regulated within traditional cultural understandings of or practices around the distribution of wealth; a permanent house or Landcruiser cannot be incorporated into cycles of reciprocal giving or exchange (Rio 2010). Here, I note that Mortensen observes that sorcery accusations, through undermining the regulation of sociality, do not operate as 'a commentary on inequality as such [in Melanesia], but refer … more exactly to a failure of the morality and management of exchange in the new context of modernity' (Mortensen 2001:509, 511). Yet, what is inequality but a failure of market-based exchange or distribution?

in this chapter, the causes of growing inequality in Bougainvillean society can for the most part be traced to its resorption within global capitalism (Mortensen 2001).[22] Hence, those accused of sorcery-related killing act as scapegoats for governmental and international economic practices over which its victims have no responsibility. Arguably, Chinese retailers in Bougainville, who have been the victims of increasingly violent attacks in recent years, are playing a similar role as straw men for the discontents of modernity and increasing inequality.

So broadly speaking, sorcery accusation-related violence, rather than being a throwback to pre-development society, often operates as a reaction to changes and inequality wrought by the destabilisation and disappointments of development and globalisation; and it represents a means through which individuals who feel disenfranchised can attempt to enhance their power through enrolling community disapproval against others perceived as acting in contravention of more egalitarian societal norms. Through depicting sorcery practices as lawless disorder or tradition in want of transformation, human rights discourse obscures a comprehension of sorcery-related violence as a misdirected response to growing inequality. It thereby misses the opportunity to make visible and critique the economic origins of this inequality of which sorcery accusation-related violence is but one symptom.

Sorcery accusation–related violence as a consequence of legal and economic intervention

In her work *Reading Humanitarian Intervention*, Anne Orford is concerned with the way narratives of international intervention *commence* with the story of the international community's response to a particular humanitarian crisis. She argues that through beginning too late in the piece these dominant narratives obscure the way in which the 'international community had already intervened on a large scale in each of the … cases [of the former Yugoslavia, East Timor and Rwanda] before the security crisis erupted, particularly through the activities of international economic institutions' (Orford 2003). In a similar vein, I want to now interrogate how the human rights view of sorcery accusation-related violence, which is localised in the present to a singular practice of 'cultural' violence, obscures a deeper understanding of the causes of such violence.

---

22 See in general also Nihill (2001:103) and Schram (2010). In a similar vein, Nibbrig has persuasively argued that gang crime in PNG increasingly represents a means through which the marginalised can make a claim for equality within PNG's new economic order. According to Nibbrig, *raskols* (loosely organised urban gang members) are motivated 'by a sense of moral indignation which is directed at inequalities originating in the colonial experience that have been further institutionalized in the postcolonial period' (Dinnen 2001:47, referring to the work of Nibbrig 1992).

The colonial and nation-state's attack on indigenous self-regulation

In PNG and Bougainville, the arrival of the technology and forms of the nation-state has undermined the ability of Papua New Guineans to regulate themselves through indigenous forms of dispute settlement including through fear of sorcery (Tombot 2010). I have written elsewhere how the processes of colonisation through 'indirect rule' — alive in the present through the operation of the developmental state — has systematically attempted to contain indigenous self-regulation through either attempting to eradicate it or through rendering it subordinate and subservient to the centralised and positivist law of the PNG state (Evenhuis 2013). While some introduced legal forms have been embraced by Papua New Guineans and Bougainvilleans, others have weakened the ability of communities to respond to violence when it erupts or regulate its imposition as punishment (Ottley 1995).

In colonial times, this weakening occurred through the administration's attempted institutionalisation of indigenous authority and dispute-settlement practices. While diverse indigenous forms of pre-contact disputing in Melanesia sought to keep the ever-present risk of societal fragmentation at bay through the continuous renegotiation of leadership and indigenous norms (in Bougainville this also occurred through 'the pursuit of warfare, the practice of initiation, and the organization of large-scale gift-exchange'; Filer 1990:9), the process of institutionalisation fixed these relationships and dispute resolution processes at a particular moment in time. In some instances the administration in Bougainville also intentionally reallocated traditional authority in order to best accommodate its needs.[23] As the lively flexibility and instability of indigenous forms of self-regulation have been undermined, the state has remained 'a distant presence with uncertain relevance for everyday life' (White 2007:4), unable to replace the authority it has displaced. Within this space various indigenous constraints on sorcery allegations and the punishment of alleged sorcerers have been loosened (this is discussed in more detail below).

While an argument can be made that the imposition of colonial rule ushered in an era of relative peace in Melanesia through reducing inter-village warfare, paradoxically many anthropologists now believe that so-called '[p]acification led to the conduct of inter-village warfare by less visible means' (Mortensen 2001:524), including through sorcery or accusations of sorcery. So looking briefly back into Bougainville's colonial past reveals that a rise in sorcery

---

[23] When the Australian colonial government established local-level councils to govern and administer justice, councillors were elected to this new level of government who did not hold traditional authority to deal with disputes to the exclusion of others who did — paramount chiefs were sometimes excluded from participating where they lacked the ability to speak Tok Pisin (Tombot 2010; see also Blackwood 1931).

accusation-related killing can in part be attributed to the various law and order interventions of the colonial and postcolonial order which undermined the role of sorcery practices in regulating pre-contact sociality.

Globalisation-induced disorder

Rapid economic and social change wrought by PNG's incorporation into the global economy, through development policies premised on economic growth and international investment, have led to an increasingly violent, inequitable and disordered society (Dinnen 2001), which, in Bougainville, has been further compounded by the conflict. This dialectic of economic destabilisation — initiated by PNG's articulation within the international economic order — dates back to the days of colonial rule where the administration endeavoured to restructure local production in order to meet the needs of the metropole.[24] Except now, PNG has shifted its economic base from an agricultural/plantation economy towards one largely based on logging and extractive industries in order to bankroll the nation-state (Allen 2013).

The destabilising effects of PNG's encounter with global capital have been grave. In rural areas across the country violent land disputes are increasingly common — particularly in areas where extractive industries operate; to date Melanesia's most violent conflicts have all been resource conflicts (Allen 2013). In turn, urbanisation spurred by the call of the modern city as the wellspring of development and prosperity has brought instability to urban and peri-urban PNG. Faced with a reality of limited formal or informal employment, the marginalised within PNG and Bougainville are increasingly turning to illegal and often violent activity as alternate forms of income. As is the case with sorcery accusation-related violence in Bougainville, much of this violence can be linked to growing inequality within PNG (Levantis 1997). In the face of economic and political destabilisation wrought by development and resource capitalism, PNG and Bougainville's police have a limited capacity to restrain violence and are themselves often perpetrators of violent human rights abuses (Human Rights Watch 2005).

The consequence of economic and political destabilisations wrought by the government and globalisation — combined with the state's inability to fulfil its assumed role of maintaining law and order — is the proliferation of urban and rural spaces where neither state nor 'traditional' authority has normative and

---

24 This attempt to render Papua and New Guinea responsive to the needs of the metropole occurred through law. Murray's 1918 Native Taxation Ordinance and Native Plantations Ordinance allocated land for plantations near each village, to 'ensure that Papuans would work the plantations by establishing a tax burden on each community' (Silverstein 2012:196) under the Native Labour Ordinance of 1892. This approach was intended to 'establish peasant production within a village economy as providing the means of subsistence and thus a subsidy for settler-owned plantation production' (Silverstein 2012:197).

regulatory legitimacy or power (Dinnen 2001).[25] This regulatory void acts as an enabling environment for excesses of violence unconstrained by shared local authority or the law of the state.

Within this understanding we encounter a paradox: while we can attribute the perceived increase in violence in PNG (including sorcery accusation-related violence in Bougainville) to various governmental and economic interventions which have produced heightened levels of societal inequality and intersocietal conflict, the logic of 'due diligence' and sovereignty prescribe only further intervention based on law and cultural transformation as a panacea for violence. Such a paradox is only possible through a 'localisation' of the immediate symptoms of violence and the concealment of its socio-economic and political antecedents (Orford 2003). The maintenance of this paradox is aided and abetted through the proclivity of human rights law to privilege the political and individual over the economic and collective (Wright 2001), which has been entrenched within international law through the traditional separation between its political and economic branches (Pahuja 2000).

The Bougainville conflict

Continuing to trace this line of inquiry, I now want to draw on the example of the Bougainville conflict and events preceding it to suggest that the perceived increase in sorcery accusation-related killing in Bougainville can be linked to the interventions of the state and transnational corporate actors, which both fuelled and prolonged the conflict. While a plethora of theories exist as to the underlying causes of the Bougainville conflict, it is largely uncontested that the conflict arose out of the unequal distribution of royalties, compensation and other benefit flows from an imposed resource extraction project that many landowners simply did not want (Filer 1990; Ghai and Regan 2006; Howley 2002; Oliver 1973). The resultant inequality among Bougainvilleans contributed to a conflict-prone environment of intercommunity and inter-ethnic tensions and jealousies (MacWilliam 2005),[26] which greatly assisted the Bougainville Revolutionary Army (BRA) to mobilise a force largely composed of disaffected youth, many of them landowners or former employees of the mine (Ghai and Regan 2006). Secondly, this conflict was protracted due to the heavy-handed military intervention of the police and PNG Defence Force — who were covertly supported by the Australian Government — which culminated in the blockade

---

25 As Dinnen (2001:44) notes, '[t]he cumulative effect of [urbanisation] is to generate an overall social pathology, in which neither the norms of the emergent social order nor those of the traditional order are dominant' (see also Goddard 2003).

26 Although this situation of inequality pre-existed the conflict, as Ghai and Regan (2006:592) note: 'In particular, many groups in Buka and on the east coast of Bougainville adjacent to the colonial administrative centre and plantations have had much greater access than others to education, employment and opportunities for economic advancement, a source of inequality that contributes to tensions and divisions'.

of Bougainville, effectively cutting off all services, communications and medical supplies to the island and leading to the deaths of many thousands of people (Lasslett 2012).

So what are the links between these interventions and sorcery accusation-related violence? In the decades before the Bougainville conflict, sorcery-related violence was reportedly rare due to the strength of community, clans and the church, and the absence of guns in the community.[27] During the conflict, when combatants displaced both autonomous indigenous authority at the village level and the law and order apparatus of the PNG state, they began to regulate communities over which they held power; '[s]ome BRA [and also Bougainville Resistance Force] commanders used their new monopoly of force on their patch to settle old disputes over land, sorcery, local economic inequalities and other grievances that had nothing to do with the[ir] … struggle' (Braithwaite et al. 2010). UN Women in Bougainville understands that some incidents of sorcery accusation-related violence during the conflict involved the murder of entire families by combatants.[28] While some communities allegedly requested and received the spiritual protection of sorcerers during the conflict, these same sorcerers were often accused of malevolent sorcery after the fighting ceased.[29]

Both media and anecdotal accounts of sorcery accusation-related violence in Bougainville suggest that many ex-combatants have retained their monopoly over community dispute settlement dating from the conflict (Toreas and Masiu 2013). Ex-combatants have carried out sorcery-related killings themselves — sometimes according to their own version of customary law — or facilitated their community to carry out these murders.[30] In the face of armed community members and ex-combatants, the police of Bougainville — who are unarmed by law — are unable to intervene to prevent killings. In the April 2013 case in Bana, police witnessed the murder of Mrs Helen Rumbali but were unable to act as her accusers were armed.[31]

The Bougainville conflict not only displaced the formal law and order system. When combatants took up arms, they also disempowered traditional leaders, such as chiefs, to regulate their own communities and contain sorcery allegations and sorcery-related violence.[32] Before the conflict, the use of sorcery, including who was given knowledge about its practice, was generally strictly controlled by tribal authority; knowledge about sorcery was usually only passed down within the one clan. Many Bougainvilleans believe that during the conflict,

---

27   Interview with Agnes Titus, sub-national co-ordinator, UN Women, AROB, 20 April 2013.
28   Interview with Agnes Titus, sub-national co-ordinator, UN Women, AROB, 20 April 2013.
29   Interview with Helen Hakena, 23 April 2013.
30   *Post-Courier* 2013; interview with Informant 1, 23 April 2013.
31   *Post-Courier* 2013; interview with Informant 1, 23 April 2013.
32   Interview with Agnes Titus, sub-national co-ordinator, UN Women, AROB, 20 April 2013.

sorcery knowledge was given to young and often non-clan members prematurely as a form of spiritual weaponry against their enemies and that since this time chiefs have no longer been able to control who practises sorcery or under what circumstances it is practised.[33] This has provoked strong community fears of sorcery, as all community members are now perceived as potential sorcerers — likely resulting in a spike in the number of sorcery allegations.[34] In summary, state and corporate-led interventions, which underpinned and sustained the Bougainville conflict, pushed out the already weak law and order of the state, further undermined traditional authority and concentrated power in the hands of people with guns and, as a consequence, fostered an environment conducive to the spread of sorcery accusation-related violence. So while the logic of human rights and sovereignty might simply characterise this practice as disorder or traditional practice in need of state intervention or transformation, a wider reading of its causes suggests otherwise.

Part 4: Responding

The ineffectiveness of both colonial and contemporary human rights-based 'solutions' to sorcery does shine some light on possible alternative, non-violent and largely non-state-reliant responses of addressing the issue in Bougainville. However, conscious that a narrow and orthodox human rights approach limited to redressing sorcery violence will be at the expense of comprehending or challenging 'economic and political structures which generate inequality' (Merry 2006) and violence in Melanesia, in closing I will also consider the emancipatory and political potential of a broader view of human rights for those in search of a more just and peaceful local and international order.

Restoring power to communities

If sorcery-related violence in Bougainville can, in part, be attributed to the deterioration of local authority to regulate violence — a destabilisation which commenced with colonisation and was exacerbated by a civil war concentrating power in the hands of an armed minority — there is a real risk that any attempt by the state to increase regulatory control of the population will result in further deterioration in community cohesion and an upsurge in violence. Instead, respecting and, where applicable, restoring power to communities to resolve disturbances of the peace non-violently (coupled with weapons disposal discussed below) represents the most obvious means of successfully responding to this issue.

---

33   Interview with Informant 1, 23 April 2013.
34   Interview with Informant 1, 23 April 2013; see also Tombot (2010).

A greater reliance on local authority does not mean that traditional forms of authority, where absent, must be reinvented to regulate communities. While loosely articulated with the state, throughout PNG and Bougainville many grassroots-level justice institutions and individuals (village courts, peace officers, councils of elders, village assemblies, church leaders etc.) have been embraced by local communities as dispute resolution mechanisms and creatively adapted to a local context (Goddard 1996, 2000, 2010); however, working with the above should not be to the exclusion of supporting other non-institutionalised forms of authority. So rather than a strategy of intervention or usurping local authority, it may be preferable for the ABG and PNG government to work towards real power sharing with and within local communities in an attempt to stem the multiplication of violent spaces within them. Clara Bal's chapter provides an excellent example of a successful community-driven response in Gor (Chapter 16).

Contestation about the legitimacy of sorcery-related killing

Keeping in mind the ineffectiveness of colonial and state-led criticism of sorcery accusation-related violence through law or rhetoric, conducting 'awareness', especially delivered by community outsiders emphasising the superiority of 'modern' human rights values, risks restaging the colonial encounter in the present and inviting resistance from those subject to its belittlement. Again, community authority is best placed to contest the minority support for the murder of alleged sorcerers (in my understanding, the vast majority of Bougainvilleans unequivocally reject sorcery accusation-related violence on the basis of current understandings of culture and widely held Christian faith which do not tolerate individuals taking the law into their own hands).[35] This is not to say that communities should not internalise the values of human rights in responding to sorcery accusation-related violence as they see fit — for example, its emphasis on the sanctity of life and human dignity or in the manner discussed towards the conclusion of this chapter. However, the potency of human rights values will always be contingent on their translation into local vernacular[36] and their alignment with local values.

---

35 Interview with Agnes Titus, sub-national co-ordinator, UN Women, AROB, 20 April 2013; interview with Helen Hakena, 23 April 2013.
36 In Bougainville, the language of human rights has been adopted by a formally educated urban minority and local NGO workers; the extent to which it resonates with the diverse cultural beliefs and conceptions of community and self within rural and remote communities is contentious.

A role for the state?

Given the low overall enforcement and regulatory capacity of the ABG and PNG government, it is appropriate that responses to sorcery accusation-related violence should be largely community based and driven. However, the ABG and PNG government could attempt to reduce sorcery accusation-related violence in two key ways.

First, the ABG has a crucial role to play in facilitating weapons disposal across Bougainville. Unless guns are disposed of, local power will remain concentrated in the hands of the minority that possess them and communities will be obstructed from keeping the peace collectively. Second, the ABG must find a way to begin to engage seriously with Bougainville's most marginalised, especially its youth, in a conversation about their desires for their lives and the future of Bougainville (Kent and Barnett 2012). Unless these youth are meaningfully accommodated within Bougainvillean society through meaningful education and work opportunities, economic and social marginalisation will continue to find violent means of self-expression.

A place for human rights?

In this chapter I have attempted to draw attention to the limited promise of international human rights law — when it operates in its regulatory and imperial mode — to address individual manifestations of 'cultural violence'. However, I am not advocating for the total abandonment of human rights as an emancipatory language which Bougainvillean, or indeed other Papua New Guinean, communities *may* wish to employ tactically to further their own immediate or long-term political or emancipatory goals. When Helen Rumbali and her sister were taken hostage, local women activists quickly alerted international media and international NGOs; the latter in turn funded the evacuation of the Rumbali family.[37] These women's strategic decision to draw on the transnational language and appeal of human rights no doubt increased the audibility of their request for assistance and helped save many lives.

Instead, I want to consider here how human rights discourse might be distracted from its preoccupation with 'harmful traditional practices' and appropriated to critique the economic structures that perpetuate global and local inequality and increasingly stratified and violent societies. From the outset I want to make it clear that I am not proposing that human rights be mainstreamed into development; TWAIL scholars such as Sundhya Pahuja have persuasively argued that the subordination of international law including human rights to the transcendent value of 'development as economic growth', 'exacerbates international law's

---

37 North Bougainville Human Rights Committee, press release 5/4/2013.

imperial quality and minimises its counter-imperial dimension, or emancipatory possibilities' (Pahuja 2011:37). Rather, I want to suggest here that the discourse of human rights — when decoupled from the civilising mission of the state or a single and unified story of developmentalism — retains a political or emancipatory potential. This political nature of human rights originates from 'the gap between the body of human rights norms in international law at any given time and the imaginative appeal of human rights' (Pahuja 2007:168). As Pahuja critically observes:

> when a human right comes up against someone to whom that right does not apply because of the particular human 'inscribed' within the right, that person embodies the limit of the right and presents to the universal an insistent factuality contesting the universal's claim to be such. (Pahuja 2007:168)

Thus, through its investiture in all humans, the consequential human rights assertion of universality and equality between humans 'carries with it a symbolic valence in its imaginative link to justice' (Pahuja 2007:84) which is unconstrained by a positivist conception of universal rights (i.e. rights as they exist in treaties, customary international law or justiciable domestic legislation). In its restive and political mode, the content of claims to human rights are as expansive and diverse as the desires and imaginations of those who lay claim to them.

The imaginative act of liberating human rights from the constraints of legal positivism raises a possibility of shifting its narrow target of critique (its colonial preoccupation with civilising culture), to the economic violence of corporate penetration within the global South. Within this broadened discursive space, human rights language has the capacity to foreground 'the extreme social, economic, and cultural dislocation felt by women, children, indigenous peoples and the poor generally when this economic penetration either fails owing to financial or structural collapse, or is instituted without regard for the environmental costs of uncontrolled development' (Wright 2001:215). A liberated human rights discourse may also be of use to Bougainvilleans as a means of rerouting misdirected and internalised societal rage induced by rising inequality towards its actual source; and of laying claim to a more just international economic order through mobilising coalitions across borders.

Conclusion

As Anne Orford reminds us, in the face of humanitarian crisis, rather than just asking 'what should we do?' it is better to question 'how did we get here?' (Orford 2003). A reading of sorcery-related violence outside the narrowing lens of regulatory human rights law reveals both its broader context — the systematic destabilisation of indigenous society through economic, social and legal interventions — and the consequential irrationality of singling out one symptom of growing societal marginalisation for remediation through state-centric law and order or re-education.

While asking the question, 'how did we get here?' offers alternative ways of knowing about sorcery-related violence and suggests some non-violent and non-state focused responses to the issue, this line of inquiry more significantly foregrounds the economic dialectic of growing inequality as the driving force behind an increasingly violent local and international order. The potentially illimitable valency of human rights offers one language to those who dare to ask for the world to be otherwise. Yet, for human rights to be of practical use to the people of Bougainville or PNG more widely, it must broaden its critical gaze from localised cultural symptoms to the underlying pathology of the current international economic order.

References

Allen, M.G. 2013. Melanesia's Violent Environments: Towards a Political Ecology of Conflict in the Western Pacific. *Geoforum* 44:152–61.

Amnesty International 2013a. Papua New Guinea Must Act after Woman Burned Alive for 'Sorcery'. Amnesty International News online 9 February. www.amnesty.org.au/news/comments/31052/, viewed 8/8/2013.

Amnesty International 2013b. Demand an End to the Brutal Sorcery-Related Killings in Papua New Guinea. Amnesty International News online. www.amnesty.org.au/action/action/32547/, viewed 11/8/2013.

Anghie, A. 2004. *Imperialism, Sovereignty and the Making of International Law*. Cambridge: Cambridge University Press.

Anghie, A. 2006. Nationalism, Development and the Postcolonial State: The Legacies of the League of Nations. *Texas International Law Journal* 41:452–63.

Australian Broadcasting Corporation 2013. Bougainville Residents Claim Compensation for Helping Sorcery Victims. Australian Broadcasting Corporation, 7 June. www.abc.net.au/news/2013-06-06/compensation-claims-for-helping-sorcery-victims/4738724, viewed 11/8/2013.

Beaver, W. 1920. *Unexplored New Guinea*. London: Sealey, Service and Co Limited.

Blackwood, B. 1931. Report on Field Work in Buka and Bougainville. *Oceania* 2(2):199–219.

Braithwaite, J., H. Charlsworth, P. Reddy and L. Dunn 2010. *Reconciliation and Architecture of Commitment: Sequencing Peace in Bougainville*. Canberra: ANU E Press.

Callick, R. 2013. PNG to Enforce Death Penalty. *The Australian*, 29 May. www.theaustralian.com.au/news/world/png-to-enforce-death-penalty/story-e6frg6so-1226652553341, viewed 8/8/2013.

CEDAW (Committee on the Elimination of Discrimination against Women) 2010. Concluding Observations of the Committee on the Elimination of Discrimination against Women: Papua New Guinea. UN Doc CEDAW/C/PNG/CO/3, 30 July 2010.

Cheatwood, D. 1993. Capital Punishment and the Deterrence of Violent Crime in Comparable Counties. *Criminal Justice Review* 18(2):165–81.

Comaroff, J. and J. Comaroff 2001. *Millennial Capitalism and the Culture of Neoliberalism*. Durham: Duke University Press.

Dinnen, S. 2001. *Law and Order in a Weak State: Crime and Politics in Papua New Guinea*. Honolulu: University of Hawai'i Press.

Dorward, D. 2003. Colonial Administration. In M. Page (ed.) *Colonialism — An International Social, Cultural and Political Encyclopaedia*. California: ABC-Clio, 128–30.

Elkin, A. 1940. The Place of Sir Hubert Murray in Native Administration. *The Australian Quarterly* 27:23–35.

Eslava, L. 2014. Istanbul Vignettes: Observing the Everyday Operation of International Law. *London Review of International Law* 2(1):3–47.

Evenhuis, M. 2014. Law as Salvation, Law as Civilisation, Law as Development: The Attempted Containment of Indigenous Law in PNG. *Griffith Law Review* 23(2):176–209.

Eves, R. 2000. Sorcery's the Cure: Modernity, Envy and the Flow of Sociality in a Melanesian Society. *Journal of the Royal Anthropological Institute* 6:453–68.

Filer, C. 1990. The Bougainville Rebellion, the Mining Industry and the Process of Social Disintegration in Papua New Guinea. *Canberra Anthropology* 13(1):1–39.

Forsyth, M. 2006. Sorcery and the Criminal Law in Vanuatu. *Lawasia Journal* 1:1–27.

Fox, L. 2013a. PNG PM Condemns 'Barbaric' Sorcery Killing. Australian Broadcating Corporation, 8 February. www.abc.net.au/news/2013-02-08/an-png-pm-condemns-sorcery-killing/4509182, viewed 25/9/2013.

Fox, L. 2013b. Two Charged over Brutal Sorcery Killing. Australian Broadcating Corporation, 18 February. www.abc.net.au/news/2013-02-18/two-charged-over-brutal-sorcery-killing/4524888, viewed 25/5/2014.

Gandhi, L. 1998. *Postcolonial Theory: A Critical Introduction.* New York: Columbia University Press.

Ghai, Y. and A. Regan 2006. Unitary State, Devolution, Autonomy, Secession: State Building and Nation Building in Bougainville, Papua New Guinea. *The Round Table* 95(386):589–608.

Goddard, M. 1996. The Snake Bone Case: Law, Custom and Justice in a Papua New Guinea Village Court. *Oceania* 67(1):50–63.

Goddard, M. 2000. Three Urban Village Courts in Papua New Guinea: Some Comparative Observations on Dispute Settlement. In S. Dinnen and A. Ley (eds.) *Reflections on Violence in Melanesia*. Sydney: Hawkins Press and Asia Pacific Press, 241–53.

Goddard, M. 2003. The Age of Steam: Constructed Identity and Recalcitrant Youth in a Papua New Guinea Village. In S. Dinnen, A. Jowitt and T. Newton (eds.) *A Kind of Mending: Restorative Justice in the Pacific Islands*. Canberra: ANU E Press, 45–72.

Hamnett, M. and J. Connell 1981. Diagnosis and Cure: The Resort of Traditional and Modern Medical Practitioners in the North Solomons, PNG. *Social Science and Medicine* 15(4):489–98.

Howley, P. 2002. *Breaking Spears & Mending Hearts: Peacemaking and Restorative Justice in Bougainville*. Sydney: Zed Books.

Human Rights Committee 2004. General Comment No. 31 [80]. The Nature of the General Legal Obligation Imposed on States Parties to the Covenant. UN Doc CCPR/C/21/Rev.1/Add.13, 26 May 2004.

Human Rights Council 2011a. Report of the Working Group on the Universal Periodic Review: Papua New Guinea. UN Doc A/HRC/18/18, 11 July 2011.

Human Rights Council 2011b. Report of the Special Rapporteur on Torture and Other Cruel, Inhuman or Degrading Treatment or Punishment: Mission to Papua New Guinea. UN Doc A/HRC/16/52/Add.5.

Human Rights Watch 2005. *'Making Their Own Rules': Police Beatings, Rape, and Torture of Children in Papua New Guinea*. Human Rights Watch 17(8)C. http://www.hrw.org/reports/2005/08/30/making-their-own-rules, viewed 8/8/2014.

Jewkes, R., E. Fulu and Y. Sikweyiya 2013. *Family, Health and Safety Study, Bougainville, Papua New Guinea*. Cape Town: MRC South Africa (unpublished).

Kapur, R. 2005. *Erotic Justice: Law and the New Politics of Postcolonialism*. London: Glass House Press.

Kent, S. and J. Barnett 2012. Localising Peace: The Young Men of Bougainville's 'Crisis Generation'. *Political Geography* 31(1):34–43.

Lasslett, K. 2012. State Crime by Proxy: Australia and the Bougainville Conflict. *British Journal of Criminology* 52:705–23.

Levantis, T. 1997. Urban Unemployment in Papua New Guinea: It's Criminal. *Pacific Economic Bulletin* 12(2):73–84.

LRCPNG (Law Reform Commission of Papua New Guinea) 1978. Sorcery among the East Sepiks. *Occasional Paper* No. 10. Waigani: LRCPNG.

Lyng, Captain 1919. *Our New Possession*. Melbourne: Melbourne Publishing Company.

MacWilliam, S. 2005. Post-War Reconstruction in Bougainville: Plantations, Smallholders and Indigenous Capital. In A. Regan and H. Griffin (eds.) *Bougainville Before the Conflict*. Canberra: Pandanus Books, 224–38.

Merry, S.E. 2006. *Human Rights and Gender Violence: Translating International Law into Local Justice*. Chicago: University of Chicago Press.

Mortensen, R. 2001. A Voyage in God's Canoe: Law and Religion in Melanesia. *Current Legal Issues* 4:509–28.

Murray, H. 1913. *Papua or British New Guinea*. London: T. Fisher Unwin.

Murray, H. 1929. *Native Administration in Papua*. Port Moresby: Government Printer.

Nibbrig, N. 1992. Rascals in Paradise: Urban Gangs in Papua New Guinea. *Pacific Studies* 15(3):115–34.

Nihill, M. 2001. Pain and Progress: Revisiting Botol Sorcery in the Southern Highlands of Papua New Guinea. *Social Analysis* 45(1):103–21.

Oliver, D. 1973. *A Personal History*. Victoria: Melbourne University Press.

Orford, A. 2003. *Reading Humanitarian Intervention*. New York: Cambridge University Press.

Ottley, B. 1995. Looking Back to the Future: The Colonial Origins of Current Attitudes Towards Customary Law. In J. Aleck and J. Rannels (eds.) *Custom at the Crossroads*. Port Moresby: University of Papua New Guinea Press, 97–107.

Pahuja, S. 2000. Trading Spaces: Locating Sites for Challenge within International Trade Law. *Australian Feminist Law Journal* 14:38–54.

Pahuja, S. 2004. Power and the Rule of Law in the Global Context. *Melbourne University Law Review* 28:232–51.

Pahuja, S. 2007. Rights as Regulation: The Integration of Development and Human Rights. In B. Morgan (ed.) *The Intersection of Rights and Regulation: New Directions in Sociolegal Scholarship*. England: Ashgate, 167–92.

Pahuja, S. 2011. *Decolonising International Law*. New York: Cambridge University Press.

Rio, K. 2010. Handling Sorcery in a State System of Law: Magic, Violence and *Kastom* in Vanuatu. *Oceania* 80(2):182–97.

Schram, R. 2010. Witches' Wealth: Witchcraft, Confession, and Christianity in Auhelawa, Papua New Guinea. *Journal of the Royal Institute of Anthropology* 16:726–42.

Schwarz, N. 2011. Thinking Critically about Sorcery and Witchcraft. A Handbook for Christians in Papua New Guinea. *Occasional Paper* No. 14. Goroka: Melanesian Institute.

Silverstein, B. 2012. Indirect Rule in a Settler Colony: Race, Indigeneity, Government. PhD thesis, La Trobe University.

Tombot, J. 2010. A Marriage of Custom and Introduced Skills: Restorative Justice Bougainville Style. In S. Dinnen, A. Jowitt and T. Newton (eds.) *A Kind of Mending: Restorative Justice in the Pacific Islands*. Canberra: ANU E Press, 255–64.

Toreas, W. and R. Masiu 2013. Women Beheaded. *Post-Courier*, 8 April, p. 1.

White, G. 2007. Indigenous Governance in Melanesia. *SSGM Discussion Paper* 2007/5. Canberra: State, Society and Governance in Melanesia Program, The Australian National University.

Wright, S. 2001. *International Human Rights, Decolonisation and Globalisation: Becoming Human*. London and New York: Routledge.

Zocca, F. 2010. Gender and Accusations of Malevolent Sorcery and Witchcraft in Papua New Guinea. *Catalyst* 40(2):192–206.

15. The Belief in Sorcery in Solomon Islands

Philip Kanairara and Derek Futaiasi

Introduction

Solomon Islands was primarily governed by customary law or custom before the protectorate era, which commenced in 1893. People still embrace their customs and cultures today even with the introduction of many changes affecting how people think and how things are done. Preferring customary ways to settle disputes, practising customary dances, tattooing, and weaving of mats and baskets are some examples of how people still embrace their customs.

People also have strong beliefs in custom rituals and magic. These rituals and magic are believed to have good and bad causes. Belief in the magic of sorcery is an example of a belief that is still strong and alive in Solomon Islands society.

Sorcery today is an offence under both state and customary laws in Solomon Islands.

State law (the Penal Code [Cap 26] Section 190) refers to sorcery as:

i) the performance of any magical ritual where there is a general belief among a class of persons that may result in harm to any person; or

ii) the possession of articles (without lawful excuse) commonly associated by any class of persons with harmful magic.

Under custom, sorcery in Solomon Islands can refer to an act or action that causes serious sickness or illness that could result in misfortune, insanity or death if no customary means of cure is given to the victim.

Sorcery can be for a good[1] or bad cause. As to the latter, two common examples in Solomon Islands of the belief in sorcery are *arua* in Malaita Province and *vele* in Guadalcanal Province.

---

1 Antisocial behaviours are low for fear of sorcery; or sorcery provides the community the reason for death, sickness, insanity and misfortune.

Arua is a term given to a sorcery practice in which a male or female takes food scraps or a piece of clothing of another person and feeds it to a snake or frog or rat. This is mainly practised in some parts of Malaita.

Vele means '"to pinch", from the tingling or pinched feeling in the arms that warns protected persons of the proximity of the *vele* magician' (Wright 1940:203).

According to Wright (1940:204), 'The usual method employed by the *vele* man is to hide by the side of a road and, as the victim approaches, to make a sharp noise, thus attracting attention. The man turns and sees the *vasa*[2] suspended from a finger. He collapses, usually in an unconscious condition.' This method is practised in Guadalcanal.

In 1932 in Ontong Java, Malaita Province, Ian Hogbin reported that:

> When a sorcerer decided to kill a man, there were several ways in which it might be done. One was to get hold of something closely connected with him, — his hair, nail-parings, or saliva, the last being the favourite. The sorcerer watched where his victim spat, and subsequently took the wet earth and worked his spells over it. Very soon the man would sicken and, if not treated, would die. Another method was to make spells over some such object as a stone, a human bone, or a few grains of sand. During the night the sorcerer took this and either threw it into the house of the victim or buried it near the door. This was equally fatal. The third way was to make an effigy out of pandanus leaf and stick skewers through it. As each one was put in, the man is said to have felt a sharp stab of pain. (Hogbin 1932:442)

He went on to say '[t]he spells, like all others at Ongtong Java, were direct appeals to the spirits of the ancestors' (Hogbin 1932:442–43).

Accusations of sorcery arise today because of several factors that include:

- jealousy due to social and economic advancement
- customary land disputes between different clans and tribes
- criminal activities within villages
- friendship breakdown.

---

2   The instrument in which the magical power of *vele* resides, a small bag made of fibre containing articles such as sacred earth, pieces of shrub or creeper, a man's tooth, and a short piece of native shell money.

Sickness, death, insanity or misfortune are widely believed to be possible results of bad sorcery.[3]

This chapter has five parts. Part 1 focuses on some common perceptions[4] about sorcery in Solomon Islands. Part 2 briefly highlights some negative social consequences of the belief in sorcery. Part 3 deals with customary governance of sorcery. Part 4 deals with state governance of sorcery, and the final part suggests some ways forward and options for law reform.

Part 1: People's views on the belief in sorcery

The Solomon Islands Law Reform Commission (SILRC) conducted consultations in Solomon Islands in 2009 and 2010 on the review of the Penal Code. Sorcery was an issue highlighted by many people as being of serious concern in society and needing to be addressed by the government. The problem of sorcery was raised by many respondents, even though it was not a subject they were directly asked to comment upon. Below are some examples of views on sorcery expressed to the SILRC from people from Choiseul, Temotu, Isabel, Western, Malaita and Makira provinces:

- Sorcery causes harm to human life. Sorcerers should be categorised as murderers. Sorcery can result in mental illness, bad luck and death. Capital punishment (death) should be the punishment for sorcerers. Sorcery is caused by power, self-defence and jealousy.[5]

- Sorcery is a main concern and is happening on a massive scale today. It is very common that when a person died, the death is often linked to an alleged sorcerer. In the past in custom, death was the penalty for practising sorcery. Sorcery should be seriously considered and its penalty should be equivalent to that of a murderer.[6]

---

3   See also Bennett (1987:18), who said: 'Solomon Islanders attributed major troubles to the actions of sorcerers. In the Melanesian's view nothing happened by chance; people attempted to channel spiritual forces to their own ends. Consequently whatever happened — be it illness, a famine, death of a pig, the falling of a branch onto a child, the achievement of leadership, or victory in a battle — all occurred because someone had access to power from the spirits. One major way of gaining access was through sorcery, with the sorcerer using magical ritual to invoke a deity, an ancestral spirit, or less commonly, a demon spirit. Sorcery was universal and, in its negative aspects, greatly feared. A form of social control, it usually restrained the more ruthless and exploitive members of the community and ensured conformity to socially accepted moral values.'
4   No detailed consultation was conducted by the Solomon Islands Law Reform Commission on sorcery. The views in this paper are the ones people expressed during the general consultation on the review of the Penal Code.
5   Frank Waetara, Toroa village, Makira Province, verbal submission over mobile phone to the SILRC, 2010.
6   Tom Firilanga, Malu'u, North Malaita, Malaita Province, verbal submission to SILRC, 2010.

Talking it Through

- Sorcery disturbs the community. Those who practise sorcery should be punished accordingly. The sorcery offence should include threat to commit sorcery.[7]
- Sorcery in Solomon Islands is an act of murder.[8]
- Law should recognise customary law that deals with sorcery. The chiefs should deal with sorcery disputes. Use of witchcraft like black magic for house breaking is common.[9]
- Evidence of sorcery could be a report from the chief. Most deaths are believed to be caused by sorcery. Law needs to recognise death by sorcery. At the moment church leaders and chiefs conducted reconciliation and counselling to parties. Penalty for sorcery should be one of deterrence purpose.[10]
- Black magic or sorcery is widespread. There are more deaths caused by sorcery than other means. Law should recognise sorcerers as equal to murderers. People report sorcery incidents to the church. One alleged sorcerer was beaten to death because of sorcery. The church has gone on missions to collect evidence used in black magic.[11]

The central message from the above perceptions is that sorcery is a serious concern in society. The variety of views suggested the state, church and community leaders should be responsible for dealing with the sorcery offence.

The SILRC is actively working on the review of the sorcery offence as part of the review of the Penal Code and Criminal Procedure Code Reference, and is currently conducting consultations on this review. The end product of the review will be a report containing recommendations for law reform which will be sent to the government through the minister responsible for justice.

Part 2: Effects of the belief in sorcery

Today in Solomon Islands, belief in sorcery is leading to criminal activities. Some of these negative social effects are criminal offences such as assault, arson and murder.

In 2012, according to the Isabel provincial police commander, unlawful activities related to sorcery had increased in the highlands of Isabel Province (Kakai 2012). In 2010, relatives of a dead man burnt down two homes in separate villages in Central Kwara'ae, Malaita Province, because they suspected their relative had

---

7   SILRC Consultation meeting with Gizo Police, Western Province, 2009.
8   SILRC Lata Public Forum Consultation, Temotu Province, 2010.
9   SILRC Taro consultation, Choiseul Province, 2009.
10 SILRC Bula consultation, Provincial Council of Women, Isabel Province, 2009.
11 SILRC Bula consultation, Diocese of Isabel, Isabel Province, 2009.

died due to a type of sorcery commonly known in the area as *kelema* (Kakai 2010). In this case, the police did not act because nobody reported the matter to them. In 2009 in East Kwaio, Malaita Province, a pagan priest who was suspected of practising sorcery was stabbed to death (Radio Australia 2009). These were some instances that suspected sorcerers were harmed and banished from living in communities.[12]

Furthermore, so-called customary healers or customary doctors sometimes take advantage of the strong beliefs in sorcery to commit sexual offences like rape and indecent assault in the name of curing or healing female victims from sorcery-belief sickness. An example is the case of *R v. Tebounapa*.[13] In this case the customary doctor who was the accused was convicted for raping the complainant. He had sexual intercourse with the complainant during a massage session that was aimed at removing a devil from the complainant. First, the accused told the complainant that if she thought about her children, she must let him have sexual intercourse with her. He told the complainant that without sexual intercourse with her, the sickness would not be cured. The accused told the complainant that the purpose of sexual intercourse was to remove the dirty water from her body caused by poison (sorcery). If this was not done, she would die the following month. Also in this case, the same accused was convicted of indecent assault because the accused during the course of curing another complainant played with the clitoris of the complainant. The accused told the complainant that he had been given power and anointed by the chiefs to do such work. He told the complainant not to be afraid of him despite the occurrence of such sexual acts.

Rape was also committed in the case of *Regina v. Sisiolo*.[14] In this case, the accused claimed to be a customary doctor. He also claimed to be someone who could predict the future. Because of his alleged background, he was allowed to cure a young girl who was believed to be a victim of sorcery. In the course of trying to cure the girl Sisiolo had sexual intercourse with her. Sisiolo claimed that a remedy to cure the alleged sorcery caused to the female complainant was sexual intercourse with her.

---

12   Authors' knowledge of the effects of sorcery.
13   *R v. Tebounapa* [1999] SBHC 1; www.paclii.org.vu
14   *Regina v. Sisiolo* [2010] SBHC 35; www.paclii.org.vu.

Talking it Through

Part 3: Customary governance of sorcery

In the past, sorcerers were killed if they were deemed responsible for the death of other persons (Ofasia 2003).[15] Such payback killing could be executed by the relatives of the deceased.

In other instances, sorcerers were banished from the village or community. In one part of Malaita, the sorcerer would be represented by a coconut placed in the *bae*[16] as an affirmation that they would not return. Sometimes they were asked to pay compensation before they left.

At present, chiefs or traditional leaders sometimes deal with sorcery because it is a customary wrong. An example was in 2010 in Malaita Province where chiefs were asked to deal with a sorcery case. A house of chiefs inquired into the matter and ordered the alleged sorcerer to pay 10 red shell valuables as compensation to the relatives of the deceased. The alleged sorcerer paid the compensation.[17]

Proving sorcery according to custom is different to the requirements of the state courts. Chiefs and other traditional elders have the knowledge and ability to prove sorcery according to customary acceptable standards. This is because although the practices or rituals of sorcery are done in secret, a person who practises sorcery is noticeable in the community. A sorcerer is suspected in the community by his or her strange behaviour. This includes strange things that are observed to happen at the sorcerer's home. For example, snakes or frogs are regularly found in the home of the alleged sorcerer or lying in cooking pots or on plates.

In North Malaita (Toabaita and Lau) custom there are two common methods of proving sorcery. These methods both involve tracing. However, people's acceptance of these methods is an issue.

The first method of tracing is to trace any contact that the victim had with the sorcerer. For example, the sorcerer might have given some food to the victim or might have taken a piece of the victim's clothes. Any illness caused to the victim after his or her contact with the sorcerer is always suspected to be due to sorcery. Further, if the sorcerer's home was frequented by snakes or frogs, or if these

---

15   See also SILRC interview with Chief John Konai, Matakwalao House of Chiefs, North Malaita, Malaita Province, 2013; SILRC interview with Rinaldo Talo, president, Malaita Local Court, Malaita Province, 2013.
16   Place where people are buried.
17   SILRC interview with Chief John Konai, Matakwalao House of Chiefs, North Malaita, Malaita Province, 2013. The authors were unable to get information from the interviewee as to how the chiefs came to the conclusion that the alleged sorcerer was responsible for the death.

were found in cooking pots and plates, this proves the suspicions according to customary standards of belief and proof. This method is still commonly known today although not used to pronounce somebody as a sorcerer.[18]

The other method of finding the sorcerer is the use of spiritual ritual (called *sule akalo*). This method involves tribal leaders who are specialised in spiritual callings to call the dead person's spirit to lead them to the sorcerer's home. At the grave the expert person will call the deceased's spirit. The deceased's spirit in the form of a firefly (*bubulu*) will lead the expert and his group to the sorcerer's house. The firefly will rest on the sorcerer's house. This method is no longer used to prove someone a sorcerer in the community.[19]

Denial of being a sorcerer is a common response of alleged sorcerers. However, in some cases alleged sorcerers admit that they have magical objects for protection and not to cause harm. In some instances, the alleged sorcerers can point out the source of their magical objects to well-known customary healers in the community.

Part 4: State governance of sorcery

State legal system

Sorcery is an offence in Solomon Islands. The Penal Code [Cap 26] in Section 190 provides:

> Any person who
>
> (a) performs any magic ritual in respect of which there is a general belief among any class of persons that harm may be caused to any person; or
>
> (b) has in his possession, without lawful excuse, any article commonly associated by any class of persons with harmful magic,
>
> is guilty of a misdemeanour, and shall be liable to imprisonment for two months or to a fine of forty dollars.

There are two problems with this provision. First, this sorcery offence provision does not fully reflect sorcery as it is known and understood in Solomon Islands society. This is because sorcery as it is known to Solomon Islanders is an act that causes serious sickness or illness that could result in misfortune, insanity or death if no customary means of cure is given to the victim. A sorcerer is

---

18 The authors of this chapter were unable to get information on why the method was not used.
19 The authors of this chapter were unable to get information on why the method was not used.

known to the victim when the victim experiences misfortune or becomes sick. While sick, the victim may repeatedly dream about the sorcerer. Or the sorcerer becomes known to relatives of the victim after the victim dies. The relatives can use the two tracing methods described above to identify the sorcerer.[20] These are the customary beliefs and perceptions as to how a sorcerer is identified. This is different to the sorcery offence as envisaged in Section 190(a) that provides for criminalisation of performance of any magical ritual where there is a general belief among a class of persons that may result in harm to any person; and under Section 190(b) that provides for criminalisation of possession of articles (without lawful excuse) commonly associated by any class of persons with harmful magic. This is because performing rituals and possessing articles (objects) are only partial factors for identifying a sorcerer in customary ways.

Second, the sorcery provision in the Penal Code has not been used to prosecute any alleged sorcerer(s) in the past.[21] The reason for this non-usage is because of the perception that the sorcery offence as in Section 190 of the Penal Code is difficult to prove.[22] This perception is due to the fact that sorcery conduct or dealings are done in secret. For instance, the performance of magic ritual and possession of harmful magic objects or articles are hidden from those who do not practise sorcery. The only people who may have a chance of witnessing the conduct or articles are close family members. Except in rare cases, these family members will not reveal the sorcerer because of the stigma that is associated with sorcery. They will not wish to be seen and considered as an evil family in the community. There was an instance that a child revealed that her mother was practising sorcery.[23] This instance is discussed below under the Local Court Act.

The perception that the sorcery offence is difficult to prove needs to be tested in court. This is because although sorcerers perform their magical rituals in secret or hide their magical articles, there are times they can be caught. For example, a sorcerer who practises *arua* often dances in the graveyard after the victim is buried. This type of practice is considered to be a ritual that is associated with harm. A *vele* sorcerer often has in possession a special *vele* bag. This object is commonly known as possessed by those with harmful magic. There might be some successful cases if cases of the sorcery offence were tried in courts, especially the local court and magistrate court.[24]

---

20 The problem with these methods is that they are not currently used.
21 SILRC email correspondence with Mr Douglas Hou of the Public Solicitor's Office, Mr Ricky Iomea of the Director of Public Prosecutions and Mr Galvin Ora of the Police Prosecutions Office. Also SILRC conversation by telephone with Mr Leonard Maina, chief magistrate of Solomon Islands.
22 SILRC email correspondence with Mr Galvin Ora of the Police Prosecutions Office.
23 SILRC interview with Rinaldo Talo, president, Malaita Local Court, Malaita Province, 2013.
24 The local court is the relevant court to deal with sorcery offences. The magistrate court is mentioned because it is the court that currently deals with matters that are under the local court jurisdiction as the local court is not active at the moment.

Another reason for the non-usage of this provision may be because of the low penalty attached to the offence.[25] This does not reflect the nature of the offence in custom as sorcery is a very serious wrong in custom.[26] A suggestion for a higher penalty to deter people from practising sorcery was proposed during consultation.[27]

Regina v. Havimana case

This is a case[28] where sorcery was discussed by the court in the context of a defence to a charge of murder. The defendant attempted to rely on the argument that he killed the victim because the victim had killed his father by sorcery. The defence alleged that the sorcerer revealed himself through two other victims (Eldon Kari and Veronica Lestro — not killed) when two Church of Melanesia Brothers conducted clearance and healing in the area. The Brothers used holy water, holy oil and prayer in their clearance and healing sessions. It was alleged by the defence witnesses that the victim in this case (alleged sorcerer) was speaking through Eldon Kari and Veronica Lestro saying that he was responsible for killing the accused's father, the late Reverend Ambrose Havimana. The alleged sorcerer was alleged to speak through Eldon and Veronica when they were made asleep by the Brothers. The High Court of Solomon Islands did not accept this method (voice identification through the victims in which the alleged sorcerer was identified) because of inconsistent evidence given by the defence witnesses.

It is not clear how the defence wished to advance its case in relation to its argument that the alleged sorcerer was responsible for the death of the accused's father. This is because it is not clear as to what would be the legal consequences of the court accepting Allen (the deceased in the case) as the sorcerer of the accused's father. That is, what benefit would the court render to the accused on the basis that the accused committed payback murder for the sorcerer killing his father? Would the court agree to extend provocation to cover that circumstance? The court in this case did not make any statement on this issue.

Local Court Act [Cap 19]

The Local Court Act allows for the local courts to deal with minor civil and criminal matters where parties are all islanders residing within the jurisdiction of the local courts as set out in their warrants that established them (Section 6). The Act allows the local courts to apply islander custom in the area of the

---

25   The maximum penalty for the sorcery offence in the Penal Code is imprisonment of two months or a fine of SBD40.
26   SILRC interview with Rinaldo Talo, president, Malaita Local Court, Malaita Province, 2013.
27   SILRC interview with Rinaldo Talo, president, Malaita Local Court, Malaita Province, 2013.
28   *Regina v. Havimana* [2011] SBHC 48; www.paclii.org.vu.

jurisdiction of the courts (Section 16). The courts can hear both the law and customary wrongs or breaches. They can impose punishment authorised by law or custom of the islanders that is not contrary to natural justice and humanity, and the punishment must always be proportionate to the nature and circumstances of the offence (Section 18).

The local courts can deal with sorcery offences both under state law (Penal Code) and under customary law. Under state law a local court can deal with a sorcery offence because it is a minor offence and if the parties are from the area of jurisdiction of the local court. However, there is no evidence (according to the authors' research) to show that a local court has dealt with a sorcery offence under state law. On its customary jurisdiction, a local court can deal with sorcery as a customary wrong. This is because sorcery is a customary wrong and custom determines the punishment for alleged sorcerers. Custom recognised death, banishment, or giving of land to the victim or victim's family as forms of punishment for sorcerers (Nanau 2011; Ofasia 2003; authors' personal knowledge). According to the authors' research there were two instances where the Malaita local court, under its customary law jurisdiction, dealt with the accusation of practising sorcery. The first case involved a wife who was accused of causing the death of her husband by sorcery. The community suspected the wife of having *arua* because she danced and talked in the graveyard in the night during moonlight and a customary ritual was performed and found that the wife was responsible for the death. During the local court hearing, the daughter of the wife testified that her mother fed a 'cat' in the bush. The daughter led the court officers to the place in the bush and they found a half snake (snake without a tail) in the area. The local court found the wife guilty of sorcery according to custom and ordered her to pay five red shell valuables to the husband's side.[29]

The second case was *Are v. Makau*.[30] In this case, the plaintiffs (husband and wife, wife accused of being a sorcerer) brought the case to the local court to make appropriate orders against the defendants for accusing the wife as a sorcerer. The facts of the case were Rebecca Koobira, wife of Are, was sick and got healing or deliverance from a Church of Melanesia Brother (*tasiu*). The first defendant, Selly Makau, went with Rebecca and witnessed the healing process. Rebecca was unconscious during the healing process. The Brother told her that she would see some signs within the next three days. During the three days, Rebecca passed blood and then she passed a dead snake on the third day. This snake was believed to be an *arua* given to her. She could feed the *arua* and use it to poison people. Selly told this story about Rebecca to others, including Are. Are (the husband) was not happy about the story and went to the local court for

---

29 The authors were unable to get further information about this case.
30 Malaita Local Court, Civil Case No. 1 of 2012 (judgment delivered 22 April 2013).

appropriate orders. The court ruled that Selly only informed others about the true happenings or story about Rebecca. The local court did not give any orders for damage or compensation to the plaintiffs. Instead the court ruled that:

i) Rebecca not to initiate any rare actions to raise suspiciousness;

ii) Parties are not to spread false news of arua; and

iii) Parties are to reconcile.

Apart from the above two cases, the Malaita local court dealt with many cases in relation to rare or extraordinary behaviour of alleged sorcerers during times of death.[31] Claimants came to court claiming compensation from alleged sorcerers, accusing them of behaving extraordinarily during times of death. The extraordinary behaviours include laughing out loud persistently, putting flowers on heads and eating a lot during the mourning period. The court awarded compensation for such claims because these extraordinary behaviours amount to customary wrongs.[32]

Provincial government level

Moli Ward Chiefs Council Ordinance 2010

At the provincial level, the Guadalcanal Provincial Assembly passed the *Moli Ward Chiefs Council Ordinance 2010* (Moli Ward Ordinance) establishing the Moli Ward Chiefs Council and providing it with powers to deal with matters within the Moli Ward in accordance with customary law and practices of the tribes of Moli Ward and for related matters. Among others, the Moli Ward Ordinance stipulated that sorcery is an offence.

Section 77 of the ordinance states:

> A person who practices sorcery in Moli Ward breaches this section and is liable to a fine not exceeding 1,000 penalty units and one pig, one chausangavulu,[33] and one chupu.[34]

> In this section, 'sorcery' means any rituals for which there is a general belief among any class of persons that harm may be caused to any person or in possession, without lawful excuse, any article commonly association in any class of persons with harmful magic, and include

---

31 These cases were mainly seeking customary compensation for the rare actions of the respondents but not accusations of practising sorcery.
32 SILRC interview with Rinaldo Talo, president, Malaita Local Court, Malaita Province, 2013.
33 *Chausangavulu* refers to 10 string shell money of one fathom each string in length.
34 *Chupu* refers to the piles of cooked food, uncooked garden produce, live pigs and shell money that are exchanged in ceremony which may be made for a range of purposes (Monson 2012:229–30).

heathen practices or black magic commonly known in Moli Ward as piro, vele, or kibokibo for which there is a general belief among any class of persons may cause harm.

All evidences in sorcery matters shall be by way of eye witness, circumstantial or admissions.

Hearsay evidence is inadmissible and cannot be accepted as evidence against a defendant.

The offence except the penalty closely reflects the sorcery offence in the Penal Code. Proving an offence under the Moli Ward Ordinance is just as problematic as under the Penal Code. Admission of guilt is difficult as alleged sorcerers do not generally confess in Solomon Islands. The closest admission of guilt that an alleged sorcerer will make is to say that he or she has something for protection and not for killing or harming someone. Circumstantial evidence could therefore be the only possible way to prove someone is guilty of sorcery. For example, in the case of someone with *arua*, facts such as the alleged sorcerer was recently in contact with the victim by giving food to the victim, and evidence of frogs and snakes in the sorcerer's home, are circumstantial evidence that can be argued in a state-supported court. However, whether a court will accept such evidence is uncertain — only the courts will give a position on this.

Part 5: Options for law reform and ways forward

The first option as a way forward for law reform is to use the local court customary jurisdiction to deal with sorcery. The Local Court Act [Cap 19] establishes the legal framework to recognise, apply and use customary law in the rural areas of Solomon Islands. It allows the local courts under its customary jurisdiction to determine or settle customary disputes or wrongs. The local courts also have the power to direct an accused or a respondent to pay compensation to a victim — more towards restorative justice. The problem at the moment is that the local court is not fully utilised to perform its customary jurisdiction. The local courts were active in the past but not now (Evans et al. 2010). Currently, the local courts are operated more in the provincial centres as opposed to the local rural areas as the Local Court Act envisaged. Also, currently, the local courts focus more on customary land disputes other than customary wrongs and breaches, and minor criminal and civil cases.[35] This makes it impossible for serious customary wrongs like sorcery, adultery and fornication (adultery and fornication are not criminal

---

35 The authors' personal knowledge with the justice system of Solomon Islands.

offences under the state law) to be settled at the local courts. The result is that people resort to self-help approaches of asking compensation and assaulting the accused in sorcery, adultery or fornication cases. This sometimes results in escalation of violence in the communities. This could be avoided if local courts functioned to their full capacity.

Under its customary jurisdiction, the Local Court Act should clarify that local courts are to have unlimited jurisdiction to order or give punishment or sentence on customary wrongs or breaches appropriate to the seriousness of the wrong in custom. This unlimited jurisdiction, however, must be subject to natural justice and humanity as provided for in Section 18 of the Local Court Act. This suggestion is made on the basis that the Act is not clear as to sentences the local court can award under its customary jurisdiction. A broad interpretation of the Act would mean that the local court has unlimited jurisdiction and can award any sentence according to custom so long as the sentence is not inconsistent with natural justice and humanity.[36] In contrast, a narrow interpretation of the Act would mean that the local court can only award a sentence for criminal matters of a fine of no ore than SBD200 or no more than 6 months imprisonment. And for civil matters the local court can only award up to SBD1,000 for damages or compensation.[37]

In the past when local courts were active, they upheld customary laws, which on appeal to the high court were also upheld. This was reflected in the *To'ofilu v. Oimae* case.[38] In that case, the high court ruled that the customary practice of determining payment of bride price would be best dealt with by the local court of the area of which both parties originated. Similarly, sorcery as a customary wrong should be best dealt with by local courts.

The second option is to devolve jurisdiction over sorcery to the customary legal system. The chiefs or traditional leaders' customary forum is good because they have the knowledge about sorcery practices.[39] Given their know-how about sorcery they can deal effectively with it. For instance, the move by the Guadalcanal provincial government through the ordinance in empowering the Moli Ward Chiefs Council to deal with sorcery is a step in the right direction. Such an approach should be carefully considered at the national level to see if it can be adopted as a solution for addressing sorcery more widely.

Finally, the third option is to consider the involvement of churches to deal with sorcery. The Church of Melanesia is involved in dealing with sorcery on request by communities by way of blessing shrines and neutralising the habitats of

---

36 This interpretation is based on custom as the determining factor subject to natural justice and humanity.
37 See warrants that established the different local courts.
38 *To'ofilu v. Oimae* [1997] SBHC 33; paclii.org.vu.
39 See Futaiasi (2011) for a discussion of the advantages and challenges facing customary forums.

dangerous spirits. Brothers of the Church of Melanesia on request visit villages to do what is termed 'clearance' or 'deliverance'. This process involves going to villages and collecting items associated with sorcery or talking to people who are suspected of practising sorcery. They usually urge those who practise sorcery to stop doing sorcery and come forward to the Brothers for healing purposes. An issue with this option is whether such church programs will accept taking a step further to settle disputes between parties as a result of sorcery.

An additional aspect that must be done if local courts, councils of chiefs or houses of chiefs, and church officials are to be involved in dealing with sorcery is for the state to provide training for them in areas of natural justice, human rights principles and other basic law principles. The training will empower them to conduct and discharge fair hearings and settlements for parties who seek remedies from them. Further, the councils of chiefs or the houses of chiefs and the church officials who are to deal with sorcery must register their groups with the local courts. This will ensure proper coordination and oversight over the groups dealing with sorcery.

References

Bennett, J.A. 1987. *Wealth of the Solomons: A History of a Pacific Archipelago, 1800–1978.* Honolulu: University of Hawai'i Press.

Evans, D., M. Goddard and D. Paterson 2010. The Hybrid Courts of Melanesia: A Comparative Analysis of the Village Courts of Papua New Guinea, Island Courts of Vanuatu and Local Courts of Solomon Islands. *Justice and Development Working Paper Series* No. 13. Washington DC: World Bank. documents.worldbank.org/curated/en/2010/01/14276330/hybrid-courts-melanesia-comparative-analysis-village-courts-papua-new-guinea-island-courts-vanuatu-local-courts-solomon-islands, viewed 22/4/2014.

Futaiasi, D.L.G. 2011. Advantages and Challenges Facing Custom Dispute Determination and Settlement: An Assessment. In *A Study of Customary Methods Dealing with Customary Land Disputes in Malaita, Solomon Islands.* LLM Research Paper. University of the South Pacific, 91–108.

Hogbin, H.I. 1932. Sorcery at Ontong Java. *American Anthropologist* 34(3):441–48.

Kakai, J. 2010. No Police Action on Burnt Homes. *Solomon Star* 2 December.

Kakai, J. 2012. Sorcery on the Rise in Isabel: PPC. *Solomon Star* 9 June.

Monson, R. 2012. *Hu Nao Save Tok*? Women, Men and Land: Negotiating Property and Authority in Solomon Islands. PhD thesis, The Australian National University.

Nanau, G.L. 2011. The *Wantok* System as a Socio-Economic and Political Network in Melanesia. *OMNES: The Journal of Multicultural Society* 2(1):31–55. www.omnesjournal.org/upload/public/pdffile/10/1.pdf, viewed 3/5/2013.

Ofasia, J. 2003. Traditional Toabaitan Methods of Forgiveness and Reconciliation. *Melanesian Journal of Theology* 19(2):6–39. www.cltc.ac.pg/LinkClick.aspx?fileticket=Dv2joj3F_mY%3D&tabid=80, viewed 20/3/2013.

Radio Australia 2009. Hunt for Three Murder Suspects in Solomon Islands Linked to Sorcery. Radio Australia 16 March. www.radioaustralia.net.au/international/radio/onairhighlights/hunt-for-three-murder-suspects-in-solomon-islands-linked-to-sorcery, viewed 10/2/2013.

Wright, L.W.S. 1940. The 'Vele' Magic of the South Solomons. *The Journal of the Royal Anthropological Institute of Great Britain and Ireland* 70(2):203–9.

Part 3: Positive Directions in Overcoming Violence

16. *Kumo Koimbo*: Accounts and Responses to Witchcraft in Gor, Simbu Province

Clara Bal

Introduction

United Nauro Gor is located in Kundiawa Gembogl District, Simbu Province, in the highlands of Papua New Guinea. The Gor Community Base Laws were enacted in 2006, along with establishment of a local police force to enforce the laws. The community made the laws because it faced many social problems. These included election-related tribal fights every five years, a high incidence of sorcery-related killings, and a general breakdown in law and order. The community, with the assistance of the then Catholic parish priest, Father Dr Jan Jaworski, village leaders and educated professionals, helped to draft the community laws. After the laws were implemented, young men and women from the community were recruited by the Royal Papua New Guinea Constabulary as auxillary police to enforce the laws within the community. The state supported these initiatives by training the local police and assigning a senior sergeant to help local police. The state also provided the Gor police with a car to carry out their tasks.

Methodology

I conducted a case study that began with researching reports and DVDs that were produced by the United Nauro Gor Association from its beginning until the present day. I held interviews with the former parish priest of Gor, Father Jaworski, whom the Gor community appointed as their village chief and also the person who helped the people to create the association.

The research involved quantitative and qualitative methods and observation.

One-on-one interviews were conducted with key individuals of Gor and also with individuals who had been directly associated with community projects.

Interviews were carried out in different locations and people of both sexes and all ages were interviewed. Group interviews were carried out with local police officers including the senior sergeant.

Questionnaires were given out to get the views of the people living in the neighbouring communities of Gor. Questionnaires were also given out to the officers in charge of community policing in Simbu Province.

There were some limitations to the data collection. Some questionnaires were not returned and the geographical location of some villages made it impossible to reach them.

Description of *kumo*

Witchcraft is called *kumo* in the Kuman language of the Nauro people. *Kumo koimbo* is a term in the Kuman language that refers to a person who has *kumo* and practises it. People in the Nauro community believe that *kumo koimbo* has existed since the days of our forefathers. During the days of our forefathers, the *kumo koimbo* did not practise *kumo* openly as is done today.

It is believed in my community that a *kumo koimbo* is a person possessed by an evil spirit which is the *kumo*. The *kumo* that lives inside the *kumo koimbo* compels and controls the *kumo koimbo* (demon-possessed person) to do things he would not otherwise do if he were not possessed; for example, causing death, eating human flesh and waste, or removing and eating pigs' hearts while the pig is alive. *Kumo koimbo* also destroy students' education by cursing them so that the student does not complete their studies.

Kumo manifests in different forms in the United Nauro Gor community, mostly in the form of animals such as flying foxes, rats, dogs, cats, goats, cows and snakes. It is believed that when a *kumo* leaves the *kumo koimbo's* body and travels out into the night to kill someone or look for its food (human waste, flesh, and pigs' hearts) the *kumo koimbo* will sleep like a dead person. People could do anything to try to wake them, but the *kumo koimbo* will not respond. They will wake up only when the *kumo* returns to them.

Ordinary people do not know how *kumo* is passed from one person to another. The *kumo koimbos* know how they pass *kumo* to another person but never tell ordinary people how they do it. The only time people know that someone has been given *kumo* is when someone is caught in the act of practising *kumo*. It often happens with little children.

Kumo koimbo kill people for the following reasons:

Money

The people believe that *kumo* kill people because of money. If a person has a lot of money and shares it among his or her relatives in the village and forgets to give some money to a *kumo koimbo* in the village, the *kumo koimbo* becomes angry and kills the person. Sometimes if a *kumo koimbo* sees that a particular family has a lot of money, the *kumo koimbo* will kill a family member — most often the head of the family — so that the family will spend the money in a way that benefits the *kumo koimbo*. For example, the relatives of the deceased will spend their money in the *haus krai*. The belief of *kumo* in my village encourages people to share.

Jealousy

Kumo koimbo also kill people out of jealousy. This often happens to business people and educated people. *Kumo koimbo* kill these people because they are jealous of them and the benefits they bring to their immediate family.

Food

Kumo koimbo also kill people because of food. If a particular family eat food such as rice, or any kind of protein, especially pork, and if they do not share the food with their neighbour who is a *kumo koimbo*, then the *kumo koimbo* will kill a member of the family. Therefore the people in the village are always careful when they eat the kind of food that they know the *kumo koimbo* likes eating as well.

Reasons why people kill *kumo koimbo*s

People in my community kill *kumo koimbo* for reasons of retribution. Firstly, whenever a young and highly educated man or woman in our community dies suddenly without any obvious cause, *kumo* is suspected.

When such young people die, it is a loss to the family, clan, tribe and community as a whole. In my community, our people take pride in their educated sons and daughters. That is because the entire family or clan normally contributes to paying for their sons' or daughters' education, especially when they are attending higher secondary school to college and university.

It takes years and money to educate a young man or woman. When such educated persons die because of a *kumo koimbo*, the pain and loss that the family and the clan feels is great because a highly educated person cannot be easily replaced.

Secondly, when young children, young men and women, or mothers die without any obvious cause, such as sickness, *kumo* is suspected. Sudden deaths of small children or young men or women in the village frustrate the community. Thus the community reacts by accusing and killing a person who is a known *kumo koimbo* in the village.

When the community kills a *kumo koimbo* it is often done in public or in broad daylight so that the entire community can see it. That is done intentionally to deter other *kumo koimbo* from killing innocent people in the village for no good reason.

Accusation

There are three main ways the people use to identify a person who practises *kumo*. Firstly, there are customary rules that the community follows during the mourning period. These are: women and men are not allowed to do marketing or sell their garden products, the people are not allowed to wash until after the mourning period, no work is allowed such as gardening or building of houses, children are not allowed to play, and no one in the village is allowed to whistle or laugh. If any of the people break one of these rules then the community will accuse that person.

Secondly, if any of the deceased's relatives had an argument with the deceased (and said something like 'you will live longer on this earth and continue to argue with me'), or if they gave food to him or her, and the person fell sick and died, the other relatives will accuse that relative of killing that person.

Thirdly, there are some people in Gor as well as in other rural communities in Simbu Province called *kumo* doctors. *Kumo* doctors are people who have *kumo* but the difference is the *kumo* doctors do not kill people but they expose other *kumo koimbo*. *Kumo* doctors act as doctors and they cure people who have been attacked and injured by other *kumo koimbo*.

When someone dies in the village and it is suspected that he or she was killed by a *kumo koimbo*, the relatives of the diseased hire a *kumo* doctor to come and identify the *kumo koimbo* responsible for the death of that person. It is a paid job.

Gor Community Base Laws

Sorcery-related accusations and killings were one of the challenges faced by the people of United Nauro Gor. Before the implementation of the laws, in every death there was more than one person being killed. Innocent people were also accused of possessing *kumo* and were discriminated against within the village. The accused would sometimes migrate to other provinces in the country, in order to protect their identity as well as their children from the discrimination. The people became aware that this evil practice was destroying their communal life and wanted to put a stop to it but they don't have a well-organised community and no one was there to empower them to take any action.

In response to this situation Father Jan Jaworski, the then parish priest of Yombar Catholic Church in Gor, began to talk with the community leaders about ways to improve these circumstances. This resulted in the creation of the United Nauro Gor Association with elected directors and executive. The people even changed the name of the community from Nauro Gor to United Nauro Gor. This made the people feel that they actually belonged to a community. The people in the community supported this idea because they knew that sorcery-related accusations and killings were damaging communal life. At the grassroots level the community really wanted to end this practice of sorcery-related accusations and killings, and also rape cases. The people in the community supported Father Jaworski and their village leaders by writing their own laws. The laws were publicly discussed and debated in Gor and the entire community (including men, women and children) took part in discussions and setting the penalty for breaching the laws. The elected executives had a final meeting and came up with the amended laws. They received formal endorsement across the community and were launched on 29 December 2006. A memorandum of understanding between the Royal Papua New Guinea Constabulary and Simbu administration was signed. The laws were presented to the people by their village chief, Bruno. The people in the community agreed to follow the laws. At first nothing happened. However, after the implementation of the Gor police the executives had a meeting and Bruno told them that the community law was working.

The people in the community are aware and have agreed that accusing someone of practising sorcery and rape are criminal cases. They won't accept compensation (which is the traditional law), but will bring the culprit to justice.

An extract of the Gor Community Base Laws that addresses sorcery-related violence appears at the end of this chapter. *Sanguma* and *kumo* have the same meaning; however, *sanguma* is Tok Pisin and *kumo* is from the *Kuman* language. The laws use the Tok Pisin term *sanguma*.

Gor police

The Gor Community Base Laws did not work at first because security was needed to enforce them. Therefore the Gor Community Police was formed. The village leaders selected strong and brave warriors in the village and recruited them as the Gor police. They also selected 30 women in the community and recruited them as policewomen. This was to show and teach the local people about the practice of gender equality. Although the memorandum of understanding stated that Simbu Province would support their training, financial assistance was not given. Instead, the provincial government assigned a senior sergeant to be with the police and also train them. The Gor Community Police received financial support from Caritas Australia and Mathew Siune, a former politician, gave 3000 kina for their training. The Simbu provincial government bought the uniforms. On my last interview with the Gor police as well as with the people in the community I noted that the Gor Community Police were not in the community performing their duties. But they were always in town helping out the regular police perform their jobs. This is because they are not being given allowances; at least some kind of income. Therefore they are doing other work to get money.

Recommendations

Creation of the Gor Community Base Laws and their enforcement by the Gor Community Police has had a very positive impact in the community. All that is needed now is more awareness to be conducted in the community to point out the positive impact the laws have had and encourage the people to continue to uphold and obey the very laws that they have made themselves.

The Gor Community Police need government assistance in terms of funding to conduct more workshops to educate the local community policemen and policewomen about basic constitutional rights of the people while executing their duties in the community.

The Simbu Government also should give allowances or income to the police in order to keep them in the village and stop the provincial police commander hiring them or taking them out from the village to perform other jobs.

Because of the fact that everyone in the community is living under permanent fear on their own land I also recommend that if we really want to cease sorcery-related killings and rape we should work in the community at a grassroots level. Community laws needs to be worked out and endorsed by the community itself.

Prior to introducing community laws the community must have an organised structure. Their leadership must be trusted and respected.

In order for policing to be effective it needs to be community based. But community-based laws and community policing will not work in a community that is not organised.

Conclusion

The people from United Nauro Gor came up with their community-based laws after the community was organised and received the structure of an organised association. The creation of the United Nauro Gor Association brought recovery of leadership and trust back to the community. Important factors were:

- the community was organised
- structure and leadership was created: a chairman, executives, body of directors and eight committees. The committees have regular meetings and the directors meet four times a year
- trust — people who are responsible and willing to work for the community
- the Gor Community Base Laws were written
- law enforcement was supported by community policing.

Community-based law and policing work hand in hand. I say this because after the Community Base Laws were implemented the community agreed that they would follow their own laws by June. However, they did not follow their own laws. The Nauro Gor Association then came up with the creation of community policing. After community policing was implemented the community leader reported to the association that the community laws were working.

After studying the United Nauro Gor Community Policing and Law, the community itself can address the issues on *kumo* (*sanguma*) and rape. However, not all members of the community will address the issues of *kumo* and rape. In order to address these issues, the community should build a good structure of leadership and should work and respect their leaders. The community should come up with a constructive and workable community. The people in the community know that sorcery-related accusations are destroying community life but they are not empowered to do anything to stop people from accusing other people. Therefore, if we want to help address this issue we should go to the community and start working at a grassroots level and empower the people to come up with a more organised community structure.

Appendix: Extract from Gor Community Base Laws and Policeing

3.1   Sanguma na Poisen [Sanguma and poison]

Mi Nauro i tok nogat tru long toktok belong sanguma na poison.

[As a person of the Nauro community I solemnly declare that I will never talk about witchcraft and poison.]

3:1   Makim man nating long saguma bai chargim em long baim K500.00 wantim threepela bikpela pik inap long kaikai igo long man em makim olsem sanguma. Bai kotim yu long Deformation of Character.

[3:1   If a person in the village accuses someone of sorcery, that person will give the accused K500.00 and three big pigs. Plus the accuser will be charged with defamation of character.]

    3:1:1 Court fine em K200.00.

3:2   Patim man o assoultim bai go long bikpela kot na kot i mekim save long em

[3:2   If a person is accused of practising sorcery and is assaulted by other people in the community, these people will be taken to either the district or the national court.]

Mas referim i go long Police, em Police Case.

[This case must be referred to the police.]

    3:2:1   Village kot bai appeal i go long higher kot wantaim bakrap report.

    [3:2:1   If the village court is biased this case will be referred to the district court.]

3:3   Killim man indai mas go long bikpela kot na kot i mas kalabusim ol man i mekim indai narapela.

[3:3   If someone is found guilty of taking the life of an accused person, he should be sent to prison. The person should be taken to a district or the national court.]

Mas referim i go long Police, em Police Case.

[This case must be referred to the police.]

> 3:3:1   Village court bai no nap long stretim, bai appeal i go long higher court long stretim.
>
> [3:3:1   The village court will not handle this case. It must be resolved in a higher court.]
>
> 3:3:2   Sapos lain bilong man indai lakim compensiation bai baim yet behind long higher court decision.
>
> [3:3:2   Compensation to the relatives of the accused may be given after the court decision is made. That is, only if the relatives of the deceased want compensation.]
>
> 3:3:3   Tambu tru long lain supportim long kilim man long sangum, sapos husait man i supportim man long kilim man bai kisim same charge olsem man kilim narapela indai.
>
> [3.3.3   People are not allowed to take part in killing an accused person. If someone supports another person in killing an accused, he or she will also be charged with murder.]

Mas referim i go long Police, em Police Case.

[This case must be referred to the police.]

3:4   Man indai ausait na ino sawe as belong indai mas karim indai man o meri igo long haus sik bilong wokim postmortem na kisim medical repot.

[3:4   If a person dies in the village and if their relatives do not know the cause of death they must take the deceased to the hospital for a post-mortem. They should get a medical report.]

3:5   Man indai long haus sik mas kisim full medical report before kisim dead body ikam autsit long planim.

[3:5   If a person dies in hospital, their relatives must get the medical report before bringing the deceased home for burial.]

17. Practical Church Interventions on Sorcery and Witchcraft Violence in the Papua New Guinea Highlands

Fr Philip Gibbs

Introduction

Sorcery and witchcraft beliefs and practices are common in Papua New Guinea (PNG), yet differ considerably throughout the country.[1] This paper addresses witchcraft-related accusations and violence in two PNG highlands provinces: Simbu and Enga. I will explain a response from the Catholic Church in Simbu Province, and then take up a case from Enga Province, illustrating the complexities of issues raised by people in an Enga faith community that is attempting to respond to an outbreak of witchcraft-related violence in their area. I conclude with some suggestions based on the interventions to date.

Highlands *sanguma*

In Simbu, witchcraft, or *sanguma* as it is called, involves a malevolent power that is said to take the form of a creature such as a rat, bat, frog or flying fox, with the power to kill or harm people.[2] The spirit-creature lives within the body of its host and even without the conscious approval of its host; the spirit-creature can take another form and roam around, eating human waste and searching for human flesh, particularly vital organs like the heart or liver (Damien 2005:128).

Because of belief in this region that spirit creatures appearing as animals like to consume corpses, people search for and kill animals in cemeteries. People in many parts of the highlands believe that if the spirit-creature is killed, then its host will die also. Moreover, by killing the host it is presumed that the spirit-creature will die, which is a fundamental belief behind the killing of people accused of *sanguma*. Sometimes negative feelings of jealousy and resentment are

---

1   See Zocca (2009). For an example from East Sepik Province, see Gibbs and Wailoni (2009).
2   In recent times people have come to view the spirit creature also in other forms — even as a helicopter or a computer virus (Bishop Anton Bal in an address to clergy conference in Mt Hagen, 24 July 2013).

involved, but those killing the accused often think they are doing their duty in the sense that they feel they have to defend the clan from a malicious power that could kill again.

Beliefs such as this are common in Simbu Province and the Wahgi Valley (Jiwaka Province), but in recent times such beliefs seem to be spreading to other provinces. Eves and Kelly-Hanku (2014) refer to the spread of this belief into parts of the Eastern Highlands. There is also recent diffusion of this belief and associated violence westwards, including to Enga Province.

Enga people have a traditional belief in *yama*, which amounts to the personification of the malicious effects of envy. For example, if someone carrying pork or another valued food item met a person on their way home and was not willing to share, then the resultant ill feeling (conscious or unconscious) could result in illness or another misfortune for the person or the family of the one carrying the food. If a family member falls sick and people suspect *yama*, they might enquire who the sick person or someone else in the family had met on their way home. People say that experienced elders or a ritual expert might see or hear signs of *yama* (such as a whistling noise), and as a consequence recite a spell telling the person with *yama* to come with a recognisable sign, such as clay rubbed around their eyes, so as to be given food or some other valuable that had been put aside for them. There is an expression for this presentation in Enga: *yama nenge yukingi* (literally: pulling out the *yama* teeth).[3]

Formerly in Enga there was no tradition of torturing or killing people thought to be possessed by a spirit-creature such as in Simbu. However, with intermarriage and recent frequent travel to and from Simbu and Jiwaka provinces, some people in Enga now refer to a new form of *yama* that involves removing a person's heart and eating buried flesh. Thus one hears in Enga today a reinterpretation of *yama* in terms of *sanguma* sorcery.[4]

Catholic bishops' statement

The Catholic bishops from the five highlands dioceses met in May 2013 to discuss the issue of the spread of sorcery beliefs in the highlands. The bishops are convinced that a remedy will be found in strengthening people's Christian

---

3   I have given an example of envy over food. Another situation could be envy over how handsome a man appears at a traditional dance festival. There are also tales of how a man going hunting at night would not tell his wife, sister or mother, lest the yama of the women follow him into the forest to trick him or ruin his hunting.
4   Talk of this new type of sorcery puts the blame on women, saying that Enga women who had gone to Simbu to buy magic for restraining unfaithful husbands had mistakenly brought back *sanguma* as well.

commitment. They produced two statements — a longer one in English to be posted in all churches, and a one-page statement in Tok Pisin to be read in all Catholic churches in the PNG highlands.[5]

Part of their statement reads:

> We Bishops challenge our priests, religious brothers and sisters, catechists, and all church leaders and ministers, and we invite other churches too, to join with us in taking a clear, unambiguous, and strong stand against all talk about *sanguma* and all attempts to lay the blame on anyone, especially at the time of sickness and death.[6]

A diocesan plan from Simbu

Because of the tradition of sorcery-related accusations and violence in Simbu, the Catholic Church in Simbu under the leadership of Bishop Henk Te Maarssen and more recently Bishop Anton Bal have taken a stand in responding to the issue.[7] During the 1980s and 1990s Te Maarssen developed a strategy with five related components.[8]

1. Help broaden people's understanding of the causes of illness and death

The *sanguma* question is 'who caused the death', which is different from a biomedical question such as 'what caused the death'. Nevertheless, biomedical explanations may be accepted and may help people to consider causes other than sorcery. Parish priests and other leaders are urged to ask health workers for a medical report. If an explanation such as cancer, pneumonia or AIDS is accepted by the family they will mourn and bury the deceased with little or no talk of sorcery or *sanguma*. I have heard of cases where they found that the death was caused by AIDS and the mourning was curtailed, talk of 'causes' was hushed up, and the person was buried with very little talk (Gibbs 2009a:7).

---

5   The full English statement can be found in the last item of tokstret.com/2013/07/27/social-concerns-notes-july-2013/.
6   People from several parishes in Enga report that the statement read at the end of Sunday church services generated discussion at the time. However, further research is required to assess any long-term effect of such efforts.
7   Just over one-third of Simbu people (34 per cent) say they belong to the Catholic Church (Gibbs 2004:179).
8   Te Maarssen (n.d.) writes, 'Since the 1980s there have been increasing problems with *sanguma*, affecting people's social lives and leading to strive (sic) in the families. Having been parish priest in Denglagu, Gembogl district from 1982 till 1993 and in Mingende 1993–2000. I vividly recall my pastoral involvement in the problem.'

2. Early intervention before or during a funeral

Whenever there is news of a death, the parish priest, catechist or a prominent church leader is to go to visit the family and be a pastoral presence there. (That presence may be required with leaders taking turns for several weeks or a month.) Bishop Te Maarssen comments:

> If the atmosphere was still quiet I would talk with them, enquire about the dead person and his or her sickness, explain the likely natural causes, show my sympathy and pray with them. This would normally stop *sanguma* talk in its tracks. I also remember where a parish councillor invited me to come for the funeral and celebrate Mass for the dead person at the grave to stop *sanguma* talk. Sure enough, the young men were annoyed and caused some disturbance on the edge of the crowd, but the presence of God caused them to call off *sanguma* proceedings. (Te Maarssen n.d.)

3. Immediate family members taking ownership

With extended families in PNG there is a wide choice as to which family member takes ownership of the situation. Hopefully it will be a person promoting peace and harmony and not one stirring up ideas of *sanguma*. Unfortunately in some cases good leadership is lacking in a family, in which case the situation can easily get out of hand. Also, divisions in the family can come to the fore at such a stressful time. Bishop Te Maarssen stresses, 'Make sure that there is no family quarrel left untreated and left unsolved. So make peace, talk it over, talk it out. At the time of a funeral, people jump on anything.'[9]

4. Promoting respect for law and order

Two years ago in the Nauro Gor community near Mingende two older women were being threatened that if two men who were in Kundiawa Hospital died, then those women would be 'buried' on the same day (the implication being that the women were witches). One woman was helped to escape across the Wahgi River to Neregaima and the local community police put the other under surveillance. The Nauro Gor community is fortunate in having a community law that forbids accusing another of sorcery or harming another suspected of sorcery (see Bal, Chapter 16 this volume). Offenders will be fined and if they do not pay the fine, will be sent to jail. Community policing, when functioning well, helps ensure relative order within the bounds of the community. The community police also discourage alcohol and drug abuse, which runs counter

---

9   Bishop Henk Te Maarssen, personal communication 28 March 2013.

to law and order. Community policing did not prevent threats in the case of the two women mentioned, but it did help avoid greater harm. I have uncovered only one case in the Nauro Gor community of some 16,000 people in the past five years of a person being killed after having been accused of sorcery.[10] There are other efforts currently to set up community law in Simbu, such as the United Kamaneku Community near Kundiawa. There have been families driven out over sorcery accusations, but no one was killed there in recent years. Both these communities and their efforts to maintain law and order are supported by churches, particularly the Catholic Church.

5. Fostering faith to influence attitudes and emotions

Sorcery is part of a worldview that has both similarities and differences with a biblical point of view, and considerable difference from a scientific post-enlightenment viewpoint. Sorcery and *sanguma* are a way of explaining the existence of evil, misfortune and death. From a church perspective, death is the most unevangelised dimension of life in Melanesia (Gibbs 2009b). Churches need to contend with beliefs that challenge Christian faith. Some other mainline churches such as the Lutheran Church also contest sorcery beliefs and there are moves towards a more collaborative approach.[11]

One of the biggest challenges for churches in PNG is to deepen people's faith commitment in a way that Christian faith can provide an alternative to the traditional worldview when it comes to misfortune and death. People with deep Christian faith are called to believe that God is the author of life and that God permits sickness and death. Various churches have different approaches to praying for the dead. The Catholic approach at a funeral is to say, 'Pray and thank God for the gift of his or her life, and if you are really sorry then pray for him or her and for us'. This requires a shift from blame for death to thanksgiving for life.

The Catholic Church in Simbu has developed a training course and distributed 600 copies to help believers find an alternative to *sanguma*. They are taught that belief in *sanguma* and employing a diviner who uses magic to detect someone to accuse is a way of thinking that runs quite contrary to belief in the power

---

10   Bishop Te Maarssen is quoted estimating 150 deaths a year in Simbu of people accused of witchcraft (Zocca 2005:117). With a population of 403,722 (2011 national census), that amounts to 1 death per 2690 persons per year, or 1 death per 528 persons over five years. The 1 death over five years in the Gor community is 1/16,000, which is approximately 30 times better than the whole of Simbu based on the Bishop's estimate.
11   Pastors and leaders from a number of Christian churches joined Bishop Bal in a workshop in January 2014 at Dirima parish in Simbu. A meeting of the Churches Partnership Program (CPP) in Port Moresby (27 March 2014), attended by leaders of seven mainline Churches, discussed the issue of sorcery and sorcery-related violence. There was general consensus that there needs to be a lot more work within the body of churches to come to a shared understanding on best practices with this issue. The CPP group also asked that they could have a representative at any further conferences on the topic of sorcery.

of God. The course acknowledges a biblical worldview and notes a number of examples where Jesus cast out demons, but Jesus never hurt a man or woman when casting out a demon.[12] Ultimately, there is the fifth commandment, 'Thou shalt not kill'. The bishop even added a line: *'Tekewe ol pasin bilong sutim tok sanguma'* (Eradicate the custom of *sanguma* accusations) in the prayer following the Lord's Prayer at mass and suggested that all priests in the diocese follow suit.

In order to back up the five-point policy just outlined there are also sanctions. If a person takes part in accusing another of *sanguma* or of injuring someone accused of *sanguma* they are excommunicated from the church until they retract their accusation (Korugl 2006:3).

Effectiveness of the five-point plan

The effectiveness of the Simbu diocesan strategy is still an open question. Bishop Te Maarssen says that 'it had a restraining effect'. Bishop Anton Bal, the current bishop, thinks that it has helped reduce *sanguma* accusations in many parts of Simbu, particularly around the Catholic headquarters of Mingende. Still, if a young person or a high-profile person dies suddenly, church leaders have to act quickly to counter talk of *sanguma*. Two cases below illustrate the strategy in practice.

Case 1: Death of Joe Mek Tiene

The late Joe Mek Tiene, member for Kundiawa-Gembogl electorate, died on 25 April 2011. His sister Josephine reflects on that time:

> When someone is dead they always talk about *sanguma*, they accuse people so then it becomes sort of a tradition, a custom to us. I have witnessed five deaths within our family but within our own family we never about *sanguma*. And when others want to talk about it I always come in between and always say 'no'. One reason is that I want to practise my faith and be firm in my faith. Second, my father Joseph Tiene was a catechist with Father Alphonse Schaefer. He was a disciplined man who taught us to practise our faith. The other thing is for the future generation so that we don't have this kind of atmosphere in the family. We have young girls in the family and if the girls go and marry in another place then they are going to accuse them if anything happens like that in their own family. And in their husband's family any deaths — they will blame them if they are known to come from a *sanguma* family. I said 'no,'

---

12 In Tok Pisin: *Jisas i no bin paitim wanpela man o meri bilong rausim spirit nogut.*

and I said 'these are my family and I have the right to say it'. When Joe died our parish priest Father Simon came and also Father Willie Kuman came and they supported us and we felt at peace. Father Jaworski came too and said that it must be a heart attack because Joe was such a big heavy man. It is not easy because when I say 'no', people try to break this fence of faith surrounding our family. People turn around and say, 'Why are you so strong against us getting a *glasman* (diviner)? Then you must be a *sanguma*. '*Kumo bitno akena ga*', 'You are holding the head of the *sanguma* and you are trying to cover up'. One day we will see who is right. The devil is confusing us. That's what I believe. I am fortunate that I have a number of strong brothers to support me, and also there is the government law, yet still people say, '*em mipela bai stretim long we bilong ples yet*' (we will deal with it according to custom).[13]

Application of strategy in this case:

- the family is united
- there is a strong person — in this instance a woman — prepared to take ownership of the situation
- she feels supported by her brothers and by the law
- she and the family are Christians and think that sanguma talk comes from the devil
- there was an immediate supportive pastoral response by the parish priest and another priest friend
- Father Jaworski (a surgeon) provided a biomedical explanation (heart attack).

Case 2: Addressing a world view

Margaret's brother, a university student, died of tuberculosis. A number of educated family members had died tragically (in car and air accidents) and the young men were attributing this to *sanguma* and started agitating at the funeral. Margaret, who is a registered nurse, consulted with her husband and then stood up and told them the biomedical reason for the death. That was not enough and she realised she had to compromise. She is strong Catholic but realised that Christian arguments might not help so she addressed the worldview of the boys and said,

> You have never seen a *sanguma* with your eyes have you? You know that *sangumas* turn into a dog or some sort of animal. So, after we have

---

13   Interview with Josephine Tiene in Kundiawa, 2 September 2013.

buried my brother you boys watch the gravesite day and night and you can kill any animal that comes. The only thing is you must not kill a human being. I forbid you to do that.[14]

Having promised them some money for small projects, and with the boys on side they buried her brother, watched over the grave for three weeks, killed several animals, but to no effect. After three weeks they gave up and stopped monitoring the grave.

Application of strategy in this case:

- there is a strong person — again in this instance a woman — prepared to take ownership of the situation
- she intervened from the beginning, when her brother was ill and as soon as she heard that her brother had died
- she provided a biomedical explanation (tuberculosis) — with only limited effect
- she and the family are Christian and cannot reconcile *sanguma* with their faith. On faith grounds she made it clear that killing a human being is unacceptable
- she argued using the worldview of the boys so that they would understand.

Elsewhere I have discussed gender violence and witch-killing in Simbu and the fact that women are more likely to be accused of witchcraft because of their weaker social and political presence (Gibbs 2012). In both the cases above, it was women exercising a strong social presence who prevented a situation that could have resulted in accusations of *sanguma* and a violent response. These cases help illustrate the five-point plan promoted by the Catholic Church in Simbu to reduce witchcraft-related killings.

Diffusion of *sanguma* beliefs to Enga Province

There have been several cases in Enga Province in recent years of women being killed or severely hurt after having been accused of practising witchcraft. The following account about one of those cases is factual except for the change of names and some places in an effort to preserve some privacy. A young man died in Wabag Hospital (Enga). Some people say that during his funeral, while people were mourning and he had not yet been buried, word went around that the dead man had called by mobile phone and named two women, saying that they had taken his heart and this had caused his death. Men rounded up the

---

14   Interview with Margaret Ghunn at Mingende, 12 September 2013.

two women and proceeded to torture them with heated iron rods and bush knives, demanding to know where they had put his heart and telling them to put it back. The women were brutally assaulted but could not respond to the men's requests. Eventually the body of the young man was buried. One woman died from her injuries. The other, terribly burned, managed to escape, spending the night partially immersed in a river and walking the next day to where she received assistance to get to a hospital in another province.

That woman survived. The doctor in his report states:

> [She] remained in critical condition for the first 10–14 days in hospital … She required three months for intensive care of her wounds … She was seven months pregnant at the time of this assault. Her baby died and was delivered on the following day. The baby also suffered from burns even while in the uterus … This act was one of the more cruel and inhuman acts I have witnessed in 35 years of medical practice, 17 of which I have spent in the Highlands of Papua New Guinea.[15]

I followed up on the incident, meeting the woman (here named Maria) shortly after she had been released from hospital. I came with her husband and it was a joy to see the two together. She was happy to see him and said that she looked forward to returning home to be reunited with her husband and children. She also wants to have her innocence declared publicly through a court hearing. For almost a year I have been meeting with the people where she comes from and it has been a learning experience for me, and for them, to find what are their concerns when faced with the prospect of Maria returning.[16]

Concerns of the community

I note that the concerns raised by the community are a mixture of fear and confusion.

- they fear being blamed and taken to court for supporting a person who has been declared a threat to society
- they fear that people might get violent again and she could be killed and anyone supporting her could be assaulted or also killed
- they are confused, saying that they are Christians, yet they admit they believe in witchcraft

---

15   The report, held by the patient, is signed by Dr Bill McCoy from Nazarene Hospital, 22 April 2013.
16   I first lived in the area she comes from for six months, some 40 years ago, and I was parish priest there for five years, starting 30 years ago, so I am not a total outsider.

- they worry too, saying that she had admitted being a witch, so why try to support such an evil person.

I will consider these four points in turn.

1. Fear of being blamed and taken to court

First, I spoke with church leaders, councillors, women's leaders, nurses and teachers and all were anxious lest they be blamed for supporting a person who had been expelled from the community. What if something would go wrong — if someone would get sick and die? In such an instance Maria might be accused again, and then those who had helped her return would also be blamed. Some said that we should get 'permission' first from those who had tortured her. Then there would be less likelihood of others being blamed.

Some were openly afraid that the relatives of the young man who had died — that is those who had tortured and banished Maria — might summons Maria's supporters to court. After all, the deceased's relatives had gone to the trouble of ridding the community of such a dangerous person and how could people contemplate supporting her and bringing her back? That would be totally irresponsible and if necessary they would seek legal means to stop such nonsense.

Local village court officials feel uncomfortable. They had heard that the Sorcery Act has been revoked, but are not clear about their role and their legal standing in cases involving such cultural beliefs and practices. Since it was such a grave matter involving terrible physical torture and the death of an unborn child they presumed that the original case would be a matter for the district court. Yet, what if a complainant raised the matter of a person or group of people bringing an undesirable and possibly dangerous person back into the community? Would this not be a matter for the local court officials?

2. Fear of further violence

Second, several people were afraid that there would be further violence. Some had witnessed the torture and public humiliation that had led to the death of one woman and the expelling of another. There had been terrible physical, emotional and verbal violence the day following the torture as she had tried to get assistance at the local health centre and been turned away by armed men. Then she was abused by both men and women as she desperately attempted to escape along the road in the direction of her parent's village.

The husband of the woman who had died took his wife's assailants to the village court and was awarded compensation of pigs and money, but that had not turned out well and he had refused the pigs offered, saying that they were too small — thus leaving a tense unresolved situation. There has been no appeal to a higher court.

Not everyone had been against Maria. Some said that they had tried to help her but were accosted by men armed with axes and bush knives such that they abandoned attempts to help lest they too be killed or badly injured. One man said that armed men had threatened to cut his leg off if he supported her. Remembering such violence and the horror of a woman with third-degree burns over 40 per cent of her body, many people did not want to risk a repeat episode. Why return and risk further violence? Could she not remain elsewhere and let memory of the whole incident gradually fade? Maria's response is that she has done nothing wrong, so why should she have to stay away as if she is guilty.

3. Confusion over belief in Christianity and in witchcraft

Third, many Christians admitted that they are confused. The group directly involved in the torture are unchurched but the surrounding community is predominantly Catholic. They renew their baptismal promises every year during the Easter ceremonies, agreeing to 'reject Satan and all his works and empty promises'. In doing so they reinforce their belief in good and evil and the way good and evil can be personified — good personified in Jesus Christ and evil personified in Satan. Like most Papua New Guineans they believe in the spiritual, supernatural, or non-empirical realm. Some would call it a magical worldview.

People seek explanations for good and evil, particularly misfortune and death. Why did the tree branch fall when he was beneath it? Why was there a car accident? Why does a person die? Such questions are often phrased using 'who' questions. 'Who' caused him or her to get sick and die?

Stories are circulating around the area: of a sow that was ready to give birth and then appeared not pregnant and without piglets. Had a witch consumed the piglets before the mother could give birth? There were other stories of people killing a chicken and in gutting it, not finding the heart. Had a witch consumed the chicken's heart? Such stories only too readily prepare listeners for stories of a witch who has removed and devoured a human heart.

The church leaders at the local parish requested a two-day workshop to clarify issues. In November 2013 we had the two-day workshop, based largely on the helpful book from the Melanesian Institute, *Thinking Critically about Sorcery and Witchcraft* (Schwarz 2011). Ideas promoted included human rights, scientific argument and Christian faith. Afterwards participants shared how two

Talking it Through

topics had made a big impression. They were alarmed to hear how before the enlightenment, thousands of accused witches had died in Europe (see Stewart, Chapter 10 and Keenan, Chapter 11 this volume). The other topic that made an impression was studying the Gospels to see how Jesus had dealt mercifully with persons possessed by evil spirits — such as the healing of what appears to be a lad suffering from epilepsy (Luke 17:14–21).

We discussed how the development of science and the enlightenment provide alternative explanations for sickness and death. Science may not provide satisfactory explanations to 'who' questions, but it can usually provide explanation for 'what' questions, and for many in the workshop, that is enough if it would forestall the prospect of multiple witch killings as had happened earlier in Europe. They resolved to request more often a letter from a doctor or a nursing officer about the cause of death, rather than resorting quickly to sorcery as an explanation.

Study of healing stories in the Christian Gospels led to the issue of belief and decision-making. Participants put it in terms of a fence. If a fence around a garden is strong and intact, then a pig cannot get inside to destroy the garden. In a similar way, they could have a 'thought fence' to regulate their minds, and not be troubled by the stories circulating. There are two possibilities here. The fence could separate real from unreal, thus allowing a person to say that they don't believe in the power of sorcery. The other possibility is to have the fence separate real powers so that being kept outside the protective fence disempowers thoughts and beliefs about sorcery. Several participants witnessed that they were no longer afraid of sorcery or witchcraft and this left them feeling confident and free — in other words ideas of sorcery were disempowered. Those Christians who continued to entertain such thoughts about witchcraft stories were allowing them inside the fence and so experienced confusion with diverging beliefs. Thus it was not a matter of believing or not believing in the reality of evil, but that faith commitment gives them a sense of security in the face of evil power.[17]

4. Why support a person who has admitted to being a witch?

Fourth, in many cases I hear people saying that the accused person admitted to being a witch. For example, in the case of Kepari Leniata, the young woman burned alive in February 2013 in Mount Hagen, most people I have spoken with

---

[17] At this point I will not dwell on the question whether Christian belief is a functional substitute for belief in sorcery.

tell me that they believe she truly was a witch because she had admitted it, and two women from Simbu had corroborated this evidence saying they had seen her cook and consume the young man's heart.

Usually such stories have been embellished as they get passed on. In response, I ask whether the confession was made while the accused was being tortured. In all cases so far it appears that confession was extracted under extreme torture. People say that they had to use torture in order to get them to admit the fact. However, how true is confession under torture? As Nick Schwarz notes (2011:51), some people confess their guilt hoping that their assailants will simply kill them and thus relieve them of the hell of continual torture.

Even before confession there is a tendency in PNG for presumption of guilt rather than innocence. If a *glasman* or diviner points to a person then they are automatically presumed guilty and how can they prove that they are innocent? Courts have dismissed cases involving accusation of sorcery due to lack of evidence. However, the person being tortured or expelled from the community has little chance of successfully claiming innocence. When the Catholic sisters came to intervene in the case of a woman being tortured near Mendi in 2012, some people called out '*sanguma i kam*' (witches are coming). Fortunately the sisters were not deterred by such claims. However, for most people it is a terrifying thought that in defending the accused, people might point to you, and then how would you prove your innocence?

Even if a person would return, claiming innocence and appearing quite 'normal', this would still be insufficient for some. A health worker gave the example of sleepwalking. He said that a person sleepwalking is not conscious of what they are doing and might have no recall of what they had done while sleepwalking. In a somewhat analogous way the *sanguma* spirit is believed to leave the body of its host sleeping. Later, the person having woken might have no idea what malicious acts the *sanguma* spirit had performed while outside the body. How does a woman wanting to return home respond to such beliefs, particularly in a context that presumes guilt rather than innocence? This is a complex issue that people admit needs a lot more clarity.

The spectrum of violence

The issues raised in the interventions recorded above provide wider lessons for a whole spectrum of violence associated with witchcraft and sorcery, particularly the form that is spreading recently in the highlands and among people from highlands communities in coastal towns.

It begins with the violence of what is perceived as evil or misfortune. A person sickens and dies for no explicable reason. Subsequently, violence ranges through accusations and rumours levelled at a person, usually a defenceless woman. Through this process the 'accused' becomes 'victim'.[18] It often begins as verbal or emotional violence that later erupts into physical violence. Physical violence may result in serious injuries, death or banishment from the community. If one survives, the violence continues in terms of being regarded as unwelcome and undesirable. The scars are there on the body as ever-present reminders of violence suffered and the threat of even more hurt if one would return home to a community that believes in the presumption of guilt rather than innocence. In fact, some say that recovery from violence from which they should have died is further proof that the accused person really does have access to superhuman powers.

A return visit

Having recovered sufficiently from her physical wounds, Maria's dream is to have the court declare her innocence and for her to return home and be reunited with her husband and children. People from her community suggested to me that her initial visit should be a brief one in order to test the response of the community. So one weekend in November 2013 she and her husband came with me to Enga. Coming closer to the area where she had been tortured, she said she was feeling comfortable, but her body language indicated the contrary as she pulled the hood of her jacket down over her face. Then, as we drove up into the hills above Wabag, upon sighting her house across the valley, she pointed and spoke just one word, 'home'. There was a moving nostalgia about the expression, as she knew it was still too dangerous to go there. She stayed the night elsewhere with her married daughter.

The next day she and her husband attended Sunday mass at the local parish church. At the end of mass a leader (a magistrate) addressed the congregation of about 500 people, noting her presence. Afterwards the majority of adults came to her warmly with hugs and lots of tears. Admittedly these churchgoers had had little to do directly with her accusation and torture. Notably, several people present who had been implicated in the accusations and torture did not come to greet her and kept their distance. Later that afternoon we returned several hundred kilometres to another province where she currently stays. Maria reflected as we drove, saying how her accusers must have been 'jealous'

---

18 The term 'victim' is an ambiguous term since, depending on the point of view, the victim could be the original person who died, or it could be the person tortured or killed, having been accused of sorcery that caused the first death.

of her because she had a good house and garden and enjoyed a happy marriage. From other cases I have encountered, jealousy seems a common motive, and a factor that calls for attention.

Trouble

Realising that the situation is far from settled, I went to speak with some of the men who had been involved in accusing and torturing Maria. They told a different story, claiming that before he died in Wabag Hospital their relative, the young man, had named Maria as being responsible for his demise.

> On the very day that the young man (deceased) distributed pork with his uncle, he felt sick and said, 'Maria must have taken my heart when I was giving pork meat (liver) to my other uncle because she asked for it and I refused and saw her longing to have the liver. When I did not give her the liver, she must have taken my liver to quench her thirst/hunger'. He mentioned her name even before he died.[19]

They strongly believe the words attributed to the deceased and hold Maria accountable for three major problems. First she killed the young man through *sanguma*. Second, when accused, she had named another woman — the one who eventually died. So therefore she is responsible for the death of the other woman. Third, since she would not put back the heart of the deceased she had to be tortured in an effort to make her do so, and in the process her baby was killed, so she is responsible for that too.

The men explained their view of the torture.

> The reason for torturing Maria was not to kill her. It was not done as a game or for fun. She was tortured when other people who have been living in Mount Hagen or Simbu said that the accused must have placed the heart in a cool place under a waterfall and she would eat it after the burial of the deceased. They said that if they would torture her she would take the heart and put it back and the young man would come back to life again. The general community believed that and they were desperate to have the life of the young man back again. So they believed that by torturing Maria, she would give the heart back and so they kept torturing her. They did not intend to kill her. So after spending many hours torturing her and when nothing happened, they released her.[20]

---

19 Interview with a male relative at Tieliposa, 22 March 2014.
20 Interview with a male relative at Tieliposa, 22 March 2014.

Moreover, the men claim that Maria could possibly be responsible for a fourth serious problem. With her away the incident is gradually being forgotten, but if she tries to come back to live there, it will raise all sorts of problems. There would be trouble and even violence if she comes back intending to stay. They say that they have paid compensation for the death of the other woman, therefore as far as they are concerned, the only prudent solution for Maria is for her to forgive and forget.

Conclusion

The account of Maria's return and the response of the men who had accused her illustrates a number of issues raised in this paper. The men who tortured Maria — and I gather in many other cases too — are not just young men with a blood lust or high on marijuana. They are people caught up in conflicting beliefs about life and death. If one follows the logic of Melanesian tradition, it will usually involve discovering who is responsible for the misfortune. Moreover, if the situation is such that life or death depends on identifying the person responsible in order to convince them to reverse the effects of sorcery, then the matter will appear most urgent. If the deceased is already buried, then Melanesian tradition will turn to the future wellbeing of the local community.

The five-point plan of the Catholic Church in Simbu confronts the logic of Melanesian tradition with Christian belief that attributes life and death to God. By having an influential person present at the funeral, drawing not only on Christian faith, but also promoting a biomedical explanation of sickness and death, the church seeks to provide an alternative understanding of misfortune. That alternative was accepted in the two cases presented above from Simbu. In the case from Enga, with little previous experience of dealing with this type of sorcery accusation, the Christian community was unprepared and there was no effective alternative offered.

It is noteworthy that recent conversation within local communities in both Enga and Simbu has included discussion on a faith level including bishops' statements read out in church and circulated afterwards. Prayer groups now have passages from the Bible as a source for reflection and discussion. People are faced with the issue of how as Christians they might respond to misfortune and untimely death. Discussion on this level is important as it leads to a direct confrontation with belief in sorcery. Thus the discourse goes beyond sociocultural and legal matters to fundamental beliefs. Admittedly, many people still struggle with seemingly contradictory viewpoints, but the conversation is ongoing and this will be important for developing strategies for preventing such violence in the future.

Maria finds herself in a difficult legal situation. She is determined that once the case of the other woman who died is resolved, she will summons to the district court the 10 or 12 men who assaulted her. But these men are close relatives of her husband. Thus it will mean taking 'family' to court. How can she settle again at home if those relatives owe her large compensation in money and pigs or, even worse, if they will be absent for long jail terms? The men have put it clearly — if she comes back there will be trouble.

From the interventions to date I offer the following six suggestions. First, there is need for both prevention and support. Comprehensive prevention strategies aim to reduce or even halt the trend of sorcery accusations and violence. Yet there are still many marginalised 'Marias' faced with a legal predicament after having suffered assault. How can such victims be supported, when the community claims that pursuit of the case will only mean more 'trouble'.

Second, the Simbu Catholic Church plan and the sorcery workshop in Enga appear to be producing helpful results. Yet that is only a beginning. Many in the Catholic community still admit their confusion and their fear of being blamed for supporting a person who is considered a threat to society. Church strategies should be pursued further and monitored for their effectiveness.

Third, the response of some other Christians — predominantly Pentecostal-type churches — is unclear. It could be that their stress on possession by evil spirits and 'deliverance' may only reinforce customary Melanesian beliefs in spirit possession associated with *sanguma*. This needs to be followed up in dialogue with various churches. Churches need to draw inspiration not only from scripture and theological traditions, but also human rights ideals. In PNG, given that most people profess Christianity, churches may play an important role in interpreting rights language and values into cultural frameworks meaningful to people in a given local context.

Fourth, the group who were actively involved in accusing and assaulting Maria did not attend the parish workshop and the majority are not active members of a Christian worshipping community. In such situations legal sanctions are important. The men interviewed admitted not wanting to participate in such violence ever again, as having had the village court order them to pay out pigs and money to the husband of one woman who died, they now realise that any future case will have legal consequences that could be very costly for them.

Fifth, about 50 people attended the workshop in Enga, and the Sunday congregation was large, including community leaders. This has helped identify a growing group of well-meaning people within the local community who are prepared to take a stand against sorcery accusations and violence. There is a similar trend around Mingende and the Nauro Gor community in Simbu. Initiatives that expand such support will be important for building a critical support base within local communities.

Sixth, church interventions to date are limited and call for wider cooperation between community, government, law enforcement, and church agencies that can promote meaningful prevention strategies building on human rights, scientific argument and Christian faith.

References

Damien, C. 2005. The Myth of Kumo: Knowing the Truth about *Sanguma* in Simbu Province. *Catalyst* 35(2):114–34.

Eves, R. and A. Kelly-Hanku 2014. Witch-Hunts in Papua New Guinea's Eastern Highlands Province: A Fieldwork Report. *SSGM In Brief* 2014/4. Canberra: State, Society and Governance in Melanesia Program, The Australian National University.

Gibbs, P. 2004. Growth, Decline and Confusion: Church Affiliation in Papua New Guinea. *Catalyst* 34(2):164–84. www.philipgibbs.org/pdfs/Growth%20 decline.pdf, viewed 19/7/2013.

Gibbs, P. 2009a. Sorcery and AIDs in Simbu, East Sepik and Enga. *Occasional Paper* 2. Port Moresby: The National Research Institute.

Gibbs, P. 2009b. Forces of Death and the Promise of Life in Papua New Guinea. *Australian eJournal of Theology* 14. www.acu.edu.au/__data/assets/pdf_file/0005/197690/Gibbs_-_Death_and_Life_PNG.pdf, viewed 19/7/2013.

Gibbs, P. 2012. Engendered Violence and Witch-Killing in Simbu. In M. Jolly, C. Stewart and C. Brewer (eds.) *Engendering Violence in Papua New Guinea*. Canberra: ANU E Press, 107–36.

Gibbs, P. and J.J. Wailoni 2009. Sorcery and a Christian Response in the East Sepik. In F. Zocca (ed.) Sanguma in Paradise: Sorcery, Witchcraft and Christianity in Papua New Guinea. *Point* No. 33. Goroka: Melanesian Institute, 55–96. www.philipgibbs.org/pdfs/SorcerySepik.pdf, viewed 19/7/2013.

Korugl, P. 2006. Catholic Church Warns against Sorcery Violence. *The National*, 20 October, p. 3.

Schwarz, N. 2011. Thinking Critically about Sorcery and Witchcraft: A Handbook for Christians in Papua New Guinea. *Occasional Paper* No. 14. Goroka: Melanesian Institute.

Te Maarssen, H. n.d. *Sanguma*: A Pastoral Approach. Unpublished paper, Catholic Diocese of Kundiawa, Simbu Province.

Zocca, F. 2005. Witchcraft and Mission in Simbu Province. In P. Gesch (ed.) *Mission and Violence: Healing the Lasting Damage*. Madang: DWU Press, 109–35.

Zocca, F. (ed.) 2009. *Sanguma* in Paradise: Sorcery, Witchcraft and Christianity in Papua New Guinea. *Point* 33. Goroka: Melanesian Institute.

Author Biographies

Ravunamu Auka is the deputy public prosecutor (courts) of Papua New Guinea and is from Kapari village, Central Province. He has held the position of deputy public prosecutor of the Office of the Public Prosecutor (OPP) for 18 years and has been in the employ of the office for 32 years. A graduate of the University of Papua New Guinea with a Bachelor of Laws in 1980, Mr Auka was admitted as a Lawyer of the Courts of Papua New Guinea in 1981. In 1991 Mr Auka was attached for six months to the Commonwealth Office of the Director of Public Prosecutions in Sydney; successfully completed the Victorian Bar Readers Course in November 1997; and represented the Papua New Guinea OPP at the Australian Association of Crown Prosecutors Conference in 2012. In addition to broad and extensive experience of conduct of trials in the National Court, Mr Auka has responsibility for conduct of all criminal appeals in the Supreme Court of Papua New Guinea.

Clara Bal is from Chimbu Province and has a degree in PNG Studies and International Relations from Divine Word University, Madang, in the year 2012. She is currently studying at the Yeungnam University, Republic of South Korea, and will graduate with her masters degree in Community Development Leadership in 2016. She has been conducting research on the Gor community's local governance structure and has recently undertaken a review for Caritas Australia. She visited Canberra in 2013 for the State, Society and Governance in Melanesia Program Pacific Research Colloquium.

John Cox is an anthropologist and research fellow with the State, Society and Governance in Melanesia Program, College of Asia and the Pacific, The Australian National University. His doctoral work on 'fast money schemes' explored the developmental values of middle-class Papua New Guineans and was awarded the Australian Anthropological Society's prize for best PhD thesis in 2012. Cox has been working in the Pacific since 1996 as a volunteer, development program manager, freelance consultant and academic researcher.

Laurent Dousset is adjunct professor at the EHESS and director of CREDO (Centre for Research and Documentation on Oceania), located at Aix-Marseille University. He has worked since 1994 in Australia, especially with the dialectal groups of the Western Desert, where he focuses on social and territorial organisation, history of first contacts, social transformations and ontological and legal aspects of the confrontation with the state apparatus. Since 2008 he has also conducted research in Vanuatu on political issues, particularly in the south of Malekula Island. He has published numerous articles and chapters, and edited or co-edited books including *Assimilating Identities* (2005, Oceania

Monographs), *Myths, Missiles and Cannibals* (2011, Society of Océanistes), *Australian Aboriginal Kinship* (2011, pacific-credo Publications) and *The Scope of Anthropology* (with S. Tcherkézoff, 2012, Berghahn).

Mark Evenhuis is a Senior Policy and Advocacy Adviser at Plan International Australia and formerly worked in Bougainville and Papua New Guinea as a human rights adviser and consultant. He has recently completed a Masters of Law and Development at the University of Melbourne.

Richard Eves is an anthropologist who has published widely on issues of social change in Papua New Guinea. Richard's work deals with contemporary issues in Melanesia, straddling the boundaries between anthropology, development and international health, with a particular focus on gender, violence and the AIDS epidemic. He also has wide experience consulting on issues of health, AIDS and gender-based violence in Papua New Guinea, having been a research adviser on two AusAID-funded projects and a consultant for Caritas Australia. He has undertaken qualitative research in numerous provinces, including Western Highlands, Chimbu, Western, Eastern Highlands, Morobe, Milne Bay and the Autonomous Region of Bougainville. In 2008, with Leslie Butt, he co-edited the important volume *Making Sense of AIDS: Culture, Sexuality, and Power in Melanesia* (University of Hawai'i Press), a collection of anthropological papers on how the epidemic is being understood and responded to in Melanesia. Much of his current research and writing focuses on gender — in particular, on forms of masculinity and how to engage men in the prevention of violence against women.

Lawrence Foana'ota OBE is a freelance researcher, Commissioner of Oaths, and honorary member of the Pacific Islands Museums Association, a regional organisation of which he was one of the founders and first chairman of its executive board until 2006. He is interested in social and cultural issues in Solomon Islands and in Melanesia generally. Recently he carried out social, health and cultural heritage impact assessments in communities along the Tina River, Central Guadalcanal, as part of a hydropower development project. In 2012 he completed a research project in collaboration with Bergen University in Norway and James Cook University, north Queensland. He was an adjunct senior research fellow with the School of Arts and Social Sciences at James Cook University from 2006 until 2013. He holds a bachelor's degree and Master of Arts in Anthropology and a Museum Management Certificate. He has written on several cultural issues and about the Solomon Islands National Museum.

Miranda Forsyth is a research fellow with State, Society and Governance in Melanesia in the College of Asia and the Pacific, The Australian National University. In February 2011 she commenced a three-year ARC Discovery-funded project to investigate the impact of intellectual property laws on development in Pacific island countries. Prior to this, Miranda was a senior lecturer in criminal law at the School of Law, the University of the South Pacific, based in Port Vila, Vanuatu, for eight years. Miranda's research interests include legal pluralism, customary law and South Pacific criminal law. She is the author of *A Bird that Flies with Two Wings:* Kastom *and State Justice Systems in Vanuatu* (2009, ANU E Press).

Derek Futaiasi graduated with a Bachelor of Laws (2008), Professional Diploma in Legal Practice (2009) and Master of Laws (2012) from the University of the South Pacific. He is a senior legal officer with the Solomon Islands Law Reform Commission.

Patrick Gesch was born in Townsville in 1944. He joined the Divine Word Missionaries and entered training for the priesthood, which included seven years in the United States. He was posted to Negrie Parish in the Yangoru district of Wewak Catholic diocese in 1973. He did his doctoral studies through Sydney University on the cargo cult-type movement of the area. In 1983 he joined Divine Word University, Madang, and has remained based there ever since, with absences doing editorial work for *Anthropos* journal, and for a stay in Manihiki in the Cook Islands.

Philip Gibbs is an SVD missionary priest living and working in Papua New Guinea. He is secretary of the Commission for Social Concerns for the Catholic Bishops Conference of Papua New Guinea/Solomon Islands and a research adviser for Caritas Australia. He has published on sorcery in the Sepik: *Sorcery and a Christian Response in the East Sepik* (with Josepha Wailoni; 2009, Melanesian Institute), and on witchcraft in Simbu: *Engendered Violence and Witch-Killing in Simbu* (2012, ANU E Press).

Barbara Gore is from Mukone village, Chimbu Province, and is a senior legal officer with the Papua New Guinea Office of the Public Prosecutor (OPP). Ms Gore was admitted as a lawyer of the National and Supreme courts of Papua New Guinea in 2008 following graduation from the University of Papua New Guinea with a Bachelor of Laws and successful completion of the post-graduate training for admission. Ms Gore has worked with the OPP, initially in the Port Moresby office and in the Goroka office, from early 2012. In mid-2012 Ms Gore was attached for a period to the Queensland Office of the Director of Public Prosecutions. Ms Gore has conducted all types of OPP prosecution matters in the superior courts in Goroka and circuit areas across Papua New Guinea.

John Himugu is an ethnographic researcher at the Institute of Papua New Guinea Studies. He has researched sorcery and witchcraft beliefs of the Huli of Hela Province, where he comes from. He was a member of the working committee set up by the Constitutional and Law Reform Commission of Papua New Guinea in 2007 to look into sorcery and sorcery-related killings in Papua New Guinea and has travelled widely to get public opinion on the matter.

Jonathan Julius comes from Marap village in the Sawos language area, just off the Sepik River. He followed his father around Port Moresby, Lae and Madang in his schooling years, and eventually went to Madang Teachers College. His first appointment as teacher was to the remote school of Ninigo in the Nahu Rawa Local Level Government area and over the course of the following years had to deal with a murderous *sanguma* movement as it affected the community. He is married to his home place and has two daughters. His destiny is to return to Marap one day.

Philip Kanairara is the Chief Legal Officer for the Solomon Islands Law Reform Commission. He joined the Commission as a Senior Legal Officer in March 2009. He is working with other officers of the Commission on the review of the Solomon Islands Penal Code. Sorcery is an offence under the Penal Code. He has completed work on Corruption Offences and the law that applies to land below the high water mark (beaches and foreshores). Reports containing recommendations for law reforms on these subjects were sent to the Solomon Islands Government in 2011 and 2012. Mr. Kanairara graduated from the USP with a Bachelor of Laws in 2006, a Professional Diploma in Legal Practice (PDLP) in 2008, a Professional Diploma in Legislative Drafting (PDLD) in 2011 and a Master of Laws (LLM) in 2012.

Mel Keenan is principal legal officer at the NSW Electoral Commission. He has previously held senior legal and policy positions with the Legislative Assembly of NSW, the NSW Aboriginal Land Council and the NSW Law Reform Commission. He is currently enrolled in the Master of Laws by research at Monash University, which is to be formally upgraded to a PhD in late 2013. At this stage of his research, his chapter is exploratory in nature, introducing the viewpoint of the legal historian.

Pealiwan Rebecca Koralyo is from Mambisanda village, Enga Province, and is a legal officer with the Papua New Guinea Office of the Public Prosecutor (OPP). Ms Koralyo was admitted as a lawyer of the National and Supreme courts of PNG in 2010 following her graduation from the University of Papua New Guinea with a Bachelor of Laws and successful completion of the post-graduate training for admission. Ms Koralyo has been with the OPP since admission and currently holds a position in the Port Moresby office in which she is responsible for the prosecution of family and sexual violence matters. In this role, she is also responsible for OPP law reform activities in the area of gender-based violence.

Author Biographies

Salmah Eva-Lina Lawrence is a PhD candidate at The Australian National University. After a career with a global business advisory firm in London and New York, she started work in international development and has worked in gender and development for the United Nations in Afghanistan and Papua New Guinea. She has a Master of Arts in International Relations, a Master of International and Community Development, and a Master of Business Administration, all from Deakin University, and a Bachelor of Arts (Hons) in Politics, Philosophy and History from the University of London. Her roots in her matrilineal culture of Kwato, Milne Bay Province, Papua New Guinea, influence her research interests. Her interdisciplinary PhD project draws on international relations, political economy and anthropology and focuses on power relations between the indigenous people of Milne Bay, and colonisers, as well as inter-gender. The underlying theme of her interests are decolonial projects and how majority world peoples have managed colonialism and the coloniality of power. She is associated with Professor Margaret Jolly's ARC Laureate project Engendering Persons, Transforming Things: Christianities, Commodities and Individualism in Oceania.

Siobhan McDonnell is a legal anthropologist who spent 10 years working as an academic and adviser on land and governance issues in Indigenous Australia before beginning a PhD on land issues in Vanuatu in 2008. In the two years she lived in Vanuatu, she worked on land and governance issues. Siobhan is currently legal adviser to Vanuatu Minister of Lands, Ralph Regenvanu. Ms McDonnell also has an ongoing position as legal adviser in the Vanuatu Cultural Centre and as a land law adviser to the Attorney-General of Vanuatu. She has provided legal advice on land and environment issues, carbon trading and World Heritage issues in Melanesia to the World Bank and to a number of non-government organisations. She is an occasional lecturer at The Australian National University and the University of the South Pacific.

Georgina Phillips is an emergency physician at St Vincent's Hospital, Melbourne, and senior lecturer and honorary fellow at the University of Melbourne, Faculty of Medicine, Dentistry and Health Sciences. She has more than a decade of experience of capacity development work in emergency medicine in developing countries including Kiribati, Solomon Islands, Papua New Guinea, East Timor and Myanmar. Ms Phillips is the deputy chair of the Australian College of Emergency Medicine's International Emergency Medicine Special Interest Group Executive Committee and is on the Committee of Management of the St Vincent's Pacific Health Fund.

Christine Stewart was awarded her PhD in Gender Studies of Papua New Guinea in 2012, building on a Bachelor of Arts (Hons) from Sydney University and a Bachelor of Laws from the University of Papua New Guinea. She has worked for many years in Papua New Guinea and elsewhere in the Pacific in the fields of law reform and legislative drafting, and brings a wealth of experience in these fields to her academic work. She is currently a visiting fellow with the ARC Laureate project Engendering Persons, Transforming Things: Christianities, Commodities and Individualism in Oceania in the School of Culture, History and Language, College of Asia and the Pacific, The Australian National University.

Jack Urame is director of the Melanesian Institute, Goroka, Papua New Guinea and has worked there as a social and cultural researcher since 2006. He is a Lutheran pastor and comes from Simbu Province. He has studied theology and social sciences, and holds a Bachelor of Theology and Master of Arts in Social Sciences specialising in Melanesian studies. Between 2006 and 2008 he was engaged on a major research project undertaken by the Melanesian Institute on sorcery and witchcraft.

www.ingramcontent.com/pod-product-compliance
Lightning Source LLC
Chambersburg PA
CBHW041248240426
43669CB00034B/2991